The Way I See It

D1571726

JÜRGEN SCHADEBERG

The Way I See It

A MEMOIR

PICADOR AFRICA

I dedicate this book to the memory of
the late Henry Nxumalo — a great and courageous journalist
with whom I was privileged to work.

First published in 2017 by Picador Africa
an imprint of Pan Macmillan South Africa
Private Bag X19, Northlands
Johannesburg, 2116

www.panmacmillan.co.za

ISBN 978-1-77010-529-4
EBOOK ISBN 978-1-77010-530-0

Editing by Alison Lowry
Proofreading by Russell Martin
Design and typesetting by Triple M Design, Johannesburg
Cover design by publicide
Front cover photograph of Jürgen Schadeberg (Hamburg, 1948) by Helmut Prignitz
All photographs are supplied courtesy of Jürgen Schadeberg

Printed and bound by

CONTENTS

South Africa in White and Black

Europe

Africa in Full Colour

United Kingdom, United States, South Africa

Germany
1941–1950

Air raid shelter, 1942

1

SLOW DESCENT INTO HELL

I was ten years old in early 1941 and living with my mother in a small ground-floor apartment attached to a shop on the Kurfürstendamm, one of the most fashionable parts of central Berlin. This was a wide boulevard full of expensive restaurants, luxury shops and nightclubs within an area that was vibrant and alive with artists, actors and writers. It was also where military personnel in their finest dress uniform came to promenade with their girlfriends.

In 1941 Germany was at the height of its power. The Blitzkrieg of 1940 had been a great success and, for many Germans, Hitler could do no wrong. However, most Berliners had no love for the Nazis and considered Hitler to be little more than a pretentious and dangerous upstart. Naturally cynical, and more sophisticated than most Germans, Berliners had traditionally sympathised more with communism and socialism than the national socialism of the Nazis. The city was no power base for Hitler and, in private, many Berliners opposed Hitler's regime. Needless to say, any overt opposition was impossible and would have been brutally crushed instantly.

The reality of war had barely touched Berlin in 1941. Although there had been a few air raids, these had caused very little damage and were dismissed by most people as merely inconvenient. People still went to work as normal and the schools continued, as though there was no war. The streets were full of people shopping and in some restaurants fine wines and wonderful food were still served as usual by white-gloved waiters. The theatres did good business, the cinemas were full, and the trains and trams ran, as always, on time.

Certainly, the war had changed little in my life and my mother remained magnificently unconcerned. A striking woman, she enjoyed parties and social-ising with her many friends; nights were spent working as an actress in the theatre, where she played small parts. She would be the maid who comes on stage bringing a visiting card on a silver plate to the lead actor. She also worked, when she could, in movies – minor roles, like a telephonist, for example. She took her calling seriously and was always posing for photographs. She also dressed glamorously, as would be expected of a potential star. Her name was Rosemarie but most of her friends called her Rosie.

We may have lived on the Ku'damm but our apartment was modest. It was attached to a driving school, the connecting door to which was permanently locked. In the main room there was a desk near the window which faced the Hinterhof, or backyard. The desk was covered with a glass plate and above it hung a birdcage, which was the home of Peter, our white budgie, who, when the window was closed, was free to fly around the room. My mother had very long red-painted fingernails and she used to tap-tap with two fingers walking along the glass plate on the desk. This was a signal for Peter to follow. He would puff up his feathers and walk stealthily, stretching out his legs in a parody of a goosestep, high, up and down. 'Come, sweetie Peterle,' my mother would whisper, making sucking noises with her lips. Sometimes Peter would fly onto my mother's shoulder and they would kiss each other.

We had a telephone in our flat and my mother spent many hours on it talking to her friends, particularly to her friend Anita. I didn't consciously listen when they were chatting, as I was usually buried in a book, but occasional words reg-istered, such as 'erotics' and 'men'. These words seemed to be of great interest to my mother and now and then, when I was present, she would drop her voice to a conspiratorial whisper so that I couldn't hear what she was saying. Sometimes Anita came to visit. She invariably looked unhappy and depressed, and when she talked her eyes kept half closing. My mother, who was interested in the occult, would often settle down with her at a table, where they would sit facing each other. My mother would then produce a pack of cards and lay them out dramatically, one by one, face up, on the table.

'I can see there's a dark woman,' my mother said on one such occasion, while

Anita watched her, mesmerised. 'She's dangerous and treacherous. You must look out.'

'I know her – you're right!' Anita said, getting agitated. My mother calmed her down and picked up another card. When she turned it over, it was the jack of hearts.

'There's a letter coming to you from an admirer. He will visit you soon,' she said, which made Anita smile again. I turned back to my reading.

I was a great reader and devoted to books. If I had any free time I would be deep in a book. I can remember my delight at discovering Tolstoy and disappearing into his stories. That way I could shut out the world around me, especially the daily raving of one man on the radio, whom everyone called 'the Leader'. I didn't understand what he was on about but his voice was menacing and horrible. He was clearly a very angry man and he frightened me.

On my birthday a friend of my mother's came to visit. He was very tall and wore a uniform. I think he was some sort of officer in the army. His name was Klaus and he brought us lots of presents from Paris – silk stockings and perfume for my mother and a pair of roller-skates and chocolate for me. The roller-skates were very modern. They had a platform with two leather bands to fit onto your shoe and two big wheels covered with rubber on each side in front and a small wheel at the back. I was very happy with the present. They weren't as noisy as my iron four-wheelers.

Klaus also brought a small, fat bottle with a long neck with some fancy French writing on it, and he and my mother sat on the sofa-bed drinking out of small glasses. The bed didn't look like a bed during the day but more like a couch. It had a red cover and lots of colourful cushions.

'Jürgen, how about trying out the roller-skates? I'll help you put them on,' Klaus said. 'It's still light outside. I'll give you one mark and you can go and get yourself an ice cream.'

Of course I was only too pleased to disappear and I left Klaus and my mother alone.

Actually, I had stopped calling my mother 'Mother' a few weeks prior to Klaus's visit, after she and I had gone to see a recent acquaintance of hers. She had met this man on a train when returning from one of her many trips into the country. As we entered his large office in the factory where he worked, I noticed that he wore a fine suit. He had a thin moustache, the sort you saw on Hollywood actors.

'Hello, Rosie!' he said, rising up from behind a very large desk. 'How wonderful to see you! And who is this young man?'

'Oh,' my mother hesitated, 'this is my little brother, Jürgen.'

I thought I hadn't heard her correctly, but when I looked across at her, her expression didn't change.

'So, how old are you, Jürgen?' the man asked me. Before I could answer, he walked over to a shelf and picked up a large box. He placed it on his desk and smiled. 'Help yourself,' he said.

In front of me was the biggest box of assorted chocolates I had ever seen. Well, I stayed in the man's office for what felt like many hours, while he took my mother on a tour of the factory. Naturally, I sampled as many of the chocolates as I could, making myself very sick in the process.

From that day on I called my mother Rosie, like everyone else. Some weeks later, I came across her birth certificate and noticed that she had changed her date of birth, rather clumsily, from 1905 to 1915. I didn't think this was very convincing. Since I was born in 1931, I worked out, if she had been born in 1915 she would have been only sixteen years old when I was born. All her other official papers gave her date of birth as 1915. Nevertheless, the man seemed to believe that I was her brother.

The Nazi regime controlled every aspect of life. A few days after my tenth birthday, I and my classmates all received an envelope to take home to our parents. It contained an official command that I was to report to the Jungvolk as a recruit, called a 'Pimpf', in two weeks' time, on a Sunday, at the school playground. All boys between ten and fourteen years old, the one-page letter said, had to join the youth organisation. We had to report to it every weekend. There was a lot about the duty of all boys to the Leader, the people and the country. This was to be the beginning of our compulsory service to the Fatherland. Also in the letter was a list of compulsory uniform items: short black trousers, one hand-width above the knee, grey socks, brown shirt, belt, shoulder strap and so on. My mother clearly wasn't very happy about this but she didn't say anything directly to me.

Wearing my new uniform, the following Sunday I duly walked to the school playground where 20 or so boys, all in uniform, were there, some of them from my class. We stood around for a while, greeting each other, all of us feeling rather anxious. Suddenly an older boy, who must have been about thirteen, stood up on the steps of the school entrance and blew sharply on a whistle. He waved at us to come closer. Then he clicked his heels together, stood to attention, lifted his right arm to shoulder height and shouted, in a somewhat squeaky voice: 'Heil Hitler! I am your Hauptjungzugführer.'

He then proceeded to give us a long speech about our duty as the Jungvolk and about the sports tests we would have to go through, like running and the high jump and long jump. He spoke about us being the future of Germany. He said we would have to become soldiers and that we belonged to the Führer. He talked about blood and honour, which was a bewildering concept to most of us ten-year-olds. We were then made to line up and taught how to stand to attention and move simultaneously as a group. We had to turn right, turn left and march and stop together. Left-right, left-right, left we went, swinging our arms in time. This went on the whole afternoon. When I finally got home I was exhausted. The following Sunday we marched to the forest where we played war games, with one group hiding from another and so on, which, actually, was quite a lot of fun.

After a few weeks of marching and chasing each other in the forest, one day we found ourselves in a cellar. This was a long room with bright, white-painted walls. In it was a long table with benches on both sides, where we were instructed to sit. On the walls were posters with lots of swastikas and slogans on them. At the head of the table sat the Jungzugführer. Once we had settled down he gave us another long lecture, this one about the life of Adolf Hitler, which we were supposed to learn and memorise. He told us that the Leader had declared war against the Soviet Union because the Jewish Bolshevik rulers in Moscow wanted to set all of Germany aflame. After further tedious speeches about the primitive life of the barbarian Soviets, we were taught to sing marching songs, none of which I could remember except the first line of one of them: 'On the lake swim corpses with their stomachs sliced open, in the throats stick knives so that the blood sprays into the sky.'

Because I was unable to remember the songs, I was instructed to write them down.

When I came home that evening, my mother had my Aunt Doris round for coffee. Doris was a very large lady, who bellowed out her words. When she roared with laughter, everything in the flat would shake.

'How was your day in the forest?' my mother asked me.

'We didn't go to the forest,' I replied. 'We had to sing.'

'That's wonderful,' my mother said, looking excitedly at Aunt Doris. 'I always wanted him to take singing lessons. You see this Jungvolk is doing something worthwhile after all with our children.'

My aunt looked suspicious. 'What did you sing?' she asked me. 'Why don't you sing for us?'

'No, I don't like the songs,' I said reluctantly, adding, 'I don't remember them.'

'Come on now, let's have it,' my aunt said.

So I half sang and half quietly spoke out the two lines about the corpses in the lake and the knives and throats. There was a long silence. Then my aunt turned to my mother. 'I told you!' she said indignantly. 'These people are evil!' And then, turning back to me, 'You don't have to go there again – ever!'

I remember being very happy at this pronouncement and going to my room, where I took off my uniform and went back to reading my book: one of Tolstoy's stories. My room wasn't much of a room actually; it wasn't much bigger than my bed. This was because it had been divided into two, with a bathroom and toilet in one half, separated by a thin wooden wall, which was not very sound-proof, with the door from my room leading into the kitchen. It did provide me with some privacy, however, and gave me the solitude to concentrate upon my latest book.

About a week later I was told that my grandmother was coming to Berlin and that she would be staying at my aunt's place. So, one afternoon, my mother and I took the tram down the Ku'damm and I was dropped in front of the apartment building where my aunt lived. My mother was hurrying to get to a rehearsal and she rushed off before seeing my grandmother. My mother did not get on with Grete, my grandmother, something I only found out much later on.

A young man opened the door. This was my cousin Peter, who must have been about 20 or so. He always looked very neat and superior and he made me feel inadequate. Looking down at me from above, he said, 'Ah, there's little Jürgen, to see his grandmother.'

My aunt had a large apartment and in the living room there was a tall bird-cage. In it perched an old grey parrot. Whenever anyone came into the room he always said 'Good morning' in a squeaky voice. He could also sing a song, 'I had a comrade, you can't find a better one', which was an old military song about a soldier who had been killed in the war. I think Peter must have taught him. Peter was passionate about the military, something that greatly distressed my aunt. I said good morning to the bird and followed Peter out onto the balcony, where my aunt and grandmother were sitting having their kaffeeklatsch.

It was a sunny autumn afternoon and the low sun shone through the yellow leaves of the birch and chestnut trees, the light playing against the wall of the balcony. It was an idyllic scene. Everything glimmered and sparkled, with the balcony wall covered with colourful daisies that grew from horizontal hanging flower-pots. I sat down next to my grandmother. She asked me a lot of questions about my mother and how we lived and whether I had enough to eat. She said that she was going to take me shopping and buy me clothes. She also asked if I would like to come and stay with her in Thuringia over the summer holidays, but I didn't like the idea of this because my mother had told me that life with Granny was very difficult. While I was busy consuming numerous poppyseed cakes (my favourite), I overheard her complaining to my aunt about her health. 'It's my colon,' she said. 'I don't have enough red blood cells. My liver isn't working any more and I have to eat minced, fresh, raw liver every day. Every day I have stomachache.'

Just then Peter came onto the balcony. 'I have to go to my meeting,' he announced. 'Jürgen – I will take you home. Come.'

Peter had a brand-new Volkswagen. He was very boastful about it. We had to thank our Leader, he told me. Our Leader was going to give all Germans a car. 'We'll all have Volkswagens!' he shouted in a self-satisfied tone as he stopped in front of our apartment. Before I could get out, he held me back and said: 'You are the future of our Germanic race and you must listen to our Leader.'

I was glad to get home. I thought Peter was mad and I felt sorry for my aunt. However, soon I was reading an interesting book called *From Double Eagle to Red Flag*, which I had found in the local library. The author was the Cossack General Krasnov and it was about the Russian Civil War. For the next few weeks I became deeply involved with the history of the Russian Revolution. At the time I wasn't aware that since the twenties many of the Berlin communists had ended up in concentration camps, had disappeared or had been murdered by the Nazis.

One morning there was a loud banging at our door and, when I opened it, I saw before me a policeman and, next to him, the Hauptjungzugführer, in his full uniform.

'Why have you not called in for duty?' the Hauptjungzugführer shouted.

The policeman, who looked horrified by the Hauptjungzugführer shouting at me, interrupted him and said in a kindly voice, 'We want to speak to your parents.'

'My mother's not at home at the moment,' I said.

The youth leader put his hands on his belt. 'You're in big trouble!' he told me.

I opened the door wider and asked them to come inside and we all stood in our kitchen.

'You must report for duty or I'll have to take you to the station,' the policeman said.

'I've been very ill. I haven't got enough red blood cells,' I said, remembering my grandmother's complaint and hoping that this explanation would quieten them down.

'You need to bring us a doctor's letter,' said the youth leader, looking somewhat puzzled. 'Meanwhile, I will expect to see you next Sunday. We have to train for the big parade.'

'Get your mother to call me at the police station,' the policeman added. 'It's important that she does so.'

I conveyed the message and the next day my mother phoned the police station. She was told that she was responsible for her son doing his duty for the Fatherland. This was the law and she had to obey it, like everyone else. My mother told me she thought it was absurd for a ten-year-old to be expected to do his duty for the Fatherland but said I had better play along with these confused people.

On Sunday, once again wearing my uniform, I arrived at the school playground and joined my group. We had to march up and down, turning right, turning left, and then marching in twos and threes and fours, all the time singing. This time, before we were discharged, we had to stand to attention and raise our right arms and sing the German national anthem, followed by the 'Horst Wessel' song. This was a long song and soon my right arm began to droop, so I had to support it with my left.

The following Sunday we had to march to a large building where there was a shooting range. We were each given an air rifle and instructed to shoot at targets. To my surprise, the group leader rushed up to me, smiling, with the target card in his hands. 'Bullseye every time!' he shouted, showing me my card, which had all my six shots in the centre. 'Come on. Do it again. I'll put up another target card,' he said. So I shot again, with much the same result. The other boys congratulated me and called the instructor, who was a Hitler Youth leader and much older than us. After examining my target cards, he announced: 'We must have him at our next tournament.' Then he turned to me and said, 'You'd make a good sniper. You must join the special unit.' Everyone looked at me with admiration. The instructor looked at our group leader. 'Bring him back on Wednesday,' he said.

Now I'm in real trouble, I thought. How am I going to get out of this? The very last thing I wanted to do was any military service. I hated all the shouting, marching and wearing a uniform.

There was a small cinema on my route home from school and often I would go and see a film there in the afternoon. This cinema, like many others, showed the newsreel after the main feature, so that you could leave after the feature film if you wanted to. This suited me fine because I never liked watching the newsreels, with their endless marching and shooting and the Leader constantly shouting. Some of the feature films I saw were very funny. Once I even fell off my chair, I was laughing so much. I loved Laurel and Hardy (in German we called them 'Fat and Stupid') and I adored Charlie Chaplin's film *The Gold Rush*.

In his silly way, despite looking clumsy and hopeless, Chaplin always somehow made good and overcame all opposition, however outnumbered he was. In the passage to our flat there was a big full-length mirror. I used to practise Buster Keaton's expressionless, deadpan face in front of it, which I trained myself to hold for five minutes. I also tried to copy Chaplin's gawky walk and Stan Laurel's bewildered look. I thought maybe I should become a clown when I was older.

In any event, the day after my shooting calamity, I phoned my aunt. I told her I didn't want to be in the sniper unit and asked her what to do. She replied, 'What did you have for breakfast last Sunday?'

'I don't think I had any breakfast last Sunday,' I said.

'You see, my boy, you were too worked up and intense,' she explained. 'This is what you do. Before you go on Wednesday morning you must have a very big breakfast. Four boiled eggs, lots of bread and butter and jam, and drink lots of hot milk. Put some chocolate with the milk. That will fix you up and you will be very sleepy. Good luck.'

My mother couldn't believe what she saw on Wednesday morning as I stuffed myself with food. To be on the safe side, I had six eggs and half a loaf of bread and I ended up so stuffed that I could hardly put my uniform on. When I arrived together with our group leader at the shooting range, a number of much older boys were already there, shooting at targets. They were all in Hitler Youth uniforms. I switched on my Buster Keaton face, which was not too difficult because I was beginning to feel sick with all that food in my stomach. The instructor saw me and made his way over. 'There is our sharpshooter,' he said, dragging me by the arm across to the range. 'Come. Show them how to shoot!' He spoke loudly so that everyone could hear.

Well, they all made space for me and I put myself in a shooting position, although I felt very uncomfortable from my over-full stomach. Someone put a new card in the box. There was total silence. I waited as long as I could and then pressed the trigger, again and again, six times. With a deliberate, erect stride, the instructor walked to the target, looked at it, and took the card out of the box. He stood with his back to us, not moving. No one made a sound. Then he turned round. He was furious. 'This must be a mistake,' he said, looking straight into my eyes as he advanced towards me.

I was scared to death. I switched to Laurel's bewildered look.

The instructor tore up the card and shouted at one of the boys. 'Put in another card!' Then he bent over and put his face close to mine. 'You had better get it right this time,' he said.

By now I was trembling and my stomach was grumbling but I shot again and scored one bullseye. The other five shots were on the card but they were not nearly good enough to make a fuss about. So, after being humiliated and shouted at, I got home a happy boy. I was not going to be in the sharpshooter unit after all.

Later that year I found my new hero in Karl May's book *Winnetou*, the chief of the Mescalero Apache. Winnetou and the white man, Old Shatterhand, became blood brothers during the American fights between the invading whites and the inhabitants of the American Wild West. It was a story about rights and peace, honour and comradeship, and its philosophy had a profound effect on me. In American films the Indians always lost and were portrayed as being devious and deceitful. This made me feel very depressed – you can't always believe what you see in the cinema.

I may have been only ten years old but I was fully aware of the nervousness of those around me whenever the Leader was mentioned. Meanwhile, the grip of the Nazi regime seemed to be getting more oppressive all the time. There were stricter regulations about what people could or could not do. I noticed that my mother and her friends often spoke in hushed voices when discussing the state of the country.

On the fourth floor of our building lived the Schultzes – Frau Schultze and her husband. Most afternoons and nights Frau Schultze worked as an usherette at the Universum Cinema down the Ku'damm, but once a week she would come and fetch our washing and clean our flat. I had great fun with her on the days she came to us. She was easily startled and sometimes I'd surprise her by jumping up from behind the sofa and enjoy seeing her run away squealing with shock, although she would often return shrieking with laughter. She knew all the popular romantic films by heart and sometimes she managed to smuggle me into the cinema, which also showed some American cowboy films.

It was my job to climb the stairs up to the fourth floor to collect our washing and here I would sometimes find Herr Schultze playing the accordion. I liked Herr Schultze, although he never said much. In the mornings I'd see him going off to work with an old attaché case under his arm, but at night, when we had to go down into the air raid shelter, which was a reinforced part of the cellar in our building, he would keep us entertained with all the latest songs. Everybody sang along to his music. The people of the Hinterhof would all sit together in the small space, which had a crate of beer in the corner. I drank my first bottle of beer in this cellar. It made me tipsy and I started to perform like Charlie Chaplin and everybody laughed.

By 1942 the air raids increased and they also became more intense. When the anti-aircraft fire got closer and louder we could hear the bombs whistling – sharp, high-pitched and shrill. I got to know that when they made that noise the bombs were far away, and that a short, ear-piercing screech meant they were closer, perhaps overhead. Then everything would shake. Once there was a deafeningly loud crash and the lights went out. We sat in darkness while the noise of the bombs continued to get louder and louder. Herr Schultze lit a candle and when I saw all the frightened faces around me I began to feel alarmed. What would happen if we were all buried under the building? However, after a short while, the noise slowly receded and finally the sirens sounded the all-clear.

I still went almost every Sunday to the Jungvolk, where we had to do gymnastics and, of course, the endless marching. I consistently mixed up my left and right when marching and became a nuisance to the group, who wanted to be the top group at the great march in front of the Nazi leaders that was about to take place. On the big day I took the washing up to Frau Schultze on the fourth floor, having deliberately put my uniform brown shirts and all my grey socks in the pile of dirty laundry. This meant that when I arrived at the meeting for the grand parade I was wearing red socks and a colourful blouse of my mother's. All hell broke loose. The boys laughed and the Jungzugführer nearly had a fit. They called the Hauptjungzugführer, who shouted at me until he got red in the face. With my Buster Keaton face on, I jabbered away about my washing and how everything was dirty. My punishment was that I was not allowed to march in front of the leaders. I didn't go back for some weeks and in the end persuaded my aunt to write a letter saying that I had to go and stay with my grandparents in Thuringia because I wasn't well.

Later, during the summer holidays, I did go and stay with my grandparents. They lived in Mühlhausen, a small town dating back to the Middle Ages, some 300 kilometres south-west of Berlin. It had a defensive wall built right around it, with look-out towers and gates to protect the centre, and narrow cobblestoned streets lined with small fourteenth-century houses with tiny doors and windows. In the basement of the town hall there was a torture chamber with some macabre machines in it, such as a wooden stretcher that pulled people apart, and coffins with sharp spikes. I remember wondering why this small town, with its numerous lavish cathedral-like churches, needed a torture chamber.

My grandparents – Gretchen and Heinrich – lived on the edge of the town in an apartment above a bakery. It seemed to be quite large but I never got to explore it because most of the doors inside the flat were kept locked. My grandmother kept the keys on a belt around her waist. We mainly lived in the kitchen, where we cooked on a big fire stove. It was here that we ate our meals and where we socialised during the day. There was a small piece of linoleum just inside the door that led off the street. This was where you left your shoes and put on your slippers. In the kitchen, by the door, there was a water tap and a round metal sink and beneath the sink a bucket in which my grandfather and I had to pee; my grandmother used the toilet that was on the staircase outside the flat. I was given the job of emptying the bucket, which I did once a day. Next to the kitchen was the bedroom. In it were two large beds with very thick feather covers, one on either side of the window. My grandmother slept in one bed and I had to sleep with my grandfather in the other, which was not very comfortable, especially as my grandfather was a very noisy sleeper and snored heavily.

Mühlhausen was situated in a valley and I remember some heavy night-time thunderstorms, with flashes of lightning and huge claps of thunder. During these storms I would see my grandmother walking up and down with a lighted candle in her hand, passing from the bedroom into the kitchen and back again. In her long white nightdress, with her white hair gleaming over her face in the flashing light, she looked like a ghost. As she paced, she would be moaning and mumbling: 'Dear God! Dear God! We're being punished. Forgive us our sins, dear God, my Father, Holy Father …' My grandfather remained oblivious to my grandmother's distress and slept on, snoring and farting his way through the storm. These nights felt like scenes from a Frankenstein movie I had seen at the Universum Cinema.

Everything in the flat was locked up, even the kitchen cupboard where my grandmother kept packets of cigarettes, cigars and packets of tobacco. My grandfather loved to smoke and he made up his own mixture of tobacco, which he kept in a tin box. He used rosebuds mixed with pipe tobacco, as well as leaves collected from the forest. These he dried, neatly laid out on a newspaper on the floor in a corner of the bedroom. On special days, like Sundays, my grandmother would give him a couple of cigars. He always complained that the cigars had been locked up too long and so had dried up. Then came the usual argument. 'Why do you have to lock up my cigars?' he would say to my grandmother. 'They've been there for years.'

'You're too greedy,' she would reply, pointing skywards with her index finger. 'It's a sin to be greedy.'

On Sundays my grandmother made us go to church, although she didn't attend services herself. My grandfather had to put on his best suit, shirt and tie and I had to wear my best outfit. The church was at the other end of the town and it took the two of us over half an hour walking along the old city wall to get there. By the time we eventually arrived the service had usually already started. We'd look inside and note who was preaching, so that we could tell my grandmother later on. Then we went to the nearest pub where Heinrich had a beer and a smoke and I had a non-alcoholic malt beer. We would walk back in time for lunch, satisfied that Gretchen wouldn't know that we had not attended the service – she was always kept informed by our devoutly Catholic neighbours as to who was preaching.

Lunch was usually a pea stew with pork knuckles, which Heinrich had prepared the day before, as he did all the cooking. During and after lunch I had to sit still on my little bench in the kitchen and try not to make my clothes dirty while Gretchen got ready to go out. When we were all ready, we left and slowly, at a pace set by my grandmother, walked for about an hour to go and see my aunt and cousins at their family's restaurant, which was attached to the town's slaughter-house. Every now and then during the walk, we had to stop because we met a person Gretchen knew. With tears in her eyes, she would whine and moan about her colon, her red blood cells (of which she had too few) and her liver, and tell the acquaintance what the doctor had to say about it all.

The restaurant belonged to my Aunt Irmgard's mother. Irmgard was married to my mother's brother Josef and they had three children. These were my cousins – Wolfgang, who was ten, Erfried, who was nine, and young Karin, who was four. Wolfgang was wild and crazy. One day when the beer wagon came to make a delivery and men in leather aprons came out to unload the barrels and roll them into the basement, Wolfgang unhooked the horses from the carriage. The wagon was pulled by two huge cart-horses and Wolfgang jumped up on one of them and went galloping down the street, shouting and laughing, with the other horse following behind. I thought he had gone bonkers. There was a big commotion, with Irmgard and her mother and the two beer delivery men in their leather aprons running down the road trying to catch them. When they finally caught Wolfgang and led him into the restaurant, he burst into loud crying and bawling, tears running down his cheeks. As soon as my aunt let him loose, however, he ran down the passage between the tables to the door, turned around and waved his arms about, laughing and jeering, mocking everybody, before disappearing through the door. This sort of performance took place every Sunday. Wolfgang was always up to something bizarre.

One day I was helping my grandmother do the washing. I sat on the floor in the pantry with an enamel dish in front of me, rubbing wet soap into our socks and underwear, while Gretchen stood over me giving me instructions. The pantry was quite big, with rows of jam jars and bottles of fruit juices on shelves and a number of salamis and a ham hanging in the corner, which looked rather old and dried up. I tried to persuade Gretchen to show me what was behind one of her locked doors and eventually, reluctantly, she agreed. 'But you mustn't touch anything,' she said. I stood close behind her as she unlocked the first door. 'Stay on the newspapers,' she instructed.

It was a big room, with curtains at the windows. In it was a large cupboard with long inlaid mirrors, a settee, and a dining table covered with a lace table-cloth. There were lots of porcelain figures everywhere, some candle-holders, and a glass cupboard full of patterned plates and glasses. On the floor leading to another door, with windows, sheets of newspaper had been laid down and I followed Gretchen, walking on them carefully. Gretchen opened the cupboard doors and I saw rows of suits on hangers and a fur coat, from which a strong smell of moth-balls exuded. 'These are Grandpa's suits and this is my fur coat,' Gretchen said proudly.

I walked up to the next door and looked through the window to see a summer room with windows all around, furnished with bamboo tables and chairs, including a rocking chair. Laid out on the table was a porcelain tea-set with cups and plates and little forks and spoons. I was about to try the handle when my grandmother stopped me. 'No, stop! Nobody goes into my summer room!' she said. 'And stay on the newspapers. I don't want to have to polish the floor again.'

'Why don't we use these rooms?' I asked.

'They will only get dirty,' she said.

She hesitated and then began going through the keys on her belt. She picked one out and opened the other door. I couldn't believe it. On the other side was an almost empty room. Here, too, there were newspapers spread out all over the floor, although where they all came from I'll never know, because my grandparents never seemed to read or buy newspapers. Actually, there were no books in the house either, except the Bible, which I never saw them read. On one side of the room I saw hundreds of eggs laid in rows along the floor, each egg with a date on it; and on the other side were rows of apples. The one piece of furniture in the room was a wooden chest in the corner.

'What's in there?' I asked.

Gretchen walked across to the chest and I bent over her shoulder to see what was in it. 'One day all this will be yours,' she said.

Inside the chest I saw piles and piles of Deutsche mark notes, in high denominations, hundreds of millions', perhaps even billions', worth. The chest was full to the top. I had heard about the economic crash of the twenties, when you bought a loaf of bread for a million marks, but I had never imagined so many banknotes really existed.

'This is worth nothing,' I said.

'It will be. One day it will be,' Gretchen replied.

Heinrich was a postman. I think he must have been a postman general because he wore a smart blue uniform with a cap on his head and on each collar of his jacket was a square of velvet with four little gold stars, which made him look very important. However, when he came back from work, he would change into his old post office uniform jacket. Often Heinrich would take me to the nearby forest to collect wild strawberries. One sunny day, on the way there, we passed through some cornfields and crossed a small stream that was so clear you could see little fish swimming about in it. We walked up a path along the bank. There were apple trees on either side and Heinrich picked some apples and we sat down on a bench that looked out on the valley on one side and the forest on the other. There was a large stone next to the bench with some writing engraved on it. It was overgrown with moss. I asked Heinrich about it and he told me that some well-known person had shot himself here on the bench. He was about to tell me the story when I interrupted him. I asked him about the long scar he had on his left cheek. I had always wondered about his scar and imagined there must have been some romantic story behind it, about swordfighting perhaps.

'Well,' Heinrich said, 'in 1915 I was in the infantry, fighting on the front line in France. One night I was sent out on patrol with two other men to see what the French were up to. That night it was very dark and we were walking through deep grass and bushes as we approached what we had been told was a deserted French village. Suddenly we heard voices and one of my men stumbled on a slope, causing a lot of noise. There was a shot and then all hell broke loose, with shooting coming from everywhere. I was knocked over by a bullet that hit me in the face – it was that bullet that caused the scar you can see now – and the two men standing behind me fell down dead. This was a terrible time. I was on the ground and lying beside me were my two dead comrades. I whispered to them but they said nothing and it became obvious that they were dead. There was nothing much I could do and so I stayed where I was, not moving, for what seemed like ages. After a while, I heard whispering voices, then someone struck a match and I saw a flicker of light nearby and smelt the aroma of some strong tobacco. Whoever it was, they must have been very close to me. Any moment the French could find me. I thought I can't stay here and do nothing, so I stood up and shouted, "Vive la France!" Now you won't believe it, but as soon as I said "Vive la France!", all around me I heard shouts of "Vive la France!" from the French soldiers. Well, I just walked away and found my way back to my unit. So that's how I got the scar.'

I still remember the glint in my grandfather's eyes as he told me of his lucky escape. I thought of the unbelievable story of Baron Munchausen, who tells of jumping on a cannonball as it left the fired gun to inspect the enemy's position … and then jumping over to another cannonball which came from the enemy's guns and returning to report to his generals.

After sitting there a while, Heinrich and I got up off the bench and walked into the forest. The forest was dense, but before you got into it there was a wide fire-break with tall grass and blackberry bushes and wild strawberries. Heinrich reached into his old attaché case and pulled out an empty milk bottle. He handed it to me and said, 'Fill it up.' The strawberries were very small but they tasted much better than the big ones we got in the shops. Another time when we went walking together we disturbed a boar, which ran away through the deep underbrush into the forest. We filled up our bottles and went back home.

When Heinrich returned from his weekly inspection tour, which meant visiting village post offices in the district, he always brought back presents he had received from the local farmers, such as salamis, eggs, milk, bacon and so on. Once I remember him coming back with a freshly slaughtered chicken. We took it down to the cellar. The cellar was divided into sections by wooden partitions, each resident of the building having a small space where they could store their coal and potatoes for the winter. Heinrich sat himself on a stool and proceeded to pluck the chicken. I got bored watching him and went out into the street. There I saw our neighbour, Mrs Raguse, running down the road. She was very big and very fat and wore a shawl on her head and a flowery apron. She was wearing slippers and she ran in a funny way trying not to lose them off her feet. Ahead of her, running away around the corner, were a number of chickens, one of which whisked past me into the entrance of our building and down the steps into the cellar. Mrs Raguse was right behind it, clumsily rushing down the steps in pursuit. I followed her, and as I got down into the cellar I heard much shouting and screaming coming from my grandparents' section.

'You thief! I am going to call the police!' I heard Mrs Raguse shout.

I looked into the partition where Heinrich was still sitting on his stool, only now with a plucked chicken in his hand and feathers everywhere – all over Heinrich and Mrs Raguse, who was pulling at one leg of the chicken, trying to get it out of my grandfather's grasp. Heinrich doggedly hung onto it.

'You stupid woman! Get out of my cellar!' he roared, as he grimly tried to retain a grip on his chicken.

Next thing I saw Mrs Raguse's chicken emerge from one of the neighbours' partitions. With a brief, wild-eyed look at the commotion, the chicken started running up the steps and out of the cellar. 'There's your chicken!' I shouted as loud as I could, pointing at the stairs.

For a moment Mrs Raguse stopped grappling with Heinrich's chicken. She looked at the one fleeing up the stairs and then back at the one coming apart in her hands. I could see the realisation dawning: even a world record-holding chicken plucker could not have plucked a chicken quite as fast as Heinrich supposedly had. With a furious shriek, she abruptly let the bird go and ran out of the cellar, while Heinrich slumped, exhausted, back onto his stool. I saw him look forlornly at his chicken, now a mangled wreck, on his lap. This story became the talk of the town.

While I enjoyed being with my grandparents, when it came time for me to go home I was happy to return to Berlin. As I walked up the Ku'damm I noticed that in front of our apartment building a new shop had replaced the previous electrical shop, which had specialised in lamps. It was now a shop selling uniforms. The long panels on either side of the shop's doorway had slogans painted on them in black, something about 'Juden', about Jews being unwelcome in Germany, about them being untrustworthy and evil. I stood looking at the display in the window, which was a shop mannequin in a brown uniform and, as I looked closer, a memory I had thought long forgotten suddenly came to me.

When we had lived in Berliner Street a long time before, there had been a vegetable and fruit shop on the corner. The owner was a kindly man, who had a very big, furry dog. The dog became my friend and I used to play with him often. The shop owner made a habit of giving me a delicious apple from his garden whenever I stopped by. One evening I was playing with the dog when one of the men at the shop, I think it must have been the brother of the owner, asked me if I wanted to come along with them. He said there were exciting things happening. And so the dog and I sat in the back of the car and the owner and his brother sat in the front.

To be honest, I don't know why they took me along, but what I saw, as we drove around the city from one place to another, reminded me of the uniformed figure in the shop window I was looking at now. We drove past many men in brown shirts who were breaking down doors and smashing shop windows. I saw them dragging old men out of their shops and hitting them viciously. Everywhere on the walls, in huge lettering, was written the word 'Juden'. I remember that we passed several large buildings that were burning. One of these was a synagogue and there I saw people being pushed and hauled, crying and screaming, onto trucks: old people, children, teenagers and women. It was a horrifying sight.

My mother was at home when I got back. She had a friend with her, whose name was Karl Hellmer. He was also in the theatre and movie business and I had met him before. He was Viennese and spoke with a funny, soft Austrian accent.

My mother said, 'Go and look in the kitchen and see what Karl has brought you,' and I went into the kitchen and there was Karl's old bicycle. I was wondering why he was giving it to me when he told me, in a sad voice, that he would no longer be needing it because he was going back to Vienna to make a film and to play the lead in a play. He said he wouldn't be coming back to Berlin for some time. Well, I thanked Karl very much and felt very grateful, although the bike needed a lot of work for it to be useful. After Karl left, I asked my mother for some money to fix it up and I went to the bicycle shop near us and bought the necessary things to make the bike roadworthy. I painted the frame blue, with some yellow sections, and fitted silver mudguards on it. The chain needed replacing, as well as the tubes in the tyres and the brakes, but, when all this was done, I rode happily down the Ku'damm feeling like a king.

I had changed schools and now attended the Grunewald Gymnasium, which I found very boring because most of the teachers were retired old men, the younger teachers having gone off to fight in the war. Some of our teachers were eccentric, to say the least. One had a glass eye and a curious mannerism. As he walked up and down the classroom dictating a text to us, he would take out a handkerchief and hold it in front of his glass eye. Then he would hit himself on the back of his head, at which the glass eye would jump out of its socket and into his handkerchief. He would proceed to give it a good clean and polish before popping it back into its socket. The performance held us entranced. Of all the classes, I most enjoyed the English class. Our teacher wore knickerbockers and a brown tweed jacket. Best of all, when he came into the class he would say, 'Good morning, gentlemen!' Most of the other teachers came in, raised their right arm and greeted us with 'Heil Hitler!'

I did not go back to the Jungvolk. I think they must have forgotten about me, especially since I now went to a different school, so I did not meet the same boys. By now I was reading prodigiously. I came across an interesting book on my mother's bookshelf, *All Quiet on the Western Front* by Erich Maria Remarque, and was soon deeply engrossed in it. The book was all about the stupidity of war, the gruesome things that happen to people and how war affects populations. It had a profound effect on me, especially as the bombing increased over Berlin both day and night.

I remember sitting in the sun outside a busy café with my mother one day. There were lots of people around, including soldiers on leave, with waiters rushing about carrying coffee, ice cream and cakes on their trays. Suddenly I saw Klaus walking towards us, making his way between the tables. He looked much thinner and very sad, quite unlike the way he'd looked when he had returned from Paris. He sat down next to my mother and looked intently at her, talking to her in a hushed tone. My mother looked distressed. I heard her say, 'I understand, but it doesn't matter.' Then Klaus got up to leave. He gave me a nod and, as he was hurrying away, he turned around and said, 'I'm going back to the front.' Later, at home, I overheard my mother talking to Anita on the phone. Klaus had been fighting in Russia, where he had been shot and had lost his manhood. So he had decided to return to the front, feeling that nothing mattered any more.

The air raids continued and several buildings immediately across the road from us were hit, leaving nothing but shattered, smouldering wrecks. These days we always left the radio on at night, tuned to a special wavelength, which emitted a sound like a large alarm clock – 'tick … tick … tick' – and I slept in our main room on the couch and my mother on the bed so that we wouldn't oversleep. When the ticking on our radio suddenly stopped, we would wake up and an announcer would provide a report about enemy aeroplanes crossing the English Channel. About 20 minutes later the announcer would say how many planes were flying over Hannover–Brunswick and towards Berlin. This was the signal for us to get up and move quickly into the bomb shelter.

It became more difficult to get enough to eat and, like everyone else, I was always hungry. There was a shortage of meat, butter and sugar, and now we had to get ration cards from the block administrator once a month. He lived around the corner from us in a small flat, which was full of propaganda posters, and you had to be nice to him if you wanted to get your ration cards. He was a big man with a short haircut, who wore some sort of Nazi uniform. Whenever I entered his room he would shout 'Heil Hitler!' and then look sternly at me. Obviously he was expecting to receive the same greeting from me, but I would just mumble 'Hi Hit'. Every time I went to his flat he would ask me if I was doing my duty at the Jungvolk and tell me that I should help collect warm clothes for our German soldiers fighting for us in Russia. Then he'd give me our ration card. The card had little squares on it, each one with a number. From time to time there would be an announcement stating the number's buying value. So one square might be enough to buy 100 grams of meat, another 50 grams of fat or sugar. Whatever the quantities allowed, however, they were nowhere near enough to last a whole month.

One day a friend of my mother's, Heinz Seidler, who was a boxing champion, turned up with a dog. He asked my mother if she would look after it because he had been called up for duty by the Waffen SS and he didn't know where he would be stationed or for how long.

'What about your wife, can't she look after your dog?' my mother asked him.

Heinz lowered his voice to a whisper. He said his wife was in trouble with the authorities and anyway he didn't get on with her any more. His wife was

Polish and had a relationship with an anti-Nazi group.

My mother agreed to take the dog, which was an Afghan hound with the amazing name of Cosima von der Windburg. Cosima was very thin, with long blonde hair, and she had no trouble settling on our couch and immediately making herself at home. Indeed, she looked as if the whole place belonged to her. I thought she was the silliest dog I had ever seen. She would just sit doing nothing and look right through me, as if I was not there at all. Over the next few days I tried to make friends with the blonde. I noticed that, unlike other dogs, she never wagged her tail. It would just stand up and the hair would hang down like a flag. I tried to play ball with her but she was not even interested in that. Finally, I fetched my pyjamas. I put the trouser part on her, with the slit at the back so that her tail could stick out, and the jacket in front. Then I put a party hat on her head and a pair of sunglasses. Cosima just sat there. No tail movement, nothing. I got out my little Kodak Retina 35 mm camera and took her picture. That seemed to make her happy. Her tail moved for the first time. The next day my mother, wearing her fur coat and high heels, took Cosima for a walk down the Ku'damm with everyone passing by looking at them. I thought they both looked silly, which made me remember another dog story.

There was this tiger trainer called Togare. One day my mother and I went to the Babelsberg film studios, where my mother worked from time to time. There we saw Togare standing in a large circular cage surrounded by ten angry-looking Bengal tigers. He had two large golden earrings the size of curtain rings in his ears and his beaming smile revealed big white teeth. He was bare-chested, but wore colourful Turkish baggy silk trousers and a small curved dagger on his belt. There were gold bracelets on his forearms and wrists and around his head a yellow band. In his hand he held a long whip, which he cracked from time to time. I still have a photo of Togare, signed by him and dedicated to my mother with love. Then a very friendly St Bernard dog was put into a tiger skin. The 'tiger' was supposed to wrestle Togare. I stood watching with my mother as they tried over and over again to film this. The dog kept losing his tiger skin, which he eventually tore apart until it disintegrated, and they finally gave up. When my mother murmured to me, 'This Togare is wonderful …', I did not reply. And when she said, 'And he told me that Adolf Hitler is a great man,' I could not believe the comment. I just kept quiet.

At home we had a very big, modern radio which had both short-wave and long-wave stations. Sometimes when I was bored I would listen to it. As I went through the short-wave, I found many stations in different languages, including Voice of America, which was broadcast in German. Here there was much talk about the Nazis and their criminal behaviour. Once I found a station that talked about the concentration camps in Germany, where people were being murdered. From far away, with lots of interference, I also came across a station called Atlantiksender, which you could only get at night. I had to be very careful. Once my mother found me listening to an English station and was furious. She said we would get into big trouble if anyone found out because it was against the law to listen to foreign radio stations. I didn't like the German stations, though, which seemed to consist of nothing more than marching music and endless propaganda about the victorious German army.

Instead I played our records. We had a wind-up gramophone and hundreds of records, which had been given to my mother by a friend who had left Germany many years before. I listened to 'Donkey Serenade', Louis Armstrong, Bing Crosby, Zarah Leander, Marlene Dietrich, and lots of American jazz songs. Sometimes when we had a party I was the music manager and I played records into the night, which I loved doing.

2

SURVIVING THE APOCALYPSE

By early 1943 the air raids were happening both at night and during the day, so life had become much more dangerous, with large numbers of American bombers laying terrifying carpets of bombs across Berlin. This meant that we'd frequently have to go to the bunker at the Zoo, which was at the other end of the Ku'damm, about five kilometres away from our apartment. Once you were in the bunker, which held about ten thousand people, you were quite safe, as the walls and roof consisted of a metre of concrete and could therefore withstand any bombs, however close.

The trouble was that we had to get there in time, before the bombing actually started. Sometimes when the alarm sirens started we took the tram, with the tram driver driving at the highest speed possible; at other times, when we were late or there were no trams, we went by bicycle, my mother sitting sideways behind me on the luggage-rack. This was an awkward journey – with her legs dangling on one side, my mother would have to lean out on the opposite side to maintain our balance.

We would stay in the bunker for hours sometimes, with the anti-aircraft guns above us making an incredible noise as they fired at the bombers. Once, after a very big bang, several soldiers were carried down from the roof and taken past us. They were moaning, covered with blood and in a terrible state of distress, their bodies a dreadful mess.

After the all-clear, we would walk slowly up the Ku'damm, passing burning buildings and newly demolished houses, smoke filling the air and ash falling all around us. The fire brigade would be frantically at work, together with the ambulance service and anyone around attending to those who had been wounded. We were always filled with apprehension on our return home, wondering if our house was still there or whether it was burning or bombed out.

One of my mother's great friends around this time was a Bulgarian opera singer named Sasho, who always wore a thick woollen scarf round his neck. For some reason, he drank copious amounts of cough medicine. Once I saw him drink a whole bottle in one go. Anyway, one day Sasho and I were walking together along the Ku'damm when the air raid alarms started to sound. 'Let's go to the bunker at the Zoo,' I said. 'It's not far.' I took him by the hand to speed him up as he was always very slow and I was starting to get nervous. In the distance, I could hear the anti-aircraft fire slowly coming closer. This was worrying because the anti-aircraft batteries fired shells that exploded high in the sky, causing shards of steel to rain down on anyone standing below. Some pieces of the shrapnel were as big as a fist. But Sasho just kept walking at his usual leisurely pace, even when we heard the drones of the first bombers overhead. Everybody around us on the street started to run and disappear into the surrounding buildings but Sasho appeared completely unconcerned, despite my urging. With all hell breaking loose around us, we managed to get into the bunker alive and unhurt. Sasho's indifference to danger did not stop when the all-clear was sounded. Together we walked back up the Ku'damm and into the side street where he had a flat. As we approached his apartment we found his home cordoned off by police and firemen, who stopped us. 'You can't go into that building. There's an unexploded bomb in front of it,' one of the policemen said.

Sasho told me to stay where I was and he continued walking down the street towards his apartment. Another policeman tried to stop him but Sasho pushed him aside, saying something I couldn't hear. I could see the bomb, a big one, lying next to a tree. Seemingly unconcerned, Sasho walked into the building. After a few minutes he came out carrying his bicycle, which he leant against the tree next to the bomb, before casually proceeding to pump up the tyres.

Despite the increasing bombing, normal schooling for all of us children continued. It was not until the summer holidays that I returned, at the insistence of my mother, to my grandparents in Mühlhausen. Nothing much had changed there since my previous stay, two years before, except that my grandfather's right arm was in plaster. Evidently, he had been picking apples on the country road nearby and had fallen out of a tree. He hadn't told anyone about the fall and for two weeks his arm was badly swollen before he saw the doctor. Now he had to walk sideways through doors with his protruding plastered arm.

I had brought a few books with me to pass the time, mostly detective stories, such as those about Sherlock Holmes, with the illustrations on the front covers showing a detective in action. When Gretchen saw these books she became very angry. 'These are the books of the Devil!' she shouted. 'I will not have evil in my house!' She tried to wrestle the books from me but I hung on and somehow we both ended up on the floor. She was on top of me, her face close to mine. Her two remaining teeth – one on top and one underneath – were bared and I saw absolute madness in her eyes. I became very frightened but managed to disentangle myself from her and stand up. Huffing and puffing like a rhinoceros, with one of my books in her hand, Gretchen went over to the stove, opened the fire door, and savagely pushed the book into the fire. It was an upsetting moment for me.

That afternoon it was hot and I went for a walk in the countryside. After a while I lay down in the grass and fell asleep. I was woken by the sound of thunder, a deep, continuous rolling, which gradually got louder and louder. Then, over the horizon, I saw the sky virtually darken and fill with rows of aeroplanes flying in formation. Soon they were right above me, too many to count, big American bombers, making the ground around me vibrate. There must have been five hundred or more planes, more than I had ever seen before. It was one of the most electrifying and terrifying moments of my life – the whole sky filled with bombers and the world thundering with an ominous rumbling sound. That evening when we were sitting in the kitchen and Heinrich was serving the stew, he told me there had been a very big air raid on Berlin. I told him what I had seen earlier in the day, the hundreds of bombers.

'This war is stupid,' I said. 'Anyway, Hitler's a criminal.'

Heinrich looked at me furiously and hit me hard on the head with the ladle, which was full of stew. 'Never say that again!' he shouted. 'You'll get us all into serious trouble.'

I licked the stew that was running down my face, realising that if Heinrich was scared, then that really was something to worry about. I also knew that as an official postman he could have lots of problems if anyone found out what we thought about the government.

A few days later I received a letter from my mother. She asked me if, before I came home after the summer holidays, I could go and see my father's brother on his farm and bring back something to eat. The food shortages in Berlin were getting worse and it was becoming harder and harder to find anything edible.

So a few days before my return to Berlin I put on my backpack and marched down the country road from my grandparents' home for the ten-kilometre walk to my Uncle Richard's farm. Here, even though I had not met them before, I was welcomed by the family. I arrived just as they were about to sit down to lunch. This had been laid out on a long table in their spacious kitchen, where I could see sausages, black pudding and fried potatoes. It was more food than I could remember seeing for ages. There were three children present, my cousins, who were all more or less my age and had red cheeks and very healthy faces. Of course they all wanted to know about the bombing in Berlin, which I told them about, while my Aunt Frieda kept offering me more and more food. Meanwhile, my uncle went outside to slaughter a chicken for me to take to Berlin, along with the eggs, sausages, bacon and bread that I had already been given. Finally, accompanied by shouts of 'Good luck!' and 'Come again!' I left.

The following day I took the train back to Berlin. The compartment was over-crowded and a few hours into the journey night fell. We were starting to pass through an industrial area with factories on either side of the railway line when suddenly there were several enormous explosions and the ground shook. The train swayed and shuddered, as though it would leave the rails at any moment. Flashes like lightning bolts leapt skywards as the anti-aircraft batteries opened up on the planes overhead. Our train picked up speed. All around I could see buildings burning, some of them exploding into flames as I watched. Faster and faster the train went in a desperate attempt to escape the firestorm around us. We had been caught right in the middle of an air raid. It was a terrifying experience and many of the passengers looked frightened. I thought we would be hit at any moment.

By some miracle, our train passed, unharmed, through the air raid and I arrived safely at Berlin's Anhalter Bahnhof late in the morning. I was not surprised to see that there was no transport home. It was obvious that the air raid had been a heavy one. Houses were still burning and people were cleaning up rubble in the streets and searching for survivors in destroyed buildings. The air was full of smoke and the smell of burning wood. Still very shaken, I began to walk home, worried that I might find that it no longer existed. However, our building was still standing and I saw, with relief, that it was undamaged. I opened our front door and there was my mother, laying out cards for Anita.

'You will get a letter from the past,' I heard her say. 'It's from a very good friend and it's good news.'

I knew what my mother was going to say next, as I had heard this so often, but instead she turned to me. 'Peter's dead,' she said.

'The Nazi?' I asked, thinking of Aunt Doris's son.

'No – Peterle,' she said. 'He must have died of shock. There were a lot of bombs falling nearby and I found him lying at the bottom of his cage.' And my mother returned to the cards and Anita.

'Poor Peterle,' Anita said, with her eyes half closed.

Before Christmas my mother went on holiday with a friend, skiing in the Alps. She sent me a postcard every week. She had left me with some money, so that I could go and have lunch every day at the lunch room next door to us. There were air raids almost every night and I found myself spending hours in the air raid shelter at the back of the house, with people I found very boring. They were all old – there was no one my age around – so I took to going to the shelter for the people who lived in the front part of the building, where the apartments and staircase were much smarter than on our side. They even had carpets on the staircase and on the landings.

It was on this landing that I discovered infinity. There were two large, full-length mirrors on the landing and, as you looked at yourself standing in front of the mirror, you also saw yourself in the mirror behind you and so on, until infinity. This made me think about time and space and I would spend hours trying to figure out these problems.

The first time I went to the upmarket air raid shelter I found about 20 people already there. They were all sitting quietly, with blankets covering their arms and legs. At the end of the passage next to the shelter sat an elderly couple in a dark corner, which was lit by a small candle. I had seen them a few times before and they were easily recognisable from the yellow stars they wore on their clothing. I went over to talk to them. I asked them why they were not sitting with the others, mentioning that it was much warmer there, as there was a small heater.

'It's all right, we are warm enough, thank you very much,' the old man said.

I sat with the elderly couple for a while and then returned to the shelter when some heavy bombing started. Everything started shaking and then there was an ear-splitting blast and the ground shook as if a terrible earthquake was happening. Finally, everything went quiet, the all-clear sounded and we went out into the street. Clouds of choking smoke and dust filled the air. The house next door was almost totally destroyed and those across the street were burning. People came rushing out of shelters to help the wounded. We all tried to help as much as we could while we waited for the arrival of the fire brigade and ambulances, which took ages to come.

The following night I was in the shelter again. This time I took our gramophone with me, and some records. I thought music would cheer everyone up. I played Louis Armstrong and Bing Crosby and a few others. Mrs Viole, the owner of the building, or at least the person who collected the rent, came over to me.

'You mustn't talk to those Jewish people,' she said.

'Why not?' I asked. 'They're very nice people.'

Pointing her finger at me, she said sharply, 'You will get us all into trouble. And stop playing that terrible nigger music!'

Unfortunately, the lack of available food was becoming an increasingly big problem for me and Cosima. I would make some porridge for her, boiled in water with some meat extract, which we used for stews. She seemed to like this but she was thinner than ever and did little more than lie around on the couch in her normal aristocratic way, taking no notice of anything or anybody. I took her for walks in the Grunewald forest, which she appeared to enjoy, but she still wasn't interested in playing with balls or running after sticks.

As I had almost run out of money to buy food, I got on my bike and went

to visit my Aunt Doris, who was happy to see me and gave me a big kiss. I said
hello to the parrot and asked him to sing me his song, but he didn't want to
know. He just stood silently on his perch, looking fed up – I think all the noise
from the bombing was disturbing him. My aunt told me that Peter was in the
army now and had been sent to the Russian front. 'Maybe he'll learn something
there and won't be such a fanatic,' she said. She gave me some money for food
and then asked me to wait. I heard her speaking to someone about me on the
telephone. Then she asked me if I had a bicycle. 'All right, I will send him over,'
she said. When she put the phone down she looked at me earnestly. 'Now, this
is top secret. I am serious! You mustn't talk about this to anyone.'

I ended up being a messenger for a group of students, riding my bicycle to
take parcels and letters from one end of Berlin to another. I only ever met two
of the students, who lived in a flat in Zehlendorf. The flat was almost empty,
apart from a table and a few chairs and lots of boxes on the floor. The students
told me not to keep notes of the delivery addresses for the envelopes or packets. I found all this undercover stuff very exciting and, when my mother finally
returned from her holiday, I kept the secret about my activities as Doris had
instructed me. On one occasion I overheard one of the students saying something about a 'white rose', which I found out much later was the name for an
anti-Nazi underground movement. (Towards the end of the war many members of this group were beheaded.)

One evening Heinz Seidler, the boxing champion, turned up to fetch his dog.
He said he was now back in Berlin. I was happy to see him because feeding and
walking Cosima was becoming more and more problematic, even though, in a
funny way, I had become quite fond of her.

We had regular electricity cuts in the city at the time, and on the night Heinz
came to visit we were all sitting by candlelight. I was seated on our tiled oven,
which was quite high up, near the ceiling where it was nice and warm, and I was
sort of falling asleep when I heard part of the conversation he was having with
my mother. I could only hear snatches and it sounded as though he was crying.
'They sent me to guard … they were all naked … all dead … I can't take it
any more … murdered …' I heard Heinz say and, then, in a clearer voice: 'Of
course, I'm lucky. They said that the sports minister protects me because I'm a

boxing champion. So I was sworn to silence and told to go back to boxing and Berlin.' Of course, neither Heinz nor my mother had noticed that I was listening to them but what they said seemed to bear out what I had heard on Voice of America, when they talked about the Nazis and the evil things they were doing. In Heinz, I had living proof that terrible crimes were being committed, and if my mother and I knew, then surely many other people did as well.

We now spent almost every night in the air raid shelter and it became a habit of mine to eat a sandwich after midnight, so much so that even when there were no air raids I always got up and had a sandwich in the middle of the night. In reality, we were very lucky that, so far, our house had not been hit by a bomb.

My mother and I often went to the Kempinski on the Ku'damm. The Jewish-owned hotel had been expropriated and it was now called Borchardt. There we could still get a meal without ration cards and we dined on a dish called Eintopf (one pot), which was made of potatoes, cabbage and carrots. Sometimes, if you were lucky, you would find a piece of pork-skin and a bone in it. The atmosphere in the Kempinski restaurant was as if there was no war or bombing going on and everything was quite normal. Well-dressed customers came through the door and were ceremoniously led to their tables by polite waiters, amid a gentle clinking of plates and cups and the low hum of people talking. Some ladies even wore their very best crazy hats. The only visible difference was that the waiters all had large pairs of scissors on a string hanging from their belts. These they used to cut out the little squares from the patrons' ration cards. One day after we had finished eating, my mother said she had to go to the theatre. 'You go home. I'll see you later,' she said.

When I got home I found that the electricity was off again and I made a fire in the oven to warm up the room. It was as I was doing this that I heard a loud knocking at the door. It was Karl Hellmer, the man who had given me his bicycle. 'I've come to see your mother,' he said.

'She's not in. She's gone to the theatre,' I told him, with the door held half closed.

He looked angry. 'You're lying,' he said. 'Anyway, I've come to get my bicycle. Give it to me. It's my bicycle anyway.'

I looked at him, puzzled. 'You can't have the bicycle. You gave it to me. It's *my* bicycle. And anyway it was unusable when you gave it to me.'

'You're an obnoxious, nasty little boy,' he said, all his Viennese charm gone.

I was left standing perplexed by the front door, wondering what had happened to someone who had been so nice and friendly and funny.

In the shelter one night a lady asked me why I was always on my own, being so young. I told her that my mother was working at the theatre and that it was too late for her to come back home because of the air raids. The woman's name was Mrs Puttendörfer and she was quite a large person, in contrast to her husband, who was very thin, short and bald. He told me they had a daughter, who was six years old and who, because of the bombing, had been sent to Casablanca, where Mr Puttendörfer had family at the embassy. Mrs Puttendörfer said that if I played rummy then I could come up to their place in the evening and play with them, and I promised I would. Meanwhile, I had noticed that the old Jewish couple had not been in their usual corner for the last few nights and I asked Mrs Puttendörfer about them.

'The Gestapo came at five in the morning a few days ago and picked them up,' she told me quietly, so that the others in the shelter would not hear. 'They didn't even give them enough time to take any luggage. Now a new man and his wife have moved into their apartment on the second floor.'

The next evening I went up the grand entrance at the front of our building to the first floor to visit the Puttendörfers. They had a large apartment. Mrs Puttendörfer led me into their living room, where there were floor-to-ceiling bookshelves full of books and a piano in the corner. They introduced me to the card game rummy and we played into the night. Both Mr and Mrs Puttendörfer were heavy smokers and rolled their own cigarettes. Mr Puttendörfer told me he was a writer and that he worked for the local paper. He didn't seem very happy with the political situation, although he was very careful not to say anything that might get him into trouble. Mrs Puttendörfer asked me what books I was reading and suggested that I have a look at the books on their shelves. I was welcome to borrow any books I wished to read, she told me. Curiously enough, their daughter in Casablanca had the same name as my mother – Rosemarie. I went to visit the Puttendörfers quite often. Mrs Puttendörfer played the piano and sang old hit songs, smiling and swaying up and down as she played. I always asked her to go on and on as I didn't want her to stop playing and singing. Mr Puttendörfer, in the meantime, would be sitting at his desk, either writing or playing patience.

One day I was alone in our apartment reading when Sasho turned up. He was looking for my mother. He had two tickets, one for my mother and one for me, for the operetta *Gräfin Mariza*, in which he was singing. He said he would like us both to come and he stayed for a while, chatting to me. He told me that the war would soon be over because the Russians were at our doorstep. He had his bottle of cough mixture with him and was still taking swigs from it when he decided it was time to leave. I went out into the street with him and then watched him slowly walk away.

My mother could not go to Sasho's operetta as she was working in the theatre that night in a musical (in which she sang the song 'Under an Umbrella in the Evening'), so I went to ask Mrs Puttendörfer if she would come with me. She said she would be delighted and so the next evening off we set, arm in arm, to the theatre. This was the first time I had ever been to an operetta and I found it wonderful. I was very proud of Sasho, who played the lead and sang beautifully. After the show Mrs Puttendörfer and I went backstage to congratulate him and then we returned home through darkened streets. I remember it began to snow and Mrs Puttendörfer hummed the lead song of the operetta all the way home.

A few days later, as I came back from school with my bicycle, a giant of a man suddenly appeared out of the darkness. He was the tallest, biggest man I had ever seen. He came right up to me. 'Do you play chess?' he asked. He had a very deep voice.

For a moment I could not answer, I was so bewildered and stunned. Eventually I said, 'Yes, I do.'

'Are you any good?' he asked, looking at me eagerly.

'I haven't played for a while,' I told him, 'but I have studied it for some time.'

'Great! Come to my flat on the second floor and we can see how good you are.'

I felt a bit overwhelmed. I asked him his name and he told me it was Hinsche. I said that I had just come back from school and that maybe I could see him later that evening. We agreed on a time to meet and I watched him disappear through the passage door. He was so tall that he had to bend to get his head under the doorway. Later that evening I knocked on the door of Hinsche's apartment and to my surprise it was the apartment where the old Jewish couple had lived. He opened the door and welcomed me in. There was a small, elderly lady standing by the kitchen door. 'This is my wife, but she can't play chess,' Hinsche said. 'Women don't play chess. They don't know how to think.'

Hinsche led me into the living room, where he had set up a chessboard on a little table. We sat down in two armchairs, facing each other. Mrs Hinsche brought us a tray with tea and we started to play. Hinsche opened with a king gambit, which indicated that he knew what he was doing. We played in complete silence and he won the first two games. However, in the third game he started to make a few mistakes. As he began to lose he started to talk.

'I am related to the Habsburgs,' he said, 'and I am also related to the British royal family.' He looked at me as if he expected me to say something.

'Check,' I said, moving my queen and attacking his king.

Hinsche picked up his king and threw it across the room, where it rolled under the settee. 'This is a rotten king!' he shouted.

I got up, thanked him for a wonderful game and left in a hurry.

In February 1945 I heard on the radio that the Russians were crossing the River Oder, which was 100 kilometres from Berlin. Ahead of the Russians were tens of thousands of refugees. The air raid shelters were now full of new people who had been moved into the apartments of some of the residents. Among them was a boy called Hans who, at fifteen, was about a year older than me. He was looking after his mother, who was blind, and they had come from East Prussia, where their home had been destroyed by bombs. Hans was very good at sniffing out where there was some food to be found, and he and I often went out hunting for food and firewood, particularly across from our building, where some of the street had been almost totally bombed. Here we searched in the cellars of the houses that had not been completely destroyed. Among the rubble we once came across the interior wall of a shop, its shelves still filled with goods. Sadly, most of it was useless – just stuff like baking powder and salt. For firewood we collected smashed window frames, furniture and broken branches from trees. In a cellar one day we were lucky enough to find a big supply of potatoes. On another day we heard that a baker was selling bread. This had become unusual and we raced off, only to find a long queue outside the baker's shop. It took about an hour before we each managed to buy half a loaf of bread, which was all we were allowed to purchase.

One day Hans came round after an air raid. 'The Gestapo house is on fire,' he said. We ran down the street and found the top two floors of the building in flames. There was no fire brigade or anybody trying to put the fire out, so we went into the building and passed from room to room, eventually finding a cupboard in a kitchen that had butter, sausages and other goodies in it. These we grabbed before we had to run off because some guards in the building started to chase us. Hans and I were a good team, and together we were able to supply food and firewood for our mothers. This became very important as the shops had virtually no food in them and everyone was perpetually hungry.

By the spring of 1945, the Russians were fighting in the villages east of Berlin. Now there was no more electricity or gas and the water had been cut off, so things were becoming desperate. However, across the road, at the corner of a side street, there was an old pump and a long stone trough for cart-horses. This provided us with a supply of spring water, where we filled up our buckets. These pumps were on many of the street corners of old Berlin.

Around this time an old friend of my mother's turned up. She was a small, dark-haired woman called Lore. She told my mother that she had a brother, Michel, who was in the air force. She suggested that we all go and see him at his base in Gatow, in Spandau, to the west of Berlin. 'Maybe,' Lore said, 'he can help us get out of Berlin and away from the Russians.' She then started to tell us stories about the dreadful, monstrous and barbaric things the Russian and Mongol soldiers did to people. What she said was terrifying and worried both my mother and me, reinforcing what we had already heard.

Michel picked us up in his car and we drove to the air force base in Gatow. 'We can't fight back, we're out of fuel,' Michel said. 'The Russian air force is attacking our men outside east Berlin and we're helpless.'

At Gatow we had some lunch in the canteen and then Michel took me for a drive in an open army car along the airfield. We passed a number of fighter planes and stopped next to a Messerschmit. 'This is my kite,' Michel said. He lifted me into the cockpit and allowed me to sit in it. 'See you later!' he shouted as he drove off. I found being in the Messerschmit very interesting and later, when he came back to fetch me and dropped me back at the canteen, I thanked him profusely.

Later that evening there were a few pilots, air crew, nurses and some ladies from the air force in the canteen. They played old hit songs on the gramophone, had some drinks and started to dance. Someone turned on the radio and there was news announcing the great success of the German army at the Russian front and about the final victory. Then there was an announcement that the American troops had taken Mühlhausen. With sudden excitement, I shouted: 'Hurrah, we've finally got peace!' One of the officers, red-faced and furious, rushed over to me and hit me in the face. I tumbled over on the floor, and Lore and my mother helped me up and shouted at the officer. Just at that moment an ear-piercing siren began shrieking. We all ran across a square to an air raid bunker, most people still with their drinks in their hands, where we sat down on some long benches. Soon the anti-aircraft fire started and then came the heaviest bombing raid I had experienced so far. Everything was shaking, howling, booming and thundering. In the dim lamplight all I could see around me were petrified faces. Then the lights went off, there was a series of thundering crashes, and dust and plaster fell on my face from the ceiling. I thought the roof was going to cave in. It felt like the end of the world had come.

After the all clear, we went out and found that the canteen had been obliterated. There was smoke and rubble everywhere, and fire trucks and ambulances were driving around. After searching frantically for Michel, we were told that he had been killed by a bomb. Lore stayed behind in Gatow to bury her brother, while my mother and I made our way home. There was lots of walking. Then we took a train and then a tram. Everything was chaotic, with troops, tanks and horse-drawn carts filled with refugees moving in all directions. When we finally arrived home, I found that the telephone was still working and I called my Aunt Doris, who seemed very agitated. 'I can't talk now but you had better come round. Be quick,' she said. I jumped on my bike and rode down the Ku'damm, which was now quite busy with army vehicles and cartloads of refugees. Other carts, packed with swaying loads, were being pulled by people. Suddenly, a low-flying Russian fighter plane came towards us. I dropped my bicycle where I stood and dashed into a doorway. The plane passed over us and dropped a splitter bomb, which exploded further up the road. As the plane curved round for another attack, I grabbed my bike and rode into a side street. I watched the plane pass down the Ku'damm, machine-gunning the crowded street, and saw all the people there desperately running for cover. Eventually I arrived at my aunt's place to find her very worried. 'All the students have been arrested,' she said, 'and I've got to leave Berlin immediately, before the Gestapo get here.' She told me she was going to be picked up by a friend and I helped her pack quickly. We put the parrot into a small travel cage. The bird was now completely speechless. He wouldn't say a thing. I left my aunt, looking anxious and forlorn, gazing down the road for her friend. I cycled back home, taking side streets to avoid the main traffic.

Back home my mother was not well. She had bad stomach pain. I went to see Mrs Puttendörfer, who told me lots of people had this stomach problem. It was something to do with the water. Meanwhile Mr Puttendörfer had been called up and had been forced to join the Volkssturm (home guard), which worried her because he wasn't very well either.

During the next few days it became very quiet outside. There was less traffic and there were no air raids. On the radio it was announced that a tank division was coming from the west to relieve Berlin. Everybody was urged to fight to the last man and the last bullet, so that we could achieve a final victory. I thought this was silly.

And then one morning it all started again. There was a barrage of heavy artillery fire. It was deafening and it went on and on. This was followed by a new sound, an especially frightening one: a screeching, piercing, long drawn-out sound, repeated over and over. This was the terrifying sound of 'Stalin's organs', which everybody had been talking about.

I reckoned my mother and I should be quite safe in our room as long as we kept away from the windows, but the dreadful sound continued all day. That night there was machine-gun fire close by and I went outside, across the yard into the passage that led to the cellar. It was pitch black, apart from a few people sitting around one little candle. Then there were some very loud bangs outside.

'They're shooting out of our windows!' Mrs Schinkel shouted out, annoyed. 'The Russians will burn our house down.'

I thought she was right. There were certainly rumours going round about the Russians burning down all buildings from where shots were fired, so I stayed in the cellar for a while until it got light. Then I went to see how my mother was doing. I found her looking very worried. Behind the permanently locked door that led to the driving-school shop, we heard heavy gunfire, so I unlocked the door to see what was happening. The shop windows were smashed, there were four German soldiers in the room and they were shooting at something or somebody up the street. One of the soldiers, a sergeant, saw me and waved me to get back. When I went back into our living room he followed me. He sat down and lit a cigarette. Seeing my mother, who was in bed, he offered her a cigarette too, but she shook her head. He then pulled out a bottle from his jacket pocket and took a swig. There was a strong smell of schnapps.

'You know everyone in the building here is complaining about the shooting,' I said. 'The Russians will burn our house down.'

'All right, relax. We'll be leaving tonight, when it gets dark,' the sergeant said. He looked exhausted. 'We've got our personnel carrier across the road and we'll push through to the west through Spandau. Happy now?'

By now the artillery fire had stopped, with only some sporadic gunfire and a low rumbling sound in the distance. Then a sudden loud banging at the main back door made me jump. When it persisted, I rushed through the passage to see what was happening. As I opened the door, the bright light blinded me for a moment, but I could see a very large person in the shadows.

'Jürgen, I've got a plan I must show you,' said a voice I recognised. It was Hinsche, sounding very agitated. As he waved his torch around, I saw that he had a long rolled-up paper in his hand. I invited him into the kitchen and he followed me. He unrolled his paper on the table. 'I've made a map for our escape,' he said. On the paper he had made some crude drawings, in several colours, of what seemed to be roads, houses and tanks. In the torchlight he looked even bigger than normal; his huge shadow jumped around the walls and ceiling. He pointed at his map. 'We can get away through this road. My wife can stay, but you can bring your mother and I will bring my chessboard. We've got to get out of here.' He continued speaking, sounding more and more determined, and then suddenly he looked at me with a bewildered and confused expression. 'I must find the king, I've lost my king,' he said. Then he abruptly rolled up his paper, waved his torch around wildly, and left. I stood in the dark and realised that Hinsche was nuts.

Making sure the back door was locked, I walked along our passage to the living room. As I got closer to the door, I heard music. I opened the door and saw that the room was lit with candles. Marlene Dietrich was singing one of her famous songs, the room was full of cigarette smoke, and my mother was dancing, cheek to cheek, with the sergeant. Two other soldiers were sitting on the bed drinking. It looked as if my mother had recovered from her illness, so I left them to it and went to bed. Covering my head with a pillow, I fell asleep.

I was woken by a deafening crash. Part of my bedroom window and sharp pieces of glass were all over my blanket. Above my head and all along the plywood wall I saw splinters of iron stuck into the wood. An artillery grenade had burst right next to my window. I had had a lucky escape, thanks to my bed being below the height of the window. The shrapnel had sliced into the wooden wall just a few inches above me. I disentangled myself from the pieces of glass and wood, got dressed and went into our living room. My mother was in bed but the soldiers, still with cigarettes in their mouths, were getting their bags and guns together, making ready to leave. All was quiet outside. I watched them from the front of the driving-school shop as they went across the Ku'damm to their personnel carrier, which was standing on the opposite side of the street down a side road. Soon afterwards the artillery bombardment and the Stalin's organs started again. Their hideous screaming combined with the thunderous bangs of the artillery made a horrendous noise.

I went to see if I could find Hans. I walked through the passage between the backyard and the side front door, where there was a staircase that led to the landing of the front house staircase. I saw Hans coming down the stairs. As I stopped to say hello to him, the front door of the passage opened and an SS man in a leather coat came rushing towards me. He looked at me and then at Hans on the stairway. 'Come on, boys, we need you!' he shouted. Hans and I shook our heads. The SS man pulled out a pistol. He pointed it first at Hans and then at me. 'That's an order,' he said.

'I have a blind mother,' Hans said.

Brandishing his gun, the SS man pointed at the door. 'Follow! Now!' he ordered.

Hans and I looked at each other and simultaneously we started to run, Hans up the stairs and I through the doorway and down the staircase to the cellar. The SS man did not have a chance – we were too fast for him – and he disappeared.

Over the next few days there was heavy fighting in the streets. Tanks rolled down the street past our house and there were constant explosions and the sound of machine-gun fire. One night I heard someone screaming and howling the whole night through. He must have been wounded in the street and no one could get to him because of the crossfire.

One morning everything quietened down ominously. The first Russian soldiers came into the building, searching for German soldiers. These Russian fighting troops ignored us totally but most of us still stayed huddled together in the shelter, trembling with fear. I think we all felt more secure staying together. Then a new group of Russian soldiers, smelling strongly of alcohol, came stumbling down the steps into the candle- and paraffin-lit shelter. One big fellow, with glaring eyes, who was swaying a lot, pulled out his pistol and grabbed Mrs Muller. As he hauled her to her feet, Mrs Muller started to cry. 'Bauch kaput [stomach sick],' she sobbed, but the big Russian just shouted at her in Russian and dragged her down the passage. We could hear her screaming. The other Russians then started grabbing some of the other women, shouting, 'Frau, komm!' There was terrible screaming from the women as they were hauled away but the Russians just laughed and shouted to each other in slurred voices.

I left the shelter and hurried up to see my mother, who had heard all the commotion going on in the building with the loud Russian voices in the yard and the heavy footsteps up and down the staircase. She had got out of bed and was dressed but she looked very frightened, especially as there were more loud voices coming from behind the door leading to the front shop. I opened our large, heavy wardrobe and signalled my mother to get inside. I had just managed to lock it and put the key into my pocket when the door crashed open and two drunken Russians burst into the room. They looked around and banged with their guns against the wardrobe, shouting something in Russian to each other. Then they went through the passage into the kitchen, where they saw my bicycle. One of them grabbed it and slung it over his shoulder. Then they both left through the door to the staircase. I was very upset about my bicycle but thought we were lucky the house was still standing and that my mother and I were still both alive and untouched. After a while I unlocked the cupboard and let Rosie out.

Later I went into our street and looked down the Ku'damm. I saw the bodies of German and Russian soldiers lying on the road and pavement. A tank was still burning, several houses were in flames and there were continual loud bursts of gunfire as some ammunition kept exploding. The personnel carrier that had belonged to the German sergeant and his men was burnt out and two charred bodies were lying next to it. They must have been the soldiers who had been in our apartment two nights previously. Just then two Russian soldiers came staggering down the road, stopping to drink out of a large bottle they passed between them. They were followed by some others, who were attempting to ride a bicycle, one swaying left and right down the road, while being pushed by two of his comrades. At a distance I saw another strange sight: a very big man in a white suit, wearing a Panama hat, was walking with slow, deliberate steps in the middle of the road. He had a basket under his arm, from which he took handfuls of leaves and gently threw them onto the dead bodies in the street. As he came closer I recognised him. It was Mr Hinsche.

As things started to quieten down, Mrs Schinkel heard a baby crying in one of the cubicles in the cellar. The cubicle was locked, so she called Mr Wüstenhagen, the caretaker, to break into it. Inside they found the Becker couple dead, lying on some blankets on the floor, with their baby between them with a rope around its neck. The young couple had committed suicide by taking some pills and had then tried to strangle their baby. Fortunately, the baby was fine and Mrs Schinkel offered to look after it for the time being.

Mr Wüstenhagen lived right across from us. He was a grumpy old man, who always wore a cap and an old leather jacket. He walked with a limp, and went unshaven most of the time. Whenever I played ball in the yard, he would complain about the noise. He was standing next to his door as I came out of our flat and he told me that the baker up the road across the Ku'damm was selling bread. He asked me whether I wanted to go with him and we crossed the Ku'damm, where we passed the burnt-out personnel carrier. I pointed out the two charred bodies, which I noticed had shrunk to half the size of a normal person, and mentioned that these must have been the soldiers who had been shooting from our house. He looked at me sceptically, bent over one of the bodies and pulled with his index finger at something that looked like a piece of pipe. 'It's a doll and this is the chain,' he said. However, as he pulled, the 'chain' became red and squashy. It turned out to be the guts of the dead man. Wüstenhagen looked rather shocked. We went on to the baker and queued for about an hour for the bread. What we finally got was very munchy and tasteless but it was food. A few days after this I saw Mr Wüstenhagen with a bandage on his index finger, and some weeks later I heard that he'd had to have the finger amputated, owing to infection.

Hans told me that he could get us jobs working for some Russians who would pay us in bread. I wasn't convinced but he kept insisting – 'we will have lots of bread' – and so we went together to an old car-repair yard a few blocks away from our area. Here there were about six Russians, some in uniform, others not, talking to each other in Russian. They were working on the engine of a car, or at least some of them were; the others were just sitting around smoking and drinking vodka, which they offered us. We declined but we repaired a number of tyre tubes for them. Then one of the Russians held something up to us. I didn't recognise what it was but Hans knew immediately. 'It's a spark plug,' he said.

The Russian who seemed to be in charge pointed at the spark plug and held up four fingers, indicating that we should find four of these. He pointed to a building further down the road. We walked down the road to a warehouse, part of it undamaged, that almost took up a whole street block. As we passed the building, we saw two Russian guards sitting in the big doorway in two large armchairs, pistols on their laps. They looked at us suspiciously as we passed. We walked along the warehouse and round the corner to the back. There were some broken windows there and we looked through them and saw rows of what looked like new cars; there must have been 30 or more. Very quietly, we climbed through the window and found ourselves in a long space with cars on either side. On closer inspection we could see that some of them had been damaged from part of the roof having fallen in. Hans started to run from car to car, looking into the engines for spark plugs. Suddenly, he turned, looked at me and put his finger to his lips. I ducked down and listened. Everything was quiet, but then I heard voices and heavy footsteps. I was very scared. I hid behind a car just as a guard, smelling strongly of vodka, stopped in front of me. Fortunately, his partner called from the other end of the building and the guard near me slowly walked back to rejoin his companion.

For what seemed like a long time we stayed still and then Hans continued his search. Finally he found a car with the right spark plugs, but the spanner he had brought did not fit to undo them. First we would have to find the right spanner. For several more minutes we searched the cars for a toolbox that we could use but it was fruitless, and so we began to search through the warehouse. Eventually, we found a small room next to the main entrance and in it was a toolbox. We could see the guards through the broken window still sitting in the armchairs outside, so we had to be very quiet, but Hans found the spanner he needed. Walking on tiptoe, we went back to the car with the right spark plugs, removed them and climbed out of the window at the back, where we had entered. We then walked over piles of rubble along the back of the building until we returned safely to where the Russians were repairing their vehicle. We gave them the spark plugs and in return they gave us a loaf of white bread each. Despite this success, however, we decided not to go back again; we suspected the Russians repairing their car were probably deserters.

One morning I was about to go looking for Hans when I saw a number of people coming out of our house and rushing up the Ku'damm, all carrying buckets or large water mugs and bottles.

'What's going on?' I asked Mrs Schinkel, as she came charging through the door into the street with a large bucket in her hand.

'Cooking oil!' she shouted. 'At the station!' And off she ran.

I ran back into our flat and grabbed a watering can from the bathroom and followed the people up to the station and across the railway tracks to the goods yard. Here there was a crowd of people, all holding different sorts of containers, standing around a tanker on the tracks, in front of which stood a Russian soldier. Out of breath, I came up to the people and stopped, panting. I heard someone say, 'He wants watches.'

I saw a woman go up and talk to the guard, showing him a watch. He looked at it, put it to his ear, shook it and put it in his pocket. Then he took the bucket from the woman and put it under the tap. When he opened it, oil gushed out. Seeing this, I turned and ran as fast as I could back home. I looked through the drawers in our desk and found an old watch that didn't work any more. I set it to the time on our alarm clock and hurried back to the oil tanker. I went up to the guard and showed him the watch. He looked at it, put it to his ear and then shook his head, before pulling up his sleeve, where I could see three watches along his arm. He compared the time of my watch with the time on the others. Then he nodded, put the watch in his pocket and proceeded to fill up my can with oil. In fact, I struggled to carry the heavy can of oil home. I had picked a big container, about ten litres' worth. Knowing how precious this essential fuel was, when I got home I filled up all the empty bottles in the apartment I could find. News certainly travels fast, and before long people were knocking on our door wanting to swap a loaf of bread or some sugar for a bottle of oil. Others brought potatoes, flour and carrots. In this way my mother and I managed to accumulate enough supplies to last us for a few weeks.

3

AMIDST THE ASHES

Some three weeks after the end of the war, in May, some form of normalisation started to appear. A new administration, formed by the Occupation Army, began to organise the population. Work gangs of women started to clear the streets of rubble. Even the bakers began to bake bread again.

Of course, because it was the end of May, the weather was becoming warmer and so the bodies lying in the streets and in the ruins of bombed buildings had to be buried quickly to prevent disease spreading. So wherever there was a piece of available soil, the bodies were buried temporarily. Usually the burial party made a small cross from pieces of sticks and put some stones on the temporary grave, as well as the dead person's identity card. On top of that they placed a piece of tar roofing board and another stone, to prevent the card from being blown away by the wind.

Mrs Puttendörfer was very worried about her husband. She had not had any news from him for almost five weeks, since he had been forced to join the Volkssturm. Of course, she thought he could have been killed. So we looked at all the graves in the neighbourhood, picking up the top stones and peering at the ID cards. I found this very sad and depressing, and we both had tears in our eyes.

There were graves in some strange places. In front of our apartment building, for example, there were two flower-beds, one on either side of the main entrance. Each flower-bed was about five metres by five metres and enclosed by a brick wall about 40 centimetres high. This was where we had buried the

Becker couple who had committed suicide in the cellar. But we could not find Mr Puttendörfer.

One hot summer's evening a month or so later, with everything feeling more or less back to 'normal', my mother and Mrs Puttendörfer were sitting outside on the wall of the flower-bed, talking together. It seemed that nobody knew about the concentration camps and the murder of the Jewish people. It really puzzled me. Certainly, anybody who came to see us denied any knowledge of the murders. I could not understand this and I argued with Mrs Puttendörfer and my mother as to how they didn't know. I began to worry about the human race and whether such things were unimportant to people. Finally, Mrs Puttendörfer, perhaps fed up with the conversation, stood up. 'Let's go for a walk,' she said. The three of us started to walk up the Ku'damm towards the Grunewald. It was a warm day, with a low sun glittering through the leaves of the trees, and before long we came across two Russian soldiers. As they walked closer to us, I noticed that the badges on the shoulders of their uniforms indicated that they were of high rank. They were either officers or commisars. They greeted us in a broken German, smiled and offered my mother a drink out of a hip flask, which she took. One of them then pointed at Mrs Puttendörfer's trousers, which were blue and sticking out from beneath her tunic. He indicated that he wanted them. We all started to laugh. The officer then put his hand in his bag, out of which he produced a large salami. He was offering us the salami for Mrs Puttendörfer's trousers! She did not hesitate and, turning away from us, took them off right there in the street. Accompanied by lots of laughter, she handed over her trousers and we went happily home with the large salami trophy.

On another day I was on Mrs Puttendörfer's balcony when I spotted a man coming up the Ku'damm. He had an army greatcoat over his arm and was walking very slowly. As he got closer, I recognised the small figure as none other than Mr Puttendörfer. I shouted to Mrs Puttendörfer, who was in the kitchen, and we all rushed downstairs to greet him. Mr Puttendörfer looked exhausted and he was terribly thin. You could see his cheekbones sticking out of his face. He never talked about what had happened to him during the final battle for Berlin. He just played patience most of the time, and in the evening, even though we often played cards together, he still said nothing about what had happened. His only concern now was to see his daughter, Rosemarie, who was due to return soon from Casablanca.

Meanwhile, Mr Hinsche was clearly going ever madder. He would give crazy performances. Once he was on his balcony on the second floor holding a red bathing costume from a pole, making a speech and calling on passers-by to listen. He drew quite a crowd, who watched from below, laughing at his antics. 'I am working with Stalin!' Mr Hinsche shouted. 'He is my brother!' Of course, lots of people laughed, particularly as he rambled on about how he was going to change Berlin into the most important city in the world and that Stalin was soon coming to visit him and so on. Gesticulating wildly, he leant over the balcony, almost losing his balance, which made us all hold our breath. Then he started to throw the flowers and pot plants at us. 'Here is peace!' he shouted, as more and more people stopped to watch and others ducked out of the way. Finally Mr Hinsche's wife came out onto the balcony and led her husband inside. I was told that from time to time Mr Hinsche was picked up by a mental institution but he always came home after a few weeks.

Early in August the Allies finally arrived in Berlin. We found out that we were in the British-designated zone and the Russians moved out of our district. This was good news and we waited with anticipation for the first sign of the British, hoping they would provide better security than the Russians. In any event, late one evening Mrs Puttendörfer, my mother and Rosemarie, their young daughter (now seven) who had just arrived from Casablanca, and I were sitting on the wall in front of our apartment building. It was a warm summer evening and some of the neighbours' children were roller-skating down the Ku'damm. Everybody was very relaxed. Then suddenly a car with a small British flag on its nose stopped right in front of us. A British officer got out and came over. He wore a beret at an angle and had a cigarette dangling from his lips while he talked, his left eye slightly closed to protect it from the rising smoke. Addressing my mother in fluent German, the officer asked her for directions to Wilmersdorfer Strasse. Before my mother could answer he took out a packet of cigarettes and offered them to Mrs Puttendörfer and my mother. His name was Captain Oswald Hammond and this chance encounter started a relationship between John (as I later came to call him) and my mother.

John came to visit us often, eventually daily; in fact, he just about moved in with us. He always brought something with him – tins of spam, corned beef and cigarettes. He was working in a special unit whose job was to catch former Nazis, as well as rocket scientists. At 26, John was much younger than my mother – she was over 40 (but officially 30). We discovered that he had a bad temper and sometimes he shouted at me over silly little incidents, such as when he complained to my mother after she gave me some chocolates that he had given to her. 'I did not give you the chocolates for you to give to that child!' he yelled. So, unfortunately, he and I did not become friends and it became more and more difficult for us to live together. I think he was jealous of anyone who was too close to my mother. He even had Heinz Seidler arrested for being too friendly with her. Finally, John suggested that it might be better for me to stay with my grandparents in Mühlhausen, where he claimed it would also be better for me to go to school. He persuaded my mother that Berlin was no place for a child to grow up and so, against my will, I was sent to Mühlhausen once more. Thuringia had been returned to the Russians when the Americans moved back to a new line further west, and so I was back in Russian-controlled territory again.

Nothing had changed in the life of my grandparents, although Heinrich's arm was no longer in plaster. He still went to the post office every day and, once a month, on his inspection tours of post offices in the outlying districts. Gretchen continued to have her colon problems and her shortage of red blood cells. Of course, there were many Russian soldiers in the streets and, unfortunately for me, in the local cinema they only showed boring Russian propaganda films. I went to the local high school and made a few friends, one of whom was a boy named Klaus who, together with his refugee family, came from the east.

I still had problems with Gretchen – or rather she said she had problems with me. Certainly, my grandmother was very strange. I remember one day I was sitting in the kitchen and eating some sort of yoghurt, which we made from sour milk. Because I found it too sour, I helped myself to some sugar, at which Gretchen exploded. She went on and on about how difficult it was to get sugar and how much trouble I had given her and how she was sick and that I was the Devil. Quietly I asked her to calm down but this just made her more excited. She rushed across the kitchen, leant over my dish of yoghurt and spat into it.

The following day at school I told my friend Klaus about my grandmother and her bad temper. He said I should move out, that it was unhealthy for me to stay with her any longer. He suggested that I go and stay with him and his family, where they had a small room I could have. So, the very same day, I packed my few belongings and walked out of my grandparents' apartment with Gretchen shouting at me: 'You'll be back!'

Klaus's family lived in a small apartment in an old building near the railway line. There was his mother, who was round and very jolly and cheerful, and there were two small children, a girl of about three years old and a boy who was about five. They had a kitchen/living room and a large bedroom, where I later discovered they all slept in one large bed. They were very poor but very friendly, especially compared with my grandparents. Klaus showed me my small bedroom, which I thought was fine. We all sat together and had dinner that evening, and there was a lot of joking and teasing around the table and an atmosphere in which I was very happy. Later on I went to bed in my little room and fell asleep immediately, only to wake up after a couple of hours scratching and scratching. When I turned on the light, I saw that my whole body was covered with bites. There were dozens of bed-bugs crawling all over my sheet. They were flat and round, and when I squashed them, blood ran over the white sheet. Needless to say, I couldn't sleep for the rest of the night.

In the morning Klaus and I walked to school together but I didn't say anything to him about the bed-bugs because I had a plan. That night before I went to bed I put on some heavy gloves, covered my head and face with a scarf, and put my socks into my pyjama trousers. I fell asleep happy in the belief that I had beaten these monster insects, but no, it didn't work. Somehow they still managed to get right into my pyjamas, and halfway through the night I was scratching and itching as badly as I'd done the night before. I would have to come up with a better plan. The following night I took some dishes from the kitchen and carefully lifted and stood the four legs of the bed in the dishes, which I filled with water. Then I hunted down all the bugs in the mattress, sheets and blanket and dispatched them. And, as a final precaution, I moved the bed away from the wall. Then I went to sleep. Well, that night I slept until the morning, when the problem started all over again just as the sun came up. Some of the bed-bugs must still have been in the mattress, I thought – until I looked up at the ceiling. There, right above me, were hordes of the creatures. I was still wondering what they were doing up there when one by one they started to drop onto me. I had to admit they were very clever insects. There was nothing else for it. I admitted defeat.

At breakfast that morning I told my hosts about the bed-bug problem. They thought it was very funny. They hadn't known about the bugs, they said, and suggested that I should come and sleep with them in the big bed they all shared together. At school I thought about my problem. Then I remembered that my Aunt Doris had a sister, Hildegard, in Mühlhausen. Perhaps she would have some space for me.

Hildegard lived in a large house near my Aunt Irmgard's restaurant. That afternoon I went to visit her. She remembered me and welcomed me warmly. She was eager for news of her sister, as she had not heard from her for some time. I told her what I knew and she thought that Doris must have gone to West Germany, since there had been no post from her. Hilde's daughter, Petra, lived with her. They were both married to military men. Hilde's husband was a colonel, who had been reported missing in the First World War, while Petra's husband, also a colonel in the army, had been reported missing in the Second World War. They offered me coffee and cake, and after I told them about my problem with my grandmother, they insisted that I stay with them. They had plenty of space and said that they welcomed having a man in the house. I was very flattered and thanked them very much. I then went back to Klaus's home, thanked his family for their hospitality, packed my few belongings and moved in with my two aunts.

My aunts had cooked a special meal for me, which we ate by candlelight in their dining room, with the window facing the street partially open. Every time we heard footsteps coming down the street, both my aunts would stop eating and talking and look expectantly towards the open window. When the footsteps passed by, they would cast a brief look at each other and then carry on with the meal. This happened every time someone walked past the window along the quiet side street in which they lived.

On the mantelpiece in the living room there were a number of framed pictures of both the mother and daughter, each with her colonel husband, and also several portraits of the two men. When I came home from school in the afternoon I'd find them sitting on the couch in the living room together, with the windows open, still listening out for footsteps. Every day was the same. Sometimes when I met one of them at the door they would come out into the street and look up and down in both directions, just in case one of their husbands was returning.

A habit I had formed from my nights in the air raid shelters was that I would often wake up hungry in the middle of the night. Sometimes I would put a sandwich next to my bed before I went to sleep, so that when I woke up, usually at about two or three o'clock in the morning, I did not have to get up to satisfy my hunger. One night at my aunts' apartment, having forgotten to make myself a sandwich, I got up and tiptoed down to the kitchen in the early hours. I noticed that a light was still on in the living room and I went and looked through the open door. Petra was sitting next to the window with her back towards me. Perhaps hearing my step, she turned around. I could see that she had been crying. She asked me to come in and join her, which I did. 'I'm waiting, always waiting,' she said. 'Sometimes I wish they would tell me he's dead.' She looked at me with tears in her eyes. 'You know, my mother has been waiting for my father since 1918, which is almost nineteen years now. But I can't wait that long, I really can't.'

I did not know what to say, so to try and cheer her up I said I would make her a cup of hot chocolate. By the time I came back with two steaming cups, she had settled down and was more relaxed. She told me that they had only been married for two months when her husband was called up and sent to the Russian front. He had been reported missing in 1943. I stayed up with her until it started to get light outside and we talked a lot about the stupidity of war.

Next day at school we were introduced to a new English teacher. His name was Mr Brakeloo and he was very thin and tall and wore a light, khaki safari outfit. Back in the thirties, he told us, he had lived in South Africa for over eight years. He said it was a wonderful country, very beautiful, with lots of sun and many different landscapes, from deserts to forests to mountains. After the lesson I talked to Klaus about asking our new teacher if we could take private English lessons with him. He thought it was a good idea and so I wrote to my mother and asked her if she could organise sending me a few hundred cigarettes.

I thought she would be able to arrange this through John. Cigarettes were in great demand in the eastern zone of Germany, and I knew their value. In fact, cigarettes were almost priceless. My thinking was that they would enable me to pay for the lessons for the next month. The cigarettes duly arrived and both Klaus and I had English lessons twice a week.

Some time later, my mother wrote to tell me that she and John had moved to a larger apartment. There was space for me there, my own room. So I said goodbye to everybody, including Klaus's family and my grandfather. I went and saw Heinrich at the post office. He said he was very sorry about Gretchen having been so difficult but told me she was very sick. I took the train back to Berlin.

The new apartment was in the Wilmersdorfer Strasse. As my mother had promised, there was a nice, small room for me and, more significantly, a broom cupboard. This would become my first darkroom. My mother and John had also acquired a dog, a miniature French poodle called Blacky – who loved to play with balls.

Photography had been an interest of mine for a while, and by now I was taking a lot of photographs. This prompted a discussion about my future. Certainly, school and further education were virtually impossible. After the destruction of the war, there was practically nowhere to study, but my mother had a friend, Eric Krueger, who was a professional photographer. He had been taking glamour photos of my mother for years, which she needed for her portfolio as an actress. Mr Krueger had become very friendly with John, who took a great interest in amateur photography. So, while my mother thought that I should go into film, where she had some connections, Mr Krueger thought that I had some talent in photography and should pursue that. John's view was that whatever I did, I should get a job and earn some money.

Well, because I liked Mr Krueger and I liked photography, I became his assistant. I picked up some basics of darkroom work at his studio and then I started accompanying him on assignments. My first job was to carry and hold the lamps for him as we went to different hospitals in Berlin, photographing cancer patients and the tumours on their bodies. This was interesting work but also an education for me in seeing the suffering of these people.

After a few weeks Mr Krueger suggested that I should learn some photography theory, so I signed up at the School for Optics and Phototechnique. At first I found the lessons very interesting and important, but after a few weeks at the school the tempo of the lessons changed. Since all the textbooks had been destroyed in the war, the teacher just dictated page after page for us to write down. This went on for day after day, until I couldn't bear it any more. I couldn't follow the complicated texts about mathematics, optics and chemistry. After a few months there, I left the school and went back to working and learning on the job with Mr Krueger.

Towards the end of the year, my mother and John got married. Aunt Irmgard came from Mühlhausen to help with the preparations and Mr Krueger was commissioned to take the wedding pictures. The wedding feast was going to be a party at our flat and I was tasked with making the punch, which turned out to be something of an error. On the day of the wedding, I started to make the punch, but, of course, to get the mixture and the flavour just right I had to keep tasting it. Unfortunately, by the time the guests arrived and the party had started I was staggering around and able to do little more than grin gormlessly at everybody. I remember Mrs Puttendörfer sitting in the corner of the sitting room smoking a cigar while the other guests and the newlyweds were being toasted by one of John's colleagues. Suddenly, one of the guests, Mr Koerber, walked into the room. He was wearing a dark dinner suit with a large and imposing medal on his left chest. All the men in the room got up and stood to attention to greet him.

'Gentlemen! Are you getting up for the man or the medal?' bellowed Mrs Puttendörfer, to everybody's embarrassment.

I started to giggle, too drunk to understand what the problem was, before slipping off to my room.

From then on things happened very quickly. John, having married a German woman, was forced to leave the Security Service. Knowing that this would happen, he and my mother had already decided to leave Europe and emigrate to South Africa. Shortly after their wedding, the furniture was packed up, Blacky the poodle was shipped off, and my mother and John departed. They left me with a small suitcase, a ticket to Hamburg, and a letter to a lawyer by the name of Jacobi.

4

HAMBURG

I spent two and a half years in Hamburg. The city was bursting with refugees, and when I arrived I had problems finding accommodation. I had no money and no prospect of a job. As I walked around the city, all around me I saw destruction. Houses were burnt out, with only jagged stone walls remaining, and rubble was piled up everywhere. On my first day I walked around for hours, carrying my little cardboard suitcase in one hand and clutching the letter for Mr Jacobi in the other, trying to find the address I had been given for him.

There were many people who looked as lost as I was. Shabbily dressed refugees walked the streets, looking dazed, pushing prams loaded with bags, cardboard boxes and bundles of clothes. I accosted locals and asked them to help me locate Mr Jacobi's address but I couldn't find it. As darkness fell, having spent the whole day on my feet, I was exhausted. And I still had nowhere to go.

Hamburg had been relentlessly bombed by British and American bombers over four nights in July 1943, and on one of those nights the city had been almost totally obliterated. On 28 July 1943, 722 bombers were loaded with an extra 240 tonnes of incendiary bombs. In just 50 minutes they dropped a total of 2 313 tonnes on Hamburg. This created a firestorm reaching an estimated heat of 1 000°C, billows of smoke 20 000 feet into the air, and a gale-force wind on the ground of 120 miles per hour. The streets were burning, the trees were burning, and the tarmac on the roads melted. People trying to escape got stuck in the hot, sticky, lethal mess and burnt to death. Almost 100 000 people were killed in those four nights of bombing.

As I walked along the streets towards the harbour I saw a man standing in front of a building. I approached him and asked him if he knew where I might find a place for the night. He told me about a refugee camp in Altona, which was about 20 minutes' walk away. Slowly, wearily, I made my way there.

Altona was a former independently run town, which was now part of greater Hamburg. The refugee camp was in an old warehouse, a large and undamaged brick building. At the entrance some officials were sitting round a table, receiving the exhausted and bedraggled refugees who were queuing patiently, seeking shelter. I joined the long queue. The conversations I heard around me were in an east German dialect. The officials at the table were painstakingly taking down everyone's details. When it came to my turn and they asked me for my ID card, I confessed that I didn't have one. The best I could do was produce my smallpox certificate. This was a large piece of manhandled and stained paper on which were a number of stamps from the Russian officials from when I'd travelled to Mühlhausen. The woman behind the table looked at my piece of paper, shrugged, looked up at me and then stamped the paper. She gave it back to me, pointing at the door through which I'd seen people in front of me disappearing. I followed them. I stepped into a room with a strong chemical smell. Clouds of white dust swirled around and settled on the floor. I saw two large women, in white overcoats and wearing white masks over their mouths and noses and goggles over their eyes, each holding a large cylinder with a nozzle and a handle in her hands. They were pumping the white substance down the necklines and trousers of all the people who entered. With their white faces, their victims ended up looking like clowns. I watched as they proceeded to go through another door. And then it was my turn.

After I had been sprayed, I found myself in a long hall-like room lined with benches. On either side were rows of bunk-beds. Newly arrived refugees were busy settling in while those who were already settled lay on their beds watching the activities of the newcomers. With my hair full of powder from the women with the cylinders, I had a heavy sneezing attack while pushing myself through the crowds until I found a free bed – all the while hanging onto my small suitcase. I took off my coat and collapsed, exhausted, onto a bed, falling asleep almost immediately.

I woke up to the noises of children crying and people hurrying back and forth. I must have slept for about ten hours because there was daylight coming through some narrow windows high up near the ceiling. After a wash in the shower room, I joined the queue for breakfast. An elderly couple behind me told me they had been in the camp for six months. They were looking for their relatives in Hamburg – a difficult task as their homes had been destroyed. They had come all the way from Danzig and had managed to escape the Russian and Polish advances.

Breakfast was some sort of porridge, plus a bread roll and a slice of white bread, dished up with a ladle from a large pot into tin army food containers. Once I had eaten I walked back to the city centre, where I eventually found Mr Jacobi in a half-destroyed building with some broken windows covered with cardboard. He was a tall, thin, middle-aged man with an ashen grey face. In fact, he seemed very ill. His room looked as though he had either just moved in or was about to move out. There were boxes of books on the floor and a number of half-empty shelves against the walls. The desk he sat behind was piled with more books and pieces of paper. He proceeded to read the letter I had been instructed to give him – which was from a friend of John's, who was a lawyer in Berlin. Mr Jacobi asked me three questions: did I have any money, did I know Hamburg, and where was I staying? I briefly told him my situation, after which he looked even gloomier.

'I wish I could help you and put you up,' he said, 'but my wife has just come out of hospital and needs to recover. We live in Blankenese, which is 45 minutes by city train along the Elbe, and we only have one and a half rooms in our home. But I could try and help you by writing some letters to people, where you could possibly get a job as a volunteer photographer. I have a friend, Mr Walter Benser, who runs a photo agency. Come back in four days and I might have something for you.'

He gave me 50 marks ('so you can get something to eat') and I left. I spent the rest of the day walking around Hamburg, or what was left of it, and had some sandwiches in a sandwich bar. Then I walked back to Altona, where I spent the next four nights in the refugee camp, again getting powdered with the awful-smelling insecticide. I talked to many refugees from East Prussia who had lost everything, including their homes and members of their families. I thought I should photograph these people and do a reportage of life in the camp but I had run out of film and didn't have enough money to buy any.

After the week had passed I went back to Mr Jacobi. This time he had some good news for me. 'Mr Benser is going to give you an interview,' he said. He told me I should go and see him as soon as possible.

I met Walter Benser, who, as it happened, was a famous Leica photographer, in his office. At that time he was the head of the photographic department of the DPA, the German Press Agency. I told him about my photographic background and my enthusiasm for photography. Mr Benser sat behind his desk, patiently listening to my nervous ramblings and smiling and nodding occasionally. He seemed to be a friendly character. When I had finished my monologue he leant forward, looked me in the eye and started to speak. 'You can have a job as a photographic volunteer,' he said. 'You will be trained in the different depart-ments, but I'm afraid there will be no pay.'

I was assigned to the photo printing section first. There were about six people working there, all women, and I worked there for three months, drying hun-dreds of the press prints that came out of the darkroom on an electric rotary dryer. I also attached the captions to the back of the prints and then prepared the prints for dispatch to the German newspapers and magazines. I then moved on to make negatives from the prints, which came from press agencies such as Camera Press, Keystone, Reuters and other international photo agencies, using special reproduction equipment. I developed the 4 x 5-inch negatives in a special developer with specific drying methods so that the negatives were ready for printing within fifteen minutes. The negatives then went into the darkroom where a number of women made hundreds of press prints. It was also my job to develop all the films of the DPA photographers – dozens on a daily basis. My next move was into the darkroom. Here I worked as one of a team with some of the women, printing hundreds of prints every day.

From time to time I was sent out into the city to photograph the many buildings under reconstruction, which was part of the rebuilding programme for Hamburg.

One day, after I had been working at the agency for a few weeks, Walter

Benser called me into his office. He looked at me very seriously and said, 'Young man, I am told that when you are in the canteen during lunch you only drink water and don't eat. Are you a yogi? You are very thin. Where do you live and what do you live on?'

I was a bit stunned. I didn't know what to say. I was worried that if I told him my real situation I might lose my job as a volunteer, so I told him I was still looking for accommodation and that I was expecting some money soon from South Africa. He shook his head in dismay. Then he offered me some paid work to tide me over. This was to take pictures every weekend at football matches, for a soccer photo display that was made by the photo department for all the tobacco and betting shops throughout Germany. These displays were changed every week. Mr Benser said he would pay me DM20 for every picture accepted and used for the display. He also said I could have a small room at the DPA house, which was used as living quarters for the DPA staff.

My room was on the third floor and it had a window that faced the internal shaft in the DPA building, which was in Schlüterstrasse, a short walk from the DPA office on the Middelweg. I settled in very quickly and was very happy there. The only problem was that the bath was in the kitchen, so you had to book the bath for late at night or early morning by writing your name and bath time on the notice-board on the kitchen door. The house consisted of single and double rooms, most of which were occupied by DPA staff and some students from the nearby university.

I duly photographed my first football match and I got to meet the regular sports photographers. They were all very friendly and told me the best positions to use for good action pictures. These were either next to or behind the goal. I spent the best part of two years sitting near the goal-posts every weekend photographing up to three football matches. It proved to be a crash course in action pictures. I had to develop a quick reaction to movement and also the ability to predict future action, which was an essential skill for my photography. Sometimes in winter, sitting in snow, my shutters froze and wouldn't work, and my colleagues passed a small bottle of brandy around to warm us up.

One day I was sent to the harbour to photograph Göring's yacht, which had been put up for auction. I was told that the yacht was moored in the non-commercial private harbour for pleasure boats, including sailing boats, which was directly on the Elbe before the main harbour. After a lot of wandering about, eventually I found Göring's yacht moored at a pier near the river. To photograph the whole yacht was impossible because there were people walking along the pier as well as onto and off the yacht along a gang-plank. Also there were a number of cars parked in front of it, as well as a crane, and trucks kept rumbling past. What to do? The only way to photograph the thing was from the other side from the open water. I walked a way down the river and found a man who was willing to rent me a boat. This seemed to be the best idea. I jumped in and rowed up the river, around the bank and into the private harbour area. There in front of me was the yacht in all its glory in full view. I got a beautiful picture of it with its reflection in the still water. I rowed around for a while, getting different angles, and then decided to head back and return the boat. As I rowed back into the river I found that it was becoming hard work. I was drifting to the opposite bank. The more I tried to row, the harder it became and the faster I drifted towards the western side.

There were a number of large cargo steamers moving up and down the river and I began to realise that if I didn't want to get into serious trouble, I would need to get back to the east side of the river as speedily as possible. I tried with all my strength to cross over, keeping my eyes anxiously on the steamers coming towards me and wondering how on earth I was going to avoid them. I also realised that the reason I was drifting was that the tide must be going out. So I tried very hard to row against the stream and eventually found myself in the middle of the river when a big cargo steamer came very close, making lots of waves. My little boat started to rock from side to side and front to back. I had to hang on for dear life just to stay in it. I gazed up at the steamer towering high above me as it passed and saw someone looking down from the deck. He was waving his arms about and shouting at me. Eventually, after further hard rowing, I ended up on the bank of a little forest near Blankenese. I must have drifted about 30 kilometres down the river. Leaving the boat tied to a tree, I took a train back into Hamburg. By this time it was pitch dark. I went back to see the owner of the boat. When I told him about my mishap and where he could find his boat, he became very angry. The next morning in the canteen when I told

The author on the job in Hamburg, 1948

people my story, everybody started laughing. They said I should have hired a river taxi.

One day I was walking from the Dammtor City Station down the Mittelweg to the DPA office when I saw a familiar figure in front of me. He was walking at a fast pace and I had to hurry to catch up with him. He turned around and we both recognised each other immediately. Helmut Prignitz and I used to play together in the Hinterhof at 133 Kurfürstendamm, when we both lived there. We had not seen each other for over four years. We were always in trouble with Mr Raguse when we played with our toy racing cars or our tin soldiers on the concrete floor of the yard, making all sorts of loud accompanying noises.

Helmut was one of two sons of Herr and Frau Prignitz; he was my age and Hans was about two years older. The Prignitz couple ran the Nazi uniform shop that had those ugly anti-Jewish propaganda slogans imprinted in their shop window. I had only met Mr Prignitz once. I remember him as a very short man with a long sharp nose. I had never talked to any of them about their Nazi sympathies and Helmut had never said anything on this subject either.

We were both very happy to see each other again and Helmut invited me to his home in Pöseldorfer Weg next to the Theatre in a Room, which was not very far from the DPA. I visited him the following day and to my surprise I found his parents there too. It seemed they all lived together in the one-roomed apartment. His parents were sitting at a table covered with coloured sheets of paper, some in shiny silver and gold. There was a pot of glue and a brush, a couple of pairs of scissors, and many bits of coloured paper chains. It looked as if they were making some sort of Christmas decoration. After we had exchanged brief greetings, Helmut asked me to come to the kitchen where he had his piano accordion. He sat on a chair and started to play. I remembered him playing in his Berlin home. I had often sat beside him, watching and listening with admiration. He was playing much better now than before, though, and had added classical pieces to his repertoire. I was very impressed. I found myself wishing that I could have studied music – but, although I loved music, I had no natural talent and was tone-deaf. When Helmut stopped playing, I enthusiastically congratulated him. Then I suggested we go around the corner for a coffee.

Sitting outside in the café's small garden, I asked him how his family had ended up in Hamburg and why he had disappeared from Berlin so suddenly. He said that he had been sent to the country in 1943 because of the heavy bombing together with a group of children until his mother arranged for him to come to Hamburg after the war. His brother Hans was in the Hitler Youth when they discovered that he was an exceptional athlete – a sport he had been developing since early childhood. He was sent to an athletics training school near Berlin to train young Hitler Youth boys. He was married now and also lived in Hamburg.

Helmut's father was a tailor. First he had gone underground and could not be found by the Denazification Commission and then, six months previously, he had turned up in Hamburg. His mother had been arrested and made to appear before the commission. She spent six months in prison, then left Berlin and also came to Hamburg. Now his parents earned a living making Christmas decorations.

A week later I went to visit Hans and his wife Inge in their small apartment. Inge looked much older than Hans and rather unwell. She had a sad face and never smiled, and her hair was untidy and fell loosely. Hans was a keen chess player, and after I told him that I enjoyed chess, too, he said that we should have a game. He put up his chess set on a small table in the living room while his wife went into the kitchen to make coffee. After a couple of games (which resulted in a draw each time) Hans started to talk about himself and his work and I told him about mine. He had a young team of athletes and every morning for four hours they rehearsed trapeze tricks. They had constructed a trapeze in a burnt-out church with only the outside wall still standing. He suggested I should come along and take some photos.

He also told me he was giving a one-man performance at an upmarket night-club in Hamburg's poshest area and asked if I could take some publicity photos for him. I happily agreed. It would be a welcome relief from my weekly football pictures. We arranged to meet up the following week at the nightclub.

As agreed, I duly turned up at 9.30pm with my camera, a tripod and a flash-pan with a flint attached to the pan, and a tin of flash powder. There were only about six people there, but they were all dressed in elegant evening clothes sitting around little tables covered with drinks. The tables were arranged in a half-circle facing a small dance floor. Hans had alerted the management that I was going to take pictures, so I had no problems setting up to photograph the event. I fixed my camera to the tripod and waited for Hans's performance, which was scheduled for 10pm. At the back of the dance floor a small band was playing dance music and one couple were dancing. When the music stopped, a group of young men appeared, carrying what appeared to be a large box with some steps attached to it. As they began putting it in position I realised this was the platform; it was about two metres off the floor. After a few moments of silence the house lights went out and a spotlight revealed Hans emerging from behind the curtain, supporting himself on his hands on two rods, each of which was about a metre long. He then proceeded to 'walk' upside down on these rods onto the dance floor. Jumping lightly onto his feet, he made a low bow to the audience, all of whom clapped loudly. I must say Hans made an impressive figure in his tight, colourful, glittering costume. After taking in the applause, he got back onto his rods, did another handstand and 'walked' step by step up to the platform.

Now it was my turn. I had put some of the flash powder onto the pan in readiness. I held it up high and with a long cable release opened the shutter of my camera with my left hand and simultaneously pressed the flint release lever with the finger of my right hand, which made a spark onto the flash powder. There was a mighty muffled explosion and a bright light. A black cloud of smoke rapidly rose to the ceiling, followed by screams and groans from above me. I was completely unaware that there was a balcony up there. When I looked up I saw a lot of black faces glaring angrily down at me and people shaking their fists. The manager rushed up, waving his arms about, and asked me to leave – he was furious. 'Get out!' he shouted, so I grabbed my equipment and got out as quickly as I could.

When I went to see Hans the next day at his flat, I gave him the photo I had taken. He had thought the whole incident very funny and he was still laughing about it. He liked the photo and asked me if I could make a dozen copies for him. After they had washed some of the soot off their faces, he said, most of the club guests had actually thought it was a big joke and part of the show.

Now Hans wanted to perform a more sensational act for me to photograph, so we brainstormed a couple of ideas and came up with the idea of his doing a handstand on the Michel. This was the most visible tower in Hamburg and belonged to St Michael's Church, which stood on a hill overlooking the harbour and city. So the following morning, on a misty day with drizzling rain, the two of us went up to the Michel and got permission to go up the tower to photograph the view. When he thought he had found the ideal spot, Hans stood on one hand so that I could take the picture. I began to get a bit worried while he posed for me because it was taking so long, but he was quite relaxed, just changing hands from time to time without changing his upside-down position. This photo was published in some local papers, but for some reason it didn't create the sensation we'd imagined it might – I think perhaps people had other things on their minds.

One night, after I had been working late in the DPA darkroom printing some urgent press photos, I walked home to my room in Schlüterstrasse in the pitch dark. It was late and I was very tired. Suddenly someone was standing in front of me and a light was blinding my eyes. 'What are you doing here?' a harsh voice demanded. 'Papers!' As he moved his torch away from my face, I saw that it was a policeman.

'What papers?' I said defiantly.

'Your ID,' he said.

'I have no ID,' I said, 'but I have my smallpox papers.' I began taking out my torn old paper, by now stamped all over by various official departments. He shone his torch on the paper and examined it. 'Are you a refugee?' he asked in a somewhat friendlier tone. I told him I was from Berlin and he proceeded to give me a ticket to appear at the magistrate's court at eleven the following morning.

This encounter made me think about the Nazis and how they were still around. I had been so busy keeping alive that I'd forgotten. I had ignored what was happening around me. I had overheard many people who still believed in the old national socialist ideas and had the same mannerisms of arrogance, superiority and pomposity used by the Nazis, especially civil servants and those working in government. I came to the conclusion that this was ingrained in the German character, along with their rigidity and inability to improvise. I spent the whole of the next day at the court. Finally, I appeared before a judge, who gave me time to arrange an ID card. I had to write letters to Berlin and

Mühlhausen to get into the system. I also wrote to my mother in South Africa and asked her to organise for me to come over.

I was given another job at the DPA. This was to photograph a certain politician the following evening at a local election. I was definitely not going to use flash powder again. I managed to borrow a flash gun for my Leica from the photo department, and they also gave me a pack of flash bulbs. This was a new type of flashlight and I had never used it before. You attached your flash gun to the camera: the flash gun held a set of batteries and a reflector and the lightbulbs fitted into the top of the flash gun next to the reflector. The flash bulbs looked rather strange. They were like normal lightbulbs but inside there was what looked like crumpled silver paper covered with a layer of transparent plastic.

I put on a tie and my best and only jacket and went to the Town Hall to photograph the speaker. He was standing at a podium on a stage and the auditorium was packed. I had to walk down the aisle to get up to the stage but then I discovered that the man was too far away for my lens, so I walked up the step at the side of the stage, moved closer to him, lifted my camera and focused. I released the shutter. There was a mighty explosion, and smoke, flames and splinters of glass came out of my flash gun. Horrified, I looked up. The speaker had disappeared! And when I looked around, the auditorium was silent, and a number of security guards were rushing down the aisle towards me.

I looked back at the podium but the speaker seemed to have vanished completely. I took a few steps forward and peered behind the podium, where I found him cowering at its back looking at me in bewilderment. As I lifted my camera to get a picture, I was grabbed by the security guards and marched out of the auditorium. I needed to give some explanation as to who I was and what had happened. I reckoned that the plastic covering of one of the flash bulbs must have been torn and that this was the reason for the explosion. I decided never to use flashlight again.

One morning towards the end of 1949 I woke up with terrible pain in my stomach. It was a very sharp pain and I started to feel very sick. I couldn't move, had a fever and was sweating profusely. I stayed in bed for the day, but when it got worse the following night I didn't know what to do. I had no one to call and there was nobody in the kitchen or on the same floor. I drank some water. Then I think I must have passed out. This went on for a number of days and I lost all sense of time. I woke up on an operating table in the local hospital. When I came round in the ward, a very kind and friendly doctor told me that I had had a burst appendix and they hadn't been sure I was going to make it as my appendicitis was advanced. He kept calling me 'Mister' and said that when I was under, I spoke a lot of English words. I had the recently discovered penicillin to thank for saving my life.

After six weeks in hospital I turned up at Walter Benser's office to return to work. He looked at me with alarm. 'You are as skinny as if you've come from Belsen!' he pronounced. Then he told me I should go to a convalescence centre and promised to arrange a stay of two weeks at a hotel in the forests near Hamburg. He also said that he wanted the address of my stepfather and mother. Since they didn't seem to care about me, he said, he was going to write them a letter.

In the two weeks I spent in the forest recuperating, I was given extra portions of food and a daily glass of two raw egg yolks in red wine. I also took long walks in the forest. All this was courtesy of the DPA and fortunately I made a quick recovery. I returned to work fit as a fiddle.

Whatever Benser had said to them in his letter, it must have given my mother and John a fright because they speedily arranged for me to join them in South Africa. I managed to get all the necessary papers I needed to emigrate and in June 1950 I travelled on a Union-Castle liner from Southampton to Cape Town.

South Africa in Black and White

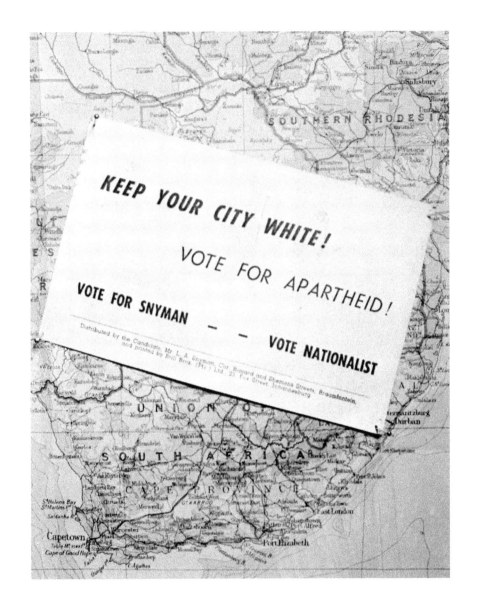

'Keep Your City White! —Vote for Apartheid!'

5

'EUROPEANS ONLY'

The voyage to Cape Town was uneventful and almost immediately on my arrival in that city I boarded a train to Johannesburg, which was where my mother and John were living.

The only other person sitting in my compartment was a middle-aged, white-haired, well-dressed man, who finally put his newspaper down, looked at me and said something in a language I couldn't understand (which, I would soon learn, was Afrikaans). I apologised to him in my broken English for not understanding him and explained that I had just arrived in South Africa from Germany, that I was from Berlin and that I had emigrated. The man became more and more friendly. He introduced himself as Dr Van Rensburg and switched to fluent German. 'Welcome to South Africa, young man,' he said with a broad smile.

I was happy to hear German again as I had spoken only English for the last ten days on the ship – I was trying to learn English but it was quite a strain.

'I am the Commander General of the Ossewabrandwag,' he told me, as if that should mean something to me.

'I see,' I said.

'I met your Führer, Adolf Hitler, and Göring, and many of the other leaders,' he went on. This was worrying me, but I didn't say anything. 'We opposed the South African participation in the war against Germany and based our policies on the Führer's teaching to fight against the British Empire, the capitalist, the communist, the Jews and the system of parliamentarianism. But we will change all this now in South Africa with apartheid.'

Not having any idea of what apartheid meant, I was nonetheless sickened at his words. I had thought I would never again hear these fascist views expressed, and here I was sharing a train compartment with a man who sounded just like one of the demented members of the Nazi Party I had been forced to listen to until the very end of the war. I could hardly believe that I was hearing the same type of extreme language once more, and from someone who was seemingly well educated. I remember having a sinking feeling in my stomach that matched my rage at his approval of people like Hitler and Göring and their lunatic and lethal ideas. How could anyone possibly say such things after a war during which millions of people were killed and millions of others had been terribly pressed?

Feeling deeply uncomfortable in Dr Van Rensburg's presence and hoping that his views were just an individual's ravings, I left the compartment and went to the dining car. Here I spent most of the night drinking beer and thinking about where I could go next and whether Dr Van Rensburg represented the general population, which I thought unlikely. If there was one thing the world must have learnt after the war, it was that racism was completely wrong and immoral. Worrying about all of this, I stayed in the dining car. When we pulled into Kimberley station, I was relieved to see Dr Van Rensburg leave the train and walk away down the platform.

We arrived in Johannesburg early on a bitterly cold morning. I stood on the platform with my suitcase feeling disoriented, not only by the unfamiliar surroundings but by my encounter with the Ossewabrandwag leader. What was I in for? Why on earth was I here?

There were two taxi ranks outside the station, first class and second class. Thinking that I could save some money, I jumped into a second-class taxi. As I was about to close the door, a big black fellow came rushing up to me. 'No, boss, no, boss,' he said, waving his hands around. I wondered what his problem was. 'This taxi is for natives only. Over there,' he said, 'you have to go to the taxis for Europeans.'

I was a little puzzled, but then I was from Europe, so ...

The driver of the taxi I climbed into was a white man. He began talking to me in Afrikaans but when I explained that I was new in the country he spoke English, and gave me a commentary about the sights we passed. We drove through the city, the business and shopping centre, where the streets were divided into square blocks, with the buildings similar to the pictures I had seen of American cities. Johannesburg certainly looked like a modern city. The majority of the people I saw hurrying along the pavements at that time of the morning were white, although I did see some black people on street corners selling newspapers. Others were riding bicycles in the traffic, alongside large American cars.

Eventually we reached the suburbs, the 'white suburbs', as the driver pointed out to me, to the east of the city centre. He pulled up outside the address I had given him in Kensington. Like the other houses we had driven past, my mother's house had a low red-brick wall with an iron gate and a neat front garden. The garden had a date palm in it and some other tropical plants. I was greeted by three black poodles, who came rushing down the steps and along the path, barking and jumping around me. My mother was sitting on the veranda. She seemed surprised to see me. 'There you are!' she said, looking me up and down. 'Blacky's had two puppies. This is Dickerchen, this is Suzie and you know our Blacky. Now, let me show you your room. John is at the office. He usually doesn't come home until five thirty.'

Later we sat on the couch in the living room and my mother told me about all the new friends they had made, the special shops where you could get German delicatessen food, about 'the natives', and how unreliable the 'girls' were. 'I had three different girls last year,' she said. 'One stole food and the others didn't clean the house properly. Absolutely dreadful. And as for our garden boy, he's always drunk. The natives are absolutely hopeless. You just wait and see what they're like. You'll be amazed ...'

On the dot of five thirty, the dogs started to bark and within a few moments John came in through the front door. He was much shorter than I remembered him and now wore glasses. He was dressed in a business suit and carried a brief-case. He was clearly not pleased to see me. 'Settled in already?' he said. He put his briefcase down, lit a cigarette and said, 'You can't stay here very long, you know. You have to find a job. There's lots of work here in Johannesburg, if you're pre-pared to work. Rosie already has enough on her hands, without you being around as well.' Then he picked up his briefcase and walked out of the room.

'Never mind him,' my mother said. 'He's got lots of problems at the office.

Of course you can stay as long as you like.'

I realised that this was not a happy house. I would have to find my way out of it as soon as possible.

The next morning I took the tram into the city and walked about the streets to get a feel for the place. It was a warm, sunny winter's day but my skin was tingling and I felt lightheaded. Later I realised this was because of the altitude, and it took me a few days to get accustomed to being so high above sea level. My wanderings took me to a park, where I found a bench to rest on. I noticed that the bench had a sign on it: 'Europeans Only'. Obviously, this was okay for me but what about the other people? Which people exactly were included as Europeans here, I wondered. Close by, some black women were sitting chatting on the grass, each of them in a sort of nanny's outfit, while they watched over a number of toddlers, all of whom were white. One of the toddlers climbed all over the bench marked 'Europeans Only', so I thought the child must be a European, while the nannies, who kept well away from the bench, were not. They had to sit on the grass. I was working this out.

It was getting hot and I was thirsty, so I left the park and found a pub. At the long bar counter, young men in business suits and ties were drinking beer and eating lunch. I found a place to sit at the counter and ordered a beer, amid a buzz of voices and the odd loud burst of laughter.

'This is the toughest piece of fucking leather off a donkey's back I've ever tried to eat – it's not worth threepence,' said a man next to me.

A red-faced, heavily built man on my right turned to the steak-eater on my left. 'We should have gone to Jeppe for LM prawns piri-piri, man!' he shouted.

I turned to the man on my right and asked him what he meant by LM?

'Lourenço Marques,' he said. 'Where you from? You sound funny, man – you from Timbuktu?'

'No, I'm from Berlin. My name is Jürgen,' I answered.

He turned to the man on my left. 'You hear this, Alan? He's a fucking Kraut.'

Alan pushed his plate with the half-eaten steak aside. 'Well, this calls for another drink – it's my round,' he said. The fellow on the right introduced himself as Jimmy.

At one end of the bar was an open serving hatch, behind which stood a middle-aged Indian man in a white jacket. He was holding a tray which the barman was filling up with glasses of drinks for the waiter, who was a short man in a bow-tie and sporting a small goatee. The barman looked angrily at the Indian waiter through the hatch. 'Don't fuck with me!' he shouted. 'You better go back to school and learn to count, boy!' The Indian waiter stood there mortified. The barman, looking around the bar, and noticing that some people were listening, said, very loudly, 'These coolies – you can't trust any of them.' He then turned back to the waiter behind the hatch. 'Okay, Gopal, get the fuck on with it!' The waiter took his tray and disappeared.

Jimmy began telling me about the king-size prawns from Mozambique that you could get at the Jeppe Station Hotel. As he was talking, a black man came into the bar. He was wearing shorts and was barefoot. I watched as he crawled behind the counter and started filling up a case with the empty bottles from beneath it. Alan, on my left, leaned over the counter, and looked down at him. 'Hey, peaboy, take my plate,' he said. He waved his half-full plate at the man. 'There is some meat for you, boy.' The man came up from under the bar counter and I saw that he was quite young. He gave us all a big smile, showing a set of very white teeth, and took the plate from Alan. 'Dankie, baas,' he said, before ducking down below the counter again.

Jimmy turned towards me. 'You have to learn how to treat these kaffirs, Jürgen,' he told me. 'They're very primitive. Just like … like children, you know.'

'They need a bloody good whipping, man. They're just a bunch of lazy shits!' said Alan.

I thought these two men were being very rude to these people and that I had better say something. 'Don't you think that you should treat people with some respect and dignity?' I asked.

'Fuck dignity!' Alan said, looking irritated. 'What do you think they've achieved? Fuck all.' He paused to take a long drink of his beer. 'Look at it this way,' he said, staring at me seriously and pointing his finger into my face. 'We've got two thousand fucking years of civilisation behind us, but what the bloody hell have they achieved? Fuck all!'

As Jimmy called for another three beers, I tried to change the subject.

'Something puzzles me – are you European?' I asked Alan. 'I mean, I see signs all over the city saying "Europeans Only", but what does that mean?'

Jimmy looked bemused. 'We're all Europeans,' he said. 'We come from Europe. My grandparents came here from England.'

At this point there was a loud ringing of a bell and the barman shouted, 'Last round, gentlemen!' so I thought I had better buy a round. After ordering, I went to find the toilet. Just off the bar was a small foyer and, through an open double door, I caught a glimpse of women sitting around tables, smoking and drinking from liqueur and wine glasses. I took my camera and, quietly placing myself behind a pillar in the room, took a few pictures. Nobody seemed to notice me until suddenly I felt a tap on my shoulder. It was the waiter, Gopal, who earlier on had been shouted at by the barman. 'You can't come into this lounge, sir,' he said, with a sheepish grin, as I was putting my camera into its case.

'Why not?'

'Because, sir, you're not wearing a tie, sir.'

As I got back to the bar, the barman was calling time and Jimmy and Alan were finishing their drinks with large gulps. 'Let's go to the Greek Taverna,' Jimmy drawled in a drunken voice, putting his arm around my shoulder. 'They don't have licensing hours there, so we can go on drinking.'

I didn't want to get into a long drinking session so I excused myself, promising to meet the two again in the bar another day.

The streets outside were busy with traffic and people hurrying along the pavements, and I soon melted into the stream. I passed department stores with displays of the latest fashions in their windows, from ladies' shoes to underwear to sportswear. There were delicatessens and camera shops and a place with a sign saying 'Bioscope'. I stopped to look at some Charlie Chaplin film posters outside and, realising that it was a cinema, I bought myself a ticket for two shillings and sixpence and went inside. I found a seat in the dark cinema, where an Abbott and Costello film was already playing, and relaxed. There was a long board in front of my seat on which an attendant put a cup of hot sweet white tea. While sipping the tea I noticed that people all around me were striking matches and lighting cigarettes and there was a lot of coming and going. The next film was another comedy, this time with the Marx Brothers.

6

KILLER'S SHEBEEN

By the time I left the cinema the streets were quieter and the weather was noticeably cooler. I walked in the direction I thought was out of the city and towards Kensington, and before long I found myself in a side road lined with suburban houses. All had small front gardens and corrugated-iron roofs, some painted red and some green, but the street was mostly deserted, except for the odd car driving past. As it grew dark, the streetlights came on and I quickened my pace.

Suddenly I heard the sound of someone playing a piano. It seemed to be coming from a house in front of me. I stood outside the gate, listening. Then in the evening gloom I saw a man sitting on the veranda in an armchair. He was wearing a Stetson hat. He was white, dressed in a suit and tie, and had a cigarette hanging from his lips. He had a tired smile on his face. 'What you up to, young man?' he said to me. 'Looking for a drink?' He got up and, raising his arm to indicate a half-open door, he said, 'Come into Killer's shebeen.'

Curious, I walked through the small iron gate and up onto the veranda. Clearly seeing that I was not a local, the man asked me where I was from. I told him my name and said that I had just arrived from Germany, and he showed me inside. I walked into a dimly lit room, where I saw a number of people sitting at a long table, its surface covered with bottles, glasses, cigarette packets, ashtrays and cards. A group of men were concentrating on a card game and three others were sitting in a dark corner on a settee and a worn armchair, in front of a low table, which was also full of bottles and glasses. All three men wore Stetsons.

The music I had heard was coming from an old piano, with candles on either side, where a man, also wearing a Stetson hat, was playing the blues. Although the piano was out of tune, the sound was compelling. The room was dense with cigarette smoke. The only lighting came from a naked bulb over the card table. Tacked onto the walls I saw pin-up posters of scantily clad young black women, advertising various products — NO MORE NASTY PERSPIRATION SMELL! MUM CREAM KEEPS YOU FRESH ALL DAY. 1 / - SMALL SIZE — and another poster that said: NAOMI — BEAUTY FOR TODAY'S WOMEN —THEY NEED WELL FITTING FOUNDATION GARMENTS. The women in the skimpy outfits offered broad, seductive smiles and gleaming white teeth.

'What's your pleasure, Mister Jürgen? We have a special tonight – one quart of Lion beer and a half-jack of Limousin brandy for two shillings and twopence. We also have Castle beer, but that would be an extra sixpence. And, by the way, call me Killer,' said the man who had led me into the bar.

I didn't know what he meant by a quart or a half-jack but I let it go. 'I'll have the special – thank you, Mr Killer,' I said.

Killer walked around the table and opened the door at the end of the room next to the piano and shouted: 'Ruth, get off your arse and bring mister here a special.' Then he told me to make myself at home, adding, 'I've got a German grandmother, you know.'

I sat down at the table beside the card players, who had so far ignored me, and saw Ruth, a very generously proportioned black woman, come waddling through the door with the special. With a bright smile, she put a large bottle of Lion beer, a glass and a small quarter-size brandy bottle (a half-jack) in front of me. Seeing my hesitation, she took the beer bottle in one hand and the half-jack in the other, leaned over me and poured both brandy and beer into the large glass. I thanked her and took a sip. It tasted terrible, awful, but it certainly had a mighty kick.

Killer sat down opposite me, lit a Lucky Strike and, in a low, confidential voice, said, 'It's against the law for blacks to drink alcohol, so they have to drink quickly when they're in a shebeen. They need to get drunk before the cops raid the place, so we call it "sip and fly", which is why we started to make a cocktail of beer and brandy. We call it the special, which is pretty appropriate, don't you think?' He looked at me with a shrewd expression. 'Now tell me what you're doing in our country, all the way from Germany? And I can tell you things about this place because I have stories, lots of stories. I was a detective in the South African police force, you know. Why don't you visit me another time, maybe tomorrow afternoon?'

From the moment I'd arrived I'd been thinking that this might be an interesting place to photograph. I was also intrigued to know where Killer had got his name from.

'I'd love to come back,' I told him, 'but can I take some pictures now?'

The musician was still trying to play a tune on the tone-deaf piano and the card players were still eyeing each other like hawks. They hadn't looked up once. I noticed that there was a small pile of money lying among the glasses and bottles in the middle of the table. Ruth carried more drinks across to the three silent men in the dark corner. I took my Leica from under my jacket and started to take pictures of the gamblers. It was very dark so I had to do a long exposure and, to keep my camera steady, I put my elbow on the table for support, pressed the camera against my forehead, and held my breath. Killer had moved over to the dark corner, where he was talking to the three silent characters, and in the meantime I took a few pictures of Ruth, who posed for me standing by the table.

I had another sip of the special, the taste still dreadful, and decided I should probably leave. It had been quite a long day and I was tired. And I still had to find my way back to my mother's house. As I was walking towards the front door, Killer came over and stopped me.

'You want to spend a penny?' he asked me loudly, so everybody in the room could hear, and then he took me by the arm and led me to a door at the back of the room. In the kitchen he whispered to me, 'The tsotsis – they've got an eye on your camera. They won't do anything in here but they'll definitely go for you outside.' Pushing me through the back door, he said, 'Come and see me tomorrow afternoon.'

I found myself in a very dark alley at the side of the house and stumbled towards the street, where some dogs nearby were barking angrily. In the distance I could see the bright lights of what I hoped was the main road and, still a bit dizzy from the special, I headed for them as quickly as I could, conscious of Killer's warning. I'd been walking for a while when I heard voices. Turning round, I saw three shadows come out of the shebeen and recognised them as the characters who had been sitting silently in the corner. I pulled myself together and stepped up my pace. Behind me, I could hear footsteps. I glanced back. Although the men were walking slowly, they were definitely following me. I began to feel very worried. Realising that, on my first day in Johannesburg, I was about to be robbed, I started to run. Unfortunately, however fast I ran, they seemed to be gaining on me. They were now running really fast.

Up ahead I saw two men standing at the corner. They looked like policemen, both men in tropical helmets and uniforms. As I got closer to them, I slowed down and pointed at the three characters coming up behind me; I was far too out of breath to say anything. The policemen looked first at me and then at the three men who were now jogging up to us and then, to my utter amazement, the policemen sprinted away up the main street. Really worried now, I ran after them as fast as my tired legs could carry me, throwing frantic glances over my shoulder. The three tsotsis, while still following me, were slowing down. Perhaps the effects of Killer's special were taking hold or perhaps it was because the street here was better lit and there was some traffic about, but to my great relief they finally disappeared. I found a 'Europeans Only' tram that took me to Kensington.

Some time later I learnt that African policemen were not allowed to carry any weapons and could not defend themselves against gangsters, who invariably had guns and knives. No doubt that was why those two fellows had run away.

John was waiting up for me in the living room, looking grim. 'You're late,' he said. 'Moreover, you're drunk, and you missed the special dinner your mother made for you.' With that, he got up and left the room.

My first day in South Africa – certainly a day to remember.

7

LOOKING FOR WORK

I had to find a job. Early the next morning I took a tram back into the city.

I browsed through some of the local newspapers and magazines in a news agency to see what was on offer. There were English and Afrikaans papers, a variety of local magazines in both languages, and also some American, British and European papers. The local magazines I looked at were of bad quality with poorly printed photos and they seemed very provincial. I thought I'd better go to a major Johannesburg daily to look for work.

The offices of *The Star* newspaper were in the centre of the city, in an impressively large and modern building. In the photo department, men in dark suits and ties were handling large 4 x 5-inch Speed Graphics, with huge flash guns. I stood watching as other men, in short-sleeved shirts, came in and out of the darkroom with wet prints in their hands. They all seemed to be very busy. Everyone ignored me. On the walls of the department were prints of girls in bathing suits and, stuck on top of a row of filing cabinets, pictures of car accidents, football and cricket matches, and portraits of sportsmen. The smell of darkroom chemicals mixed with tobacco pervaded the room.

Eventually I managed to attract someone's attention, a young man not much older than me, who was carrying a large camera.

'What are you up to?' he asked me with a friendly smile.

'I would like to speak to the head of the photo department,' I told him, rather nervously.

A busy Johannesburg street, 1951

'Hey, boys, this oke wants to speak to Jimmy!' he shouted for everybody to hear.

'He's gone for tea,' someone passing by said, holding a wet print in his hand.

'Where do I find him?' I asked.

'In the canteen, where else?'

'Where's the canteen?' I asked, looking over the man's shoulder, as he put a print onto a viewing board on the wall. The print was of a couple of men shaking hands in front of a microphone on a platform.

'What the fuck! Do you think I'm your information service?'

Someone tugged me on the arm and I saw that it was the young, friendly photographer. 'Come on, I need a cup of tea,' he said. 'I'll take you to Jimmy.'

I followed him along some long passages, and as we walked we introduced ourselves. The photographer's name was Peter. Eventually, we reached the canteen, which consisted of a long passage with plastic tables on both sides and a counter at the other end. There we walked up to a middle-aged man sitting at a table with a group of other serious-looking fellows.

'Jimmy, someone wants to see you,' Peter said and turned towards me. 'This is Jürgen.'

Jimmy looked up at me suspiciously. 'What can I do for you, young man?'

I introduced myself as a photographer from Germany and, as briefly as I could, I gave him my background. With everybody at the table watching, Jimmy pointed at my Leica, which was hanging over my shoulder. 'If you come here with that miniature camera, you haven't a hope in hell of ever getting a job in South Africa,' he said.

Well, that was that, so I went back home to ponder what to do next.

My mother had told me about her friends the Baeckers, and when I got home I found they were visiting. Mr and Mrs Baecker and their four children were sitting in the living room having coffee and cake. Mr Baecker was a serious-looking man and Mrs Baecker had a long face with rabbit teeth, like her children, and wore a flowery dress. The children seemed to be dressed in their Sunday best, the boys wearing ties, and looked very respectable. I saw my mother had brought out her best silver and cutlery, which made me wonder what the special occasion was. It turned out that the family were devout

Catholics and that today was Confirmation day for the youngest boy, who was ten. The family had come to celebrate with my mother, who seemed exceptionally excited. She kept giving me special looks and smiling at Mr Baecker in an admiring way.

'Jürgen, isn't it wonderful,' she said when she saw me come in. 'Mr Baecker has asked you to accompany him to his mine in the Karoo. He is one of the mining tycoons in the Northern Cape.'

'You flatter me,' Mr Baecker said, standing up and walking over to me. 'I am not a tycoon. But, Jürgen, come along if you like. It might be interesting for you to see what it is like in the bush, see a bit of real Africa.' He put his hand on my shoulder. 'We leave next week Monday, first thing.'

I thought this sounded quite exciting and especially good for pictures, so I stayed around talking with the Baeckers, although the conversation was uncomfortably full of talk about 'the natives', how lazy and unreliable they were, how stupid, and how impossible it was to get them to do any work.

The following Monday I was on a bench-like seat in a huge American Ford heading off to the Northern Cape. Walter, Mr Baecker's older son, sat next to me. Mr Baecker drove with his right arm resting on the door of the open window, steering with the fingers of his left hand. He was totally relaxed. We drove through mostly very monotonous, flat countryside, a khaki-coloured landscape of cactuses and thorn bushes, freckled with brown, reddish rocks. Small farms were dotted here and there.

After driving for over four hours, we reached the outskirts of Kimberley. Here the landscape changed to virgin land, with small thorn trees and, in the distance, some stony hills, which I learnt were called koppies. The sky was a deep blue and the winter sun as bright as a spotlight. Mr Baecker pulled up near a group of coloured people sitting on the other side of the dusty dirt road.

'Hey, boys – De Beers Road?' he shouted, waving his right arm outside the window.

Two of the fellows got up slowly and walked to the car. 'Gyrr, baas,' one of them grunted, giving us a toothless smile. He had an old worn cap on his head. 'Waar kom baas vandaan?'

The other fellow came around to my side. He stuck his head into the window next to me and a strong smell of stale beer entered the car.

'We've just come from Johannesburg and we're looking for the Savoy Hotel,' Mr Baecker said in an authoritative voice.

The fellow closest to me removed his head from my window, staggered backwards, then stood to attention. Lifting his left arm like a traffic policeman, he shouted, 'Oor daar!'

In the luxurious dining room of the Savoy Hotel, where we had lunch, we were the only guests. African waiters in white gloves were eagerly attentive. I hardly finished my plate before it was whisked away and I found another course in front of me. It was a magnificent meal, typical, I would discover, of South African hotels in the British style: roast lamb with mint sauce, baked potatoes and green beans.

Mr Baecker had not talked much on the drive but now he started to tell me the history of Kimberley, the discovery of diamonds, and the Big Hole, which we were about to see. The Hole, the biggest in the world, was created between 1871 and 1914 by fifty thousand miners digging with picks and shovels. Twenty-two million tons of earth had been excavated. The Hole was 463 metres wide and 240 metres deep, and the mine had produced 2 720 kilograms of diamonds. After lunch and the history lesson we got back into the car and drove to see it. It was quite amazing to me to think of those thousands of people spending all their lives digging this huge hole to get little shiny stones out of it.

As we drove out of the town, the tarred road ended and I had to close my window because of the dust blowing in, although it was very hot in the car. I began to doze off. I must have been sleeping for some hours because when I woke up the sun was setting ahead of us in a bright red-orange glow. The landscape was flat, with no trees or buildings anywhere, just semi-desert as far as the eye could see. Just before dark we arrived at a small town called Postmasburg. We drove up the main street, the only tarred road, past a small town hall, a post office and some shops and stores, and drew up outside the Grand Hotel. The town reminded me of the American Wild West that I had seen in cowboy movies – the narrow, straight, dirt roads, low wooden buildings and covered walkways with signs like the Friendly Store and the Goodwill Pharmacy, which had a poster outside saying: *'Constipation, that's the root of your indigestion – Partons Pills 30 for 1 /– 50 for 1 / 6'*. I took quite a few pictures.

Walter and I shared a room. It had two single beds and a cupboard next to a small window. Outside, the now fading landscape, hills in the background, was lit up in a bright orange glow by the setting sun. Walter seemed to be a moody type of boy. He hadn't said much during the journey and all my attempts at conversation elicited only grunts and morose looks.

The following morning, after a breakfast of fried eggs, bacon, pork sausages, baked beans and toast, the three of us were back in the Ford driving over dusty roads towards Mr Baecker's mine. After another long, hot drive through a landscape of small bushes and red rocks, with hills in the distance, we passed clusters of stone heaps. These were occupied by communities of meerkats, most of which dashed into their holes as we passed by, although a few remained on guard, standing on their hind legs, watching us. Here and there the flat landscape was broken by termite heaps, some very large ones formed in and around thorn trees.

Eventually we arrived at a settlement with huts and tin shelters. We saw some Africans walking along the road, the women carrying bundles of wood on their heads. We stopped at a barracks with a sign over the door saying 'Asbestos Mountain. District Kuruman. Office'.

Mr Baecker and Walter went into the office while I wandered off into an open field of antheaps and bushes, where I took some pictures of this strange landscape. I shot a few exposures of the wide open space dotted with thorn bushes in the foreground but after a while I began to find this rather monotonous. I carried on walking until I came to a road, a path really, my shoes stirring up the dust. The sun was high up into the sky and it was getting very hot. Suddenly a group of bedraggled-looking African men, a few of them wearing a type of miner's helmet, came stumbling and shuffling past me. Up ahead was an assortment of makeshift corrugated-iron huts. I saw some children sitting in the shade of their walls and a couple of skeletal dogs lying in the dust, who slowly got up, giving me wary looks and wagging their tails.

The path ended at a tunnel leading into a mound. Some of the miners who had come past me were busy pushing a cart on rails into the tunnel. No one took any notice of me, so I followed them. The tunnel sloped downwards and it was lit by paraffin lamps. I came to an open space where other miners were hammering at the rock with small pick-axes. It was difficult to breathe in the clouds of dust that were penetrating my clothes and lungs. I tried to take some pictures but had difficulty keeping my lenses clean.

After spending some time in the mine I went back to the makeshift huts, where I took photos of some of the men and women, who seemed to realise I was not from the mining company. They started to talk to me, first asking me questions about who I was and why I was taking pictures. Then a few people began telling me that they were getting sick from the mine dust and that some people had died from breathing problems. One woman, who said she was a nurse, told me that the workers were getting asbestosis in the lungs. I was shown a sick man who could hardly move or talk. I photographed everything I saw and took some notes.

By now the sun was setting and it was getting cold, so I walked back the way I had come. Inside the office Mr Baecker was sitting at a large desk, and two other men, both wearing khaki shorts and shirts and with deep brown suntans, were with him.

'Where the hell have you been?' Mr Baecker said. 'This is Mr Van der Merwe, the mine manager. He's been looking for you. You can't just walk about in the native area.'

I apologised and explained that I had been talking to some of the miners and their families and friends. I told them what I had heard – that it seemed that the asbestos was causing lung problems for people exposed to the dust when working in the mines. Mr Van der Merwe rose from his chair and stepped towards me with a furious expression on his face. His large balloon-like stomach was showing through the split in his khaki shirt, as he pointed his fingers at me and then prodded my chest. 'Dit is nie jou verdomde besigheid, jong,' he said. 'You don't come here and poke your nose into our business – you hear me?'

Mr Baecker also got up and told me to mind my own business. Then he said we'd been there long enough and we should go back to the hotel.

We visited several more asbestos mines over the next few days, but a sour note had been struck. I was ordered not to talk to anyone or go anywhere near the mines themselves. My first trip into 'real Africa' was, in the end, disturbing and depressing.

Back in Johannesburg I still had problems, not least of which was to find a darkroom and get a job. Finally, after much searching, I found a company called Photo Agency, which sold and imported photographic studio equipment and cameras. It was run by two enthusiastic young German brothers named Horowitz, who were very helpful and sympathetic towards me.

I also met Jack Levine, a chemist, who ran Muller's Pharmacy in the centre of town. He had a large photo section supplying darkroom chemicals, camera equipment, films and cameras, and he was a wizard at photo chemistry. Jack kindly sent me to Mr Loeb, a German Jew (as was Jack), who had a 'develop and print' business. Mr Loeb took me on as a printer in his lab. I started work-ing in the darkroom alongside two young Afrikaans women, who spoke only a little English. Here we made small enlargements, sometimes postcards, of ama-teur photographers' pictures of visits to the Kruger National Park or holiday snaps on the beach. I worked on an enlarger and printed from a roll of 35 mm film. So, for example, I would print three prints of frame 7 or two of frame 9, or six of frame 12, and so on. I had to judge the exposure and the grade of paper I needed for each negative, with no time for test strips. At the end of the day Mr Loeb would go through our day's printing to see what was acceptable. He was very strict about the quality he wanted for his clients.

The two girls drove me a bit mad after a few days, as they kept their radio on all day, listening to lots of melodramatic radio dramas in Afrikaans, in which they were intensely involved. To leave my hands free, my enlarger was turned on and off with a foot switch, which was very handy; when it sounded as if the radio stories were reaching their climax, I could press the foot switch lightly, which did not connect the power fully but created a spark. This made the radio crackle just when the drama reached its climax, to the great dismay of the girls. I must confess that I very much enjoyed doing this.

During lunch I sat with Mr Loeb in his office and we would enjoy a cup of tea and eat sandwiches. It was strange for me to hear how much Mr Loeb missed

Germany. Odder still was his conviction that Hitler had actually not been so bad. After all, Mr Loeb said, Hitler had got Germany back to work again after the terrible times after the First World War. He had built the autobahns and even produced Volkswagen cars for 'everyone'. Of course I argued with him, trying to make him aware of what had really happened and about the reality of the concentration camps, but my efforts were to no avail. He simply did not believe me when I described what it was like to live in a really fascist state, where millions of people were killed for being Jewish or disabled or politically unacceptable.

I liked Mr Loeb and I think we both enjoyed our lunch-hour chats. However, he had some sort of nervous problem, which was distracting: every 20 seconds or so his head jumped to his left side over his shoulder and his left shoulder jerked up and down. This made it difficult for him to make enlargements in the darkroom.

One day I asked him if I could make some prints for myself in his dark-room. As long as I locked up in the evening, he said, it was all right with him. For some time I had been thinking about my trip with the Baeckers and the pictures I had taken of the asbestos mines. I went to see Jack Levine, who gave me some credit to buy some photographic paper. I spent a couple of evenings printing a set of prints for my asbestos story. Once I had developed some good pictures, I phoned the Medical School at the University of the Witwatersrand and the Johannesburg General Hospital to find out some more about asbestosis. I discovered that very little research had been done, but there did seem to be an awareness of the danger of asbestos dust for the miners who were exposed to it. Indeed, a connection had been made between the tumours found in tissue culture experiments done in 1942 and 1950 and asbestos exposure. There was further research available about the dangers of asbestos dust from countries such as Sweden, Italy, the United States and Britain.

On Friday afternoon, after I'd received my first South African pay packet, of £4.15s, I took my photo essay, my first piece of photojournalism in South Africa, which I called 'Fireproof Killer Dust: Asbestos', to the Johannesburg papers. The *Sunday Times* said I didn't have 'enough proof', the *Sunday Express* said, 'We don't touch the mines,' and the *Rand Daily Mail* said that although it was a 'good story', they didn't have space to run it. After I had been to see eight editors and feature editors, I gave up. I spent my very last pennies on posting the story to *Stern* magazine in Hamburg but, unfortunately, they did not publish it.

8

PHOTOGRAPHING THE BOERS

I worked for Mr Loeb for six weeks more and then I got a job with Werner's Studio, as an all-round dogsbody. Werner's Studio was owned by two brothers, Werner and Fritz Isaac, who were immigrants from Germany, which they had left in the thirties. Werner was the photographer and Fritz ran the business. Together they had built the studio into a major concern. They had studios in all the satellite towns around Johannesburg and along the Reef, about 50 kilometres to the east and west of the city.

I started at the Johannesburg studio, which was run by a woman in her fifties with a British background. She told me she had been a housewife until Fritz had given her the job four years ago. He had taught her how to set up portrait shots – using a small spotlight from back to left, one from above, a soft reflector front to left, a soft front light right and so on. She had been shown how to make the sitters look their best (chin on shoulder) or how to maximise the front view of a sitter (shoulders set slightly sideways). She told me all the other studios were also run by middle-aged women, all using the same standardised system. None of them knew anything about photography.

Then there were the wedding operators. These were freelance and semi-professional photographers who, for £5 per wedding, made standardised shots of the bride and the moment when the ring was placed on her finger. Sometimes the wedding group came to the studio. All the standard shots were made by the studio ladies. When the proofs were ready to be viewed by the customers, the studio ladies took the orders. The service included making up a colour chart for the hand colouring of the black-and-white prints – for the eyes, a person's complexion and hair, and anything else that was relevant.

As the general dogsbody, for my monthly pay of £75, I was to go and photograph weddings, do portraits at the studio and generally help out.

To be able to do my job more effectively, Fritz suggested I should learn to drive and so off I went with Werner in his car on my first country trip. Werner was in his fifties, almost bald, tall, heavily built and stone deaf. He talked in a clumsy, throaty way. He preferred to speak German, but his English was very good and was actually easier to understand than his German. Werner was an excellent lip reader and we could communicate very well except, of course, while driving, as he could not see my lips. This put me on edge, knowing that he couldn't possibly concentrate on the road ahead if he was busy trying to read my lips whenever I had a question.

Werner drove all the way to Bloemfontein. Then we turned off the highway onto a dirt road and he pulled over. It was time for me to take the wheel. He got out of the car and told me to slide over into the driver's seat. Well, I had never driven a car before and this was a big car by anyone's standards. It was an 8-cylinder 1934 Buick, wide and long, with two rows of facing seats in the back. I was very nervous while Werner explained the gears, clutch and brakes to me, before telling me to drive. Off I went, at first jerking and grinding the gears, but finally I got the beast under control, by which time Werner, sitting beside me, had fallen fast asleep. Fortunately, there was little traffic, only the occasional horse or donkey cart or car, and gradually, with Werner snoring gently beside me, I learnt how to manoeuvre round bends, which were corrugated and slippery with dust. After almost two hours, we arrived at a town called Koffiefontein and I happily drove down the main street. As I stopped in front of the Royal Hotel, Werner woke up.

In front of the hotel there were large posters announcing our arrival – 'Werner's Studio for Your Portraits – Your Wedding and Your Family'. We unpacked the car and put up some large, framed colour pictures of portraits and group pictures, which had been taken previously, along the front of the hotel. The hotel lounge was to be our temporary studio and here we set up our lamps and spotlights and hung up a large backdrop. Werner gave me a portfolio of pictures and an appointment form and sent me off to the post office, police station, town hall and stores to promote our photography session and make appointments for sittings.

I had problems communicating with the people in the municipal offices, as they all spoke guttural Afrikaans, which I battled to understand. The trouble was that white Afrikaners did not like to speak English and they were quite hostile to me when I addressed them in that language. However, owing to my accent, they invariably found out that I was from Germany and after that they became terribly friendly. In fact, many of them told me how much they loved Germany and how sad it was that Germany had lost the war.

I made a few appointments for the following afternoon. Next morning I did some more canvassing, this time in the busy main store, where you could get anything from tobacco to underwear, from shoes to soap. The store was run by two white, English-speaking, middle-aged men and the shop was full. Most of the shoppers were coloured people. As I understood it, this was a social group that lived in the Cape Province in South Africa and came from mostly Malaysian stock. They had originally been slaves and had mixed with the Khoekhoe, the original inhabitants of the Cape and southern Africa, and then with the British and Dutch. They spoke Afrikaans too but, unlike the white Afrikaners, I found their way of speaking musical and rhythmic. It seemed to me that they were not accepted by the whites, had no vote and were treated as second-class citizens, just one rung higher than the blacks or Africans.

Most of the customers were barefoot, although some were wearing old shoes, and their clothes were plain and tattered. For the most part they looked poor and downtrodden. I saw one man bought two cigarettes at a time and another a small packet of tobacco. I saw a woman buy a small tin of condensed milk, another a single tin of corned beef. To be honest, I didn't think they would be candidates for Werner's Studio, but the store was full of laughter and jokes and there was lots of shouting and shrieking from the women.

Back at the hotel the first customers were arriving and I got busy doing the make-up for the males. Most of the men wore hats at all times, especially the farmers, so when they took their hats off for the photos their foreheads were totally white, in contrast to their deeply sunburnt, nut-brown faces. This meant that I had to bridge the contrast with layers of dark make-up on the forehead. I also had to make the ladies more elegant. This meant slimming down their noses by applying dark shadows on the sides and using a highlighter on the bridge. In the meantime, Werner took the pictures, posing the sitters singly or in couples, or doing a family group, with or without babies.

Werner asked me to photograph the babies because he had problems communicating with them and I developed a method that seemed to work. I would put the baby or toddler on a small table. I'd have the camera facing the child. In one hand I held a long cable release and in the other a feather duster which I would use to tickle the baby's face, while making funny noises. Then I would pull the feather duster away and the toddler would start to laugh, or so I hoped!

My last job was to take down the names and addresses and fill in the colour chart, the eye and hair colour and so on, the number of films shot and a short description of the sitters, before taking the deposit.

The hotel bar and foyer were full of waiting customers when we started and we worked late into the night. Then, when everyone had gone, we packed up the studio and loaded the car. By the time we went to bed, the kitchen and bar had closed, but Werner and I were too exhausted to eat anyway. I slept soundly, until I was woken by the maid, who came into my room and put a cup of tea, white and sweet, next to my bed. This was the custom at the time in most hotels.

The next morning, before we left, I dashed off to the post office to send a packet of the previous day's film and the addresses of the sitters and their colour charts to the Werner head office in Germiston. And then off we went, with me driving, towards the next town. Werner said that from now on we would only be able to spend one day in each town, since the towns were only about two hours apart.

On the way he gave me a quick lesson in how to give traffic signs (turning right, turning left) with my right arm out of the window – cars back then had neither indicators nor brake lights; you just drove with the driver's window open at all times. When we were in more built-up areas, where there was a bit of traffic, Werner told me to wave my arm up and down to show that I was slowing down and, when stopping, to raise my hand upwards. To turn left I had to wind my arm in an anti-clockwise direction and to turn right to swing it out straight and keep it there.

We drove south through a number of towns and villages (or dorps), stopping for a day and night at each. We went through the same routine each time: unloading the car, building up the studio in the hotel lounge, canvassing, making up the sitters and then photographing them. Werner let me do most of the driving and I became pretty good behind the wheel.

During our trip, we spent an extra day at a bigger town called De Aar and then, after another two towns, we reached a place called Deelfontein. After we had set up the studio lights in the hotel lounge, I turned them on to test them. The lights blew – not just the electricity of the hotel but the whole town! So, along with the rest of the inhabitants of Deelfontein, we had no lights. Unfortunately, the problem was that the town's generator was damaged and we were definitely to blame (which was bit embarrassing) because the town was on a 125-volt system, whereas our lights were 220 volt.

Werner always carried an electronic flash for emergencies but we discovered that the battery for it, which was from a motorbike, was flat. There was only one option. The Buick, which was parked conspicuously in front of the hotel on the only, very long, main street of the town, was our only hope. I took the flashlight battery and connected it to the car battery. Both batteries were 12 volt so I hoped it would work. Then I sat down on the running board to wait, which gave me time to observe the scene around me and take some pictures.

Across the road fruit and vegetable sellers had laid out their wares on the pavement on colourful hand-made mats – small pyramids of potatoes, tomatoes and other vegetables of various sizes. On the stoep of a general store large adverts were painted on the wall: *Only Lions Drink Our Beer – Lion Beer. Lucky Strike – A Man's Smoke. Ricory Instant Coffee & Chicory*. People were coming and going, going about their business, and the street was alive with colour. Some of the women wore colourful blankets around their shoulders.

I saw a man approaching from down the road. He was wearing the type of floppy khaki hat worn by the locals. As he came closer I could see that he was struggling to walk straight. He stopped in front of me. His trousers were hanging below his belt, his eyes were red and glazed, and his skin looked like leather, as sunburnt as most of the locals' faces. Trying to steady himself, he staggered up to me.

'Hey, Mr Werner, take my picture,' he said, waving his arms about.

Then he sat down clumsily next to me on the running board and breathed alcoholic fumes into my face. I told him my name was Jürgen, not Werner, and that he had to make an appointment to have his picture taken.

'Take my picture now,' he said, standing up and swaying in front of me. 'I'm Walter Bennett and this is my place. You see' – he pointed around him – 'I'm telling you. The hotel and all the houses belong to me. It's all mine. Now take my bloody picture.' He began to get red in the face, so I got up, took my Leica off my shoulder and shot a picture of him. He looked at me, satisfied, then turned and slowly staggered into the hotel bar.

After another hour charging the battery I disconnected it from the Buick's and went back into our makeshift studio in the hotel lounge, where Werner was getting anxious and sitters were patiently waiting. Luckily, my plan worked and, with a bit of imagination, we started, bouncing the flash off some white boards. Later that afternoon the power came back on and we used a transformer from our 220-volt lights to adapt to the 125-volt power. This solved the problem and luckily we didn't blow the town's lights again.

Next morning we were back in the Buick driving towards Beaufort West, a larger town on the main Johannesburg to Cape Town road, when I tried the car radio and found, for the first time on this trip, a station with good reception. The station played Louis Armstrong's 'Blueberry Hill' and Nat King Cole's They Tried to Tell Us We're Too Young' and lots of other songs I loved. After an hour we hit the main road. What a pleasure it was to leave the dirt roads behind and have a smooth ride on the long, straight tar road. There was no traffic and, in my off-key voice, I sang along with wonderful Nat King Cole. Fortunately for Werner, he couldn't hear a thing. Two hours later I steered the Buick into the parking place of the Central Hotel.

In the foyer on a pile of local newspapers, I was amazed to see a picture on the front page of none other than Walter Bennett, the drunk who had insisted I take his photo – only this time he was wearing a clean shirt and tie and looking sober and smiling at the camera. 'MULTI-MILLIONAIRE COMES TO TOWN' was the newspaper headline, and the story below it was of how Walter had made his millions as a sheep farmer, having arrived from the East End of London as a poor eighteen-year-old.

Werner and I went through our usual routine. Maybe because it was a weekend, we had more sitters than we'd had in the smaller villages. Before we left on Monday morning for our next town, I went to bank the money we had taken in the last ten days. It was a very considerable amount: well over £2 000.

Beaufort West was as far south as we planned to go on this trip, so we turned the Buick around and headed north, back to Johannesburg. The return trip took ten days –another ten dorps and small towns, and ten days of photographing people. I was looking forward to returning to city life. The places and hotels we had been to so far had been uniformly dull and provincial. Furthermore, the atmosphere in the areas we had visited had also given me another unpleasant taste of racist South Africa.

In a small town called Loxton, which was about two hours' drive from Beaufort West, we drove up to the Grand Hotel. As Werner and I got out of the car and started placing our samples of framed pictures against the hotel veranda wall, I was startled by a number of loud cracks. The noises came from the end of the veranda. I saw two men sitting in armchairs in a corner, each pointing a rifle into the sky and shooting at something I couldn't see. I walked over to them. They were both dressed, like so many of the white South Africans I'd encountered, in floppy khaki hats, khaki shorts and shirts, and they had sunburnt faces. There were quite a number of empty beer bottles lying beside them on the floor. Suddenly, one of them fired his rifle and I heard a zinging sound, as if the bullet had hit some metal. As I got closer, I saw what they were shooting at. It was the weather-cock on the church tower opposite the hotel. Whenever they hit it, they laughed excitedly. They were completely unaware of my presence.

We had a lot of sitters that afternoon – family groups, grandparents and babies. We also photographed a sergeant, who was English-speaking. He said he was head of the police station in Loxton, and he was dressed in his gala uniform for the occasion, complete with a row of medals. He refused to be made up, which upset Werner, who told him, in his throaty voice, that if he refused to put on any make-up, then he would only photograph him if he wore a hat. This led to a long argument, during which I put a bit of brown make-up on my left hand and smeared it on the unsuspecting sergeant's forehead. After a lot of grumpiness and some laughter, Werner eventually got the pictures he thought acceptable.

Later, while Werner was busy with a sitter setting up the lights, and as I was making up a young post office girl's nose, out of the corner of my eye I saw a short man walk into the studio. He was wearing black dungarees and a large white Panama hat, and carrying a parcel wrapped in newspaper under his arm. I didn't take much notice of him. I was under pressure keeping up with the stream of sitters waiting to be made up for Werner and I still had a group of telephone operators' rather large noses to retouch. All of a sudden there was a big commotion and some shouting. Startled, I looked round to see that the short man in the Panama hat had Werner by the arm and was pulling him away from his camera on its tripod. 'Look!' he shouted. 'Look at my eyes!' He unwrapped the parcel he was carrying and pointed indignantly at a framed picture.

Werner of course couldn't hear him. He stood looking down at the incensed man, with his mouth and eyes wide open and a puzzled expression on his face, while the man in the Panama hat kept pointing down at the picture and then up at his own eyes.

'What colour are they?' he demanded, waving his finger from his eyes to the photo in the frame. 'Hey, wat maak jy? Are they blue, eh … and not shit colour? I want my money back. You're a bunch of fucking crooks and that's no shit!'

Werner made a hopeless attempt to talk but managed only to bring out some weird throaty sounds, so I pushed myself between him and the ill-tempered fellow.

'Sir, can we sort this out to your satisfaction?' I said, trying to calm the man down.

He looked at me, his expression enraged. 'Who the fuck are you?'

'I am Jürgen from Germany and I'm going to sort this out,' I said.

'Well, you better sort this out! I am the mayor of Loxton and I ordered a big picture of myself for the town hall and my eyes look like shit! I also had twelve of these smaller prints made for the members of the town council and my staff.'

'Sir,' I said, 'we can sort this out for you. I will send a telegram to head office to send you, by special post, a new set of pictures with your blue eyes.'

Werner, in the meantime, was acting as if nothing had happened. He just carried on taking pictures of the family group he'd been busy with, who had been
watching the scene with great interest. As he was deaf, I don't think Werner
was ever really aware of the dramas that might have been taking place around
him and the potential for disaster, which was probably just as well. Anyway,
the angry man calmed down and I worked out what must have happened.
Apparently, about a year back, when Werner had last been to Loxton, he had
taken the mayor's picture. The colour charts must have been mixed up during
the processing at head office and the mayor's blue eyes shaded brown.

By now we were behind schedule and it was after eleven at night when we
finally started to wrap the studio up and pack the Buick for the next day's journey. I was totally washed out. The hotel bar was already closed but, as I passed
a small lounge next to it, I heard boisterous laughter and I looked inside. A
group of men were sitting around some low tables, which were loaded with
empty bottles, glasses and large ashtrays full of cigarette ends. I was hesitating
in the doorway when one of the men saw me. I recognised the sergeant we had
photographed earlier. He was no longer in his gala uniform, but wearing a pair
of shorts and a hideous Hawaiian shirt, which was the latest fashion in some
circles.

'It's the Kraut photographer!' he shouted. 'Come and have a drink, my
friend.' And taking me by the arm, he dragged me into the lounge. I was too
tired to resist. I sat down at one of the tables and said I would love a beer. I
looked at the group of characters on either side of me. They all seemed to be
pretty plastered. Next to me sat the blue-eyed mayor of Loxton. He was holding an empty glass in his hand, which he kept looking at, trying desperately to
focus on it. On my other side were the two shooters from the veranda, both of
whom looked completely pie-eyed.

'Anybody got a drink for our Kraut?' shouted the sergeant.

There was no response except from the corner of the room, from where a
drunken voice exclaimed: 'We need more beer!'

Then the mayor stood up, lifting his empty glass high. 'Jawohl!' he shouted.
'Ein Glas bier!' Then he slumped back down onto his seat.

The sergeant began staggering towards the serving hatch that led into the bar, mumbling 'We need more beer ...' He rattled the hatch door and banged against it with his fist. One of the shooters produced a rifle from under his seat, got up and swayed over to join him. Using the full weight of his body, he jammed the butt of the gun against the door of the hatch, which finally flew open. Everybody clapped and roared with laughter. The sergeant then tried to squeeze through the hatch into the bar but he was way too fat. He looked at me. 'Come on, skinny,' he said. 'You can make it.'

I thought things were going too far. I knew there were laws which forbade liquor sales after hours. 'What about the law?' I said.

'I am the law!' the sergeant replied, pushing out his chest.

And so I climbed through the hatch into the bar and passed a dozen bottles into the sergeant's eager hands, at which all the people around the tables suddenly livened up. I took this as an opportunity to escape to my room. I didn't need a beer.

Finally, Werner and I were back in Johannesburg. Despite having spent a number of weeks with him, travelling and working, I had never managed to have a proper conversation with Werner. Certainly, life for him must have been very frustrating, I thought, although he had told me that he had a fiancée who was also deaf and that they planned to get married the following year and live together in his flat in Johannesburg. I once asked him what happened when he and his lady had an argument. He looked at me with a puzzled expression and said, 'No problem – I turn the lights off.'

After Christmas, my mother gave a New Year's party. There was a Christmas tree in the lounge, candles were lit and the sitting room was bright with decorations. The Baecker family were invited, and the three poodles yapped and jumped up and down in excitement when they arrived. Mr Baecker wore a bow-tie and party hat, and the two boys were both dressed in suits and ties and had tiny fancy paper hats sticking up on top of their heads.

Christmas was the hottest time of the year in Johannesburg – it was midsummer – and with all the candlelight in the room it quickly became hot and sticky. John was also wearing a suit, a dark woollen one, and a silly gold cardboard pointed hat.

My contribution to the occasion was a big bowl of fruit punch, into which I had poured generous quantities of brandy, vodka, sherry and white wine, which I disguised with lemonade, ginger beer and tinned fruit salad in syrup. Soon everyone was discarding their heavy jackets, taking off their ties and rolling up their shirtsleeves, and before long we were all singing along to my mother's old pop records from Berlin.

I watched Mr Baecker dancing with his daughter Gerda. They had a problem negotiating their way around the Christmas tree and at one point almost staggered right into it, accompanied by roars of laughter. Everybody looked happy. My mother gave a solo dance performance, showing off her legs, which ended with her flopping onto Mr Baecker's lap, which John did not seem to like very much, although he tried not to show it. He pulled my mother up by the arm, but he must have pulled too hard because my mother stumbled over Blacky, who emitted a series of squeaky barks, which made the other two dogs join in until there was a full concert of howling dogs. The Baecker children and Mrs Baecker joined in the laughter and noise, and general pandemonium continued. The party carried on into the early hours of the morning. I decided my punch was a great success. Certainly some of our guests were going to start 1951 with hangovers.

For a while I worked at Werner's Studio head office in Germiston. This was an old building, dating back to the early 1900s, on the edge of town. On the deep, shady veranda stood some long tables, and this was where the colouring of the black-and-white prints was done. With a transparent oil colour specially made for photographic prints, this work was also done by women, all of them middle-aged and white.

By now I could drive quite well and Fritz sent me off to get a driver's licence. He owned a fleet of old American cars, ranging from Cadillacs to Chryslers, Hudsons, Pontiacs, Chevs and Oldsmobiles. All dated back to the early thirties and most needed overhauls and engine repairs – they burned oil at a terrific rate. Sometimes I found myself engulfed by smoke in whichever car I was driving.

And, finally, I found a darkroom in Johannesburg. It belonged to a red-headed Russian photographer called Knute and it cost me ten shillings a day.

The Drum Beat

Drum cover, February 1955

9

WORKING WITH AFRICANS

In mid-1951 I heard about a native magazine called the *African Drum*, which was looking for a photographer. I was told that they had no money and that it would be an unsatisfactory position because the magazine 'was about natives'. Everyone told me it would be disastrous for my career. It was totally unacceptable for a European to be working with natives. Well, I disagreed. In fact, I thought 'working with the natives' was an excellent idea and so I went to the *African Drum* office and offered my services.

The office was on the first floor of an old building in the centre of Johannesburg. A door bearing the proud sign 'The African Drum: Africa's Leading Magazine' told me I had come to the right place. In one room, furnished with two desks and some filing cabinets, I found Bob Crisp, the proprietor and editor. Bob was a large man, a bit overweight and red-faced, and a well-known and celebrated South African cricketer.

I introduced myself.

'When can you start?' was his immediate reply. 'We pay ten shillings per picture used.' Then he walked to the other desk, where a black man in a bow-tie was sitting behind a typewriter. 'Come and meet Henry – Henry Nxumalo, our chief journalist.'

Henry got up and greeted me with a big smile. I noticed his teeth were rather brown, which, I would later learn, came from smoking untipped cigarettes. He and Bob showed me some issues of the magazine, which was similar in size and style to traditional picture magazines in Europe and the States. However, in comparison, the layout, printing and photos were extremely poor and unprofessional. Later I discovered that there were only three people on the staff – Henry, Bob and an Italian lady, who was the secretary and spoke poor English.

I agreed to have a go.

Henry had an appointment the next afternoon in Lady Selborne township in Pretoria, with the director of the Native Affairs Department, and he said we should go together. When I asked him how we were going to get there, he looked puzzled.

'Don't you have a car?' he asked.

'No, I don't,' I said.

He put back his head and laughed. 'Well, then you're the first white man I know who doesn't have a car.' He looked at me, amused, and said, 'You know, it's very difficult to get to Lady Selborne and *Drum* doesn't have a car either, so we'll need to take a train to Pretoria and then find a taxi or take a bus and, of course, because you're white and I'm black, we can't use the same transport. So we'll have to go separately.'

I thought this was a bad start. I felt it was up to me to think of something.

Having arranged to meet at the *Drum* office in the morning, I took the tram home to Kensington. Sitting in the tram I suddenly had a thought. I jumped off the tram and walked to Fritz's home, which was nearby. As luck would have it, Fritz had just pulled up in his car in front of his house and was busy unloading bags of wholesale shopping. I helped him carry his purchases into his house and told him about my transport problem. He didn't hesitate. I could have one of his old cars for a while, he said, to help me out. In return I offered to photograph a wedding for him whenever he needed an operator.

I picked up Henry the following morning in a 1934 La Salle that had seen better days. The car rattled and jerked along, leaving a pungent cloud of smoke behind it. After a while the engine calmed down and we were enjoying a reasonably smooth drive towards Pretoria when suddenly I noticed two traffic cops on motorbikes following us. I began to get nervous, especially when one of them overtook us and waved us down. I stopped the car and the two cops got off their bikes and came walking towards us. They were dressed in dark-grey uniforms, long riding boots and jodhpurs with flaps on the sides. They came right up to the car and then, to my

Henry Nxumalo

consternation, slowly began to walk around it, inspecting it carefully. I was glad I had my driver's licence. Finally, one of them stopped at the passenger's side.

'Is this a V-12 or a V-16?' the traffic officer asked, putting his head through the window next to Henry, who looked paralysed with fear.

'I don't know,' I answered, getting out of the car and preparing for the worst, not that I had any idea what the worst might be.

'Would you mind opening the bonnet so we can have a look?' said the other traffic cop, who was now standing next to me. So I opened up for them to see the engine, which was enormous, at least twice as long as the Buick's engine. The two cops put their heads under the bonnet and conferred. They decided it was not a V-16 but a V-12.

'It must have something like 155 brake horsepower,' one of them said with admiration. I gave him an encouraging smile.

As they were about to return to their motorbikes, one of them turned to me and said, 'You'd better get your engine fixed and rebored or it's going to cost you. You're burning a lot of oil!'

I thanked him for his advice and we went on our way.

Henry told me he had been in the South African army during the war. 'But, you know, we blacks weren't allowed to carry guns to fight the Germans. We were just used as supporting troops and guards. The funny thing was that the blacks guarding the Spitfires on the front line airfields were only armed with spears.

Henry had been based for a year in England as a clerk and, after a few months, worked in the Information Department, writing news stories, before he was sent to Egypt for two years. He started to write essays and had his work published in the *Pittsburgh Courier*, a prestigious black newspaper in the States. I was very impressed. I liked his frank, no-nonsense, unaffected character and his enthusiasm for journalism. And he had a great sense of humour.

As we drove through the centre of Pretoria, the centre of apartheid and the seat of government, I noticed that many of the people walking along the pavements were in uniform. There were fountains in the streets and rows of beautiful jacaranda trees in full bloom. In the suburbs we passed huge mansions with well-kept, lush, tropical gardens.

At the entrance to Lady Selborne township there was a police station with a

large sign that said: 'By order! To enter this area without a permit is against municipal law, and you will be punished.' We were early for our appointment, so Henry
told me to drive on into the township so that I could see what a township was like.
We passed the office of the Native Affairs Department, which was a long barracks-
like building, where we had our appointment later that afternoon. The further in
we drove, the bumpier the dirt road became. The surface was strewn with rocks
and it took all my concentration to negotiate the big La Salle around the obstacles
while avoiding the large potholes in the middle. We drove along streets of houses
and shacks on either side, very different from the beautiful properties we had
just driven past in white Pretoria. Most had corrugated-iron roofs, small fences
and miserable gardens. Poverty and squalor were everywhere. Barefoot children
in torn shirts and dresses ran around playing in the streets, and when they saw
our car, some came running alongside us, laughing and shouting. I saw a group of
women with buckets and bottles queuing at a water tap. Other traffic on the road
consisted largely of carts pulled by extremely skinny and tired-looking horses.

When we came to a brick house with a low wall in front and a garden, Henry
indicated to me to pull over. I stopped the car and we both got out. We walked
through the gate and onto the porch of a typical suburban house. The fly-screen
door opened and a large man in shirtsleeves appeared, his shirt open at the
neck, his tie loose. He had a huge smile on his face. He greeted Henry enthusiastically in Zulu and pulled him towards him, giving him a bear hug.

'This is Moses Morena,' Henry said. 'He's secretary of the African National
Congress in Lady Selborne.'

Moses invited us in and we sat in the lounge and drank iced tea. Henry
told Moses about our planned visit and interview with the Native Affairs
Department director, a Mr Van der Merwe. Van der Merwe was an outright
racist and hated blacks, Moses told us. He was introducing all sorts of new rules
in the township, which included the carrying of permits for anybody moving
in or out of their houses. 'We're having police raids on non-residents, arrests
of people without passes in front of their homes, and cars are being stopped
from coming in and out of the area,' he said. 'Frankly, he's terrorising the residents.' The angrier Moses got, the more animated he became. 'Van der Merwe
is forcing through the new 1950 Population Registration Act with barbarous

brutality. As it is, the township is over-populated and the minister of native affairs has declared Lady Selborne a black spot.'

Henry explained that a 'black spot' was where a township was unwanted and too close to a white area.

Half an hour later Henry and I were sitting in Van der Merwe's office with the man himself. He wore a military-style khaki shirt and khaki shorts, which went down to his knees, and long grey socks. He had a short military haircut. He glanced at Henry and then looked at me with cold, unsympathetic eyes.

'Now, Meneer Schadeberg, what sort of Bantu paper are you from?' he asked me in a heavy Afrikaans accent.

'We're a new publication,' said Henry. 'We run a pictorial magazine catering for the African population in South Africa. We look at the social scene, sport, entertainment and political life in the non-white world.'

Van der Merwe kept his eyes on me, as if Henry had not spoken. His eyes narrowed. He seemed to have developed a twitch.

Henry continued. 'Currently, we're working on a feature about your department, which seems to be rather insensitive towards the African population in Lady Selborne in applying the recent new laws.'

Van der Merwe opened his mouth and for a few moments kept it open, without making a sound, appearing to be thrown off balance. Finally, he turned and looked directly at Henry, and when he spoke there was anger in his voice. 'I forbid your cheeky disrespect to our government. We are only applying the law.'

While he was talking I started taking pictures of him. He turned back to me and said, 'No pictures.' Then, in a softer, more friendly tone, he said, 'We don't allow pictures of members of this department. But I tell you this. We look after our natives. They're a very simple people, something someone like you probably doesn't understand. They need controlling or we'll have chaos. So we're doing this for their own good. We built this country and we know what's best for it and the people living here.'

'Sir,' interrupted Henry, 'we are not your natives!'

'Nxumalo!' Van der Merwe shouted. 'I don't like your cheeky, insolent manner!'

This was getting us nowhere, I thought, so I stood up and Henry did likewise.

Orlando township, 1951

We left the office and took a walk. Henry thought he had a good story anyway, from talking to Moses, and he had a better idea about Van der Merwe now too. As we walked, followed by a growing group of children, I took some photos for the story, which I thought would illustrate the poverty of the township.

In the car on our drive back to Johannesburg we laughed about Van der Merwe's typical white man's problem when addressing a 'non-white' person and a white person together. When speaking to Henry, his tone had been consistently superior and aggressive, whereas when he spoke to me, a white person, his voice was normal and relaxed. Clearly, there was nothing more perplexing for a white man in authority than to have to speak to a white person and a non-white person at the same time.

It was too late for Henry to catch a train to his home in Orlando township, about eighteen kilometres south of Johannesburg, so I offered to drop him at his house. Here there were only dirt roads and long rows of small, plain brick houses on tiny plots. There were no trees and plants that I could see. The township had no electricity and there was only one water tap outside each house.

I met Henry's young wife, Florence, and their three small children, Henry, Suzette and Joey, and was invited to stay for dinner. I accepted with pleasure, happy to be in a home that clearly vibrated with joy and affection. Florence was a nurse at Baragwanath, the biggest hospital in the southern hemisphere, and she had many interesting stories to tell. After the children had gone to bed Henry went off to buy some beer from a local shebeen and the three of us sat talking. The more I learnt about the living conditions of non-whites in South Africa, the more it shocked me. I got home to Kensington in the early hours of the morning.

Henry and I went regularly on stories together and we developed a strong friendship. The stories varied widely from stories around sports events, such as boxing or football, to colourful personalities and crime. We also interviewed many local politicians.

Once a month we had an editorial meeting with Bob to discuss the next issue, and at one of these we were introduced to a new member of the team. This was a man named Todd Matshikiza. He was a happy, chatty fellow, full of laughter and, like me, he was a freelancer. Todd came from a musical family and

Todd Matshikiza

was an accomplished pianist and composer. He also played the xylophone in a jazz trio. He became *Drum*'s music editor. He drove a little Morris Minor and, being very short, almost disappeared behind the wheel, which made driving with him somewhat unnerving, as I was never quite sure how much he could see of the road in front of him.

It was decided that I should do a number of stories with Todd about the music scene in Johannesburg, and it was through Todd that I was introduced to the African jazz world and its talented musicians. We spent a couple of weeks at music sessions, interviewing musicians and taking pictures.

First we went to George Goch, a small township on the edge of the city, where we interviewed Kippie Moeketsi, a genius on the sax, and perhaps the greatest jazzman ever to come out of South Africa. He was often called the South African Charlie Parker. Kippie followed the American greats and played at the famous Jig Club, together with General Duze, who was also his neighbour. The club was in the territory of the Co-operative Gang, who danced with knives and guns in their hands and thought gambling, shooting and stabbing was normal. Kippie told us that life was tough for a black musician, particularly when playing in areas that were so dangerous. Later on we went next door and met General Duze. He was sitting on a little bench outside his house strumming his guitar, toddlers playing around his feet. Together with blues singer Dolly Rathebe and an all-black cast, General Duze had performed in a film called *Jim Comes to Jo'burg*. Todd told me he was planning to interview Dolly in the next few weeks.

Drum didn't have a darkroom, so I made all the prints for the magazine at Knute's. It wasn't very long before I found myself in financial difficulty. The ten shillings *Drum* paid per picture used did not go very far, even though Jack Levine had given me some credit for film and paper. It wasn't long before I was in the red and getting desperate. I couldn't ask *Drum* for more money. They were only just surviving as it was. I discussed my precarious financial situation with Knute one day and he had a good suggestion of how I could make some quick cash.

10

GOING TO THE BALL

The Traffic Department Ball, which was held annually at the Johannesburg City Hall, was a grand affair. Knute said if I got permission and could get an exclusive arrangement with the organisers to take the official photographs, there was good money in it for me. I rushed about making enquiries and succeeded in getting the booking. The only snag was that I had to raise £30 to secure an exclusive arrangement. Very kindly, Knute lent me the money and I was able to sign the agreement with the ball organisers.

Now I needed a sales lady to take orders for prints. Fritz suggested a young woman from Boksburg named Joyce Potgieter, who worked for him from time to time on their country trips. Joyce was keen and we agreed to meet up an hour before the event. I got myself a white tuxedo, which was very fashionable in South Africa, and we met in a little tearoom across the road from the City Hall. I thought Joyce was very glamorous. She had a fancy blonde hairstyle, golden earrings, red cheeks, crimson lipstick and hazel eyes with long lashes. Her fingernails were long and red and she had a lot of heavy shiny rings on her fingers. She gave me a long deep look, which made me a bit nervous, and took a packet of cigarettes out of her bag. Extracting a single cigarette, she held it in her hand and pushed the lighter along the table until it was in front of me. She sat holding the unlit cigarette in her hand next to her mouth; she looked at me, then looked at the lighter on the table in front of me. I was perplexed at first but then the penny dropped. I picked up the lighter and lit her cigarette. I had just been given my first lesson in white South African etiquette.

Joyce had brought an order book with her, as well as a small folder containing sample pictures from one of her previous jobs on the dance floor, and she clearly knew what to do. We walked across the road to the City Hall. In her party dress and very high heels, Joyce had a little trouble keeping up with me. Despite her elaborate make-up and throaty Afrikaans accent, I found her rather sexy as she swung her hips.

Couples were already arriving for the ball, all of them white, and all dressed beautifully. The men wore white or light-blue tuxedos and the women the kind of elaborate party dresses you would see at a debutantes' ball in American movies.

The City Hall interior was huge, with a stage at one end, where a big band was setting up, a big dance floor in the centre, and rows of tables with white cloths at the other. Indian waiters were dashing back and forth between rows with trays loaded with drinks.

Once the ball got under way, Joyce and I moved from table to table, offering to photograph the people at their tables, either alone or in couples or groups. At first it was quite frustrating and we didn't get too many takers, but as the liquor started to flow and the dance floor filled up, the mood started to change and suddenly we got very busy, with many people calling us over to take their picture. I battled to change film in time for the demand. Joyce took the orders and collected the cash. In between photographing we had a few drinks at the packed bar and, as the evening went on, I started to feel quite jolly myself.

At one point, Joyce and I were standing in a corner in the crowded bar, rather squashed together, and we began kissing. To my surprise, this turned Joyce into a wild nymphet. We were being pushed from one end of the crowded bar to the other by groups of tipsy drinkers and somehow we got separated. I ended up with a very cute young woman in my arms who dragged me onto the dance floor where we started to do the tango. Then I saw Joyce, looking upset, standing by the door. I excused myself from the cutie and pushed my way through the dancers to get to Joyce, whose make-up by now was rather smudged and her fancy hairdo in total disorder. 'You are no gentleman, leaving me alone in this hellhole!' she said – with some justification, I have to say – but she calmed down after I asked her to dance.

We carried on working hard until the early hours of the morning, which was when the guests began to leave, their faces an indication of the severe hangovers to come. Finally, we finished and Joyce and I found another tearoom, which was already open for the new day's business. Joyce gave me the orders and the addresses of the people we had photographed. While I had a lot of work to do printing the photographs, I was overjoyed to see that the evening had earned me £800. This was a small fortune.

In fact, my work that evening at the ball enabled me to pay off all my debts and I was even left with enough money to buy myself a second-hand car – for £300. I became the proud owner of a little green Austin 7. It was full of new technology, which delighted me. It had indicators, small arms with red light-bulbs, which swung out for turns to left or right, and a light at the rear, which turned red when you touched the brakes. It also had a roof-rack. All in all, it was much better than the huge La Salle, which smoked and guzzled petrol and which I now returned, with thanks, to Fritz.

I invited Joyce to the cinema. I splashed out on tickets for the South African première of the Bette Davis film *All About Eve* at the Colosseum in Commissioner Street. Joyce said her car was in the garage for a service, so could I come and pick her up at her family's house in Boksburg.

Mr Potgieter opened the door to my knock. He was a big man with a small moustache. 'Hey, Juerrchen,' he greeted me. 'Hoe gaan dit? Kom binne. Jy is welkom.' He took me through to the lounge, where he introduced me to Mrs Potgieter. She was much smaller than her husband and, in contrast to his dark suit and white tie, had on a housecoat with a floral design. She had curlers in her hair. She greeted me in English and told me that Joyce was getting ready. She offered me a cup of tea. 'We normally don't speak English in this house,' she added, 'just Afrikaans.'

I found myself sitting in an armchair with a cup of tea in my hands opposite Mr Potgieter, who continued to talk to me in Afrikaans. After a while he began to realise that I didn't understand very much of what he was saying, so he threw in a few badly pronounced German words. I still hadn't a clue what he was trying to say, so I just sipped my tea and nodded my head at him. Eventually, Mr Potgieter groaned, shook his head from side to side and, with obvious reluctance, switched to English. 'You must learn to speak Afrikaans,' he said. 'It's very close to German. And we all like Germany. They should have won the war, not the bloody British. I've no doubt that Hitler, Napoleon and Caesar were the greatest men of civilisation. Certainly not the Jewish imperialist Churchill. And don't forget that it was Kitchener who started the first concentration camps and they killed our women and children.'

He kept on like this in a monotonous tone, as if he was making a speech, talking about the Boer War and how the British took away their independence and how they spoilt the natives.

'Piet is a dominee in the Dutch Reformed Church,' Mrs Potgieter said.

Then Joyce walked into the room. She was wearing a flashy evening dress, black with gold embroidery, gold gloves, very high-heeled shoes, lots of make-up and a small hat with a profusion of flowers on it. My first thought was that she looked rather silly and overdressed. Anyway, I got up rather quickly and, with relief, said goodbye to her parents.

'Auf Wiedersehen, Juerrchen!' said Mr Potgieter.

Joyce looked at my Austin 7 disapprovingly and stood by the passenger door, waiting for me to open the door for her. 'What did you get this tiny jalopy for? I look foolish sitting in this thing. What would my friends think?' she said as we set off. She asked me to stop at a store to buy her some cigarettes – 'Two packets of 50 Viceroy, cork-tipped' – and then, as we were approaching Johannesburg, she said: 'You know, we need to talk.'

'What about?'

'Not now, later,' she said mysteriously.

I parked the car in a side street behind the Colosseum. Before we got out I leaned over to her, held her waist and tried to kiss her.

'Don't be silly, you're smudging my make-up,' she said and pushed me away. Then she sat, stiffly upright, until I realised she was waiting for me to get out of the car and walk around to open the door for her.

In the foyer of the Colosseum we stood in a queue together with middle-aged men and women in evening dress. The women had little decorated handbags on chains and wore high heels and the men were in dress shirts. Many of the men were overweight. I could see their large stomachs protruding from their tight shirts.

The cinema was packed to capacity and the audience clapped when the curtain opened. From below, an organ rose slowly onto the stage, with the organist, his back to the audience, already at the keyboard and playing the British national anthem. The audience rose to its feet, as did I, although hesitantly. Joyce remained seated. Then, almost with one voice, the audience sang 'God Save the King', after which the organist played a few more hit songs before a short film was shown to which everybody had to sing along. The text appeared on the screen line by line and a small ball jumped from word to word or syllable to syllable, while everyone sang heartily. After that came *African Mirror*, a local newsreel. Among other items, it carried a piece about white tourists watching Zulu mine dancers and showed a clip of Dr Malan, the South African prime minister, opening a new memorial to the Boer War in Pretoria.

Finally, it was the turn of Bette Davis and the feature film, which I enjoyed very much.

Afterwards, as we drove back to Boksburg, Joyce was very quiet.

'I don't see what you have with Bette Davis,' she said suddenly.

'I think she's a great actress and a wonderful star,' I said, not wanting to start an argument, especially while I was driving.

'I think you're infatuated with that woman,' she said.

When I pulled up in front of her parents' house she looked at me and said, 'Now, we'd better have a talk. You're keeping bad company. You're mixing with kaffirs and working for a native rag. I haven't told my parents, but if they should find out, you'll get us all into trouble!'

Her words disgusted me. 'Don't you realise how unfair the apartheid system is,' I said, 'how we're hardly treating the native people here like humans? How revolting it is to have an apartheid system where people are treated according to their colour, rather than their ability and character?'

'Are you mad?' Joyce said. 'Given half a chance, the kaffirs would destroy South Africa, like they've done the rest of Africa.'

'And you think that justifies what's happening here?' I said.

'We built this country, we were here before them, and we're keeping this country. Whatever it takes. And we don't need do-gooders like you around. So change your ways or you'll start to have a really tough time and lose any white friends or support.'

'Well, that's life, babyface, and you'd better know that I'm just going to continue what I'm doing,' I said.

Joyce's shocked expression, as she realised that I wasn't going to be persuaded to change, was something to see, and for once she opened the car door by herself. She stalked up the garden path to the house without saying another word. Somehow I was relieved. I had sensed this might happen and I realised that I should've known better, that what I was doing was totally anathema to the majority of white people, and Joyce was a classic case of the majority. She may have been very pretty but her philosophy made my stomach turn.

If she thought she was going to frighten me by telling me that I would have a 'tough time' and no 'white friends', she was wrong. I had just survived one of the most brutal dictatorships that Europe had ever known. Her dire warnings didn't faze me in the least.

11

'MR DRUM'

At our next monthly *Drum* meeting we had another new member join our staff. Robert Resha was a journalist in his early thirties and wore a moustache and a short goatee beard. He was an active member of the African National Congress. Bob Crisp said Robert would be in charge of the sports section.

Bob suggested that I should get more involved with the design and production of the magazine and also that I should try to find some black photographers to help me. This worried me because I couldn't see how we could afford to pay them, as *Drum* had no money and Bob had problems with the limited distribution: the only official distribution agency at that time, the Central News Agency, refused to distribute *Drum* because it catered to blacks only. They had plans, they said, to create a black distribution network, which would be called the Bantu News Agency, but this was sometime in the future.

'If we don't get the circulation up,' Bob said, 'we're going to die. Any ideas about how we can promote ourselves better to get the circulation up?'

I remembered something that had been done in Germany by a news magazine there.

'Mr Drum!' I said.

Everyone looked at me as though I had gone mad.

'You have a photograph in *Drum* of someone called "Mr Drum",' I continued, 'who has a copy of our magazine under his arm. You then say that Mr Drum will be walking up and down the main street of your township on a specific day and, if you recognise him and you have a copy of *Drum* on you and say, "You are Mr

Drum!", you'll win five pounds.'

Silence. I looked around the room. Henry was sitting in his chair behind his desk leaning back and grinning at me as he puffed on his pipe. Todd sat on the edge of his desk, dangling his short legs, and our newcomer, Robert, looked at me approvingly.

Looking very pleased with himself, Bob turned to Henry. 'Well, Henry, you are now "Mr Drum",' he said, and everyone laughed.

'However, more importantly,' Bob went on, 'I have some very good news for us. We've found a financier, Jim Bailey, who's prepared to join us in our publication of *Drum*. He wants to become our partner in the business. He's the son of a former mining magnate, Sir Abe Bailey, who was one of the world's richest men and the biggest landowner in South Africa. This is going to change the way we operate and give us a secure future. It has also allowed us to buy a car for the office. It's a second-hand Plymouth, a '49 model and in mint condition. So look after it!'

After this everybody started talking at once. Despite the good news of a partner for the magazine, Bob didn't seem as pleased as he'd tried to sound. He explained his unease. He said he had heard that Abe Bailey had been an outright exploiter of African people and that his vast fortune had been made in part by capitalising on their seemingly unsophisticated tribal customs. Well, this started a long and involved argument about exploitation, capitalism and blood money, all of which conflicted with ANC values and socialist, communist-leaning policies. Certainly, capitalism was frowned upon.

We moved on, finally, to the business of the day. Todd and I were told to do a story about a dilapidated dance hall in Sophiatown, which the police had threatened to close down because of heavy drinking there. Meanwhile, Henry was going to do a story about Dr Xuma, the former president of the ANC, who lived in Sophiatown.

In the following weeks we were all very busy. I photographed Henry with a copy of *Drum* under his arm and began looking at layouts of international picture magazines such as *Life*, *Look*, *Picture Post*, *Stern* and *Paris Match*. This was to gain a better idea about the direction we should take in designing *Drum*. I also managed to organise a loudspeaker system for the 'Mr Drum' project. Robert got us half-a-dozen teenagers from the ANC Youth League to sell *Drum* copies

Mrs Xuma talking to Henry Nxumalo, 1951

for the search for 'Mr Drum', so that we could get the campaign going. Our trial run was set to take place in the main street of Germiston township. We needed permission for this from the Germiston Native Affairs Department, which Bob Crisp was sorting out.

Sophiatown was situated to the north-east of Johannesburg, and was inhabited by a combination of African and coloured people, with some Indians and whites. Also, Henry told me, apart from being the only suburb in Johannesburg with a racially mixed population, its residents owned their own houses. We took a tram ride to the township a few days after the meeting and I took some pictures as we walked along the streets: groups of children playing outside, a couple of men playing a board game on a veranda, some people unloading a horse cart full of furniture and mattresses. I took a picture of a young fellow sitting on the doorstep of a house playing the guitar.

Dr Xuma's house was comparatively grand and it stood out against the other houses in the street. As we approached we saw an elegant lady easing herself into a large American car parked outside. Henry went up to her. 'Hello, Mrs Xuma,' he said, 'how lovely to see you.'

'Mr Nxumalo, Alfred is expecting you,' the woman said, in a strong American accent, smiling and extending her hand. Then she put the car in gear and drove off.

We walked into the house, met Dr Alfred Xuma in his lounge and settled down into comfortable armchairs with cups of fresh coffee that had been prepared by Mrs Xuma before she left.

This brief meeting with Mrs Xuma made an impression on me. She seemed markedly different from most of the other black South Africans I had seen, and not as dark-skinned as some of the local people. She appeared to be more like a sophisticated Westerner. I had a similar impression of Dr Xuma, who I learned had spent about fifteen years in the United States. Both were self-assured and confident, unlike the local Africans, who often appeared insecure, particularly in the presence of a white person, no doubt owing to the continuous humiliation they endured under apartheid.

While I was taking photographs, Henry conducted his interview. Dr Xuma talked about his presidency of the ANC between 1940 and 1949 and about

Dr Alfred Xuma, 1951

being replaced when the younger ANC members charged him with being anti-communist. He had been accused of participating in 'gentlemen's politics' and not fighting aggressively enough for black people's rights. Henry was very pleased with the interview and it became the pilot for a regular Henry Nxumalo column called 'Masterpiece in Bronze'.

That same evening I went back to Sophiatown with Todd in his Morris, the idea being that we would do the piece on the notorious dance hall. The venue was not so much a hall as a shop or store, with the ground-floor windows boarded up with sheets of plywood, blankets and bits of curtain. The powerful sound of jazz trombone and saxophone hit us as we entered into a place that was jam-packed with people and tobacco smoke was thick in the air. Couples were jiving and shuffling to the sound of Vy Nkosi's trombone, which, as Todd wrote later, 'rocked tremors into the bowels of the earth'. It was certainly an amazing sound within a vibrant and exciting place and one where any drunkenness was dealt with very swiftly, with the offending person immediately ejected.

On the personal front, it was now about time for me to find somewhere else to live. John, my stepfather, was becoming more and more unpleasant and, predictably, did not approve of my association with what he called 'communists and natives', on account of my work on *Drum*. I still had some money left from the ball but the ten shillings per picture used was barely paying my costs, let alone providing me enough to live on.

I phoned Fritz and we arranged to meet at Werner's Studio in President Street. When I arrived I found Fritz busy photographing a wedding group. He was fussing around, arranging the bride's train on the carpeted steps in the studio. He had a young man of about my age helping him set up the shots. I noticed that he was very smartly dressed in a tweed jacket, a silk neck scarf, suede shoes and tight corduroy trousers. He was introduced to me as Fritz's new assistant, Ian Berry. Ian told me he lived in Benoni, a fashionable satellite town east of Johannesburg, a bit further out than Boksburg, and that he was planning to start a photographic studio there. He had recently arrived in the country from England.

When they had finished with the wedding party, Fritz and I went to a tearoom in Eloff Street, where I suggested my working for him over weekends, photographing weddings. He was short of photographers and liked the idea. The demand for wedding photos across all six studios had escalated. I asked for £6 per wedding and he agreed, provided that, if necessary, I would cover weddings on the East Rand as well as in Randfontein and Krugersdorp to the west of Johannesburg. The arrangement suited me perfectly, especially as I wouldn't have to develop the films or make prints myself. I only had to hand in the exposed film to the relevant studio. It would make it possible for me to carry on working for *Drum*.

From then on, on Saturdays I photographed one or two Christian weddings and on Sundays I went to the Johannesburg Synagogue and photographed Jewish weddings. Sometimes I had to travel between 50 and 80 kilometres between the small towns but I didn't mind. I enjoyed driving, and all the time I was seeing more of South Africa and understanding the country better.

The launch of our 'Mr Drum' project in Germiston township was an exciting day. Bob Crisp drove the Plymouth, with a loudspeaker mounted on the roof, and Robert Resha sat inside with the microphone. In three African languages he started announcing that 'Mr Drum' was in the area and that if anyone had a copy of *Drum* magazine on him and said to 'Mr Drum', 'You are Mr Drum', they could claim the £5 prize. At the same time, six youngsters were loaded with copies of the latest issue and they moved up and down the streets, selling them to anyone and everyone they could. I sat in the back seat of the car, handing out more copies as our young sellers ran out. From time to time, I got out of the car and took pictures of the crowds of people congregating on the main street as we drove slowly up and down.

On cue Henry strolled among the crowds with a copy of *Drum* under his arm. He did not have to wait long before he was recognised, and there was a big commotion and lots of laughter and Henry presented the prize.

Afterwards we drove to the nearest store and bought some cold drinks and took them back to the car where Henry, Robert, Bob and I sat drinking and chatting. We were all feeling very excited about the project. Bob suggested that we do this every week in all the townships on the Reef. While we were talking, we saw a police car stop in front of the store. Two policemen got out of the vehicle and walked inside. After a short while, they reappeared at the door, each with two parcels under their arms.

'Look at those bastards collecting their pay-off,' Bob Crisp said angrily.

The two policemen seemed to hesitate. They stood still, looking all around them, with very puzzled expressions on their faces. Then, clearly disturbed, they dashed to their car and drove off in a hurry. That was when Robert, who still had the microphone in his hand, noticed that he had accidentally switched it on ... Bob's remark had been amplified through the speakers on the roof.

I liked Bob. He had a laid-back manner and a good sense of humour and there was much more to him than met the eye. I'd read an article about him in a local magazine, which stated that he had been a tank commander in the North African desert during the war. He had been seriously injured several times, and was decorated for bravery by Montgomery. He had climbed Kilimanjaro (twice), farmed minks in England, written for the *East Anglian Daily Times*, and was known to have been a crooner in a nightclub in Alexandria, while somehow finding time to be a famous cricketer, author and adventurer.

For the next few weeks we went every Saturday into the various townships with our 'Mr Drum' circus. Overall, the campaign was a great success and it increased the sales, as we had hoped.

I had begun making the monthly schedule for *Drum* and doing the layouts and cover design. It was a lot of work and I had to drop the Saturday weddings for Fritz. It was all I could do to make the Sunday ones. This meant that my income was improving but I still couldn't afford to rent a place of my own. I went to speak to Bob Crisp. He was sympathetic but asked if I could hang on until the new year, when the new financier would be in place. I said that I would.

One day Todd turned up in the office with a young woman who impressed me with her good looks, liveliness, intelligence, energy and humour, despite the fact that she wasn't very well dressed. She wore men's shoes, a long, badly fitting skirt and a man's jacket.

'I told you about her,' Todd said, smiling, as he introduced us. 'This is Dolly Rathebe, our famous blues star.' He asked me to take some portraits for his story about her and I got permission to use Werner's Studio the following day. We also arranged some new clothes for Dolly. I didn't have much experience of photographing models or stars but I think I learnt quickly. I thought it would have been more interesting to make these pictures in a broader environment, with some background related to the film she had starred in, *Jim Comes to Joburg*,

Henry Nxumalo handing out prizes during the 'Mr Drum' competition

but Bob had asked me to photograph Dolly with a packet of Max cigarettes. So I had my first experience of trying to do a commercial shoot. I did it reluctantly, as I was a bit of a puritan and didn't want to mix my style or prejudice my reputation as a documentary photographer.

Time passed very quickly as I continued to go on many social, cultural and political stories with Henry, Todd or Robert Resha. Robert's heart wasn't really in our assignments and most of the time he just talked about the political problems in South Africa, the ANC and the meetings he was organising. I thought he would have been better suited as the political correspondent for *Drum* rather than as its sportswriter.

On 25 November 1951 Todd and I went to the Ritz Dance Hall where there was a special show, promoted by a well-known fellow called Mr Abe Mokgale, and Dolly was performing. The Ritz was an old music hall for non-Europeans and, while it was a bit dilapidated, it was well known for its swing music and jazz shows. When we arrived, Dolly was on stage singing with the African Inkspots under Philemon Mokgosi. People were dancing and jiving, the men with their hats slightly askew, some with cigarettes hanging from their lips, looking cool. I took lots of pictures, but kept having to sidestep the drunks who were staggering around, falling onto the dancers and coming up to my face mumbling incoherent words at the camera. Couples were jiving or, when the pace slowed to a sentimental waltz, just swaying together to the music. Later the two top female vocalists, Dolly Rathebe and Emily Kwenane, gave an outstanding performance and the crowd stopped dancing to listen to these two singers. They clapped furiously and continuously after their performance. It was well after midnight when we left the Ritz. I told Todd I thought it was a great evening.

Driving in my little Austin 7 towards Kensington to my mother's house, a whole lot of fire engines came racing past me with their sirens blaring. The next day we heard that the Ritz had burnt down in the early hours of the morning. I thought it a terrible shame as it was the end of the only real dance and stage hall for non-whites in Johannesburg.

12

ANC CONFERENCE 1951

In early December we had another new member of the *Drum* crew, Anthony Sampson, who was to be the circulation manager. Fresh out from England, he was difficult to understand at first. He spoke very fast, swallowing his words and using a vocabulary containing many words that were new to me. His body language indicated someone who was socially awkward and easily embarrassed.

The Defiance Campaign was planned to begin in 1952, its aim to compel the government to repeal a number of apartheid's unjust laws. These included the much-hated pass laws, the Group Areas Act, the Separate Representation of Voters Act, the Suppression of Communism Act, and the Bantu Authorities Act. These were the acts that were the bulwarks of the apartheid system, although of course there were many others in place at the time and to come in the future.

Bob wanted Henry to interview some of the people involved in organising the campaign and suggested a road trip for me and Henry in the Plymouth, starting in Maseru in Lesotho and ending at the ANC conference in Bloemfontein which was scheduled later that month. I would drive and Anthony would go with us.

Lesotho (still Basutoland at the time) was a mountainous, landlocked British protectorate and Maseru was its capital. This was a modest town with government buildings in its centre and rows of stores. In the passageways between the stores and on their verandas people sat selling vegetables. Many of them had travelled down from the mountains on horseback, and wore colourful blankets tied around their shoulders and pointed hats made out of woven grass.

We went to look for Patrick Duncan, the judicial commissioner, whom Henry was to interview. We found the Englishman in his office and he offered us tea, which was served by an African man dressed in an old-fashioned askari-style outfit. Duncan, in shirtsleeves, was relaxed and affable. He was actively involved in the South African anti-apartheid movement and was planning to join the Defiance Campaign the following year. This had been an important decision for him, since his father, Sir Patrick Duncan, was a former governor-general of South Africa. He was of the view that it was important for as many whites as possible to join the campaign to reduce the possibility of racial clashes. The more whites who joined, the greater the hope for everyone in South Africa, including the whites, he said.

We spent the night in a hotel in Maseru, where we each had our own thatch-roofed rondavel, and enjoyed a wonderful dinner. Anthony told us that he was friends with Jim Bailey, our new financier, and that he had been at Oxford with him. Evidently, Anthony had been working for a bookshop when he received a telegram from Bailey asking him to come and work for him in South Africa. He hadn't had to think twice. He hopped on a plane and flew straight out.

In the middle of the night I woke up feeling ill and struggling to breathe. I found myself staring at two big cats, which had climbed onto my bed. I discovered the hard way that I was allergic to cat hair.

The next morning, about 20 kilometres from Maseru, we stopped at a village called Thaba'Nchu. This was the home of the ANC president, Dr JS Moroka. I was still feeling dreadful from my cat hair allergy, but I took some pictures of Dr Moroka and his family before Henry's interview. Then I retired to the back seat of the car.

On 15 December 1951 we arrived at the ANC conference. It was being held in Batho, an old-established township just outside Bloemfontein, and it was where the ANC had been formed in 1912, 39 years before. The conference took place in an old church hall and was attended by about 350 delegates. Dr Moroka was already there, and he was on the platform addressing the delegates. He demanded that the prime minister, Dr DF Malan, and his government repeal the unjust apartheid laws. If they refused, mass demonstrations and defiance of these laws would follow.

Over the next three days I managed to photograph most of the leaders of the ANC. One of these was a new face, a young man who had just been elected national president of the Youth League. He was a very striking and imposing person, tall, self-confident and charismatic. His name was Nelson Mandela. Bloemfontein being the hotbed of Afrikaner nationalism, many of the conference participants were understandably anxious and nervous about this conference with its strong defiant message. Mandela was one of the few delegates, I remember, who remained relaxed and calm, despite the possibility of imminent dangerous disruptions.

I also met the anti-apartheid activist and Communist Party editor of the South African *Guardian* newspaper, Ruth First. When I photographed her, she was wearing large dark glasses and was dressed in a conservative suit, and she had a number of books under her arm. When I told her I was from Berlin, she asked the usual question: 'East or West?'

'When I grew up in Berlin there was no East or West,' I said. 'However, now my former home is in the West.'

'Have you been to the German Democratic Republic?' she asked.

'You mean East Germany? Yes,' I said, 'my grandparents live in the East.'

Ruth then became very curious and she asked a lot of questions, such as what I was doing at the ANC conference and how I liked it in the East German Republic. When I said I wasn't impressed by the East German/Russian dictatorship, the comment seemed to displease her. She took off her sunglasses and looked intently into my eyes. 'Young man,' she said, 'you still have much to learn. Stalin and the Soviet Union and the German Democratic Republic are in reality the only nations supporting our anti-apartheid movement.'

Well, I thought that I would not start an argument that would get us nowhere. For me, this was another illustration of how detached the South African people were, even well-educated ones, from Europe and the United States. They had such little knowledge or experience of world history that they would swallow any propaganda fed to them. So I retreated gracefully, offering Ruth some prints of the conference for her paper.

An interesting and pleasant man I met at the conference was Mahatma Gandhi's son Manilal Gandhi, who was an editor of the *Indian Opinion*, a Durban

Nelson Mandela and Ruth First at the ANC conference, 1951

weekly paper. He had been imprisoned several times by the government for his anti-racist and anti-apartheid activities and was set to participate in the Defiance Campaign. Manilal strove hard to emulate his father's way of thinking and living and spoke to me about his appreciation of the full depth and significance of his father's conviction, his belief that purity of heart was the most important factor in defeating racism and evil.

After the third day at the conference we set off back to Johannesburg, with me driving and Anthony and Henry asleep on the back seat of the car. It was late at night and the narrow road was pitch dark. The landscape to either side was flat and the road ahead stretched for miles. Temporarily blinded by the lights of some oncoming traffic, I suddenly heard a loud crash and the car shuddered to a halt, steam sizzling out of the engine.

Anthony and Henry woke up with a fright and we all leapt out of the car. In front of us on the tarmac, moaning and kicking its legs, was an enormous ox. Horrified, we all stood in front of the car, which was badly smashed, staring at the poor animal. None of us knew what to do. Cars were stopping and people getting out to see what was going on. One of them, a big Afrikaner in shorts and a khaki shirt, wearing a floppy bush hat, came up to us.

'Jissis, man!' he said, and then, in Afrikaans, 'We need to clear the road!' He produced a pocket-knife and gestured at Henry, who was still looking sleepy. He handed the knife to Henry and, still speaking Afrikaans, said, 'We have to put the poor thing out of its misery.' Henry looked completely bewildered but the big Afrikaner was unmoved. 'Come on, boy,' he urged, 'cut its throat!'

By now quite a crowd had gathered and cars travelling in both directions kept pulling over. Poor Henry, intimidated by the big Boer, started to cut into the throat of the suffering animal with this tiny pocket-knife. Part of his hand and then his arm disappeared into the ox's throat while the beast continued to groan until, finally, it died. Henry looked shocked. As a black man from the city, he had probably never killed anything bigger than a chicken, if that, but the white Afrikaner had automatically classed him as a simple rural tribesman or farm labourer, who no doubt did this type of thing every day. Eventually, with the help of some onlookers, we managed to move the ox and the car off the road to clear the traffic and the three of us got a lift to the nearest town,

Kroonstad, where we spent the rest of the night in a crummy hotel. The following morning we arranged for the damaged Plymouth to be picked up by a garage, and we took a train back to Johannesburg, Anthony and I in the carriage for whites and Henry in the one for non-whites.

13

UNDER NEW MANAGEMENT

I expected Bob would be furious about his smashed-up car and I was anxious about going into the office the next day, but I thought it was better to face the music and get it over with, so I went in early. Henry and Anthony were the only two people in the office. Bob was nowhere to be found. Then I was told that Bob wasn't just out – he had left *Drum* altogether. Apparently, he had had a disagreement with Jim Bailey, the new financier. Anthony was taking over as the editor.

This was quite a blow. I thought Bob was a great person and an excellent editor. And I wasn't at all certain about Anthony, who was not just inexperienced in journalism but also awkward socially, especially around black people. Anyway, I had lots of printing to do, so I spent the next few days in Knute's darkroom. Then I received a call from Anthony to say he wanted to introduce me to Jim Bailey. He also told me that they were moving *Drum* to the offices of the SA Associated Newspapers (SAAN) group in Main Street.

At the appointed time I turned up at the new office. Jim Bailey came to greet me, hand outstretched and a broad smile on his face.

'How are you, old chap?' he said.

He ushered me and Anthony into his office, sat down behind his desk, and picked up a long steel ruler. Then he leant backwards, until his chair back was touching the wall behind him, and began to talk. 'Right!' he said. 'It's all change. I don't want any more of the "African Drum, Bob Crisp missionary magazine" stuff. That's condescending and paternalistic, as is the tribalism and African culture nonsense. I don't want any more poetry or ethnic romance and bloody folklore. Johannesburg is a modern city and our readers are modern Africans. So I want editorial on the politicians, the sportsmen, the cover girls and dancers. I want you to talk to the gangsters, organise a beauty competition, speak to the man in the street and get *Drum* up and running as a contemporary magazine that everyone needs to read.'

Watching him wave the ruler around, holding forth bombastically in his very Oxford accent, I thought him quite affected.

'Jürgen, we need pictures,' he went on. 'Lots of them. And they've got to be excellent. Each one telling a story and each one a top-class image. I want *Drum* to become the *Life* magazine of Africa, and to do that it's got to have images that really work. Don't forget that most of our market has difficulty reading.'

Just then the door to the office opened and Henry's head popped round. 'You wanted to see me, Mr Bailey?'

Bailey waved him in and Henry perched on the edge of the desk. 'I was wondering what you three white guys were up to,' he said.

Bailey burst out laughing. He chuckled away for a while and then grew serious. 'Well, Henry, what we need is to meet with black intellectuals to get a better idea of what our readers want to know. We've got to make *Drum* relevant to the black population. We've got to make *Drum* a vital part of their lives.'

In his capacity as editor, Anthony suggested that my function on *Drum* should be to find us some African photographers and, if I couldn't find any, to train some intelligent youngsters in photography. I was also to be responsible for the magazine production, schedules, layouts and picture editing.

My financial situation was becoming seriously problematic. The last of the money from the Traffic Department ball was almost gone and I now urgently needed to find a new place to live. Things with my mother and John in the Kensington house were deteriorating and John wanted me out of the house as soon as possible. He never stopped making remarks about my working with undesirable people and it was creating a very unpleasant atmosphere.

I told Bailey that we needed to discuss my payment, as an all-rounder and as a freelance photographer. Also, I said, we needed to set up a darkroom in the *Drum* offices. Our own darkroom was essential if the magazine was to produce great images and teach black trainees.

Anthony Sampson, 1952

Bailey looked at me and said: 'Don't worry – we'll see you right.'

That wasn't enough reassurance for me. 'Look,' I said, 'I need to discuss my financial position with you. Now.'

Bailey looked displeased. 'We'll talk about it later,' he said.

I left it at that but I wasn't altogether happy. In the meantime I began getting costs for darkroom equipment and the building of partitions in the office, and I had these typed up for me by Deborah Duncan. She was Patrick Duncan's sister and she had recently joined the team. She was very friendly and I liked her.

The following day Anthony asked me to accompany him to Sophiatown, where he was doing an interview. In the car I gave him my list of costs for the photography department. It was early January, the hottest time of the year, and a Saturday, which was market day. All the suburban white people had come to town to do their shopping and they were everywhere on the streets, with their bags and parcels, crossing in between the cars, ignoring the traffic lights and making it difficult for me to navigate my car safely through the crowds.

Eventually, I found our way to our destination, which was the Church of Christ the King, an Anglican mission in Sophiatown. There we met the resident priest, Trevor Huddleston. He was a tall man with short hair and a rather long chin. Dressed in a long black cassock with a cross hanging on the belt around his waist, he was an imposing figure.

Trevor asked us to join him at lunch and led us into a large room with long tables and benches, where we had a simple lunch of chicken and rice and red wine. During the meal, Trevor talked a lot about the evil of apartheid and the full horror of racism. 'Apartheid', he said, 'is an attack not only on the nature of man but upon the nature of God Himself.'

As we were leaving, he mentioned one of his students, Arthur Maimane. Arthur was one of his brightest students and had many talents, but he had a particular passion for journalism. Trevor asked if we might give him a chance to work with us on *Drum*.

In the meantime, Henry had arranged a meeting at the *Drum* offices for Jim Bailey and Anthony with a group of various political and intellectual figures. I was also invited to the meeting, which I attended. Sitting in a circle were Mr Selope Thema, editor of the *Bantu World*, a white-owned weekly newspaper, a

Johannesburg businessman named Job Richard Rathebe, who was a social activist, and Dan Twala, also called 'Mr Sport, the man who gets things done'. Also there that day was Andy Anderson, the printer of flyers and posters for the African National Congress, who had a print shop in Commissioner Street.

Bailey began proceedings by talking about the new *Drum* and his vision for it – stating that we needed to know what the average African in the street really wanted to read in a paper. Mr Thema then started a long and pedantic speech about the literary aspect of African writing and poetry and its cultural significance to contemporary life until Andy Anderson eventually interrupted him.

'We want more pin-ups on the front cover,' he said.

This caused Bailey to convulse with laughter, which made Thema lose all momentum. His speech tailed off and a general, somewhat boring discussion started. I started to take pictures of the people at the meeting.

Bailey turned to me. 'Jürgen, what do you think?' he asked.

After thinking for a few moments, with everybody looking at me, I said: 'Some 50 per cent of your potential readers are of the female species, so wouldn't it be a good idea to make sure that *Drum* caters for them as well?'

Bailey guffawed loudly, chortling and chuckling. 'Well, you'd better get us some smashing cover girls!' he said.

The following day as I walked past Anthony's open office door he called out to me. 'Jim left a note for you,' he said.

Bailey had approved the darkroom, but he had slashed my budget by 50 per cent. The money he'd allocated made a proper darkroom unworkable. I had put the darkroom budget together very carefully, mindful of costs, with the help of the Horowitz brothers of Photo Agency. We had kept the costs to the absolute minimum.

I looked at Anthony and asked where Bailey was. 'He went to Colesberg to organise the auction of some of his racehorses,' he replied.

I knew that Colesberg was halfway between Cape Town and Johannesburg and that Bailey had a massive sheep farm there where he also bred racehorses.

'What about my pay?' I said, really distressed.

'You'll have to speak to Jim about that. But he won't be back for about three weeks because once he's finished in Colesberg he's going to Cape Town.'

I was very worried. Without any certainty about my payment, I could not make any of the important decisions I needed to. My personal financial situation was close to perilous. I asked Henry what he thought I should do. Unfortunately, he had a similar problem and Anthony obviously had no power to do anything to help us. Bailey had offered Henry £40 a month as chief reporter and assistant editor, which was clearly inadequate. He said he thought Jim was a bit scatter-brained and suggested that when he came back, the two of us should corner him together.

We were very late printing the January 1952 issue of *Drum*, owing to our office move, and by 26 December, when it should have been available on the streets, we were just starting to print it. Because SAAN and the printing works were in the same building as our offices, there should have been no problem. However, we printed on an old four-colour tabloid machine, which had been bought second-hand in India, and was very slow. Also there was a worldwide shortage of newsprint, which accounted for the poor printing quality of *Drum* and the occasional erratic timings of print runs. All of this made my life difficult as I was responsible for all aspects of production, including block making, the quality of the photos and the layouts. I also had to oversee the machine run, which kept me very busy for a full week.

One day Anthony asked me for lunch at the Phoenix, which was one of the few restaurants in downtown Johannesburg. He said Jim had not been happy with the meeting we'd had with the political figures, whom he had found dull and boring, so he had asked Henry to organise a session with a group of gang-sters and burglars, to get their ideas on how to make *Drum* more relevant.

'Why would our readers want to know what gangsters think?' I asked. 'I'm baffled by Jim and what he wants.'

'Well, he thinks that gangsters are the heroes among the Africans because they defy apartheid, drive big expensive cars, dress stylishly and look like Hollywood stars.'

I was not at all convinced by this argument, nor did I think it reflected the thinking of the Africans that I came across day to day.

Of course, creating a *Drum* darkroom was hopeless now that the budget had been cut so harshly but, desperate to get it going, I went back to talk to the Horowitz brothers about what I could get for the money I had available. It turned out that there really wasn't enough for a decent enlarger, or indeed for any of the necessary bits and pieces. It wouldn't even cover the chemicals, paper and film. There was, quite simply, nothing that I could do until Bailey returned.

In the meantime I did some research about African photographers but it was rather dispiriting. It seemed there were none. I even approached the amateur camera clubs throughout South Africa to see if they had any African or so-called non-European members. I spoke to picture editors on local papers but, astonishingly, none of them had any non-white photographers on their staff or even on their freelance lists. Finally, I discovered that the *Bantu World* used some freelance black photographers, but after meeting with them I remained disheartened. They knew very little about photography and expressed no interest in working for *Drum*, even as freelancers.

The trouble was that the few Africans I had met who were interested in photography had never had the chance to study it or to work somewhere as trainees. There were no books on photography or photo magazines that I could find in the city's main libraries. It was true that some of the photo laboratories, of which there were few, had black technicians on their staff, but their work experience was limited to making up chemicals, drying prints, dispatching them and general cleaning. They certainly did not know photography.

Out of the blue I got a call from Bob Crisp, who offered me a job on a new Sunday paper he was setting up, called *Egoli*. I hesitated for a while but I finally turned his offer down. I preferred working on a magazine rather than a Sunday paper. And I really liked working with Henry and Todd. They were very professional and we all got on well. Whatever happened, we always ended up having a good laugh, however depressing a situation or story might be.

I thought Fritz's assistant, Ian Berry, might be an option for Bob. It seemed that Ian wasn't working for Werner's Studio any more and I only had his physical address in Benoni, so off I went in the Austin to find him, taking Henry along for company. Henry also wanted to visit an old friend from his army days who lived there.

Ian had just set up his studio and was very proud of his new lighting equipment. Equally, though, he was interested in Bob Crisp's offer, which he said he would follow up on. He was about to go to a fireworks display at the Benoni lake where there were some celebrations going on connected with the founding of the city in 1887. It was a potential opportunity to take some good photographs, so we decided to accompany him.

The celebrations were just starting, with the elite of Benoni on a platform making speeches. Ian got busy with his Hasselblad and flash, while Henry and I strolled around. There were the usual funfair stands where you could win a stuffed teddy bear by shooting at tiny moving ducks or throw soft balls at targets to win a little doll. I took a number of pictures with my Leica of people and children having fun. The finale was the fireworks display and eventually Ian turned up, having finished his shoot of the celebrities.

'What are you doing with that little camera?' Ian asked me, looking rather puzzled, as he inspected my Leica. 'No flash?'

I explained to Ian about 35 mm cameras and available light photography, and he became very excited. This was exactly what he was looking for in photojournalism. Smaller, more versatile and easier to use, the new 35 mm cameras were on the point of revolutionising photography.

By now it was getting rather late and we still had to visit Henry's old comrade from the war. We drove into the township looking for the address Henry had, but it was dark and there was no electricity and the streets had no names, just the houses with very long identifying numbers, which were difficult to read. For a long time we drove up and down, street after street, becoming ever more frustrated. Then, just as we were about to give up, we found Henry's friend in a little corrugated-iron shack in the backyard of one of the matchbox-sized houses.

We entered a tiny room with a bed as high as a bar stool, its four legs standing on a pile of bricks, which was common in many African homes, where the space below was used for storage. The room was barely lit by a lamp, which gave out a strong smell of paraffin, and in a dark corner, next to the bed, was Henry's friend, sitting in a battered old armchair.

'Solomon!' shouted Henry. Arms outstretched, he went to embrace his friend, who, with difficulty, rose to his feet.

Solomon looked much older than Henry. His hair was snow white, he was unshaven and he spoke in a soft, croaky voice, all the time gasping for air. Solomon fell back into his armchair and invited us in a wheezy voice to sit down. Henry and I sat on the bed, which was covered with a thin, worn blanket. The whole room smelled of desperate poverty. Solomon and Henry spent an hour or so, chatting in Zulu, reminiscing about their time in Egypt.

In the car on our way back to Johannesburg, Henry told me that Solomon was a hero, who had rescued two white South African soldiers from a burning truck in the desert. He was now terribly ill with tuberculosis, but received no help from the government.

Bailey was back.

Although we had arranged to confront him together about pay, Henry was out on a story and I felt the matter couldn't wait. I walked into Jim's office, prepared for an argument. He smiled and invited me to sit down.

'I've come to see you about my wages and the darkroom budget,' I said.

Immediately, his expression turned humourless. 'I'm very busy at the moment,' he said, 'so that'll just have to wait.'

I looked at him with astonishment. For a moment I had to breathe deeply. 'This can't wait!' I protested. 'I can't work for *Drum* any more. I've supported this magazine long enough and way beyond what I can afford.' I got up and turned to leave.

'Sit down, Jürgen,' Jim said.

Reluctantly, I lowered myself back onto the chair. 'Look,' I said, 'I've got to have a monthly fee for my work as production manager, photographic editor and designer. And I also want £1 sterling per picture used in the magazine. Also, we need to agree on a credible budget for building the darkroom.'

Jim's eyes were cold. 'I'll pay you £40 a month for your editing work and 15 shillings per picture used,' he said.

At that moment, there was a short knock at the door and Anthony popped his head round. 'You got a minute, Jim?' he said, and seeing me, 'Jürgen, come and see me when you're finished.'

I turned back to Bailey. 'What about the darkroom budget?'

His response was to burst into his usual croaking laughter. His whole body shaking with mirth, he waved me away. 'Later, later ...'

I left the room and lit myself a Lucky Strike. I had been planning to rent a one-roomed apartment in Claim Street, close to the office, for £25 a month. This now seemed like an illusion unless, of course, I should quit *Drum*. These were the thoughts that were going round and round in my mind as I left the *Drum* office and walked along the corridor. I passed a number of open doors, through which I could see members of the different SAAN departments in shirtsleeves working on the production of their newspapers. Then I saw a very tall man come out of an office and walk towards me. He was wearing red braces over a white shirt, with his collar unbuttoned and a loosened tie.

'Aren't you the photographer who works for *Drum*?' he asked.

Beneath a small red logo on his office door saying Time-Life Magazines was the man's name: Ted Hughes. He invited me in and got straight to the point. 'I need a photographer who knows his way around the townships and who can communicate with African people.'

'I don't speak any African languages,' I said.

'That doesn't matter. I've heard that you've got a good rapport with the natives and that's what we need. Someone who can get into the townships and cover the stories we want. I'll pay you £40 per call or per day, whichever is the longest, as long as you can commit to being on call at any time. Is that okay with you?'

Well, was I happy! In fact, for a while I was almost speechless. 'That's perfect,' I said. 'When do I start?'

'Have you heard of a man called Nelson Mandela?'

'Of course,' I said. 'He's making quite a name for himself. I photographed him a couple of months ago.'

'Well, be here tomorrow at 2.30. I have an interview with him and I'll need some good shots.'

Later that day I went to see Anthony. I told him about Bailey's penny-pinching and uncompromising bull-headedness. I told him there was no chance of a darkroom. I told him I couldn't continue working for *Drum*. Anthony tried to calm me down. I should realise that Jim was under tremendous pressure, he said, because he was selling his sheep and stud farms. He was also planning

to make *Drum* part of a newspaper group which would see the magazine distributed throughout all of English-speaking Africa. 'You can be part of a real
adventure,' he said, 'and have a wonderful future. Look, even I'm only being
paid a paltry salary but I can see where this is all heading and some hardship
now will pay off later. To be honest, the only real money I'm making is from
articles I do for the London *Observer*. I've just had one accepted on the ANC
conference, which is good news.'

'Where's Jim going to get all the money to finance his delusion about becoming a newspaper tycoon?' I asked.

Anthony smiled. 'In reality Jim is a multi-millionaire and his money is held
in trust by Syfrets, so don't worry about that.'

'And the darkroom?' I asked. I was still upset.

Anthony said we should have another look at the budget, which, he agreed,
needed to be increased by 25 per cent over what I had costed originally and that
we should purchase even more equipment than I had specified.

14

'WE NEED MORE CHICKS!'

'Henry has arranged for us to meet a group of gangsters tonight,' Anthony told me, 'so let's meet later. We'll go to the Rand Club and pick Jim up there. Oh and by the way, I've appointed Arthur Maimane as our sports editor.'

'What about Robert?' I asked, surprised. I realised I hadn't seen Robert Resha around for some time.

'Jim doesn't like him. He's too much of a communist. Well, to be accurate, he's a Stalinist actually. He could've been useful with his ANC connections but we need to keep him at arm's length.'

I had met Arthur Maimane the day after Trevor Huddleston recommended him to us when he'd paid a visit to the *Drum* office. I had liked him. He was laid-back but spoke his mind.

That evening Anthony and I, in my little Austin 7, arrived at the Rand Club in the centre of town. Outside the gate a ragged group of black teenage musicians were playing a swinging township number on pennywhistles and a battered guitar. Their evident poverty was in stark contrast to the imposing colonial building and its beautiful foyer, where Bailey signed us in. In the lounge of this gentlemen's club hung life-size portraits of Cecil Rhodes and Jan Smuts, the comfortable armchairs were green leather, and the only audible sound was the soft humming of two ceiling fans. Uniformed waiters slid quietly between the groups of club members, unobtrusively clearing and replacing glasses on the small tables beside them. Jim and Anthony settled deep into two chairs facing each other and started talking, loudly, in their pompous Oxford voices.

'I've just finished reading about the life of Randolph Hearst, the newspaper and magazine tycoon, biggest in the world,' Jim said. 'He had enormous political influence in Washington. That film with Orson Welles – *Citizen Kane?* That's the way to do things.'

They discussed their ambitions for *Drum*, how it should reach all corners of Africa, and be published in all languages, and how to build an African newspaper empire. Then they started to talk about Shakespeare, agreeing how much African society reminded them of his plays, given the language they used and the African lifestyle. I thought it was all rather surreal.

As we left the Rand Club and walked through the foyer, Bailey asked the concierge for an envelope. He took a £5 note out of his pocket, slid it into the envelope and sealed it. Then he wrote his name on the envelope and handed it back to the concierge, asking him to keep it for him until the next day. 'It's not safe to have too much money on you,' he said.

When Jim saw my car he burst out laughing. 'Let's take my car,' he said, chortling away. He led the way to where his Hudson, a large American battle-cruiser, was parked and handed me the keys. I should drive, he said, because I knew the way to Henry's place.

As I drove through the dark streets of Joburg towards Orlando township, I listened idly to Jim and Anthony's conversation. They were onto Charles Dickens now. When they were studying at Oxford, it seemed, they had read a lot of Dickens and Shakespeare and saw resonances of both in South Africa. They said how lucky they were to be in a country where they were surrounded by Dickensian and Shakespearean characters. Then, referring to Todd Matshikiza's original inventive style of writing as 'Matshikese', they said that perhaps they should encourage creative writing in *Drum*. What about a short story competition?

When I turned into Henry's street I saw a figure in my headlights waving at us. 'You're late,' Henry said, climbing into the car.

With no streetlights (no electricity at all) in the township, it was very dark, but Henry directed me. There were few people about, although we passed some odd shadows walking along the dusty road. Finally we came to an open field. The road had deteriorated to nothing more than a rutted, uneven path and this made the Hudson, with its very soft springs, bounce up and down like a boat on the sea. Up ahead was what looked like a farmstead, with a number of cars parked around. Stumbling in the dark, we followed Henry up some steps and through a fly-screen door. We could hear voices and bursts of laughter. We walked into a large sitting room, which was dimly lit by a paraffin lamp and a few candles, where six figures were sitting at a large wooden table, covered with many bottles of brandy and beer, glasses and overflowing ash-trays. Conversation stopped. Dark faces and shiny gleaming eyes watched our approach through clouds of cigarette smoke.

Henry introduced us and then pointed out the names of the faces in front of us: Don, Lucky, Whitey, Kort Boy, Blackie, Cooleye. We all sat down except Bailey, who started to make a speech. In short, he talked about the aim of *Drum*, which was to give the black reader, especially the reader he referred to as the 'city African', what he wanted. However, to do this, we needed help to get closer to modern Africans and to know what they really wanted in a magazine.

Of course, all the gangsters started to talk at once.

'Chicks – we need more chicks!' Don shouted out.

Lucky, with his cigarette hanging on his lower lip, slowly rose to his feet and in a boozy voice loudly proclaimed: 'No crime. We want no more crime in your *Drum*, Mr Bailey.'

Meanwhile, Bailey had had a word with the proprietor – the 'shebeen queen' – and ordered more brandy for the table. The drinks kept coming and voices rose. Everyone seemed to be talking at once, shouting out their ideas and arguing among themselves. It became difficult to understand what anyone was saying or whether any of it made sense. Henry tried to bring some order into the group but he was rapidly becoming as drunk as the rest.

Then Jim Bailey rose to his feet and made an extraordinary statement.

'I have the authority and expertise and I am duly empowered to make any of you a cardinal!' he announced, startling the circle of gangsters into sudden silence. 'Now listen to what I'm going to say and do exactly what I tell you to do.'

With a sinking heart, I realised that Bailey had some kind of drinking game in mind. I had heard about the Cardinal Puff. Invariably the result was that everyone playing it would become catatonically drunk – which was exactly what happened. The game went like this: the victim had a glass of brandy half filled and he had to lift it, holding the glass with thumb and one finger, and say, 'I drink to the health of Cardinal Puff for the first time tonight.' He then had to take one sip from the glass, bang the glass on the table once, then touch his left knee with his left index finger, then the right knee, lift his left foot off the ground then his right, and lift his behind off the chair. He had to repeat this sequence twice more, first lifting his glass with thumb and now two fingers, etc. If you made a mistake, you had to finish your drink and start again with a filled glass. Everybody had a go. Jim encouraged this by saying how important it was to become a cardinal. The night ended up with passed-out bodies all around the room.

The drama of the night, for me at least, had not ended, however. When it came time to pay the substantial bar bill, Bailey looked totally uninterested. Despite being one of the richest men in Africa, of course he had no money on him. With the shebeen queen becoming increasingly angry, Anthony roused himself enough to see if I could help pay; he had some money on him but not enough. Feeling very annoyed, I searched through my pockets and gave him all the money I had. Then, climbing over the pile of intoxicated bodies, we left, having achieved, in my view, nothing whatsoever.

Back in the car and now driving towards the city, with a red sun rising in the east, Jim said: 'I learnt that old drinking game in the Air Force. It guarantees to put all but real heroes out for the count. One thing I do know is that to get people to tell the truth, you have to get them drunk.'

When we returned to the Rand Club, Bailey tried to recover his envelope with the £5 note from the porter, but the envelope could not be found, which was very annoying for him – and for me. I had asked Jim if he could help me with some cash as I was skint.

'What a bore,' Jim said when he realised he was going to be five pounds short that morning. Then to me, 'You'll have to get some money at the office.' I told him not to worry, I'd get some petty cash later.

'Jolly good chap!' he said. Then he slapped me on the back, turned around and walked back into the club.

Nelson Mandela in his law office

That afternoon I was due to accompany Ted Hughes to his interview with Nelson Mandela. I decided to take my Rolleiflex because it would be more practical than my Leica. I turned up on time at Ted's office, but out in the street he couldn't remember where he had parked his car. It took a lot of walking up and down a number of side streets before we finally found it – a huge white Cadillac convertible. Ted got behind the wheel, rolled his window down and, with his right arm on the door and his left hand on the wheel, Nat King Cole playing on the radio, he cruised lazily through the city. Eventually we found a parking spot near Chancellor House next to the law courts and walked up to Mandela's office. We were very late.

Mandela was standing behind his desk, books and papers under his arm. Ted apologised for being late, but Mandela said he couldn't wait as he had a meeting with one of his clients. I quickly took out my Rolleiflex and managed to expose two frames before Mandela left his office, telling Ted to make another appointment.

I printed up all my week's photos, including the Mandela pictures, in Knute's darkroom. Then I went to Ted's office to deliver the Mandela prints, at the same time handing him my bill for £40. Ted wrote me a cheque there and then. Then he asked me if I would be available the following week for a couple of days. Of course I agreed. Finally I began to feel secure enough to rent the apartment I had been waiting so long to move into.

Back at *Drum* I made up the schedule for the February issue with the help of Deborah Duncan, who kindly helped me out once more with the typing.

We had another woman on the Drum team now too. Dolly Hassim, from Cape Town, was appointed women's editor. She started a new column, called 'Heartbeats', replying to readers' letters about love and relationship problems.

Dolly was a very nervous person and Anthony told me she was what was called in South Africa a 'play white'. 'Play whites', he said, came from a mixed marriage in the Cape, and often moved to Johannesburg where they passed themselves off as white people. There they lived with all the privileges bestowed on whites but with all the insecurities that went with being neither properly white nor black.

Anthony had bought himself a motorbike and, after a few lessons, learnt to

Esmé Matshikiza, Deborah Duncan and Todd Matshikiza

ride it. One day after lunch I climbed onto the back of his bike and, at break-neck speed, we whizzed through the city centre to the Phoenix Restaurant. Over a bottle of wine, we talked at length about the future issues of *Drum*. I felt flattered that someone like Anthony, who was highly educated, seemed interested in my opinions and actually appeared to pay attention to them.

He told me about a friend he thought I should meet, David Macrae-Taylor. A fellow jazz fan, David had his own weekly radio show, and we became good friends. I visited him at his flat, sometimes with Anthony, where we would spend hours listening to music and discussing the relationship between American and South African jazz, the latter now becoming an active vehicle for the anti-apartheid movement. David was a tall, thin man in his mid-thirties, almost bald, and a heavy drinker and smoker. He often fell asleep while we were listening to his latest records.

I was spending quite a lot of time with Todd Matshikiza and other musician friends, taking pictures at various places where the music was vibrant and exciting. My love of South African jazz grew. One story Todd and I did together was about the Manhattan Brothers. These were four close-harmony singers, led by the distinguished and brilliant Nat 'Dam Dam' Mdledle. The four had decided, after eighteen years without a female singer, to team up with blues queen Emily Kwenane and we saw them perform to a packed audience in a small hall in Krugersdorp township. It was a wonderful event. Their outstanding performance of 'The Landlord Blues' had everyone shouting with delight.

15

PUMPY NAIDOO AND THE CRIMSON LEAGUE

Attracting more writing talent to *Drum* was something that had come up at a few editorial meetings, and it was decided that we should move ahead with the short story competition Jim and Anthony had talked about. A prize of £50 would be awarded for the best story. We also wanted to make our presence felt further afield in the country and Jim was keen that we open an office in Durban, where *Drum* then had no contacts. A trip to Durban was the next thing to organise. And so it was that I found myself behind the wheel of the Hudson heading down to the coast, with Anthony and Jim in the back of the car, enjoying long discussions about the Bloomsbury Group and Virginia Woolf while I did my best to keep my eyes open. They talked about how much influence and publicity the set had generated in the early twentieth century, their literary achievements and their unconventional relationships. Only half listening, and trying to concentrate on the road, I confess I didn't understand much of what they were saying, but I got the impression they were hoping to recreate the Bloomsbury Group lifestyle here, in South Africa, among black intellectuals.

By 4am, still driving, and with Jim and Anthony now fast asleep in the back, I was getting very tired. The journey from Johannesburg to Durban was long and arduous for a single driver, and manoeuvring the cumbersome Hudson along the winding roads through the Valley of a Thousand Hills was challenging. As we got closer to the coast it grew noticeably warmer and more humid, and tropical vegetation was a pleasant change from the dryness of Johannesburg. Finally, as dawn was breaking, I drove through the deserted streets along Durban's beachfront.

I found a beach and parked the car. Although I was exhausted, the sea looked too tempting to ignore, so I put on my bathing costume and woke Bailey and Anthony by pressing the hooter of the car for a full minute and shouting, 'Here we are! By the Indian Ocean!' They weren't impressed, so I left them there and ran into the sea. It was wonderfully refreshing and I swam for a while, enjoying jumping and diving into the breaking waves. Finally tiring, I walked up the still deserted beach. I saw my two passengers sleepily climbing out of the car and stretching. I waved at them. Then I flopped down onto the sand on my stomach and fell sound asleep.

I don't know how long I slept for, but it must have been several hours because when I woke up it was boiling hot and I heard children laughing and shouting. I opened my eyes and saw people all around me, running into the water, playing ball games, women in saris with toddlers, some running and some doing somersaults. The sunlight was dazzling in its brightness. For a while I didn't know where I was. When I tried to lift my head I felt a severe pain in my neck. I tried to get up but I couldn't bend my knees. I realised my back was so sunburnt I was almost roasted.

Eventually I managed to stand and, step by agonising step, I staggered on the hot sand towards the car, only to find that it had disappeared. There were lots of cars in the parking area but no sign of the Hudson or my fellow travellers. The sun was high in the sky and I was scorching hot. I found a stone bench under a tree and sat there, with my back, neck and legs on fire, feeling sick and dizzy.

Suddenly I saw the Hudson drive up and stop. Anthony and Bailey climbed out and cheerfully walked up to me. When I showed them my sunburn and explained my extreme discomfort, Bailey responded typically – convulsive, chortling laughter. He kept chuckling while I painfully got to my feet and hobbled over to the car. He and Anthony took me to the beachside hotel they had gone and booked into while I was busy frying on the beach. The hotel organised some cream for my burns, but I felt very rough. I was furious with Bailey and Anthony for having left me asleep with my pale skin in the full sun.

I thought it was callous and selfish of them. I spent the rest of the day in my room recovering.

At breakfast the next morning, Jim and Anthony told me about an Indian bar they'd discovered the previous evening. They had met some interesting characters, people they thought could provide stories for *Drum*, and I could get some sensational pictures. We agreed to meet up after lunch and all go back there together. Meanwhile, I decided to do my own research. I'd noticed that the hotel was run by Indians, who seemed very efficient and competent, so I spent the morning making some enquiries. They told me about the Victoria Street Indian Market and the danger of pickpockets, the Goodwill Lounge run by Pumpy Naidoo, a jazz and boxing promoter, and Benny Singh, a boxing trainer and promoter. I was also told to watch out for the Crimson League, a brutal gang that was at war with the Salot gang, who controlled the area around Grey and Victoria Streets. They extorted money from business people and shopkeepers, were extremely dangerous and were known to be killers.

Living in Johannesburg, I was yet to discover segregated beaches. As I strolled along the beachfront, I confronted this apartheid reality. The beach I had found myself on when I got roasted was the beach for Indians. There was a different beach for Africans, and one for whites. I decided I should get some pictures in the next few days.

After lunch Jim and Anthony showed up and off we went to the Indian bar, which turned out to be in Victoria Street, opposite the Indian Market I'd been told about. It was a seedy, dingy space, with dozens of men in shabby suits sitting at long wooden tables or standing about with bottles of beer in their hands and cigarettes dangling from their lips. We had just sat down on a bench at one of the tables when an unshaven man, clearly plastered and rather wobbly on his feet, sat down next to us.

'Sir, I have information for you,' he slurred, putting his face up close to Jim's. 'We go to your car and I will take you to the house.'

'Let's have a drink first, old chap!' said Jim, leaning back.

I had picked up my Leica and pointed it towards a group of characters standing next to the bar when suddenly a nasty-looking, angry-faced man stormed towards me. He grabbed me by the arm and pushed me backwards over the bench onto the floor. 'No photos!' he shouted. As his heavy beer-smelling breath hit me in the face, I felt a knife at my throat. In a raw, coarse voice he whispered in my ear, 'I'm going to carve out your tonsils and spit down your windpipe.' Then he got up and walked back to the bar. As I got up slowly, pulling myself together, I saw Anthony and Jim leaving the bar at high speed, followed by the drunk.

I left the bar rather more slowly and walked up to the Hudson. Bailey was already in the driver's seat and had the engine running. I slid into the back seat beside the drunk. As Jim put his foot down, the drunk said in a slurred voice: 'Sir, they could have killed you, sir, the Crimson League are bad men, sir.'

Driving through the market traffic was tricky, with people jaywalking and trucks unloading crates of vegetables and fruit, but eventually we got into some quiet side streets. The drunk directed Jim uphill into the suburbs of Durban. On a steep hilly road he told us to pull up opposite a large house surrounded by a high wall.

Jim turned around and looked at me. 'Ah, I say, Jürgen, take a picture.'

I looked at him, astonished. 'What?' I said.

He pointed at the house across the road. 'That house, I say.'

'Why? What for?' I asked.

Then Anthony butted in. 'The house is the headquarters of the Durban prostitution ring,' he said.

'Ja, all the hookers come out of there, I have seen it myself – they pick them up in big cars,' the drunk spluttered into my face.

I was bewildered. I could not understand how Anthony and Jim would do a story about a prostitution ring in Durban without researching the story first. What was the point of taking a picture of a house that a very drunk man you'd picked up in a bar pointed out to you, and claimed was a brothel? Anyway, I got out of the car and took the picture. Then I got back in and asked Jim, 'Now what?'

In fact, the prostitution racket story came to nothing – neither Jim nor Anthony ever mentioned it again. When, much later, I told Arthur Maimane about the character who'd put a knife at my throat and threatened to carve out my tonsils, Arthur laughed. He said they picked up these expressions at the movies – all the crooks in South Africa emulated the Hollywood gangsters in the films they watched all the time. They wore the same shoes and hats and copied the body language of actors like Humphrey Bogart and Edward G Robinson and got the fast talk in Peter Cheney and Raymond Chandler detective novels. 'That guy in the Durban pub had been waiting to frighten someone like you for some time!' Arthur reckoned.

The next place we went to in Durban was the Goodwill Lounge, following up on the lead I had been given. Here we met its proprietors, Pumpy Naidoo and his brother Nammy. They were both very large, heavy men and gave us a warm welcome. We enjoyed some excellent curry and heard some interesting and useful information about the Durban scene. Pumpy recommended a freelance journalist called GR Naidoo as being very familiar with Durban social life – GR later became *Drum*'s bureau chief in Durban – and he also gave us dates for some future boxing and music events he was promoting. The Goodwill Lounge would become my base whenever I visited Durban.

We paid a visit to Benny Singh's boxing gym, where he had trained many well-known South African boxers, such as the former South African welterweight champion Baby Batter, Jolting Joe and Alby Tissong. When we arrived, Benny was training the national lightweight champion, Homicide Hank. He was a friendly man and I managed to get a picture of him, with his boxing gloves, facing the camera – this made the March *Drum* cover.

When we got back to the hotel I told Jim and Anthony I was going to the seafront to photograph the various activities on the separate apartheid beaches. Anthony wasn't happy about my wanting to 'waste time and film taking boring pictures of silly people on beaches' and Jim agreed with him.

'What are we paying you for?' he said.

'You are paying me peanuts and I pay for my own film!' I retorted angrily.

The beach for 'Whites Only' extended along the total length of the promenade, which was lined with hotels and restaurants, with the dolphinarium and a children's playground at the end. There was a sign in three languages, English, Afrikaans and Zulu, saying

'UNDER SECTION 37 OF THE DURBAN BEACH BY-LAWS THIS BATHING AREA IS RESERVED FOR THE SOLE USE OF MEMBERS OF THE WHITE RACE GROUP.'

'Whites Only' Durban beach sign

Indian women on the beach

I took some interesting pictures on the 'Whites Only' beach: there were hundreds of people here, in bathing costumes, sitting on deckchairs, sunbathing, playing ball games and making sandcastles, while children splashed about in the waves. There was a fenced-in area with trampolines, where a few people were jumping up and down and doing somersaults, watched by a dozen or so spectators.

At the end of the promenade was the Indian beach. Here Indian children played happily in the same ocean; on the firmer sand some children were doing acrobatics and somersaults, standing on each other's shoulders; and on the soft sand women in saris sat chatting, keeping an eye on their offspring. I spotted a lifeguard on duty and I went up and asked if he could set up a mock rescue for me, which he happily organised. Everybody participated with enthusiasm and I got some realistic pictures of a sea rescue.

After the Indian beach was a sign: 'For Natives'. Here I came across a strange sight. I saw a number of men standing at the water's edge with their trousers rolled up. Each was holding an empty milk bottle tied to a long string. They proceeded to throw the bottles into the sea as far as they could and then pull them in by the strings. When they held them up for inspection I could see there was only a little water inside. Patiently they repeated the exercise, slowly filling these bottles up with more seawater. I asked one of the bystanders why they were doing this and was told that these were people from rural Zululand who came to Durban to collect seawater, which they believed had healing properties and would cure sick family members. They were afraid to get into the water themselves as they couldn't swim, but it wasn't easy to fill up a bottle by any other method. I took off my sandals and pulled up my trousers. Then I waded out into the water and filled up everybody's bottles – to the delight of all.

As I strolled back the way I had come, along the promenade and to the hotel, I gazed out at the wide ocean and the white-crested waves rolling in and breaking on the sand on each of the separate beaches, and thought what a strange system the government had constructed.

16

BETHAL

At our last editorial meeting Henry had come up with a strong story, which he believed would be suitable for our March issue, when we would be celebrating *Drum*'s first anniversary.

About 200 kilometres east of Johannesburg was the district of Bethal, a potato and mealie farming area where, in 1947, the Reverend Michael Scott had conducted an investigation into and produced a report on slave conditions on farms. From what Henry said, it appeared that nothing had improved since the Reverend's report about beatings, killings and forced labour conditions. He wanted to investigate further and expose the truth of the current farm labour conditions there. Everyone agreed that Henry should research the story and that I should go with him to get some pictures.

Back in Joburg after a dreary trip home from Durban, there was some good news. The darkroom was finished. This would make life much easier for me as it meant I wouldn't always have to go running off to the other end of town to print in Knute's darkroom.

At our editorial meeting we caught up with Henry on his progress on planning the Bethal story. He was going to go under cover. If he could get work as a labourer on one of the notorious Bethal farms, he would be able to experience and investigate the conditions at first hand. The assignment carried a big risk but Henry was undeterred. I was to go with him to the labour office when he signed up and get some pictures.

There were a large number of African men, many of them in tattered clothes and worn shoes, hanging around outside the labour office. A small group were playing a card game on the surface of a big box, which elicited much noise and excited shouts. Henry went into the office while I strolled around outside taking a few pictures and trying not to attract attention. I peeped through a grimy window and saw Henry standing in a queue in front of a desk, behind which two white men were sitting. The men were filling out papers. As each man stepped up to the desk, one of the white men held up a pencil, and one by one the men in the queue stretched out their hands and touched it. Most of these people were illiterate and so, instead of signing, they touched the pencil with a finger. I watched as Henry stepped up and conformed to the practice in his turn by touching the pencil. I managed to get a picture of him doing this. I had noticed that I was being eyed suspiciously by a black policeman who had come through the door out of the office, so after that I moved away from the window. About ten minutes later Henry and his group came through the main door, followed by another policeman. They walked towards a truck standing nearby. When Henry passed by me, he winked and dropped a box of matches, pushing it in my direction.

As I walked back to my car I opened the matchbox. Inside I found a piece of paper with the name of the farm to which I presumed Henry was being sent. So now it was a matter of waiting for a message from Henry from the farm. After two weeks and no word, we began to get worried. It was decided that I should drive to Bethal to see if I could find him.

After two hours of driving through flat, boring landscape, passing mealie and potato fields and the odd farm building with the ubiquitous stand of tall bluegum trees like an oasis in the desert, I arrived in Bethal. It was a typical South African country town — one main street flanked by the usual stores, a town hall, a couple of banks, a hotel, a post office, bars and petrol stations. I started making some enquiries. I must have appeared strange to the locals — as if I had come from the moon — what with my small car looking very out of place among the farmers' trucks and bakkies and my pronounced German accent, but I managed to get the information I needed. I saw several white farmers in khaki shorts, shirts and large floppy hats, ordering their black workers to load supplies onto their trucks. The workers were barefoot and dressed in rags.

Some were wearing filthy potato sacks, with three crudely made holes for head and arms.

Having got directions, I set off to find the farm where Henry was supposed to be working, the name of which, Sonneblom, he had scribbled on the piece of paper he'd tucked into the matchbox. After driving for some time I spotted a sign that said 'Sonneblom Plaas – Van der Merwe – Privaat' and I turned onto a dirt road with potato fields on either side. In the distance I saw a long row of workers, some carrying large baskets, some bags, slowly moving towards me, bending down and scratching with bare hands through the soil, picking up potatoes and throwing them into the baskets and bags behind them. Riding up and down on horseback alongside them was the 'boss boy', cracking his whip. I stopped the car and got out. I opened the bonnet and bent my head to look at the engine, hoping to give the impression of having had a breakdown, while I surreptitiously took pictures with my telephoto lens of the line of workers.

Suddenly I recognised Henry as one of them. He had seen me too.

I closed the bonnet, jumped back into the car and did a three-point turn as quickly as I could in the narrow dirt road, so that the Austin was facing the way out of the farm. Then I opened the door of the passenger seat and pressed the hooter, which gave out a miserably squeaky sound. I saw that Henry had dropped his basket and had started to run towards me. My heart was racing. Henry stumbled into the car as I put my foot on the gas and the Austin jumped up and down the rough dirt road, engine straining. Henry, out of breath, started to laugh as we looked around and saw the 'boss boy' giving chase. He looked like a wild cowboy on his horse, with his whip rising and falling. We turned onto the main road and I put my foot down – getting as much from my little seven-horsepower engine as it was possible to get. Luckily, the Austin's horse-power did the trick and we left him far behind.

Adrenalin pumping, we couldn't stop laughing about Henry's escape. But we weren't done with Bethal quite yet. At Henry's suggestion we went to visit one of his friends, Mr Gert Sibande, the 'Lion of the East'. Sibande was chairman of the Bethal branch of the ANC and he lived in Emzinoni township. He was also a great crusader for better working conditions for farm labourers. Sibande spoke about the brutal conditions on most of the farms going as far back as 12 April

Workers in Bethal

1929, when a case heard in the Bethal Magistrate's Court found a farmer guilty of tying a labourer by his feet from a tree and flogging him to death. He had poured boiling water into the man's mouth when he cried for water. In 1944 Philipp Lebovo had been beaten to death for attempting to escape from a farm in Bethal and in 1947 a farmer had assaulted two labourers, setting his dogs on them, flogging them and chaining them together for the night. There were many more cases which never came before the magistrate's court and which were never uncovered or punished.

Henry and Sibande had been together during the Bethal farm investigation with Michael Scott in 1947, and Gert Sibande was born and bred on a farm in the district. He had spent his life fighting for better conditions for the farm workers.

When it started growing dark outside, Sibande lit a paraffin lamp and produced a couple of beers for us. Henry and I sat on a bed covered with a faded, once colourful Basuto blanket, while George sat on an old wobbly chair. His white teeth and the whites of his eyes glinted in the reflection of the lamp. I could see how much these two men, friends since childhood, enjoyed each other's company as the hours went by, with the two of them chuckling together and remembering old stories.

Sibande then started explaining the contract system, which meant that two-thirds of the farm labourers on the Bethal farms were sent there under false pretences, having been promised either soft jobs in Johannesburg or 'dairy work' in the Springs district. A man from Nyasaland had described how the representatives of a farm labour agency in his country had offered him a contract to work in South Africa as a waiter. It was only when he arrived in the country that he realised he had been tricked and was actually contracted to work on a farm in Bethal. Then there was Joseph, a boy only fourteen years old, who was recruited by an agency in the Northern Transvaal to work in a clothing factory in Springs, only to discover that he and other unsuspecting boys like him were victims of this scam; they ended up working on a farm in Bethal for a wage of £2 a month.

In 1950 Casbert Tutje, from the Cape Province, together with three friends, was recruited by the Siz' Abafane Agency in Natal and sent to a farm in Bethal to work as labourers for £3 a month. On Christmas Day they were invited to a party by a family who were living on the neighbour's farm. The farmer would not grant them permission to attend, so they left the compound without leave. When they returned to the farm the next morning, the farmer punished them severely by beating them. Then he handed them over to the police. They were brought before the court on a charge of desertion and each was sentenced to two months. The farmer arranged that their term of imprisonment be served on his farm, where they were again thrashed by the 'boss boy'. Casbert sustained serious internal injuries and ended up spending several months in hospital.

Sibande told us story after story, and we talked until the early hours of the morning. The next day we went to visit some of the farms in the district notorious for their brutality. Unnoticed, we managed to get into the labourers' compound on one of these farms. These compounds were like jails, with high walls and filthy conditions. They were often attached to the cattle kraal where the air was filled with a strong animal stench. The labourers were regularly checked at night. Many of them wore potato sacks, like the ones I had seen in Bethal, with holes for the head and arms, and they slept on sacks instead of mattresses. Many of the workers we met were young boys, some no older than thirteen.

On one farm we were caught by the farmer, so I had to pretend to be a German tourist photographing landscapes. With my purposely exaggerated German accent I managed to get away with it. Henry, I made out, was the 'boy' I had employed as my driver and interpreter.

17

RITUAL MURDER AND A DERBY IN BASUTOLAND

Arthur Maimane had been researching 'muthi' murder and had heard a story with an angle that might be interesting to *Drum* readers. The killing of human beings for their body parts, used as 'muthi' (medicine) in some traditional healing practices, was not openly spoken about. The angle in Arthur's potential story was to do with the murder of a young boy in Basutoland. The Paramount queen of Basuto was rumoured to be involved in this killing. It was decided that I should travel to Basutoland with Arthur to see what we could uncover.

Before we left, while Henry feverishly typed up his story, I made enlargements of my Bethal pictures to lay out the pages for our March issue. I put my picture of boxer Homicide Hank on the cover and oversaw the paper go to press.

Arthur and I first went by train to Kroonstad to pick up the Plymouth, which by now had been repaired, I in the almost empty section reserved for whites, with a compartment to myself, and Arthur crammed into the over-crowded section reserved for 'natives'. There was no way we could break the law – the trains were continually watched and inspected by the Railway Police, who were determined to do their duty to keep South Africans apart.

We reconnected in Kroonstad, took delivery of the Plymouth, and drove through the Orange Free State, passing fields and fields of sunflowers, their heads turning in unison towards the sun. We drove through Maseru, and turned off at a sign to Leribe. From here the dirt roads were difficult going, bumpy and narrow, and led us up steep, rocky mountainside and down into deep valleys. As we drew close to Leribe, to our surprise we found ourselves surrounded by hundreds of Basutos on mountain ponies all riding in the same direction as us. The riders wore colourful Basuto blankets and a variety of hats, and some had long decorated sticks hanging by their sides. I noticed a few wearing old-fashioned swords. Groups of riders appeared over the horizon and came galloping down the hills as we came into a wide open valley. The sound of hundreds of galloping horses was like thunder, and the billowing dust clouds thrown up by the horses' hooves were an extraordinary sight.

By pure chance we had arrived on 12 March, the day of the annual Moshoeshoe Derby in Leribe. This was the day when thousands of Basutos and racing enthusiasts from different parts of the small mountain kingdom converged in the valley of Leribe for this traditional race meeting. It was an exhilarating experience and, for me, an unexpected opportunity to take lots of pictures.

A wire fence marked the track for the race and many of the spectators, still sitting on their ponies, were already lining up around the fences on either side. A member of the Basuto Mounted Police blew his horn and the race began. The horses flew past the spectators, the heads of whose ponies were hanging over the wire fence, in a blur of dust and colour, and raced along the track through the thick grassland.

I spent some time photographing the atmosphere, which was excited, tense and joyful. We seemed to have moved into another world, a world of the past. Arthur eventually jolted me from my hypnotic state and said, 'We have to move on. We have a job to do!'

Arthur's contact, Father Francis, was stationed at a nearby Catholic mission. He had been expecting us. He was dressed in robes and had a large cross on a chain hanging on his chest. On his head he wore a dilapidated Panama hat. He had wide intense eyes which glinted from his bearded face. In a deep and powerful voice he told us that ritual murders had been on the increase recently in Basutoland. Expanding a bit on the practice, he told us that an individual, 'often a powerful person or group, a traditional chief or leader, will commission a herbalist or healer – a sangoma – to make up a medicine, or muthi, which should strengthen their or his personality, improve agriculture or protect them against war or any enemies'. The sangoma in question, whom Arthur was hoping to interview, worked for the Royal Paramount family. Father Francis gave us a piece of paper on which he had drawn a map of the way to the village where the sangoma lived. It was a roughly drawn map showing a path going over a couple of steep hills and mountains. I was busy wondering how well the Plymouth would handle this when, to my and Arthur's horror, we were told we had to go on horseback. Neither of us had ever even sat on a horse, let alone ridden a pony over a mountain pass!

After much explaining and a great deal of hesitation, with Father Francis smiling uncertainly and wishing us Godspeed, we mounted two sturdy ponies and off we set to seek out the sangoma.

'Be careful!' Father Francis called after us.

I think Arthur and I were more worried about falling off than anything else at that moment, and the Basuto mountain ponies certainly seemed to have a will of their own. My pony refused to walk next to Arthur's. It insisted on walking behind his, while Arthur's mount insisted on leading. We found ourselves riding uphill through a rocky landscape, following the map Father Francis had sketched for us. Occasionally Arthur turned around and gave me a large grin. He looked much more comfortable than I felt. After about an hour of steady uphill riding we came to a deep slope looking down into a valley through which at its deepest point we could make out a river snaking along. On the other side of the valley was a range of mountains covered by heavy dark clouds. Arthur had gone ahead and he (or, rather, his pony) had found a path that led down the slope. My pony followed Arthur's down the narrow zigzagging path, cautiously, step by step finding its way along the narrow track. I began to feel rather wobbly so high up on the animal. Maybe one shouldn't sit on one's pony while moving down a steep incline? Maybe I should get off – but how? On my right was a steep ascending mountain and on my left the downhill descent. It was definitely no place to dismount!

After what seemed like hours we eventually reached the bottom of the mountain, thanking our brave and clever mountain ponies by stroking their necks. I thought my pony felt very pleased with itself. We rested for a while, giving the horses a chance to recover. The heavy clouds over the distant mountains had come closer and there was the occasional flash of lightning. Later, as it was getting dark, we raced through the bush country, which was now engulfed in heavy rain and lightning accompanied by thrilling peals of thunder echoing all around. We were soaking wet and the rain stung our faces like sharp pins. We crossed the river, splashing our way through the water, and then we were going uphill again, the ponies breathing heavily. Finally, we came to a small settlement of thatched-roof rondavels. A couple of older women silently led us to an empty hut, where we spent the night. When we told them we were going to the Paramount Queen's clan village, they looked at us disapprovingly. The next morning, after a couple of hours riding through flat rocky highland, the track led steeply uphill. High up against the horizon, we saw the outlines of three horsemen with their pointed hats and blankets flowing from their shoulders. They looked at once mysterious and threatening. Arthur and I stopped for a few minutes, and then rode beside each other. Arthur looked worried. There was a mist rising up the slope and a profound silence all around. Then, in a hushed, shaky voice, Arthur said, 'They look menacing ...' His words did nothing to console me. Even our ponies kept still and quiet, lifting their ears. Their breathing was the only sound.

As we took the long uphill slope at a walking pace, the three horsemen suddenly vanished over the top. We came to a group of large thatched rondavels and a walled-in compound. We saw no people about except a few children, who ran away from us, screeching as we approached them. We dismounted and were walking up to what appeared to be the entrance of the compound when two elderly men, dressed in what looked to me like fancy dress, appeared. One wore an ancient pointed helmet from the German Kaiser time and a colourful military coat with epaulettes and a leather shoulder strap and belt. His hand was on the handle of the sword that was hanging at his side. The other man, also clutching a sword, had a leather strap around his forehead with a large bobble on it. They were totally silent, did not reply to our questions and refused us entry into the compound, silently threatening us with their swords – one man waved his sword in our faces and made angry noises when I pulled out my camera. Apart from these two jokers and a few children, there seemed to be no other living soul around.

It was clear that nobody was prepared to talk, so after hanging about in this inhospitable place for a few hours, we decided to call it a day.

Five days later we were back in Johannesburg empty-handed. Father Francis did not want to be quoted and so, in the end, there was no story.

For me, however, the trip was by no means wasted. The first thing I did when I got back to the office was process my films of the horse race. I was pleased with the results and I made a few prints.

Bailey was back in town. He called everyone to a meeting in his office, where he proceeded to give us a long lecture about how we were going to open *Drum* offices in the Gold Coast, Nigeria and East Africa. Editions of the magazine for these different markets would have to be produced in Joburg and then shipped to West and East Africa. He talked about the success of our birthday March issue and Henry's Bethal story and so on. Then he grew serious and, looking sternly at me and Arthur, dismissed our entire Basutoland trip out of hand. 'You two twits mucked up a good story,' he said. 'Total waste of money and time.'

Arthur tried to explain why we had no interviews or photos but said he had enough material to write a good story all the same, based on reports of court cases that had been published the previous year, in 1951, about incidents of 'muthi' murder, not only in Basutoland but also, as far back as 1940, in Swaziland. These murders were widespread throughout southern Africa, he said, so the story was no problem. Pictures, however, he said, were impossible to get because no one wanted to talk. People were all scared of the sangomas, who might put a 'spell' on them.

Jim was unimpressed. He merely shrugged. Then he looked at me questioningly. I started telling the meeting about the horse race and the amazing pictures I had got, but Anthony interrupted me. In a cynical voice, he said, 'Boring. You are wasting film and paper, just like your pictures of the Indian beach. Gymnastic pictures. Boring!'

I thought I would leave it at that.

Henry and I had both decided in any event to give notice to *Drum* at the end of the month, which was the following week. Neither of us felt we received adequate pay for the work we did. We received £40 per month and I got paid

1 os. extra per picture used. I spent that money to buy film, and for my camera and car costs.

Shortly after we had officially handed in our notice, Jim summoned Henry and me to his office. His face wore the usual dour expression he adopted when he was confronted with something unpleasant. He looked as if there was something foul-smelling in his nostrils. First he was impatient and irritable. Then he started to wince. Then he gazed out of the window.

Henry and I sat patiently. Finally, Jim turned back from the window. First he scowled at Henry, and then he scowled at me. 'I will give each of you a £5 raise,' he said.

As we were on our way out of his office, Jim called me back. 'Ah, I say, Jürgen – we'll see you right.'

It was not the first time I had heard those words and it wouldn't be the last.

18

ARRESTED WITH DOLLY

Todd Matshikiza had arranged for us to do a photo feature about Dolly Rathebe, the blues queen and film star. She brought a few dresses and her bikini along to the *Drum* office, and Deborah had organised a few bits and pieces to make her look more glamorous – some high-heeled shoes, make-up, scarves and a wide-brimmed straw hat. Dolly was full of laughter and fun. We got into the Plymouth and drove to Zoo Lake, which was a well-kept public park with a small lake in an upmarket white suburb of Johannesburg. Beautiful old willow trees trailed their branches in the water and Dolly posed for me beneath one of these trees, leaning against the trunk. With the sun reflected in the water and shining through the branches, and Dolly in a loose flowery dress looking up into space, it made a terrific picture. She changed poses and I continued taking pictures, including some close-ups.

After a while I noticed that we were being watched. A small but curious group of onlookers had gathered on the grass. Among these was an elderly couple, the man in a straw hat and carrying a walking stick, and his partner in a tweed costume, and a short lady with thick make-up (which was noticeable from ten metres away). The man waved his stick in our direction and shouted in a squeaky voice: 'This should not be allowed!' On the road nearby, out of the corner of my eye I spotted a police car cruising slowly past, its driver and passenger obviously watching us.

Dolly and I ignored the growing crowd around us and left quietly.

As we were driving back to the city, Dolly suddenly said, 'What about the bikini?'

'We need to go to the beach,' I answered, joking.

'Four hundred miles,' Dolly mused. 'Have you got enough petrol?'

Then I had an idea. Close to Kensington, the suburb where my mother lived, was a mine dump. Mine dumps were composed of deposits of finely ground sandstone, which formed into piles when brought to the surface by goldmining activities. Much of Johannesburg was surrounded by mine dumps, some of them huge, but the one I was thinking of was right at the edge of Kensington. It was a small dump, about 30 metres high. Its flat top was the size of a football field. The sand was golden, almost white. Perfect for bikini seaside pictures.

We were nearing the end of March and the air was fresh and vigorous, an early sign of autumn in Johannesburg. I drove onto the sandy foot of the mine dump and stopped. As I was about to get out of the car, Dolly looked at me.

'I am not going to pose in my bikini in front of these "whitey" suburbans,' she said in a serious tone.

'Take it easy,' I said. 'We are going to the top.'

We grabbed our bags, I my camera bag and Dolly her bag full of various dresses, hats and accessories. Laughing, we stumbled up the slope of the sandy mine dump. At the top we stopped for a minute to catch our breath. I stood at the edge and looked around. Down below I could see our car, which I'd parked in the road opposite the suburb's last house. Then I noticed a man in the garden. He was wearing a straw hat and watering his plants with a hosepipe. And now he was looking straight up at me.

I turned to Dolly. 'Let's move over there,' I said, indicating the centre of the dump.

Dolly started getting herself ready for the photo shoot. She put on her bikini and a wide-brimmed straw sunhat. I started to photograph her in various poses and outfits. Dolly was easy to work with – she was a natural – and we were both enjoying ourselves. There were lots of jokes and much laughter.

After using up four rolls of film, carefully avoiding getting any of the fine sand into the camera, I thought I had enough. I closed my camera bags while Dolly slipped her dress on over her bikini and got her things together. When I straightened up, I saw a shadow come over Dolly's face. I turned around to see what she was looking at. Two uniformed policemen had appeared over the top of the dump and were making their way towards us, slipping and stumbling clumsily on the sand, one losing his cap in his rush. I turned back to Dolly and saw two more heads appearing over the top behind her. All four men broke into a run. As they closed in on us, breathing heavily, they all started shouting at once.

'Wat doen jy hier, seuntjie?' shouted a big fellow, who I assumed was a sergeant judging by the stripes on his uniform. He came up close to me and, with his face inches from mine, hissed into my ear. 'Moenie beweeg nie, boy!' Don't move, boy.

'Soek bewyse!' another policeman screamed in a piercing voice – Look for evidence! And they all rushed back and forth, examining the ground like bloodhounds, peering down at the sand. The sergeant got out of my face and strode over to Dolly, who was standing quietly in the middle of all the chaos.

'Trek jou rok op, meisie!' (Pull your dress up, girl!) he demanded loudly.

Dolly looked at him without expression. Then, without taking her eyes off his, and with one leg slightly leaning forward in a fashion model pose, she lifted her dress above her knees.

'Ek wil jou broek sien!' (I want to see your underpants!) he shouted.

Slowly, very slowly, Dolly pulled her dress up a little further.

The sergeant's face was turning red. 'Moenie cheeky wees, hoor!' he shouted. 'Hoor jy my?' Don't be cheeky, you hear me!

Dolly's dress reached her crotch. You could just see her bikini bottom.

'Okay!' the policeman snapped. 'Let's get down.'

Now looking somewhat embarrassed, he began pushing Dolly towards the edge of the mine dump. I started to complain to one of the other policemen, asking him in my strongest, deliberately exaggerated German accent if they were from the Gestapo, but he did not seem to understand me. We slipped and slid down the dump. Next to our car now there was a pick-up van and a police car and two more policemen, one of whom was chatting to the man I had seen earlier watering his garden in his straw hat.

As we were coming down, the policeman who was hanging onto me shouted at the two below, 'We got ourselves a bloody Kraut!'

Dolly Rathebe on the 'beach'

As I brushed the dusty sand off my clothes, I walked up to the sergeant. 'What is this all about?' I asked him, trying to control my anger.

'You will soon find out,' he said.

Then the man with the straw hat came up to me and, in a stern voice and looking earnestly at me, he said, 'You should be ashamed of yourself.'

Two of the policemen threw Dolly into the back of the pick-up van while the sergeant took me by my arm and led me to the police car, where he pushed me into the back seat. I was taken off to a police station in downtown Johannesburg. After a number of phone calls to the *Drum* office and calls in Afrikaans, which I couldn't understand, the police officer behind his desk put down the receiver and looked at me slowly, shaking his head.

'You come to our country and think you can do as you like. We have laws, you know. The Immorality Act forbids sexual intercourse between Europeans and anyone non-European, between white people and black, coloured or Asian people. Prison for nine months without the option of a fine.' He leaned forward, folded arms on his desk, and looked seriously into my eyes. 'We don't mix with these people. You should know, as a German, they are different, like children. You can't trust them. They are lazy.' He picked up a letter opener and leaned back in his chair, playing with the pointed end. 'Let me give you an advice: get yourself a job with a decent newspaper – not this communist black rag. You could do well for yourself here in South Africa. We have a great future for the country with our new government. It would also be a great advantage for you if you learn to speak Afrikaans.'

He got up, giving me a friendly smile. 'You can go now,' he said, pointing to the door.

I got out as quickly as I could.

When I got back to the office, Dolly was already there. Henry and the *Drum* driver had collected her and the Plymouth from the Marshall Square police station. They were all sitting in Anthony's office, joking and laughing about our adventure.

I was still upset about the whole incident, which revived my memories of the Nazi period in Germany, and I thought I should do something about it. I went to see Johnny Johnson, a reporter at the *Rand Daily Mail* and the *Sunday*

Express, the latter a tabloid sister paper of the *Sunday Times*. He and I had become friendly in the SAAN canteen. I described what had happened and he wrote a story which was published in the *Sunday Express* the following Sunday with the headline 'YOUNG WHITE MAN ARRESTED WITH NATIVE GIRL ON MINE DUMP'. The story was reasonably fair. The headline, however, upset a few white people, especially my stepfather John, who, when I paid my mother a visit, almost threw me out of their house. And when my mother tried to calm him down, they both ended up having a shouting match.

Sometime in late March, Henry brought a youngster into the office and introduced him to Anthony and me as his nephew, Bob Gosani. We needed a switchboard operator and Henry thought he might fit the bill. Bob was a young coloured man, seventeen years old and tall and lanky. Anthony took Bob on, and Henry showed him how to operate the switchboard. He was a disaster – Bob was almost totally incomprehensible when answering calls. On the very first day he transferred a call to me, saying, 'Hey, man, I have this dude on the line – he wants to talk to Anthony but you are the wrong switch, man.'

The next day Anthony asked me if I could use Bob in the darkroom. I was very busy at that moment but I reluctantly agreed, for Henry's sake, and put him onto cutting up negatives to put into sleeves and to start to number and caption all the negatives I had shot in the last six months. Bob learnt very quickly and I thought he might well make a good assistant in time.

19

DAY OF UNITY

On 6 April 1952 Ted Hughes and I went together to Freedom Square in Fordsburg for the launch of the Defiance Campaign. We watched, awestruck, as the square filled to capacity and beyond. Literally thousands of people came from all over to attend. There were representatives from most of the South African provinces and different anti-apartheid organisations and movements. They came carrying banners and singing freedom songs. As we arrived, Walter Sisulu, Dr Moroka and Yusuf Cachalia were on the platform. They spoke in turn and were loudly cheered by the crowd, who showed their approval of the leaders by giving the ANC thumbs-up sign and shouting, 'Afrika! Mayibuye Afrika!' It was very moving and emotional, and I found myself deeply affected by the soul-stirring atmosphere.

On our way back to the office Ted talked about the race problem in South Africa. He didn't think the racist government would last very long. It was out of step with the current zeitgeist, especially since the world had recently conquered the racist Nazi gang. I told him I had heard many African politicians saying they believed the same thing – that the apartheid system was too ridiculous to last. We arranged to follow the Defiance Campaign and Ted gave me carte blanche to photograph all of the campaign's future planned events for Time-Life.

Meanwhile, on the first Saturday of every month, choosing a different township each time, the *Drum* team continued with the 'Mr Drum' promotion. With Henry as our key man, we would make our way down the main street, selling

Nelson Mandela, Dr Moroka (left) and Yusuf Cachalia, 1952

copies of the magazine and giving away the £5 prize to the person who identified 'Mr Drum'. The short story competition had also been launched and we
were getting some interesting tales from readers.

At the next monthly editorial meeting, to plan the May issue, Anthony
introduced us to a young journalist named Barney Desai. Until it was banned,
Barney had run a paper called *New Age* and was now editor of a publication
called *Spark*, which was supported by the ANC Youth League. Anthony thought
Barney might do some freelance writing for *Drum*.

We were just getting down to business when suddenly Bailey came into the
office and joined the meeting.

'I say,' he said, looking at me as he sat down, 'let me tell you – we need girls
on the cover of *Drum*! The cover sells *Drum*.'

'I can be the talent scout!' Henry offered, to loud laughter.

Then Barney brought up the 'tot system' in the winelands of the Western
Cape as a possibility for a story worth investigating and writing about. This was
a system widely used on farms, where farmworkers received payment for their
labour in the form of a daily measure of residue wine instead of money. This
was wine of a very poor quality that couldn't be sold on the regular market. The
effect of this system of payment was that most of the farmworkers, male and
female, became alcohol dependent, and the effect on their families, children
and the communities in the area was disastrous. The tot system was widespread
throughout the Cape.

Jim liked the idea. He suggested Barney do some further research and that
Anthony and I travel down to the Cape the following month to visit some
farms. While we were there, he said, we should go about finding a stringer for
Drum in Cape Town.

Later that day – early evening – Anthony and I went along to Andy Anderson's
print shop at the end of Commissioner Street. Andy had been among the group
of interesting people called to Bailey's office when he took over the publication
of *Drum*. Andy was from Basutoland and his print shop had become a regular
haunt of many of the leadership in the ANC. Some of them would spend the
evening there once or twice a month overseeing the printing of the organisation's posters, flyers and other documents, and over time these gatherings

became quite social affairs. The print works was a former bakery and it still had the old oven. Since it was illegal for non-whites to own or consume alcohol, bottles of brandy were hidden deep inside the oven and, when necessary, Andy would use a long baker's shovel to extricate them. Every so often Nelson Mandela, Walter Sisulu and Robert Resha visited the print works and I took photographs of them there from time to time. That Defiance Campaign year was a particularly busy one for Andy. He would be rushing between his two printing machines while the rest of us sat around talking, drinking brandy out of cups and eating the curried chicken pieces we had bought from the corner café nearby. Many of the discussions would move towards predicting the future of South Africa. Whites were in the minority and the ANC was getting stronger. Since the announcement of the Defiance Campaign, membership had grown to over 100 000. The belief, in 1952, was that the apartheid government wouldn't last much longer – a few more years perhaps. There was a feeling of optimism in the air.

Sometimes we had a lot of fun. One evening we created a new cabinet for a democratic South Africa: Walter was to be the prime minister, Nelson the minister of justice, and Anthony the minister of communication. I was to be the minister of entertainment.

Towards the end of 1953 a new face emerged in the regular group who socialised at Andy's. To me, the newcomer did not fit in at all. In fact, I thought he was totally out of place. Everybody seemed to approve of him, however, and they called him 'Doc'. He was fair, slightly bald, and had blue eyes. He talked with a heavy Afrikaans accent. I couldn't understand what he was doing in the company of revolutionaries. I started to tease him – 'What is an Afrikaner doing here with members of the ANC?'

Then Walter Sisulu took me aside and told me Doc's story.

Doc came from a very large mixed-race family in the Cape. In stark contrast to him, all his brothers and sisters were dark-skinned. When he was sixteen years old he left the Cape and moved to the 'City of Gold' to seek his fortune. In Johannesburg he discovered that everyone treated him as a white man. And so he became a 'play white'. After working at a number of garages he got a job as a trainee mechanic at the Palmietfontein Airport. There were quite a few former South African Air Force (SAAF) pilots and mechanics working there, and after some years Doc learnt to fly. He then joined the Air Force himself. In 1950 South Africa supported the western-led war effort to fight North Korea and the government commissioned its No 2 Squadron to go to Korea, where it was attached to a United States bomber wing in Pyongyang. The whole SAAF No 2 Squadron, Doc among them, became legendary for their bravery. They were famously known as 'the Flying Cheetahs'. They received two Legion of Merit awards, Silver Stars and other medals acknowledging their bravery. A total of 176 Air Force medals were awarded to this team. Doc returned to South Africa a celebrated war hero.

When, unexpectedly, he was exposed and it was discovered that he was a 'coloured' person, not a white man, the SAAF was so embarrassed and bewildered that in order to keep him quiet they eventually offered to pay for him to study anything he wished and for as long as it took. He decided to study medicine at Wits University – hence his nickname.

All of what he was telling me, Walter said, was totally confidential. I never did find out Doc's real name or the name he'd adopted as a 'play white', nor the new name he was given after he left the Air Force. We all just called him Doc.

My new darkroom trainee was catching on very quickly. Bob Gosani was now developing films and making contact prints. I showed him how the enlarger worked and he began to make enlargements too. I also bought him a Yashicaflex, a cheap Japanese copy of the Rolleiflex. It was a bit tinny but it did the job. From time to time there was a need to make a head-and-shoulder portrait and Bob was beginning to do well at these.

One morning I drove with Ted through Newclare township in his convertible Cadillac. We had the roof down and, with me perched sitting on top of the back seat taking pictures and Ted driving in his usual leisurely style, one hand on the steering wheel and his arm on the door, we had a lot of fun. We were followed by a horde of shouting and laughing children. The road was bumpy and the Cadillac swayed on its soft springs – it felt like being at sea. I had a problem standing up and taking pictures not only because of the motion, but also because of the policemen patrolling the area in vans with loudspeakers, announcing their plan to declare the Western Areas 'black spots' and to remove them in 1953. The areas in question were the townships of Sophiatown, Martindale and Newclare. Some activists had already painted large graffiti on walls saying 'Hands off Western Areas'. The police threw me and Ted some very puzzled looks. Perhaps they thought we were crazy tourists, but whatever they thought, they didn't bother us in the least. We continued in our mission to document what was going on in South Africa.

Henry, meanwhile, had been busy trying to arrange a meeting of 'non-white' intellectuals for a friend of his, someone he had met while he was stationed in London. This was Peter Abrahams, a South African novelist, journalist and astute political commentator, who was currently visiting South Africa.

Born in Vrededorp in Johannesburg to an Ethiopian father and mixed-race mother, Peter had been classified 'coloured'. He left South Africa in 1939 to work as a journalist in London and had recently published a book entitled *Wild Conquest*, about the Boers who, refusing to live under British rule in the Cape, had trekked up north in 1835. Henry had arranged, with the help of James Phillips, an anti-apartheid activist and trade unionist, whose Scottish mother lived in a suburban house in Doornfontein, which was relatively close to the *Drum* office, to host the meeting.

Peter was a lively and intelligent-looking 35-year-old man with large bright eyes and a moustache. When we arrived at Mrs Phillips's house in Doornfontein, everybody was already there and had settled down in her small lounge. In one corner was Selope Thema, editor of the *Bantu World*, a medical doctor named J Thuynsma, Walter Sisulu, and James Phillips. In an armchair at the back of the room was Nelson Mandela. Dr Thuynsma was in the middle of telling a story that had all the elements of a human tragedy … about a light-skinned coloured man who had been treated as white all his life and who had many white friends, who had been an officer fighting in the Second World War. Suddenly, overnight, he was classified 'coloured' and became a lost man. He had to adapt to a new way of life and adjust to being a 'non-European' – his whole world had fallen apart. There were many similar stories. One was about an African girl who lived with an Indian man and how they were not allowed to sit together in a cinema for 'Indians'.

After many stories and much discussion, everyone at the meeting agreed that the Day of Unity had arrived. Coloureds and Indians needed to put their faith in Africans and their ability to lead the ANC into an organisation for all 'non-Europeans'. From this time onwards everybody who was 'non-white' would be 'African'. After some time had gone by, I noticed that Henry had disappeared and I went to look for him. I discovered him staggering about in the kitchen, helping himself to large glasses of brandy. This was Henry's dark side, and a side with which I had become familiar. From time to time he couldn't help himself and became totally, as they would say, 'motherless'. I dragged Henry out of the house and drove him to the office, where I left him fast asleep, passed out on the carpeted floor.

On 26 June the Defiance Campaign went into action for the first time. A group of volunteers walked into Boksburg township without the necessary permits. They were promptly arrested. There was no violence or resistance as they entered the police station and were taken to prison. That same evening there was a meeting at the Garment Workers Hall in Johannesburg which was attended by several Defiance Campaign volunteers. As a group of leaders left the building late in the evening, after the curfew hour for black people, they were arrested by the police. Among those arrested were Nelson Mandela and Yusuf Cachalia. On 30 July the police raided the offices of the ANC and the homes of Dr Moroka and other leaders, confiscating documents and correspondence.

There were so many events connected to the Defiance Campaign happening all over the country that it was difficult to know what to cover next. The white newspapers didn't cover any of the events. Many hundreds of people were arrested. They refused the option of a fine and were given prison sentences, usually of between two and six weeks.

In the meantime, at the *Drum* office I found that Bob had done well enlarging his prints but there was a problem. His pictures needed better timing and composition, so every Monday morning I sat down with him and we studied books about design and graphics, art books and magazines like *Life* and *Look*, plus a number of photographic books I managed to find in bookshops and libraries. I found that Bob, like many South Africans who had never been exposed to the visual arts, was open and receptive and picked up visual understanding and design very quickly.

Early in August Manilal Gandhi and Patrick Duncan were in a group of

Yusuf Cachalia arrested by Major Spengler

Defiance Campaign protesters

volunteers who defied the permit regulations in Germiston township and were arrested and taken to prison. A few days later the ANC leaders involved in the Defiance Campaign, including Dr Moroka, Walter Sisulu, JB Marks, Nelson Mandela and James Phillips, were arrested and charged with contravening the Suppression of Communism Act. They were later let out on bail. On 26 August a group of 28 women, led by Amina Cachalia, marched into Germiston township and were stopped by the police. The women started to sing and dance. They were then led to the police station – and given a two-week prison sentence.

During the subsequent court case of Defiance Campaign leaders, Dr Moroka handled his own defence independently of the other trialists. In doing so, he fell out of favour with the ANC. (At the December conference Chief Albert Luthuli would be elected president.) Outside the court crowds were demonstrating and singing freedom songs. I rushed from one event to another with little time to eat or sleep – it seemed as though the whole country had gone into a state of upheaval and nobody knew what was happening where and when.

When I handed my prints over to Ted, he had some bad news. He was leaving South Africa. He would be replaced by a new Time-Life representative shortly.

By this time I had managed to move into my own home, a small flat close to the centre of the city. Owing to the jobs I had done for *Time*, I was in a much better financial position, so I also swapped my Austin 7 for a brand-new Beetle, which was a better way to travel as it had more power than the old seven-horsepower heap. Very proud of my new car, I went to visit my mother. She had just returned from her weekly shopping trip to Fatti in Johannesburg, where you could get all the German delicatessen foods, and she invited me to stay for a special German dinner. I wanted to accept but was worried about John, who was expected back from work any moment. 'Don't worry, he will be proud of your new car and of you working for *Time*,' my mother said optimistically.

Although John gave me a sour look, the three of us sat down for dinner and managed to have a reasonable conversation without quarrelling about my work. When I left I thanked my mother and John for their hospitality. John, with a cigarette hanging from the corner of his lips, his left eye slightly closed against the rising smoke, said with a grin: 'Give my regards to your nig-nogs.' Black humour, I suppose you could say.

20

THE 'TOT' SYSTEM AND A GRACIOUS HOSTESS

The additional research Barney Desai had done on the 'tot' system in the Cape had turned into a long and detailed report, which included statistics and details of the worst cases to be found on specific wine farms. It was time to do the story.

It was a crystal-clear, frosty winter morning and the sun was rising into a bright blue sky as I drove to Anthony's apartment to pick him up. Anthony was still half asleep and dozed off in the passenger seat – he didn't say a word from the time we left till we came to the flat, open countryside of the Orange Free State. Anthony still couldn't drive, so it was going to be me behind the wheel for the next thousand miles to Cape Town. I kept the car at a steady 60 miles per hour and relaxed. There wasn't very much traffic on the road. When Anthony finally woke up, we talked a bit. He was amazed by the wide open spaces, first of the Free State and then the Karoo. The road stretched straight ahead – I could see easily ten miles or more – and the landscape was flat, interspersed with clumps of thorn bushes, termite heaps, the occasional mound of earth and, far in the distance, koppies and rocks. I had been told that the road had been built by Italian prisoners of war. There were no towns or houses for hundreds of miles. Sometimes we drove parallel to a railway line and passed goods trains.

Roughly halfway to Cape Town, we stopped at Colesberg. This was where Jim Bailey had his stud and sheep farms. We had some tasteless coffee and sandwiches at the local hotel and left at about 4pm, heading for Beaufort West. Anthony pushed his seat back and fell fast asleep again. I had bought myself some bottles of Coke to keep awake. We eventually arrived at Beaufort West at nine that evening. I parked the car in the grounds of a garage and fell fast asleep myself.

At sunrise, both of us looking and feeling rather bedraggled, we found a café and had a hearty breakfast – bacon, fried eggs, baked beans, tomatoes, potato cakes and sausages. Beaufort West was a typical 'one main street' town, with the usual stores on either side of it and one hotel. Most of the inhabitants were coloureds and, as in many of these country dorps, poverty was everywhere apparent. Many of the local people were dressed in rags, and were barefoot.

The scenery became more interesting as we were now in mountain roads where the landscape gradually changed from uniform dull and dusty to green valleys and rolling farmland. These were the winelands of the Cape, the districts where we were going to explore our 'tot system' story.

Anthony and I were both looking forward to seeing Cape Town and the sea. As we got nearer to the city, I stopped at a garage to fill up. I asked Anthony to give me the address of Lady Bailey, Jim's mother, who had invited us to stay at her house. Anthony looked through all his pockets and then opened the boot of the car to look in his travel bag but he couldn't find it. 'I must have left it in the flat,' he said. Now what? I thought. I asked the petrol attendant to bring me a phone book but I couldn't find the right Bailey in the directory. Anthony tried to remember the address. He said he thought Jim had said it was a house somewhere between Cape Town and Muizenberg, which wasn't awfully helpful. We tried to phone the *Drum* office from the garage, but Jim was not in, so we drove around between Cape Town and Muizenberg, seeing if something would come to us. In a suburb called Claremont we asked a local police station for help, and thankfully, eventually, we succeeded in finding Lady Bailey's address.

We drove up the driveway of her home and parked the car. In front of us was a large, impressive mansion. A petite elderly lady with grey hair, wearing a large straw hat and holding a garden rake in her hand, came up to us.

'We have come to see Lady Bailey,' Anthony said in his public school accent, swallowing his words.

'Oh, you must be Jim's friends from his newspaper venture!' the lady said, looking from Anthony to me with a friendly smile.

After we had formally introduced ourselves, she called a man over, who seemed to be her gardener. She asked him to show us to our rooms and then she left, still carrying her rake over her shoulder, strolling down a garden path. At the end of the path she turned and smiled again. 'Dinner at eight,' she called.

'Let's go for a swim in the sea!' Anthony said when we'd put our bags in our rooms.

I was exhausted from all the driving but I thought maybe a swim would freshen me up, so we got back in the car and I drove to Muizenberg. Here we found the beaches packed and Anthony suggested we drive a bit further along the coast, towards Simon's Town, which turned out to be quite a long way along a narrow road past Kalk Bay and Fish Hoek. Actually, I was glad I'd allowed myself to be persuaded. With the mountain on our right and the 'villagey' Cape streets, with shops and restaurants, nestled below it, and the sea on our left hitting the rocks and sending white spray into the air and an occasional flurry of wind, it was an exhilarating and invigorating drive. Just before Simon's Town we found a small beach hidden away between rocks. There were no people on it. I rushed down to the water, dropping my clothes as I ran, and dived straight in. Anthony was taking his time. As I swam around a rocky point I saw him standing on the beach, undressing slowly. He waded into the water and I left him to it. I swam into a narrow sandy gap, where I sat down to catch my breath. I was surrounded by rocks, isolated and hidden from the world, and I felt very relaxed. Suddenly I had a strange feeling that I was not alone. I turned around and there was Anthony – stark naked, standing on a rock, looking at me with a strange glaze in his eyes. Then he turned and disappeared behind the rocks. When I swam back to the beach he was getting dressed. I came out of the water and was just putting my clothes back on when suddenly I was grabbed from behind. Anthony put his arm round my neck, pushed me down on the sand, jumped on top of me and started to wrestle with me. He was very strong but I struggled and slipped out of his grip. I grabbed the rest of my clothes and ran up to the car. Perhaps the sea or the long trip, I thought, must have made him bonkers, but, even so, wrestling games at our age seemed to me foolish and inappropriate. After a while Anthony came back to the car. He opened the door and sat in the passenger seat. Neither of us spoke. On the drive back to Lady Bailey's house, I attempted a humorous remark or two about Anthony's strange behaviour on the beach, but he would not be drawn. He remained silent all the way.

I had almost finished dressing for dinner and, in my best outfit, was struggling to put on my one and only tie, when Anthony came into my room. He approached me from behind, lifted my left arm behind my back and said, 'There's a spider on your back.' As he said this, he pushed me down onto the bed and lay on top of me. His breathing was heavy and his breath smelt stale. For a moment I was totally shocked, as though I had been struck by a thunderbolt. When I'd managed to wriggle out of his hold, leaving him panting on the bed behind me, I left the room and, still very flustered, walked down the staircase and into the dining room. Lady Bailey was already sitting at a table laid for three with the tall gardener, now dressed in a waiter's outfit, standing behind her chair. I sat down beside Lady Bailey and made an excuse for Anthony. I told her he was feeling unwell but might join us a little later.

'How is James?' Lady Bailey asked. 'Is he settling down? He's a restless soul.'

She seemed rather worried about her son and his health. His habitual heavy drinking, she believed, stemmed from his time in the RAF. She asked me a lot of questions about *Drum*, the work we did and the stories we covered, and she seemed interested in hearing about our roles on the magazine. She said she approved of our efforts to create a voice for the rejected people of South Africa.

Lady Bailey introduced me to the waiter-gardener, whose name was Simon. He had worked for a close friend of hers who had recently passed away and she had 'adopted' him as her personal assistant. Simon was very clever, she said, and a great help to her.

As we were finishing our simple meal, Anthony came in. He apologised to Lady Bailey for not having come down for dinner but said he had been feeling unwell. Giving me a sidelong glance, he sat down and joined us for a drink.

Lady Bailey looked at each of us in turn and then said in a stern voice, 'Now let's stop this Lady business. You can just call me Mary.'

After Simon had brought him a drink, Anthony asked Mary to tell us about her adventures flying solo from London to Cape Town, which she had done 23 years before. She gave a modest smile. The flight was unremarkable, she said.

'But, Mary, I heard that you encountered sandstorms, wind and heat, and that your DH60 Moth flipped over! Not to mention snowstorms and fog – at least that's what I was told. In fact, what you did was a remarkable achievement.'

I tried to imagine this indeed remarkable feat. A woman flying solo in 1929 was definitely unusual and courageous.

There followed some more talk about Jim. When he had lived with her in Cape Town, Mary said, he sometimes used to disappear for days, mixing with riff-raff; once he was gone for over a week and she'd had to phone the police to find out if anything had happened to him. 'He's my youngest,' she explained with a mother's rueful smile.

It was getting late and I decided to excuse myself. I left Anthony and Mary talking and went upstairs to my room, where I puzzled over Anthony's behaviour. To be honest, although I was aware that there was such a thing as homosexuality, I had never been 'confronted' with it, and certainly not in this way. Perhaps I was particularly naïve. Anthony's sudden physical overtures, if that was what they were, had taken me completely by surprise. I had thought we were friends, but now I began to wonder what Anthony thought. Here was a highly educated man, and an intellectual, who had always treated me as an equal despite the fact that I had had no formal education whatsoever. He always agreed with my ideas, acted as though we were intellectually on a par and gave me to believe that we were friends working together on a common project.

The following morning we drove out together to the winelands in the Stellenbosch district. During the whole trip there Anthony remained silent, beyond giving monosyllabic replies to one or two questions I asked and offering a few words if they related to the job we were about to do.

The farmhouses we saw were built in the Cape Dutch style with beautifully kept gardens and neat gravel pathways lined with old, exotic trees. On the first farm we visited, we managed to find the foreman in charge of the farmworkers, who swiftly dismissed any suggestion of wrongdoing or involvement with the tot system. He got quite irritated by our questions and eventually asked us to leave. By then it was almost noon and turning into a very hot day. As we drove

along, vineyards on either side of us, we came across a group of about 20 farmworkers, men and women, on their lunch break. They were sitting in the shade
of a couple of small trees, eating off tin plates and drinking from large tin cups.
Two of the women had babies on their backs. We tried to talk to the workers
but quickly realised we should have brought along an interpreter as they only
spoke Afrikaans. Some of them appeared intoxicated and we asked to taste the
drink in their tin cups. They laughed and offered their cups to us. It was wine.
We tried our best to communicate with them in a mixture of English and our
very poor Afrikaans and managed to work out that they were given a large tin
cup of wine twice a day, that they lived in the farm compound for free, and that
they received 20s. pay each week.

Jim had been keen that we look up a journalist friend of his, Jackie Heyns,
who was in Cape Town. Anthony and I thought Jackie might be able to help out
with Afrikaans, so we went to see him at his home in District Six. Jackie was a
jolly man of about 30 years old with a twinkle in his eye, who told jokes while
keeping a straight face. He told us that his family came from Cape Town and
that his parents had moved to Johannesburg in search of a better life. They were
very disappointed by the City of Gold. Jackie loved to write, so he decided to
move back to Cape Town and find a job in journalism. When I asked him how
he had met Jim Bailey he laughed. 'I met Jim at Back o' the Moon,' he said. I
thought this was another of his jokes until Anthony, laughing – the first time
he'd cracked a smile since the bed incident – explained. 'That's the fun shebeen
Jim took me to in Sophiatown – very amusing people, all sorts, gangsters,
politicians, intellectuals and musicians. The shebeen queen is a great character
called Fatsy – lots of fun.'

Jackie said he would come with us on our mission, so the following morning
we picked him up and drove to Paarl, a small town at the foot of a mountain
range and another wine farming area. It was near noon when we got there,
which meant the time for a lunch break for the farmworkers, and we drove into
the vineyards. Beside a compound, which we knew were the labourers' living
quarters, we saw a corrugated-iron structure and a queue of farmworkers, all
with tin mugs in their hands. They were being supplied with their wine rations.
Jackie and Anthony identified the foreman and they began talking to him while

I started taking pictures. Our plan that day was that Anthony would pretend to be a rich tourist looking to invest in wine.

I took pictures of the wine being poured out of a large barrel into each person's mug – one by one, men, women and young boys, not older than fourteen, stepped forward to have their large tin mugs filled. Some drank as they walked off to sit under a tree to give them some shade from the hot sun. Like the labourers we had seen the day before, these farmworkers were dressed in rags; some wore tattered shoes but many were barefoot.

We visited a number of wine farms on that and subsequent days and found that on most of them the 'tot' system was the norm. We also spoke to a few farmers, who either denied that they were practising this system or admitted only to practising it occasionally on weekends.

We agreed we had enough information and photos for our story, and after a few more days in Cape Town, and having been unsuccessful in finding a suitable stringer for *Drum* there (Jackie was planning to come back to Joburg soon, so he was out), we decided to return to Johannesburg. Lady Mary invited me to come and stay with her anytime I came to Cape Town again.

All the past week Anthony had been uncommunicative. It was becoming tiresome for me and stressful. I found it impossible to work productively under these circumstances and so I was looking forward to getting back to Johannesburg. I drove non-stop all the way, other than to fill up with petrol. Anthony kept intensely quiet. Most of the time he slept – or pretended to be asleep.

Beautiful as the Cape had been, I was very glad when I finally saw the lights of Joburg in front of me.

21

KILLER TALES

One day over a cup of milky white, heavily sugared tea at the local tearoom, which was run by a Greek family, I was about to take my first sip from my plastic cup when out of the blue Jim said: 'Are you having lots of fun with all the black wenches?'

I nearly scalded my lip. Whether it was my reaction or the question itself, I don't know, but Jim cracked up. He broke into peals of laughter, chortling noisily, and slapping me on the back. When he steadied himself, he looked me seriously in the eye and said, 'We need more pin-ups. Maybe a regular full back page.'

'Getting more girls into *Drum*' had become a regular refrain of Jim's, and that was what he wanted to talk about today. In the course of our conversation I told Jim about my experience on my second day in Joburg, when I had found myself walking around Doornfontein and come across a shebeen run by a character called Killer. Jim got very excited. He wanted to go there. He wanted to meet Killer. 'It will be jolly good fun!' he said.

So the following Saturday evening, Jim and I walked into Killer's shebeen. It was already dark outside and there was little traffic on the road. The main room was smoky and there was still only the one bare bulb hanging over the long table, where half-a-dozen characters were sitting hunched over their drinks. Everybody looked up. After inspecting us with openly curious expressions, they resumed their dazed state, gazing straight ahead or looking down at their drinks.

Big Ruth waddled up to us. 'Hey, man,' she said to me with a smile, 'where's my picture?'

I had come prepared. I had made a few prints of Ruth and the card players from my previous visit to Killer's. When I gave the prints to her, she looked at the picture of herself and started to squeal and giggle. She then led us into another dimly lit bare room. Killer was sitting cross-legged on top of a table holding court, three young African women, who were sitting together on a dilapidated couch, hanging on his every word.

'What have you got here?' Killer said, looking at us and pushing his hat back with one finger. 'I see Jürgy, the German sharp-snapper, but who is that smiling Mister Simple?'

I looked around. Jim was standing behind me with a frozen smile on his face.

'Oh, that is Jim, from England,' I said.

Killer invited us to sit down and ordered Ruth to bring everybody a special. The girls shifted to make a place for me and I sat down between two of them. Jim lowered himself into an old armchair. Then, pointing at each of the girls in turn, Killer introduced them: 'We have here three of the hottest beauties with personalities – on the left the African supermodel Patience Nthuli, next to our own film star, Ribbon Dlamini, and then Rhodesian blues and jazz singer Dorothy Masuka.' Then, ignoring us, he continued: 'Now where was I?'

'How you wiped out the Ndondis!' the girls shouted almost in unison.

'Okay …' Killer got himself into a comfortable position and lit himself a smoke. 'In 1942 the whole of Germiston was in the grip of terror. There were running battles between the Boom Town gang and the vicious Ghost Town gang. The location was divided into two parts – between 4th and Brammer Streets the Boom Town gang ruled, and between 7th and 13th Streets the Ghost Town gang ruled … and between 5th and 8th Street was no man's land – this was where all the battles took place between the two gangs.'

The door opened and Ruth came in with a box full of drinks. She dished out the special – a quart of beer and a half-jack of brandy, how could I forget! – and we all filled up our large glasses with beer topped up with brandy. It still tasted awful – at least to begin with. As it went to your head, in my experience, it gradually got pleasanter … I was squeezed between the two cuddly, voluptuous

Dorothy Masuka, 1952

young ladies and began to enjoy myself.

Killer in the meantime lit another cigarette and had another drink. Suddenly he looked at me and said sharply, 'What is your Limey up to?'

I turned around to see Jim pushing his notebook into his pocket. In his best Oxford accent, he said, 'I must say, old chap, I am spellbound by your fascinating anecdotes.'

For a moment Killer was floored. Then his eyes grew cold and steely. 'I am not your "old chap",' he said. 'And what is this silly English you are speaking? You better watch out or you will be put under your own spell!'

Then Dorothy got up and in a high-pitched tone started to sing. 'Killer – Killer – Story-Teller – Catch the Gangster – Kill the Mob.'

It broke the tension and Killer started to laugh. 'Let me go on with the story,' he said. 'While all this fighting was going on in Germiston township, a group of delinquent boys was hanging around Germiston station and speaking in some sort of Zulu slang – that is when they were called "the Ndondis". They started by cleaning cars and just loafing about, then began pickpocketing and stealing in the township. In the meantime the Ghost Town gang steadily lost ground and the Ndondis fought their way into township terrorism – housebreaking, shoplifting and carrying off dames they fancied from functions. In about 1948 the Ndondis were joined by a boy called Danger, who had returned from a reformatory. Danger had pluck and seemed to be a pleasant, respectable boy – but he was sinister, with piercing eyes under a forward-bent head. He quickly became the leader of the gang and more boys joined. They raped, stole, stripped and robbed people at night and made lots of money.'

By now the girls were leaning forward, watching Killer intently, as the suspense built.

I was quietly sipping my drink, absorbing the atmosphere, when all of a sudden I got a prickly feeling. At first I thought it was the effect of the special, but then I realised that Dorothy had put her hand gently on my leg. Patience, meanwhile, had slipped off the couch and settled down on the floor at Jim's feet. Jim was mesmerised by Killer. His face had a glazed look and he didn't take his eyes off him.

'Now,' Killer carried on, 'most of Danger's brothers were members of a football club called the Eleven Experts, so Danger and his boys decided to start their own club, calling it the Fast Eleven. There were some tough characters among them. There was Manual, who was dark, stubborn, cruel and daring … he was the chief knife-man. Then there was Shorty, a good-looker, who was the brains behind the club; Mickey was stubborn and full of guts … and Chicago – he was tall, dark and merciless – a knife-man too.

'At a party in 8th Street Danger quarrelled with someone about a girl and shot the girl point-blank. He was arrested and sentenced to five years. This weakened the gang and another gang, called Dead Man's Gulch – the DMG – came into existence in the south of Germiston. They began to fight the already weakened Fast Eleven, who recruited new blood into the gang – some young boys – so the Fast Eleven managed to keep going in the face of the new threat, the DMG. They terrorised shopkeepers, extracting protection money and on Fridays, pay-day, they got money from factory workers.'

After a short drink and smoke break, Killer took up the story again.

'I joined – "undercover" – a body-building club and infiltrated the Fast Eleven to organise that the club curb all these evil activities. I was head of the detective branch of the police for the East Rand townships at the time. The body-building club consisted mostly of coloureds and Indians, so me, a white man, could pose as a light-skin coloured and get away with it.'

Sipping away at my drink, I was growing mellower and mellower, and Dorothy kept on feeling me up. She was very young, only about seventeen years old, and despite her confident exterior, she was unsure of herself.

'On the Sunday,' Killer continued, 'myself with the body-building club attacked the Fast Eleven. There was a bloody fight and a number of gangsters went to hospital. The Fast Eleven were still confident and they went to the houses of some of the body-building club saying to whoever was at home, "Get yourself mourning clothes for you're going to lose your sons." On the following Friday the Fast Eleven went round to the factories as usual to collect their protection money. The body-builders were waiting for them again and beat them up … they had followed them from their doorsteps to their late-night parties, which they often attended, to the factory. The Fast Eleven tried to make peace but in the end they had to terminate their activities. This was the end of the Ndondis.

'Most of the DGMs were eventually arrested for murder and housebreaking, but in their absence a new gang called the Vultures gained power – but this is another story for another time.'

Killer climbed down from the table and left the room while we all clapped loudly.

As I was getting up from the couch, Dorothy grabbed me by the hand and pulled me past the other girl through a door at the back of the room into a small bedroom. By this time I had consumed many specials and was feeling very giddy. In fact, I was sozzled. I staggered after Dorothy and onto a very big bed, where I fell asleep with Dorothy softly singing an African lullaby.

I awoke to light shining through the curtains. At first I couldn't remember where I was, but after a while I recovered. I was alone on the bed. Slowly I climbed off it, went to the window and pulled the curtains aside. I saw a small garden outside and, on the pavement, people hurrying off to work. In the kitchen I found Killer, still wearing his hat, sitting at a table, drinking coffee.

'How did you like Babyface?' he asked me.

I told him Dorothy had a great voice. Then I asked him where Jim was. He told me that Jim had left late the night before – he had had to put him into a taxi because he was so plastered. I asked Killer if we could use his story for *Drum* and he got quite angry. Under no circumstances whatsoever, he said, did he want to get involved with the press. And that was that.

Two days later Jim called me and Henry into his office. He looked very seriously at both of us and we were expecting the worst. Then he started to smile.

'Thanks to you,' he said, addressing me directly, 'we have a top crime story.'

He suggested that Henry should write an investigative story about the Germiston crime scene and its history. He passed Henry some notes and asked me to write down everything I could remember about Killer's story. I told Jim what Killer had said but he didn't seemed concerned. Henry looked doubtful. It was hardly a 'top crime story'. Big crime had moved to Alexandra township north of Joburg, where the Spoilers gang was operating.

A few days later Todd Matshikiza asked me if we could meet with Deborah Duncan at her place sometime after work. That evening I went to see Deborah and Todd at Deborah's flat in Hillbrow. Her two-roomed apartment on the tenth

A knife fight in Alexandra township, 1952

floor was tastefully furnished. There were shelves in the living room bursting with books and family pictures on the dresser. There was a warm, comfortable atmosphere there. Todd, quite relaxed, was sitting on the couch smoking a cigarette and sipping a drink.

Deborah offered me a drink and I sat down next to Todd, curious to know what these unlikely friends had on their minds. Deborah was someone who always had a smile on her face, but tonight she looked serious. Puffing on a cigarette, she came straight to the point.

'What do you think of Anthony?' she asked me.

What's this all about? I wondered. I didn't answer immediately but then, looking at Todd, I said, 'Anthony can be very moody …'

'That's it,' Deborah said. 'He's unstable. He's always in a huff. And he's very temperamental. Everybody on the staff is complaining about his spitefulness and inconsistency.'

Todd was nodding. 'We thought we should talk to Jim. We need another editor. What do you think?'

Before I could reply, Deborah said, 'Anyway, he has no journalistic experience – he worked in a bookshop before he came to *Drum*.' Then she added, 'I can't work with him any more. I can't cope with his insolence.'

I knew exactly what they were saying and, in fact, I agreed with them. Anthony could be very vicious sometimes. I was having a hellish time coping with him myself and his lack of journalistic experience didn't help. But Jim and Anthony were close friends, and personally I didn't think Jim would agree to make any changes. Complaints might actually make matters worse.

I asked Todd and Deborah whether either of them had spoken to Anthony about his moods and they said they hadn't, thinking it would probably aggravate the situation. I offered to have a word with Anthony, try to make him aware of the problem and, without mentioning names, let him know that this was how most of the staff felt.

About a week later I found Anthony in the office. He was in a good mood because one of his articles had been published in the London *Observer*. I took the opportunity and asked him for lunch at the Phoenix. We had a meal and a bottle of wine and chatted generally about *Drum* matters and Jim, who was away on one of his trips to West Africa and London. Then, trying to be as diplomatic as possible, I got onto the topic of Anthony's temper and his angry outbursts at the office. A little more courtesy and politeness, I said, would go a long way with the team, who were all devoted to *Drum* and passionate about what the magazine stood for, but were taking strain working in a bad atmosphere.

Anthony looked astonished. He was completely unaware of how people felt. He was very upset and I began to feel sorry for him. He thanked me for informing him. Perhaps talking to him helped, I thought, because over the next little while his attitude towards the staff improved.

The issue of what to put on the *Drum* covers came up for discussion time and time again at editorial meetings. Jim was persistently in favour of 'girly' pictures, while others of us felt we needed a balance. Some covers, we felt, should rather illustrate lead stories or showcase a particular issue or the people we profiled.

For some months now I had been designing the covers together with Mr Janssens, a Belgian graphic designer, but we had a big problem when it came to quality. The old tabloid printing press we used was not able to print high-quality colour. Coupled with this there was an international shortage both of newsprint and high-quality paper. The black-and-white photos in the magazine had to be made on a 65 screen block, which gave you an extremely grainy picture almost without half-tones.

I had to jazz up the covers with lots of colour and a lively design. I usually cut out the black-and-white photo of the figure – the girl or the musician or whatever person or persons were to be on the cover – and made some sort of colourful design with the headlines of the stories inside. Everything was discussed with Mr Janssens, who was a very gentle, quiet person. He would then make up the four-colour design for the works to make the films for the plates. Mr Janssens left in late 1953 to return to his home country and I had to find another designer. This was a gentleman with the strange name of Mr Wigglesworth, and he and I worked on covers together for many years.

Jim's ongoing campaign to haul in as many girls as possible meant that the *Drum* office was always full of young women who wanted to become models. The job of sorting them out for possible cover pictures fell to me. Some girls were in their early teens and very shy and embarrassed, and many came from poor backgrounds and had no suitable clothes. Jim wanted lively, swinging, well-dressed successful African women – but, unfortunately, in 1952 they were few and far between. I didn't have the time or inclination to start a modelling school for *Drum*, so I depended solely on luck, trying out as many of the young girls as possible in front of the camera. After some desperately chaotic days I discovered a small selection of talented models for different covers. Some of these young women would eventually go on to become semi-professionals working as models in advertising.

The process gave me an idea, though. We had recently added a new member to our *Drum* crew. This was Mr Fairbanks and he was an experienced advertising manager. I asked him if he could contact one of the department stores that catered to Africans as well as whites and ask them if we could photograph and publish photos of their latest fashion ranges using African models. Everyone jumped at the idea and within a week we had the go-ahead.

I selected the Johannesburg Library as a location. It was a picturesque, grand colonial building in the centre of the city with an imposing stairway and a well-kept garden. I went to see the head librarian to ask her permission to use one of the library's storerooms for the girls to change in and to keep the dresses. She was a stern Afrikaans woman with a domineering manner. She wore a long skirt down to her ankles and a dark cardigan over a shirt with a black tie. She looked at me irritably and said, 'I am not having any native girls dressing in my library – it's against the law.'

'What law?' I asked, but she didn't reply.

She turned sharply away and began walking back towards the library counter. Then over her shoulder she said, 'No natives in my library.'

We arrived at the library in a kombi, which had been lent to us by the department store, packed with the models we'd selected for the shoot, dozens of dresses and a dress designer. My star model was top jazz singer Thandi Klaasen. She was a lively young woman with a slim figure and a sparkling energy about her. I started taking pictures with the models on the top of the library steps. A few moments in and I noticed that we were attracting an ever-increasing audience. Some of the whites watching made insulting remarks, one of which was

Anthony Sampson lending a hand

to call me a 'kaffirboetie'.

We had parked the kombi in the road next to the library and it wasn't long before we had traffic cops telling us we had to move it. They also told us we couldn't 'use a van for dressing and undressing purposes'. Then I saw the head librarian standing at the top of the steps, arms folded, looking angry. 'You are disturbing the peace and blocking the entrance to the library – you must leave or I will call the police!' she boomed.

Despite all of this intrusion, somehow I managed to shoot a set of pictures which, to my knowledge, was the first set of fashion pictures with African models produced in the Union of South Africa. These images were published in *Drum*.

22

TOO MANY MARTINIS

Early in 1953 the editorial judges, one of whom was Peter Abrahams, made the final decision on the winner of our short story competition – the first Drum Literary Short Story prize. The response had been overwhelming and over a thousand stories were submitted. Peter declared a story called 'Mob Passion' by Can Themba of Sophiatown to be the most promising literary work of all the entries.

Henry and I duly drove to Sophiatown to find Can Themba so that Henry could present him with the £50 winner's cheque. His address took us to a busy street in Sophiatown, and as we got out of the car a brass band came round the corner, leading a wedding party and followed by dozens of smiling, dancing children chanting 'Happy happy!' They in turn were followed by a small horsecart filled with youngsters with big smiles. I took quite a few pictures before we went to Can's house. The street was lined with typical family homes: red-brick houses fenced off from one another by low walls, each with an iron gate and short brick pathway to the front door, usually with small bushes and trees on either side.

On a stoep with a red polished floor we found a scholarly-looking man sitting in a dilapidated rocking chair. He was wearing horn-rimmed spectacles, a white well-ironed shirt and a conservative dark-blue tie. Can was surprised to see us and expressed great pleasure when Henry told him the good news.

Can was born in 1924 in a township in Pretoria and, after completing his schooling, had won a scholarship to study at Fort Hare. He graduated in 1947 with a first-class degree in English. Now he was a teacher at Madibane High School in the Western township.

I took a photo of Henry presenting the cheque to Can on the stoep and then asked him if I could take a picture in his room, which he rented from the family who lived in and owned the house. It was extremely tidy. There were bookshelves full of textbooks and literary magazines. On his desk books were piled one on top of the other, and there were papers and open textbooks. I asked him to sit behind his desk at the keyboard of his typewriter (a modern one, not the usual upright typewriter) and he happily obliged. He told me that most of the time he could only write after midnight because that was the only time it was quiet. He had to keep the windows open – especially in summer when it got very hot – and it was just too noisy to concentrate with children playing in the street, drunks shouting and performing, and loud music coming from the neighbourhood's radios.

One month later Jim offered Can a job as a reporter-journalist on *Drum*, which he immediately accepted. He gave notice at the high school and joined the staff.

Most of the *Drum* crew had shortened Anthony's name to Tony, so from now on I called him Tony too.

I had always loved jazz and I couldn't get enough of it. Apart from the live shows I got to see in various townships, I was a regular listener to David Macrae-Taylor's weekly radio programme. When it was abruptly cancelled one day, I went to see Tony in his office to ask if he knew why. I wondered whether it might have had something to do with David's previous two programmes, which had focused on black American jazz and black South African jazz. As far as I knew, this was the first time that the state-controlled South African Broadcasting Association (SABC) had devoted any time to local 'African' music.

Tony hadn't been aware of these two particular programmes, nor had David been in touch with him, he said, but he wanted to know what musicians David had featured. One of the American musicians, I told him, was Nat King Cole. David had told his listeners that Nat's recording of 'Straighten Up and Fly Right' in 1943 had gone gold, which meant that it had sold over a million copies. Then he had talked about Nat's latest, perhaps greatest, hit, 'Tenderly', which sold

Can Themba at his typewriter

over eight million copies. He had gone on to talk about South African musician Edmund 'Ntemi' Piliso and his tenor horn, and how Piliso had started a new group called the Alexandra All Star Band. He also talked about Thandi Klaasen, my library steps model, whose 'Cow Cow Boogie' had become legendary. When Thandi was jiving, jumping, snapping her fingers, clapping her hands and throwing her hips around, the house would scream for an encore – 'Again Cow Cow, Thandi! Again!' He said Thandi was now singing with the big band the Harlem Swingsters, with 'Gwigwi' Benjamin Mrwebi as the leader (he was often nicknamed the 'Alto Sax Maniac') and that they were currently on tour in Cape Town.

Tony was rather taken aback – 'This is amazing if he said all this on air' – and he suggested we pay David a visit. So later on Tony and I walked together to the apartment building where David lived. It was an old eight-storey early-twenties building in a narrow street next to Joubert Park. In the twenties this had been a very popular upmarket area for the younger liberal generation, singles and couples. By the time I arrived in Joburg in 1950, sadly these old buildings had become neglected and dilapidated. They would soon be pulled down to make way for more modern and larger buildings. Nineteenth-century buildings in Joburg had all but disappeared.

The lift in David's apartment block wasn't working, nor was there any light, so we walked up the staircase to the third floor. We knocked on David's door. There was no response but we could hear faint music coming from behind it. We banged harder and eventually we heard shuffling noises inside and the door opened slowly. In the dim light all we could make out was a strange-looking figure – one arm raised up in front of him.

'Oh hell, it's you two,' said David in his perfect English radio announcer's accent.

He led us into his room and sat down on the floor in his usual corner with the record player next to him and his speakers on either side blasting Count Basie. The floor was strewn with records and record covers and empty Coke bottles. There was an overflowing ashtray next to him and his usual bottle of gin plus some glasses.

'Sit!' David ordered, so we sat down on the floor, making ourselves a little more comfortable by using some scatter cushions that were also lying around.

We could now see why David's left arm had been up in the air when he opened the door to us. It was sticking out in front of him at shoulder height and covered in thick white plaster of paris. He had a white bandage on top of his bald head. Leaning against the wall with his legs stretched out on the floor, with all his bandaging, he looked rather freakish and grotesque, the image not helped by his teeth, which were dark and decayed.

Eventually we got the full story. After his recent radio programme, when he'd talked about African musicians, he was called in to see the management of the SABC. He was told in no uncertain terms that they didn't want to talk or report about Bantus or natives, who, they said, had their own newspapers. David should stick to white jazz – there were plenty of excellent European (by which they meant white) musicians in South Africa. David had argued with them, resulting in his programme being scrapped. He had gone out and drowned his anger in a nearby bar with a number of pink gins. When he got into his car to go home, he'd suddenly felt giddy and drove into a lamp-post in Eloff Street. Then he crashed into a parked delivery van and panicked. He got out of the car and ran as fast as he could. He ran for several blocks until he was tackled by some pedestrians and taken to a police station, where he was charged with drunken driving, disturbing the peace, and damage to public property. Then he was taken to hospital and plastered up. Now he was out on bail.

There wasn't much to say after that, so we listened to a few more numbers from David's latest jazz records, and after he fell asleep, we left.

One late afternoon Tony asked me to come with him to see Jim – 'We've got a picture of a lifetime for you!' he said.

Jim was sitting behind his desk and he gave me a friendly smile. 'Now look here,' he said. Then leaning across the desk and putting his face close to mine, he looked intensely and deeply into my eyes and, in a purposeful soft voice, said, 'Look into the eyes when death takes life.'

I thought Jim had gone nuts. I looked at Tony with a question mark on my face. When neither of them spoke, I said, 'I don't understand. Who is dying?'

'Anybody,' Tony replied.

I was still confused.

'Life passing out of a live body,' Tony said.

Tony and Jim exchanged meaningful looks, as if they had discovered the wheel or the steam engine or something. Slowly, I was getting it, but I couldn't quite believe what they were asking me to do. I said that maybe if it was some-one important under special circumstances, then it might make sense, but the whole suggestion was immoral and stupid. And you couldn't photograph life leaving a body. Then I got up and excused myself.

The next day Tony came up to my desk. 'Get your camera and let's go,' he said.

Thinking there must be an emergency, I grabbed my Leica and hurried after him. He was already starting his motorbike when I climbed onto the back seat. We roared off at high speed. I tried to ask Tony where we were going but he either would not or could not answer as we raced through the city in a southerly direction. Near to Orlando township we came to a busy road and finally, after a very hair-raising ride, Tony stopped in front of the gates of Baragwanath Hospital. 'Where do we find the head matron?' he asked the guard who approached us. 'We've got an appointment.'

The head matron was a large woman, stern and authoritarian in her matron's outfit. Tony started to tell her about *Drum* and its aims and then cut to the chase. 'Anyone dying in the next few hours in your hospital?' he asked in his best Oxford accent.

The matron looked at us. 'I don't understand your question,' she said. She had a slight Afrikaans accent.

Tony was happy to explain. 'Our photographer here, Jürgen, wants to get a picture of the facial expression, especially the eyes, when a person dies,' he said.

The head matron was furious. She glared at me in disgust. 'This is preposter-ous, young man!' she hissed. Then she pursed her lips angrily, got to her feet and pointed to the door. 'Get out!'

Neither of us said a word the whole way back to the office. The subject was never mentioned again.

South African Associated Newspapers' offices were at 176 Main Street. It was a big building with a large foyer. The group produced three newspapers

– the *Sunday Times*, the paper with the biggest circulation in South Africa, the *Rand Daily Mail*, the liberal Joburg morning paper, and the *Sunday Express*, a smaller tabloid paper. *Drum* had its own entrance in Polly Street, a narrow one-way street on the left side of the building. SAAN occupied the whole block up to Mooi Street to the right and Marshall Street at the back of the block, where the printing works was based. This was also where the newsprint was delivered and the final printed papers were collected for distribution.

There was a staff canteen in the building for whites only. The only black person in the canteen was 'Simon', but everyone referred to him as 'the tea boy'. Every day he pushed a trolley around the different departments, going from office to office and floor to floor. On it was a huge urn of hot tea, plus milk and sugar. The tea we drank was strong, white and very sweet. Simon always had a big smile for everyone. In the evening he served tea in the canteen. Sometimes when I had been working late in the darkroom and all the tearooms in the neighbourhood were closed, I went to the canteen for a cup of tea and a bacon sandwich. It always cheered me to see Simon there with his friendly smile.

The canteen was a busy place, with lots of people coming and going, reporters, subs and staff from the printing works and various other departments. A number of times a woman came and joined me at my table. I noticed that she dressed well, usually in a pleated skirt, a colourful blouse, high-heeled shoes and a bright-red silk scarf around her neck. One day we got talking and she told me that she was the editor's secretary at the *Sunday Express*. She spoke with an Afrikaans accent and she was a heavy smoker. The cigarette butts she put out in the ashtray were always red from her lipstick. Her name was Gertrude. Sometimes she tried to converse with me in fairly broken German – her grandfather was German. Gertrude was at least ten years older than me, which made me slightly uneasy.

One evening I was sitting in the canteen drinking my tea and worrying about my schedule for the next issue, which had to be delivered to the printer the next morning – Deborah Duncan, who usually typed it up for me, was on holiday – when Gertrude sat down beside me.

'What's the matter, Jürgy?' she said. 'You look down in the dumps.'

I told her about my problem: that the printing works urgently needed the schedule to make up the pages for the print run and I needed some typing help.

Gertrude drained her cup and got up. 'Come on, my boy. I'll look after you. Let's go to your office – I've always wanted to see the *Drum* office.'

The editorial room was deserted – all the staff had left for the day – and in no time at all Gertrude had typed the pages I had written out in longhand with my somewhat defective spelling. As we were making some copies on the copy machine, I suddenly got a strong whiff of Gertrude's perfume close up. She was touching my rear. Things moved quickly after that. She pulled me over with wild excitement and somehow we ended up rolling around on the office floor. When the phone on one of the desks suddenly rang, I got up to answer it. Gertrude stood up, straightened her clothes, took her lipstick and a small mirror out of her handbag and began painting her lips.

'Thank you, Jürgy, that was nice,' she said, when I put down the receiver. 'I must introduce you to my niece. She'll be at a party tomorrow night – she's nineteen and an actress in a play and it's their wrap party. You'll love her!'

She put her lipstick back in her bag, gave me a quick kiss, put her stilettos back on and walked to the door. 'See you tomorrow at 7.30,' she said. 'Totsiens!'

The following evening Gertrude and I met at the office and walked to the Carlton Hotel on the corner of Eloff and Commissioner Streets. We went through the foyer to a spacious reception room with a large sign outside in Afrikaans, which I didn't understand. The reception room was full of self-conscious-looking people. Everyone was speaking Afrikaans but they looked different from the Afrikaans people I had come across so far – the women more dressy and elegant in evening dresses and high-heeled shoes and most of the men in dark suits and ties. Some looked quite prosperous, but others were more bohemian-looking in corduroy jackets and silk scarf neckties. Everyone had a drink in one hand and a cigarette in the other.

A couple of black waiters with white gloves went from group to group offering drinks on trays. I grabbed a glass off a passing tray and gulped it down rather quickly, which made me almost choke. Gertrude was standing behind me, and as I turned round she laughed. 'You must be careful – these martinis are laced with lots of vodka,' she said.

Suddenly a high-pitched laugh came from the back of the room. 'That's

Etricia!' Gertrude said. She took my hand and pulled me through the crowd to the end of the room. There, surrounded by men, stood a beautiful young woman, laughing and joking with them. When she noticed Gertrude she gave her a big smile and waved. As we approached she gave me a long, intense and distinctly coquettish look. I was instantly bowled over. No woman had ever looked at me so deeply and meaningfully.

'Etricia, this is Jürgen, the German I told you about,' said Gertrude.

Somehow I suddenly became very daring. I took the empty glass out of Etricia's hand and said, 'Let me get you another drink.' I had to get away from that look – I didn't know what it meant. I found the nearest waiter and took his tray, loaded with full glasses, and offered drinks to both Etricia and Gertrude. Then I took one for myself, before handing the tray to one of the young men standing next to Etricia. Moments later, with all the martinis in my head and dazzled by the smouldering looks Etricia kept giving me, I began to feel somewhat befuddled. A lot of things were running through my head – the movie with Ava Gardner, who had that same sort of look, the Bette Davis look, myself at the Berlin scene when I had to go on parade and wore red socks and my mother's colourful silk blouse and the Hauptjungzugführer went red in the face, shouting at me when I put on my Buster Keaton face, which I had rehearsed for that occasion. Now, in my intoxicated state, I did my deadpan Humphrey Bogart. This succeeded in putting off Etricia's two young men, who excused themselves and beat a hasty retreat. I then switched to Marlon Brando (I had recently seen *A Streetcar Named Desire*), which, I noticed, worked better with Etricia than Bogart. Etricia kept smiling and looking at me with that special, hungry look. Brando reciprocated. Then he grasped her by the hand, put his hand around her slim waist and pulled her through the partygoers, Gertrude trotting along behind in her high-heeled shoes. In the foyer he scooped Etricia up into his arms and strode out of the hotel.

There was a line of taxis waiting at the entrance, and Gertrude signalled to one of them.

In the cold night air Brando began to falter slightly. Then suddenly he was gone and it was just Jürgen there on the pavement, trying to put a tipsy girl on her feet, seeing her legs buckle under her, and quickly picking her up again.

Gertrude helped me put Etricia into the taxi and, as I was climbing in with her, she pushed me out. 'I'll take her home. Too many martinis,' she said. 'See you tomorrow!' And off they went, disappearing down Eloff Street into the traffic, leaving me standing on the pavement in a dazed state. Brando was nowhere to be seen.

Next morning, with a thumping headache, I arrived late to the monthly *Drum* editorial meeting. There were several newcomers. Can Themba, wearing a tie and looking like a very respectable schoolteacher, was talking about the transport system for black people. He spoke in a very educated and knowledgeable way. This, of course, pleased Jim and Tony, who kept up a long intellectual conversation with Can, leaving the rest of us behind. Also there was 'Gwigwi' Mrwebi, the famous 'Alto Sax Maniac', who was to be in charge of circulation; Sy Mogapi, who was going to work with Arthur Maimane on sports stories; David Sibeko, our new man on the switchboard, a very talkative, humorous character; and Dan Chocho, who was to take care of the office.

The *Drum* photographic department was increasing in size. Apart from Bob Gosani, who was doing very well, taking some outstanding pictures and covering some good stories, my new darkroom assistant, Victor Xashimba, was also doing well, learning the basics of developing film and making enlargements. Soon Victor was taking care of the darkroom and we got a new recruit, Sydney Andrews, who started working with him.

Arthur was writing a new series for *Drum* featuring a private eye called 'The Chief', in the style of Peter Cheney and Raymond Chandler, which I illustrated with photographs, using a professional actor who looked tough, smart and in control. Arthur completely looked the part and was a sharp dresser himself. When he sat down at his typewriter, with a cigarette hanging from his lips and his hat on the back of his head, he looked just like a black version of Raymond Chandler.

We had begun to publish short stories in the magazine regularly now. This included a story by a writer named Bloke Modisane, which we needed to illustrate.

By chance, a while back I had been invited to a party one evening at the home of a local artist by the name of Bill Papas and his wife Aroon. Bill was of

Greek origin and this bohemian couple lived in an old farmhouse near Gillooly's Farm on the road to the airport. Bill was a clever and original illustrator. Using nervous strokes, which gave a strong sense of movement, he produced fascinating and unusual pen drawings – perfect, I thought, to illustrate *Drum*'s short stories. He was very keen to try and so I began to drop by regularly, taking him stories to illustrate. Out came the rum and Coke, Bill's favourite drink, while we sat, often for hours, going through the text to find the most appropriate part to illustrate. Of course, the rum and Coke helped the creative juices flow.

After my silly performance at Etricia's theatre party, which left me feeling very embarrassed, I swore to myself never to drink martinis again. But Etricia had been on my mind all of the next day and finally I got up the courage to go to the *Sunday Express* office to see Gertrude and ask how I could get in touch with her. Gertrude was sitting at her typewriter in a little office next to the editor's office. She looked up at me and gave me a big smile. 'There is our heroic knight! Etricia is very impressed. You rescued her before she passed out,' she said.

'I didn't know that she was going to pass out,' I said.

'Well, she did, Jürgy,' she laughed.

Gertrude told me Etricia was on tour with the theatre company and she thought they were performing in Krugersdorp for the next few nights. And so the following evening I drove to Krugersdorp to see Etricia at the theatre. Krugersdorp was west of Johannesburg and about a 45-minute drive. Eventually I found the little theatre, a former cinema, in Commissioner Street next to the town hall. I got there late and the performance had already started. I found a seat at the back of the auditorium, which smelt of stale tobacco and dust. On stage the set was that of a typical provincial lounge and three actors were in mid-scene. The play was in Afrikaans so I couldn't understand a word, but I got that they were having an argument and shouting for someone who seemed to be off stage. Later Etricia came on stage in an evening dress. She appeared to be very upset and looked angrily at the older man, who was dressed in uniform, who then hit the other man. The performance seemed to me to be very amateurish and I found my attention wandering. As my eyes adjusted to the light, I looked around the theatre and saw that it was less than half full – which didn't surprise me. In fact, I noticed one or two couples quietly tiptoeing out through the side door. After the show I went backstage to look for Etricia, who was very pleased to see me. I invited her for a drink.

We found a ladies' bar in a hotel not far from the theatre and sat in a corner. The place was very noisy and full of drunks trying to sing an Afrikaans song – they were totally off key. 'Let's go somewhere else,' I said.

Although it was only 9pm the town was deserted. No traffic, not a soul around, and there were no open bars or restaurants that we could find. So we sat in my Beetle talking for a while and shared something of our backgrounds. Etricia told me she never knew her father, who she thought was German, and that her mother had passed away some years back. Her uncle, who ran an Afrikaans literary group, had adopted her. Later I drove Etricia home, dropping her off at her uncle's house, which was in one of Johannesburg's northern suburbs. We arranged to meet again at the theatre in Roodepoort, where the play would be staged the following week.

One day I received a call from Father Trevor Huddleston, who asked me if I would take some pictures of his Church of Christ the King in Sophiatown. He had received a trumpet from Louis Armstrong – Satchmo himself! – and had arranged for it to be handed over to one of his students, who was also a member of his St Peter's Huddleston Jazz Band. He wanted me to take some pictures of the occasion. The student's name was Hugh Masekela.

It was early evening and I needed someone to help hold the floodlights since I hated using flashlights, which were still very unreliable with the Leica shutter. As there were very few people left in the office at that time of the day, I asked Deborah to come with me to help set up the picture. There were four of Hugh's friends there, also members of the band, and everyone was very excited when young Hugh opened the case and gently took out the trumpet. He held it up and studied it, his eyes shining. When he brought the instrument to his mouth and blew a tune, it was a magical moment. Deborah held the floodlight and I was shooting away to make a sequence of this extraordinary event.

I thought a lot about Etricia and her unfortunate family history, and I hoped that I might meet her uncle some day. The following week I drove to Roodepoort, not far from Joburg, to see her, but this time I didn't sit through the whole performance again. I waited in a nearby bar until the show was over.

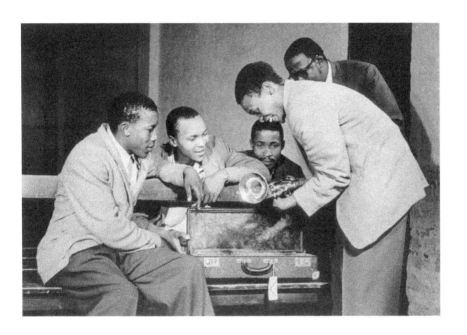

Hugh Masekela with the trumpet given to him by Louis Armstrong

The smoke-filled bar was full of middle-aged men in farmers' floppy hats and well-worn sports jackets sitting on bar stools in front of their drinks and staring into space. The barman, a small bald man, stood in the corner behind the bar, and whenever one of the characters gave him a sign he would take a bottle from behind the counter, open it, and skilfully slide it along the bar counter until it came to a stop directly in front of the customer. He must have had a lot of practice.

Suddenly the door opened and everyone in the bar looked round. Etricia came through the door smiling at me. I must say I was happy to see her as I was about to leave the depressing bar and wait for her outside. We got in my car and headed home to her uncle's place. On the way there Etricia talked a lot about how unhappy she was about the play but how she had to continue the tour for another three weeks. Maybe afterwards, she said, we would have more time for each other. So I dropped her off at her uncle's home and we arranged to meet again – this time in Springs, 50 kilometres east of Joburg, where the show would be performed the following week. For the next three weeks I drove from town to town on the outskirts of Johannesburg, picking Etricia up after the performance and taking her home.

One morning we got some information about a problem in Newclare township, just to the west of Joburg, so I jumped into my car and drove straight there. A railway line ran through the middle of the township. North of the line lived a mixed community of black South Africans and south of it the community was mainly a migrant one, mostly Basutos from Lesotho. Nearly all of the men in this migrant community came to Johannesburg to work on the mines. The Basutos were heavily armed and could often be seen carrying machetes, menacing-looking axes and pointed spears. The residents on the northern side of the railway line had formed a group calling themselves the Civil Guard to protect themselves from 'the Russians', the Basuto group they claimed was responsible for attacking and murdering residents on their side of the tracks. The conflict between the two groups had now escalated to clashes and bloody fights.

That day there was a heavy police presence on the bridge dividing the two groups who were assembling on either side shouting insults at each other, waving their weapons and uttering war cries. When it began to grow dark, the two groups slowly retired into the streets of their respective areas. I drove around for a while and ended up on a side road on the Civil Guard right side, where I bought myself a Coke in a nearby store. I sat drinking it in the car, waiting to see if something was going to happen.

I woke up as the sun was rising, feeling cramped and uncomfortable after an uneasy sleep in my small Beetle, to see what looked like hundreds of very agitated people running past, waving sticks and assegais and pikes. Hurriedly, I got behind the wheel, started the engine and followed them. As they ran along the railway line leaving the built-up area and onto the dirt roads, I took some pictures. After a few hundred metres they began climbing over the fences and crossing the rails – many of the men had already clambered onto the opposite bank. I turned back towards the bridge, which was still guarded by policemen, crossed over it and drove to the road on the other side, where a group of Civil Guard men and some women were crossing from the north. I was now on a road between the open fields with, to my right, the heavily armed Civil Guards still crossing the railway line, climbing over the fences and slowly surging across the fields towards where I was parked. Coming towards me on my left was a large group of Russians tightly bunched together, wearing blankets, brandishing their spears and machetes, and stamping their feet on the ground. Realising that I was about to be in the middle of a clash between two rival aggressive gangs, I thought perhaps I should have said something to the police on the bridge. The two groups were converging on me, moving ever closer, each group making threatening noises and doing their best to intimidate the other, jumping up and down and shouting war cries. I stood in the road, hanging on tightly to my Leica, feeling the tension.

Just as it looked as if the two groups were about to charge at each other, a truck came up the road loaded with armed police, who jumped off and made up a line along the road facing the groups. Then another truck arrived, also loaded with police. Slowly, and to my immense relief, the two groups began to retreat to their respective positions.

As I was about to drive off in my car, an officer came up to me and claimed it was all my fault! He told me my presence had encouraged the Civil Guard to cross the railway line. I had better watch out, he said, or he would have to arrest me.

Later on I photographed the Russians holding a meeting of some 300 men, all wearing blankets and waving weapons, while one of the leaders gave a long speech in Sesotho. Every time he made a point, the crowd got up and cheered and shouted. One of the police trucks had parked nearby and a police officer, followed by two of his men, approached the menacing group. He spoke to the leader in Afrikaans. When he finished, the whole group of Russians got to their feet brandishing their spears and machetes and shouting war cries. The officer and his two men ran back to their truck at high speed. I was left on my own standing in the middle of this group, taking pictures. Gradually the crowd began to relax and settle down. Then some of these characters wanted me to take their pictures, which I was happy to do. In this rather volatile atmosphere they took time out to pose for the camera while I snapped away furiously.

I spent the rest of the day driving around the area to see if anything was going to happen, when unexpectedly I saw Tony on his motorbike. He was on the bridge talking to a policeman. When he spotted me, he drove up to me on his bike and said with a worried look, 'Are you okay?'

'I couldn't be better,' I replied. 'Why?'

He told me that people at the office thought I had got involved in the battle with the Russians, and as nobody had heard from me since yesterday ... Then, before I could respond, he asked if I had got any 'smashing pictures'. He parked his bike and joined me in my car and we drove to a nearby white suburb where we had some tea in a Greek tearoom. I ordered a ham and tomato sandwich, but after the first bite I just couldn't swallow. I realised I hadn't slept properly for 24 hours and was too hyped-up to eat anything.

After I told Tony what I had seen and what pictures I had taken, he suggested I stay on and wait for any new developments. He would go back to the office to develop the film and write the story.

As was usually the case when a significant and important happening in the 'non-white' world took place, no white newspaper or news agency was cover-ing the story, so we thought it might well make a good story for *Drum*. Tony took off on his motorbike while I continued to drive around Newclare township looking for action. I took many pictures of people in the street going about their normal business. However, whether this was shopping or working in a motor repair shop, I saw that all of them carried weapons or had them close by and there was a feeling of high tension in the air. I noticed this on both sides of the opposing groups … and the police were standing by hanging, onto their guns.

Except for a few clashes, nothing much happened that night, so the next morning I drove back to the city. First I went home and had a shower and then I went to the office. The films had been developed and I got busy making a set of prints to send to London for the *Illustrated London News*, with which I had previously worked and to which I'd sold a number of photographs. I then made a layout for *Drum*, including a cover, of the Newclare–Russian War.

One morning as I sat down at my desk Henry came up to me. He showed me a letter and asked me what I thought about it. It was an anonymous letter addressed to 'Henry Nxumalo – Mr Drum' and signed 'George'. There was a phone number on the letter, which showed the exchange of a town called Koster, about 112 kilometres north-west of Joburg. The writer said he was a journalist who worked for the 'Argus group' as a stringer in the Rustenburg district, mostly covering court cases. He wanted assurance that this letter would be treated with great confidentiality. He also mentioned that he suffered from a severe case of polio.

'George' said had been collecting information about extremely violent cases of white farmers seriously mistreating African labourers in the Rustenburg district. There was a court case pending against the owner of a farm called Harmonie, one Johan Snyman, who was a wealthy, religious and respected member of the community. Snyman had previously been convicted of assaulting his labourers but had got away with fines. Another case had been brought against Snyman's son and his foreman, Jantjie Tlhamo, who were accused of whipping to death a labourer named Elias Mpikwa.

George also had information of other cases of assault and murder by white farmers of their black labourers in the district – he had a complete file. One such farmer was Pieter Breedt, who had beaten an African labourer to death. George had written to Henry because he had seen the story Henry had written about Bethal farm conditions in a 1952 issue of *Drum*; he thought *Drum* was his last chance for getting the facts about these murders into the open. He had tried many times to get the story into the papers of the Argus group but his reports had been ignored. If Henry was interested in following up this story, he should phone him.

Henry and I took the letter to Jim and Tony. It was decided that we should go to Koster and meet with George, and while Henry got some more information about the small town, I could look around the Rustenburg district, locate the Snyman farm and hopefully take some pictures. Jim suggested that I take along some magazines about birds in the north-west Transvaal. Early the next morning we arrived in Koster and eventually found George's house. It was a strange moment. He was encased up to his neck in an iron lung and we had to talk to him via a wide mirror which reflected his face. He told us that his condition meant that he spent half the day in this contraption but he was still able to continue his research work. He gave us a file containing all the relevant court notes as well as some newspaper cuttings. Johan Snyman, he said, had been refused bail so he was still in jail, but his son and the foreman had been released on bail and were back on the farm. Another case some months back, details of which were also in the file, was that of the two Gouws brothers, who were found guilty in the Rustenburg court of assaulting a farmworker, Joseph Mokwatsi, with a sjambok and jumping on his head with their boots. They had broken the man's neck.

As we'd agreed, Henry remained in Koster to look around for more information and I went to Harmonie farm. I drove up the dirt road to the homestead, parked, and walked up the steps onto the stoep. I stood at the door armed with my books about birds in the Northern Transvaal ... and my camera.

A small woman appeared and looked at me suspiciously through the screen. 'What do you want?' she said, in Afrikaans.

Putting on my best, strongest German accent, I introduced myself as a bird watcher who was keen to photograph birds in the area to add to my collection. Just then a heavy-set young man in a khaki shirt and shorts came up behind her. 'What the hell do you want to photograph birds for, man?' he asked me, in English but with a strong Afrikaans accent. I explained that I was working on a book on wildlife and birds in the north-west Transvaal.

'There's a lake about three miles north where there are lots of birds breeding,' he said after a minute. 'You can go there if you stay on that road.' He pointed in the direction of the road behind the farm building. They seemed to believe my story, so I asked them if I could take a picture of them in front of their farmhouse and they readily agreed.

As I drove along the road I took some pictures of Africans working on the land and also of the 'boss boy' – Jantjie, I thought – who posed for me with his sjambok over his shoulder. Then I thought I'd better leave before they got suspicious, so I drove back to Koster to meet Henry. I found him dressed in rags and barefoot, carrying a bundle over his shoulder. He grinned at me and told me he'd collected enough information. Now he was ready to go and get a job on Snyman's farm – could I drop him at the farm gate? I told him I thought the assignment was too dangerous. I also pointed out that, in reality, they could well kill him. But Henry said he had spoken to Tony on the phone, who agreed that he should go ahead. With great reluctance I drove back to the farm and dropped Henry at the Snymans' gate. I watched him walk off with his bundle over his shoulder.

I drove back to Joburg and anxiously waited for Henry's call, which came through from Koster five days later. I went and picked Henry up. He was quite shaken. Snyman's son had torn up his pass and kicked him hard in the back several times. He had had to work from 5am till 7pm, weeding in between the mealie plants. In the evening the labourers got half-cooked porridge with a little milk and half a cup of brown sugar – this to be shared among eighteen men. They had to sleep on a bare concrete floor with only a few mealie sacks for covers. Henry was also sworn at by Jantjie for working too slowly. I could see he was exhausted. His hands were torn and sore and he had a painful back.

Back in the *Drum* office, after Henry had written his story and I had developed my photos, Jim decided that we should hold the story for the following year for *Drum*'s birthday issue in March 1954. In any event the case was still pending and he said we should wait for the verdict.

A few days later I drove to Springs, the last satellite town along the Reef east of Joburg, to pick up Etricia from the theatre. It was late and the play had finished when I arrived at the stage door, where I found Etricia waiting for me.

She jumped into the car.

'You're late,' she said in a sulky, moody tone.

'I'm sorry, I was working late,' I replied.

'I had arranged for you to meet my uncle,' she said.

Janho was a large man with short grey hair and a round, protruding stomach, who shook my hand vigorously. 'Welcome – welcome, young man,' he said. He spoke English with a heavy Afrikaans accent. He led the way inside, through the living room which, I noticed, was bare, as though no one lived there, except for a couple of items of obviously new furniture. As we walked towards the back door, I overheard him say softly to his niece: 'Jy het 'n goeie een ge-catch.' My Afrikaans may not have been good but I knew what he was saying. Through the back door, there was a small lawned garden and a large square building, light-red in colour. Jan pointed at it. 'This is our new Afrikaans Literary Centre,' he said proudly.

Basically, it was a hall, divided into a sort of living room, which had a large green carpet on the floor and some armchairs, a green settee and a rocking chair. The chair was rocking. I looked closer and could just discern a small person in a colourful but worn outfit and an old floppy hat, so you could hardly see his face. 'That's old Dawie, my cousin, he's our driver,' said Janho. Dawie didn't look up, just continued to rock. There were lots of brand-new-looking children's toys all over the floor – a fire engine, a tricycle, some wooden building blocks – and a small blond-haired boy sitting playing with them. Next to him was a grey-haired elderly lady in a floral-print dress. She was tiny compared with Janho.

'Meet Saartjie, my wife,' Janho said and then, pointing at the boy on the floor, he added, 'and we have just adopted Hanno.'

I smiled at everyone.

'Here is Jürgen,' Janho continued, 'Etricia's new friend she has talked so much about.' He led us round the furniture and we climbed over the toys into the second half of the hall. Here there were a few rows of benches and chairs facing a small platform on which was a stand with a microphone and some half-a-dozen chairs. 'And this is where we meet to read and discuss Afrikaans literature. I am going to England soon to see Winston Churchill.'

'Oh, that's interesting,' I said, rather surprised and wondering what Churchill might have to do with Afrikaans literature. I was none the wiser after Janho explained. He stepped onto the platform and turned to face us. Adopting a stately pose and using what I can only describe as a regal tone, he announced: 'We, the South African Literary Society, have spent many hours deciding on a deserving recipient for our annual literary prize and have chosen to give our £100 prize to Mr Churchill for all his literary works ... and I will personally donate it to him. You might know that Mr Churchill spent some time in South Africa when he was a young man.'

Janho then stepped down from the platform and, with his tiny wife, Saartjie, on his arm, led us back into the furnished part of the hall. As we followed he turned around and said: 'And Saartjie got her gift from me – the beautiful boy Hanno.'

Tea was served to us by Saartjie. She was very quiet – in fact, she never said a word – and I presumed it was because she didn't speak any English. During our conversation I decided it might be wisest not to talk about my work on *Drum* or anything related to the racial problem in South Africa. As had happened so often in South Africa when I met white male Afrikaners, Etricia's uncle told me how much he admired the Germans and how sad it was that they had lost the war. He was of the opinion that the whole world had conspired against them.

In the car on the way home I asked Etricia how her uncle got all this money to afford all the new furniture and toys that were in evidence. 'Oh, he gets it from department stores on appro,' she said nonchalantly. 'He keeps the stuff for a few months and then has it returned. And then he goes to another department store for another appro order.'

Etricia and I had taken to kissing passionately in my car. When I suggested we might take things further, she was very clear. 'I won't sleep with anyone before I get married,' she said.

Drum was doing a story on 'Who's Who in the African National Congress?' While I was doing the layout, every inch of space on my desk covered with photos of politicians, Ian Berry turned up unexpectedly one day. 'Hey, lad, what are you up to?' he asked. He looked his usual dandy self with his neatly trimmed beard, silk scarf around his neck under his shirt collar, neat sand-coloured corduroy trousers, a sports jacket, and suede shoes. Two rangefinder Nikon cameras were slung over his shoulder. He walked around the desk and looked over my shoulder at the assembled mass of photos.

'Who are these characters?' he asked in an inquisitive tone.

'ANC,' I replied, getting to my feet. 'Let's have some tea.'

We went to the canteen and Ian filled me in. He had taken Bob Crisp up on his offer, but *Egoli* had closed down and now he was freelancing. He was keen to know what stories we were working on and asked if he could come along on some stories from time to time.

When I got back to the office, David was sitting at the switchboard. 'Hey man,' he called out to me, 'the old man wants to see you.'

Jim had just returned from another of his trips. In London, he told me he had met Tom Hopkinson, who had been the editor of *Picture Post* from 1940 to 1950, and Tom had been very interested in *Drum*. He had agreed to give us a monthly crit of the magazine. Jim asked me to get in touch with him and arrange for copies of *Drum* to be sent to him, along with any ideas and problems I might have relating to layout and production.

Picture Post was considered to be a pioneering example of photojournalism at its best, at one time selling over 2 million copies weekly. It had campaigned loudly against the persecution of Jews in Nazi Germany. A picture story entitled 'Back to the Middle Ages' featured photos of Hitler, Goebbels and Göring juxtaposed with photos of Einstein, Thomas Mann and writers, scientists and actors who had either been murdered in concentration camps or had managed to escape to the United Kingdom or the United States before and during the war. One of the escaped journalists was Stefan Lorant, who had pioneered the picture story for the *Berliner Illustrierte* and the *Münchner Illustrierte* in the late twenties, and who wrote the best-selling book *I Was Hitler's Prisoner*. He had to leave Germany when the Nazis closed down the magazine and persecuted many of the journalists. He fled to Britain and founded *Lilliput* and then *Picture Post*. By 1940 he feared the invasion of Britain and fled to the United States. *Picture Post* became the most important and successful propaganda medium for the Battle of Britain.

When Jim and I were finished talking, as I was leaving he told me he was giving a small party that night on his farm in Lanseria. He said I should come – 'We can have a lot of fun!' Then he called after me: 'Bring Can and Henry!'

When I told Henry and Can about the invitation they were surprised, but not over-enthusiastic. Both said they had other arrangements for that evening. I decided to go anyway and drove on my own to Lanseria. I had been to Jim's place out there, Monaghan Farm, once before. Once you were on the property you still had to drive about a mile along a rough, narrow path until you came to the Crocodile River, which hopefully was dried up, then go across a concrete ditch over the river bed and up to Jim's farmhouse.

Inside the house was a room with a wooden table and some chairs, a large open fire, an old couch past its prime and a couple of worn armchairs. This was where I found Jim. He was sitting on the couch with a young girl beside him. She was playing the violin (or rather making scratchy sounds on it) and both of them kept dissolving in fits of laughter, shrieking with hilarity. I sat down on a chair next to the table while the two of them continued fooling around, laughing their heads off. Every time the girl managed to get a few bars out of a couple of recognisable tunes, Jim would snatch the instrument from her and send the bow screeching across the strings. I sat quietly watching the pair's antics when Jim suddenly noticed me. 'Oh, how are you, old boy?' he cried. Pointing at me with the bow, he said, 'This is Jürgen.' Then pointing at the girl next to him – 'And this is Barbara Epstein, the great violin maestro.' Barbara seemed very young to me – I thought she looked about fourteen – but what I found fascinating was that she mimicked perfectly Jim's movements and his laugh. What was more, she talked just like Jim too. Looking at me with her dark eyes, she asked if I could play the violin. I said I didn't play any musical instrument, nor could I sing.

'Why not try?' she said, holding the violin out to me, while I smiled and shook my head. 'See how well Jim plays!' This was followed by more shrieks of laughter from both of them.

Looking around the poorly lit room, which was illuminated only with a paraffin lamp, Jim asked, 'Where are the boys?'

'I am sorry, Jim, they are otherwise engaged,' I said.

'What a bore,' Jim said, making his usual grimace of disappointment and annoyance. He turned back to Barbara. 'I would have been delighted if you had met Can Themba. He's our African intellectual … what minds and characters we have on *Drum*.' Then he looked at me with a meaningful smile. 'Now look here, Jürgen, let's make you a cardinal …'

'Oh, smashing, Jim, let's!' said Barbara excitedly, getting up to the table and passing the brandy bottle and a glass to me. 'Let us Puff him!'

When she stood up, it struck me how small Barbara was. Her hair was cut very short, which made her look even more like a tomboy.

'I am already a cardinal, don't you remember?' I said to Jim.

From outside, the sudden loud sound of a motorbike coming up the hill intruded on the moment and, to my relief, diverted Jim and Barbara from the drinking game. To be honest, I was getting tired of the heavy drinking culture at *Drum* and in the country generally. I enjoyed the occasional glass of beer or wine and will admit that a few times in my short adult life I had been terribly drunk, to the extent that I forgot what happened before I passed out. But I also suffered from severe hangovers, and after one of these heavy drinking bouts I always felt nauseous for three or four days.

Actually, I had observed that many of the writers in the *Drum* office had got into the habit of taking long breaks, from which they returned in a jollier mood, making jokes and teasing one another. The aroma of alcohol mixed with tobacco was constantly in the air, giving the place a party atmosphere.

Jim looked expectantly towards the door and Tony, followed by Jackie Heyns, came in. They had met up at Andy's printing works where the ANC's new pamphlets had just been printed announcing the forthcoming meeting in Kliptown to herald the creation of the Freedom Charter.

When everyone settled down and had drinks in their hands, Barbara announced that Jim was a maestro on the violin and instructed everybody to listen to his creative musical talent. Chortling happily, Jim picked up the instrument again and scratching, high-pitched, grating noises filled the room once more, while Barbara screeched and shrieked, which in turn produced hilarious laughter from Tony and Jackie.

Eventually Jim stopped playing and the conversation picked up. It became more serious as Jim talked about the future of *Drum* becoming the leading news medium in all of Africa, with the bonus of great literary input by such writers

The Drum *office*

as Can Themba. When I pointed out the obvious, namely that half of Africa was either French- or Portuguese-speaking, everybody went quiet for a moment and looked at me as though I was off my rocker. Then, 'Never mind,' said Jim. 'They will all speak and read English soon enough.'

I was continually fascinated by how isolated people in South Africa were from the rest of the world. Nobody here, for example, ever talked about the Cold War or the Korean War or about what was going on in Europe or the United States. Anyway, I thought I'd better take my leave as the next day was going to be a busy one for me at the *Drum* office. In fact, I left without anyone noticing. They were too busy pouring drinks and clowning around with the violin again.

Later that week I met Etricia and we sat talking in my Beetle, parked outside her uncle's house. Etricia was beginning to think about her future. She was tired of acting, she said, because it was too limiting for her. Also there was too much travelling and she had to work with some unpleasant people who had no talent. She decided she was going to be a concert pianist and had been taking some piano lessons. She could already play some Chopin and other classical pieces. I thought this change of direction was a good idea, as I had heard her singing and thought she must have a musical talent. With no parents and dependent on a crackpot uncle, I felt moved by Etricia's dilemma.

Two weeks later we were married at the Joburg Magistrate's Court and Etricia moved into my one-and-a-half-roomed flat.

In order to give Can Themba an opportunity to use his talent better, Jim and Tony decided to start a new magazine, small in size (7 x 10 inch) and 60 pages in length, using the overflow material from *Drum*. Can would be the editor. Can was delighted. He brought in one of his former students, Casey Motsisi, as his assistant. They decided to call the magazine *Africa!*

Karabo Moses Casey 'the Kid' Motsisi got his nickname from Stan Motjuwadi. They had grown up together, gone to school together at Madibane High and had both sold sweets on trains to get extra pocket money. Later Stan would also work for *Drum* publications. Can had been Casey's English teacher at Normal College in Pretoria, where Casey edited the college magazine.

Casey was a man of slim build and he had an innocent, kindly face, and always a twinkle in his eye. With his signature witty and humorous touch, he started to write columns for the new magazine as well as for *Drum*. He was the black Damon Runyon. His first column was 'Bugs' and later he wrote 'On the Beat', which was about Joburg's shebeen life. He became known as the Shakespeare of the shebeens. 'No nooze is good nooze, but no booze is sad nooze indeed!' Casey described Sis Fatty, queen of the Back o' the Moon shebeen, 'heaving her massive frame in that infectious giggle of hers', and he wrote about many of the other famous booze joints of the time in his column: 'Falling Leaves', 'The Church', 'The Classic', 'The White House' and 'The 39 Steps'.

'I don't go out for my columns,' he always said, 'my columns come to me.'

Africa! was a monthly covering a range of topics. Regular features were sports by Sy Mogapi, 'Mrs Dube's Diary', which dealt with relationship problems, intended to appeal to housewives, crime stories by Henry Nxumalo, some short stories, a series by United States writer Langston Hughes, and Arthur Maimane's detective stories, which he wrote under the pen name Arthur Mogale. The magazine was poorly designed, printed on flimsy newsprint, and cluttered with *Drum*'s overflow photos, but it became very popular.

Around that time people were raving about a book called *Knock on Any Door* by an American writer named William Motley, which had come out in 1947. The book contained the quote 'Live fast, die young and become a good looking corpse'. This became a catch-phrase for the *Drum* crew.

The arrival at *Drum* of Can Themba and Casey Motsisi resulted in a more light-hearted atmosphere around the office, and there was plenty of laughter and joking … and more drinking.

We had received some disturbing reports from former prisoners who had been incarcerated at the Fort, the notorious Johannesburg prison, which we felt needed further investigation. The conditions in the prison sounded alarming, with reports of brutal beatings and even murders.

A while back I had set about finding out how to take pictures with a hidden camera. After some enquiries I discovered a camera made in Germany called Robot. It was half the size of a Leica and had a clockwork motor which you wound up – similar to the winding system for the action news film camera. The Robot took the normal 35 mm film with a square format and you had 50 frames in the normal 35 mm cassette. When you wound up the spring system you had 25 frames and the film wound onto the next frame automatically. The camera had a 40 mm f2 lens so you could pre-set the distance and hide the camera in your clothes and, using a cable release, expose frame after frame. You could also conceal the camera inside something – for example, in a loaf of bread, a book or a milk carton. The Robot became our secret camera to expose situations such as police brutality or criminal activities where no cameras were allowed.

I tried to investigate how to get our Robot camera into the Fort, but it seemed impossible. After a number of meetings with Henry and Tony, Henry offered a solution: he would get into the Fort as a prisoner. He thought that if he could get arrested for being in possession of liquor, he wouldn't receive a long sentence – maybe no more than two weeks – which would be enough to get a story. I said I thought it would be too dangerous, but Tony agreed with Henry.

A few days later we were sitting in Back o' the Moon, with Can and Casey encouraging Henry to drink more. He needed little coaxing and it wasn't very long before he became roaring drunk. Can started to quote Shakespeare and Dickens and a few other writers mixed in between – 'It is the best of times – and will be the worst for Henry' – and Casey said, 'I am crying for Henry – to keep from laughing.' Once Henry was drunk we dropped him in front of the Sophiatown police station with a bottle of brandy one-quarter full. Then we parked at a distance and watched.

Henry staggered up to the main entrance, swinging the bottle of brandy, where he started to shout and sing in Zulu. When nothing happened he took to staggering up and down the station's car park. A police van pulled up and parked and we all held our breath. Some white policemen got out and rushed into the station, completely ignoring Henry. A little while later, about half-a-dozen policemen came out of the main door of the station, dashed across the car park and scrambled into the police van, driving off at high speed. We all started to laugh as Henry, looking very forlorn, made his way towards us and got back into the car. So much for that idea. At the office the next day all Henry had to show for his endeavours was a bad hangover.

A week later Henry was arrested on a pass offence and sentenced to two weeks in the Fort.

When he was released he told us about the 'tausa', also known as 'the Monkey Dance'. This was a ritual which took place in the prison yard. After their return from work duty, the male prisoners, all jammed tightly against one another, were ordered to squat. Then each prisoner in turn had to undress until he was naked while a white warder, standing with his hands on his hips in front of him, watched. The naked prisoner then had to jump up and down (like a monkey), turn around in mid-air and then bend down with his arms outstretched. This humiliating dance was designed to dislodge anything illicitly held between a prisoner's legs – or elsewhere. After this 'performance' the prisoner picked up his clothes from the ground and the next man in the queue, stripped naked, repeated the dance.

Arthur and Bob started scouting out various buildings that might overlook the Fort, from which one could see into the yard where this humiliating dance took place. They eventually found a nursing home whose windows gave a good view. In the meantime I managed to find an old 4 x 5-inch camera at SAAN with a very long telephoto lens, which I think was used for photographing cricket matches. It was extremely heavy and needed a strong, stable tripod.

I never got to carry on working on the Fort story, however, as I left *Drum* at short notice for the following reason.

Tony asked me to come and have a look at his new apartment in Killarney on a Saturday afternoon. David Macrae-Taylor was also coming along, he said, and bringing his latest jazz records. The apartment was in a rather old but well-kept two-storey building. I was the first to arrive and Tony showed me around. I told him that he was very lucky to find such a perfect place. He seemed exhilarated, but nervously on edge, as he paced from room to room, turning left and right. Then he led me back to the lounge and asked me to sit down on the couch. He offered me a whisky and put on a record. I asked him when David was coming. 'Oh, the silly clot, he can't come,' Tony said. 'He forgot he had another appointment.'

All the while he was walking nervously up and down in front of me, the whisky bottle in his hand, from which he took a swig now and then.

I started to talk about the prison story we were working on.

Interrupting me in mid flow, Tony said abruptly, 'I'm having a bath,' and, with that, he disappeared. I sat there for a while, contemplating my drink, and heard some splashing noises coming from the bathroom. I wondered whether I should leave, but I waited a little longer, leafing through a *Life* magazine that was on the coffee table. Suddenly the bathroom door slammed open and a stark-naked Tony, wide-eyed and breathing heavily, came into the room, making straight for me. He sat next to me on the couch. With eyes that I can only describe as gleaming or raving, and breath that smelt strongly of whisky, he grabbed me, putting his arm around my waist and touching me up between my legs, breathing heavily all the time.

In a state of shock I struggled to release myself from what I perceived as the clutches of a maniac. I managed to free one arm and give him a hard punch in his guts. As I wrestled and battled to get away from him, I shouted: 'You're bonkers! Let go of me!' Then I ran to the front door, wrenched it open and fled. As I was leaving I glanced round. Tony was lying on the couch, groaning and hyperventilating. Out on the street I got into my car and was just about to start the engine when I realised I had left my Leica camera on the coffee table. For a moment I hesitated but I was too upset to return to the flat. I drove home to Etricia.

On Monday morning I was at my desk at the office, working on some page layouts, when Tony came in. He had a furious expression on his face as he approached. 'You feather-brained idiot,' he said, 'abandoning your expensive Leica!' He threw my camera onto my desk and stalked off to his office. At the door he turned around. 'I want to see all the layouts for the final pages this morning!' he snapped. Then he went into his office and slammed the door behind him.

Of course it was impossible to finish the final layout for the last section because some of the copy was still to be written and some of the photos had still to be printed up. So I went into Tony's office and told him why I couldn't do what he'd instructed.

He wasn't impressed. 'You barmy German, with your codswallop ideas,' he snarled.

He brushed past me and left his office, leaving me standing there, speechless. I saw him walk over to Deborah's desk and say, in a loud voice and acid tone,

'Deborah, take Bob and Arthur with the large camera to the nursing home and photograph the tausa dance at the Fort – now.'

Without any further thought, I cleaned out my desk, collected my cameras, put them into my camera case and left the office.

When I got home, Etricia was sitting on our bed surrounded by books and sheet music. A violin concerto was playing on the record player. She looked up at me and smiled. 'I am studying the theory of music,' she said.

I walked over to the record player, lifted the arm off the record and put it on its rest. Then I switched the record player off.

'What's wrong? You look angry,' Etricia said.

'I left *Drum*,' I told her.

My wife's response wasn't what I needed right then. 'You don't want to work with those idiot natives anyway,' she said. 'What happened? And what's going to happen now?'

I sat down on the bed beside her. I would work as a freelancer, I said, although I hadn't actually given this any thought. Then I told her about Tony's crazy behaviour the night before. Etricia got quite mad. She said she had never trusted Sampson. She said again that she was glad I'd left *Drum*. Then, after a brief pause, she said, 'But what about my piano lessons? We need to buy a piano. How are we going to pay for it?'

I told her to relax. I would think of something.

23

THEATRICAL INTERLUDE, A ROAD TRIP AND BACK TO SOPHIATOWN

The next day I went to see Taubie Kushlick at the National Theatre. She was a larger-than-life lady in her early forties, who spoke with a powerful theatrical voice. And she was tough, tough as nails. I showed her some of my pictures, which she liked, and we agreed, after a bit of argument about my fee, that I would make a set of publicity photographs for the foyer of the National Theatre of the dress rehearsal of the play she was currently directing, *She Stoops to Conquer*.

Next I went to see Leon Gluckman in the small office he occupied in Bree Street. I found him sitting behind his desk, which was piled with files, books and pieces of paper with notes, smoking a long, thin cigar. Leon told me he knew my work on *Drum* and also that he would soon be staging Shakespeare's *King Lear* at the Wits University Great Hall. He was playing Lear. Once rehearsals started, he said, he would call me to take photos.

Then I went to visit Fritz Isaac at his home. He was very pleased to see me, but he also had some sad news to share. 'Werner is very ill,' he said. 'I booked a country tour for him and now he can't go.'

I said I could do the tour for him but I didn't think Etricia would be happy about my being out of town for six weeks or so.

'No problem,' Fritz said. 'She can go with you and be your assistant.'

I said I would give it some thought and let him know.

I went to the SAAN offices and dropped off a letter in the foyer for Jim. In it I said that owing to Tony's unexpected behaviour it was impossible for me to continue to work on *Drum*.

For the next couple of weeks I kept busy taking pictures for Taubie and Leon, making the prints at Knute's darkroom. Etricia was agreeable about coming along as my assistant on the Werner tour and we began to make preparations for our trip. We were busy packing when the doorbell rang.

I opened the door and there stood Jim, looking his usual dishevelled self – his shirt was half unbuttoned and skew, his sleeves were rolled up and his crumpled tie hung unevenly. Standing slightly sideways, a frequent stance of his, he gave me a broad smile. 'How are you, old chap? I was getting concerned about your disappearing act,' he said.

I invited him in, introduced him to Etricia and asked him to sit down in our only chair. I sat next to Etricia on the bed.

'Now let's get to the point, young man,' Jim said in a more serious voice. 'What's your problem?'

I told him that Anthony was making it impossible for me to work with him and also that his bitchy behaviour when it came to the *Drum* crew, which had recently escalated again, was making him very unpopular.

'He tried to rape Jürgen!' Etricia burst out. Then, turning icy eyes on Jim, she added: 'Several times.'

Jim looked at Etricia and then at me and, predictably, burst out laughing in the raucous, bizarre way he had, with his mouth side-open.

'What's so funny?' I said angrily.

Jim tried calming me down with his usual smiles and some soothing talk but I was still very annoyed.

'Now look here,' he said, 'Tony is going back to the United Kingdom some-time next year, and maybe in another six months or so I will have a new editor on *Drum*. In the meantime, maybe you could cover the odd story for us and continue supplying pictures to us as usual, as a freelance photographer.' Somehow we agreed that he would be my contact and that I wouldn't have to go through Anthony. He then invited me and Etricia out for a drink but we declined as we were about to leave for our country tour.

After picking up the big old Buick, the studio equipment and advertising photos from Werner's Studio headquarters in Germiston, Etricia and I travelled through the Northern Transvaal during the hottest season of the year. I had trouble coping with the heat and after a day's work, setting up the studio, making up some of the sitters and photographing them under a hot spotlight, I would be totally knocked out. I flopped in an armchair while Etricia fanned me with a large piece of board.

On one of the shoots, where I had been taking pictures of some pretty young girls, whose day jobs were probably in the post office or as secretaries in one of the dorps nearby, I noticed Etricia giving me angry, resentful looks followed by suspicious glances. Later that evening when we had finished and went to our hotel room, she seemed moody, in a huff, and avoided my attempts at making conversation.

'What's the matter, don't you feel well?' I asked.

'You liked that blonde,' she said bitterly. 'You took hours to photograph her and fussed around her for ages.'

I told Etricia I was only doing my job and that the girl, the blonde one she was talking about, wouldn't sit still and I had had problems taking a decent picture. Also she kept blinking and I couldn't be certain of getting a picture with her eyes open. Etricia didn't talk to me again until after breakfast the next morning – after which she behaved as though nothing had happened. So I forgot about the incident. When we returned to Joburg after our six-week tour, we had done rather well financially. I bought Etricia a piano, which made her very happy and earned me lots of compliments and fussing over. We also decided we should find a bigger apartment or maybe even a house with a garden.

One evening Henry turned up at our apartment. In his trademark bow-tie and his brown suit, hat pushed slightly to the back of his head, he looked very dapper. 'We all miss you,' he said as he came in and sat down on the piano stool. We chatted for a while and I told him I had read his prison story in *Drum*, which I thought very impressive, very courageous. It must have been tough for him in the Fort, I said. Then, 'Oh, I forgot –' he said and, reaching into his inside pocket, he pulled out an envelope which he handed to me '– a telegram arrived for you at the office.'

The telegram was from Camera Press in London and it said: COVER THE SOPHIATOWN REMOVALS WHICH IS IMMINENT – REGARDS TOM.

I made some enquiries about the removals and discovered that the first of these was due to take place in Sophiatown on 12 February 1955 – so I had a few days to prepare. I still had a lot of printing to do, so for the next few days I spent my time in Knute's darkroom, working and listening to jazz on the radio.

One evening late at night there was a newsflash on the station I had tuned into, Springbok Radio, read out by broadcaster and commentator Eric Egan. He announced 'considerable police activity in and around Sophiatown'. Without waiting to hear more, I grabbed my cameras, got straight into my car and drove as fast as I could in the direction of Sophiatown. It was pouring with rain – a typical Johannesburg summer storm had just broken – and I could barely see where I was going as sheets of rain hit my windscreen. I thought that maybe I had got my dates wrong. The removals were scheduled to begin on the 12th, which was still two days away.

When I got to Sophiatown, the rain had almost stopped and there were police everywhere. I parked behind some police cars and army trucks and walked up Victoria Street where, by now in almost complete darkness, a group of about a hundred policemen had lined up. Some wore the dark-blue uniform with helmets, some wore khaki uniforms, some khaki coats with caps. Most were armed with rifles and they carried their leather ammunition belts over their shoulders. I thought it was rather a motley crowd and the men themselves seemed unsure about what they were doing there. Suddenly a resident came out of his house wearing pyjamas and slippers and walked along the line of policemen – he looked as if he was taking inspection. I started taking pictures.

Further down the road in a side street police were breaking down doors and ordering people to move their furniture outside, where it was loaded onto trucks. I carried on taking pictures and had to use a flash as it was almost pitch dark and there were no streetlights in the township. This seemed to upset the police. They started to complain, but I deflected them by saying I was 'official'. They were such an odd group of men, in such a mixture of uniforms, I felt sure they had been hastily collected from the different police stations in the area.

Many of the Sophiatown residents were entirely unprepared for the move two

Sophiatown graffiti

days earlier than scheduled. And because of the date change, no ANC demonstrators and protesters were present. I kept on taking pictures throughout the night
as the police kept up their relentless harassment of residents, many of whom were
in a state of extreme shock and despair. As the sun rose and lit up the scene, more
trucks arrived. These were full of African policemen. In Sol Street, a road with
rows of terraced houses, I took pictures as they jumped out and were ordered by
a white officer to break down the doors of the houses and load the furniture onto
trucks. There were hundreds of these trucks, all lined up and waiting. I followed
some of those that were carrying gangs of demolition crews and took pictures as
the men jumped out and climbed onto the roofs of some of the shacks at the back
of the properties. They then tore down the corrugated-iron roofs, using large
sledgehammers, and threw them to the ground.

By now it was early morning and more and more people were coming out
of their houses looking about and looking lost. Some residents had decided to
go to work and they started queuing up at the bus stop. And all the while police
cars drove around the streets.

Robert Resha didn't recognise me at first. He was standing on a corner
wearing a long raincoat and a floppy hat. He confirmed that the ANC campaign
against the forced removals had been planned for 12 February and that it was
now redundant. As we were standing talking, we heard several sharp, ringing
sounds, coming from several directions. 'It's too late,' Robert said in a desperate voice. 'They're hitting the telegraph poles with bats and iron bars. This was
supposed to have happened the night before the removals to tell people to dem-
onstrate.' Gradually the ringing became less frequent. I left Robert and went off
to try to get a few pictures of the boys who had been designated to bang against
the poles, but it seemed they had been chased off by the police.

Finding myself suddenly in front of the door of Back o' the Moon, I decided
to go inside and see if I could get a cup of coffee or a Coke.

'Hi, Mr Jürgy,' said Fatsy. 'Come to see your friends?' She started giggling,
her whole body shaking. 'They all come to my nice place.'

And there sat Anthony, Can Themba and Bob Gosani, each with a bottle of
beer in front of him. They looked very surprised to see me.

'What are you doing here?' Can asked.

Waiting for a removal truck, Sophiatown

'We tried to get hold of you ...' Bob said.

I looked at Bob. 'Why are you sitting in a shebeen?' I asked. 'Shouldn't you be out there taking some pictures?'

'We just got here,' he said.

'Anyway,' said Anthony, 'it's all over, too late, the ANC demonstration and defiance was disrupted by the change of the removals date.'

I asked Fatsy, who was standing behind me, if she could please make me a cup of coffee. 'Of course I'll make you a cup of coffee,' she said. 'Now listen. Let me tell you all –' and she looked at the trio who were gazing up at her '– I ain't going to Meadowlands, no way! I'm staying right here in Sophiatown and so is Back o' the Moon. And there you have it.' And with that she turned and wobbled away to the kitchen.

Can looked at me and said, 'Are you coming to Tony's farewell party at Jim's on Coney Island?'

This morning Can had a pin in his mouth, which was an upgrade from the usual matchstick. This disconcerting habit always made me slightly apprehensive. The matchstick jumped from one corner of his mouth to the other while he talked and sometimes it disappeared altogether. Then it would suddenly reappear and go back to moving from one corner to the other. An unconscious but well-practised habit – but I was relieved to see the pinhead now, glinting against his lip.

'It was the best of times, it was the worst of times,' Can said, looking at Tony. *A Tale of Two Cities* was very popular amongst the Sophiatown intellectuals and at *Drum* everybody quoted lines from the book, even more so than from *Knock on Any Door*. 'Don't worry, Tony, this historic milestone and memorable event in our evolution will always be with you and you will return one day to see a new South Africa.'

Bob picked up his bottle and downed the rest of his beer as Fatsy came back with my coffee. 'I'd better try and take some pictures,' he said. He took his camera and left, swaying slightly. I drank my coffee while Tony and Can carried on debating Shakespeare and Dickens and comparing their work with that of contemporary African writers. They hardly noticed me leave.

I drove through the morning rush-hour traffic to Klute's darkroom in

Sophiatown destroyed

24

A NEW EDITOR AND A CATFIGHT

One block up from Polly Street was the Federal Hotel. 'The Fed' was a favourite haunt of journalists and reporters. It was where most of the *Sunday Times* writers could be found, and this was where Jim and I walked to get a drink. Over a beer he asked me if I would come back to work on *Drum*. Tony was about to leave. His offer took me by surprise and I sat contemplating it in silence for a few minutes. In truth I missed Henry, Arthur and Todd, and the rest of the *Drum* gang.

'We'd have to talk about my salary,' I said. 'And my fee per image.'

Jim looked a bit pained, as he always did when money and payments were discussed, but didn't say anything.

'I'm doing very well now with my freelance work,' I continued. 'Also Etricia is expecting, and we have to rent a larger place, maybe a house. So as a production manager and picture editor I need a monthly salary of £100, plus £2 for every picture published by *Drum* publications. And that's that.'

As I talked, Jim had been looking more and more miffed. He scrutinised my eyes with doubtful, probing looks but I gazed back into his unflinchingly. I was determined. Then his expression suddenly changed and he burst out laughing, chortling and guffawing away in his usual manner. Then he stretched out his right arm and offered me his hand. So we shook hands and I was working on *Drum* again.

I asked Jim who the new editor was going to be. He told me that the position was to be taken by a multi-talented South African who until recently had been the parliamentary correspondent for the *Rand Daily Mail* in Cape Town. His name was Sylvester Stein. Stein loved photography and magazines, was a liberal and very courageous.

Etricia was indeed expecting. As we prepared for our first child, we needed to find a bigger space. She had spoken to her uncle about renting a house and now he said he could get us a house, with a garden, in Edenvale. Etricia was very excited and ready to move right away but I told her we should look at the place first. I also had some reservations about the suburb, which was predominantly Afrikaans, not to mention close to Jan Smuts Airport and a long way from the centre of Joburg, where I would again be working. After a lot of arguing, I agreed to make the move to Edenvale and a few weeks later we had a house with a large garden, spacious enough that I could also have my own darkroom.

Sylvester Stein was a serious, intense man in his mid-thirties, with horn-rimmed glasses. At our first meeting in his office, my impression was that he wasn't altogether sure of himself and his role as editor, but I was pleasantly surprised that he spoke English with a normal South African accent and not, like Tony and Jim, as though he had a plum in his mouth. His desk was piled with magazines like *Life* and *Look*, layout sheets and photos.

We talked for a while about ourselves, and he told me that he came from Durban, had studied electrical engineering and for a short time had been a taxi driver in that city. He had joined the Navy and served on a minesweeper during the war. After that he'd worked for a time as an actor in London theatres before returning to South Africa and getting a job as a reporter on the *Rand Daily Mail*. He and his wife had four children. As we talked, Sylvester relaxed and we both thought that we could work well together.

There were a lot of changes at the *Drum* offices. There was a new publication, a Sunday tabloid called the *Golden City Post*. The editor was a Scotsman, Cecil Eprile. And there was a new sub, an American named Hank Margolies, who gave the appearance of always being extremely busy, running around with a cigar between his lips, holding bits of paper in his hand and roaming from one room to another. Hank was in his fifties and heavy-set and he had a strong American accent. Arthur Maimane was filling in as news editor. The darkroom was taking some strain as it now had to accommodate both papers and the work of all the new staff. Along with all this change, we also had a new office car – a Land Rover – and a new driver, Peter Magubane. I got to work as quickly as I could, but with all this chaos I was amazed that we were able to bring these two publications out at the same time.

One Saturday afternoon, while I was at my desk working out the layout for the next issue of *Drum*, Bob Gosani came to me, looking miserable, and said, 'We have no fix. I can't develop my films.'

During the five months I had been away from *Drum* the darkroom had become very chaotic, with no one in charge of checking and ordering supplies. We were short of chemicals and photographic paper and we were urgently in need of fix – Hypo – essential for developing films and for making photographic prints. We had a problem. Bob's pictures had to go to press on Monday morning. I tried the darkroom at SAAN but everybody was out and, being a weekend, all the photographic shops were closed.

Then Bob came up with an idea. A neighbour of his in Fordsburg, Gopal Naransamy, was an amateur photographer. He might have some fix for us. Gopal welcomed us warmly and was indeed able to help us out with a few pints of Hypo. His home smelt of spices and incense and his living room was filled with Hindu religious figures, lighted candles and various colourful objects. Gopal enthusiastically showed me his photographic prints, small photographs he had taken of his family and of Hindu religious ceremonies. He was very proud of his pictures, which he developed himself in a small darkroom. I tried to encourage him but in truth found his photography rather poor. They demonstrated little sense of timing and composition. He told me that for many years he had worked for a well-known company as an administrator and storekeeper, doing the filing and book-keeping, and that he was looking for a new job. I suggested he come and see me at the *Drum* office the following week – I thought he might make a good supervisor for the darkroom and photo department.

As we were about to leave, I noticed a delicious, strong curry smell coming from the kitchen. Unable to resist, I followed the aroma and knocked on the open door, where two women in saris were working at the stove. Gopal quickly followed me in and introduced me to his wife and her sister. I tried to talk to his wife, saying I was very keen on cooking curry and maybe sometime they could give me a lesson, but both women seemed embarrassed and uncomfortable and could not be drawn into conversation.

The following week I went to see Jim in his office. I told him we needed someone to relieve the pressure on the photo department, which was becoming unmanageable from having to serve three publications: the two monthlies, *Drum* magazine (including the West and East African editions) and *Africa!*, and now, too, the weekly *Golden City Post*. Jim told me Can's endeavour to edit *Africa!* was something of a disappointment; circulation hadn't increased but rather declined and he had decided to discontinue the magazine in the next few months. He also brought up the fact that he had taken on several new members of staff. He would need to think about my request for a darkroom supervisor.

He was giving a party on Coney Island at the weekend, he said. I should come – it should be fun. Coney Island, so named by Jim, was a picturesque spot on his land next to the Crocodile River to the west of the main entrance.

Sylvester Stein's first editorial meeting started with introductions to the new members of the *Drum* crew. These included Bloke Modisane, who had been contributing short stories to us for some time, and a newcomer, Es'kia Mphahlele, who was the new literary editor.

We were all settled down for the meeting when Sylvester announced some bad news. Bob had been in a car accident the night before and was in Baragwanath Hospital. All we knew so far was that Bob, who had been driving, had had to have a lung removed after hitting his chest against the steering wheel. His passenger, a young journalist on the *Golden City Post*, had been killed. Sylvester said he would be going to the hospital after the meeting and anyone who wanted to visit Bob could join him.

He then discussed new stories. 'Next year the Olympics are taking place in Italy,' he said, looking at Can. 'Why are there no Africans or non-whites participating? We have a great number of excellent African sportsmen, don't you think, Can?'

Can's pin disappeared into his mouth. 'Baaa … yes, you don't have to be an intellectual, have any language skills and there's little call for initiative.' And the pin reappeared between his lips, moving from the left to the right side.

Sylvester looked somewhat puzzled. He turned to Henry. 'What do you think?' he asked. 'This could be our lead story and create an awareness about the exclusion of non-whites from international football competitions.'

Henry said he had also been thinking along similar story lines, had done some research and felt it was important to follow up. And the timing was perfect. So it was agreed that our next main lead for the March 1956 issue would be about the Olympics for South Africa's Africans.

Just before the meeting closed Sylvester had another announcement to make: that Can would be his number two as associate editor – which made Can's pin deftly move more swiftly from side to side.

I went with Sylvester to visit Bob. Baragwanath Hospital consisted of one large building surrounded by many small barrack-like blocks scattered in a sprawling complex. These were the wards, and after much searching we eventually found the ward where Bob was. He was lying in bed being interviewed by two policemen. He looked a mess – his chest and part of his face were heavily bandaged. Sylvester got very upset with the police sergeant, saying that Bob was in no condition to be interviewed. The police claimed that Bob's passenger had been killed in the accident, which had happened in a white suburb, and that another car had been involved. The accident had resulted in several seriously injured people. The car Bob was driving was full of bottles of alcohol. Bob himself had appeared extremely drunk.

I did not go to Jim's party at Coney Island but I was told it went on for the whole weekend. On Monday morning the office was deserted, except for good old Joe Bloomberg, our sub-editor, a most gentle and peaceful member of the *Drum* staff, who always remained unruffled despite the constant hurly-burly and bustle around. Occasionally he would drop a wise or apt remark. Most of the crew turned up that afternoon, hungover, unstable and wobbly.

I found it difficult to understand that both Jim and Tony, and now Sylvester, it seemed, tolerated and even encouraged this drinking behaviour. Their argument that most of our black writers were intellectual geniuses on a higher plane and therefore their eccentric, erratic behaviour was almost to be expected, even acceptable, made no sense to me. Can now often disappeared for several days at a time. When he returned, he acted as though all was well. His writing, particularly his short stories, was highly regarded and he was respected as an intellectual, but his frequent absences made it impossible to bring the paper out on time. Can's behaviour influenced the other *Drum* crew members, except for Casey Motsisi, who spent most of his time in one shebeen or another, the sources of the material for his regular columns. Casey wrote vast amounts of copy and was always ahead of schedule. He was a personable young man, full of wit and humour.

A few weeks later my phone rang in the middle of the night – in fact, it was 3.30am. It was Todd Matshikiza, sounding rather tipsy. 'Please, Jürgy, please come and take me home. We're stuck here in Sophiatown and need to get home … please, Jürgy!'

Actually, these late-night calls were becoming a habit and it was quite a long way from Edenvale to Sophiatown. I found Todd and Henry inside Back o' the Moon, totally drunk and about to be kicked out. I drove Henry to his home in Orlando and Todd to his house in White City, which was beyond Orlando. Both fell asleep in the car and I had some trouble returning them to their waiting wives. By then it was 5.30. There seemed to be no point driving all the way home, so I went straight to the office. I managed to get a cup of tea in the canteen from Simon as he was opening up.

The drinking problem was weighing on my mind. I thought it must be part of the South African culture. I like the odd drink and I've already admitted to overindulging now and then. In my travels for Werner's Studio throughout the country, from town to town and hotel to hotel, I knew that hotels were really only glorified bars. The laws were that in order to get a licence to run a bar and to sell alcohol, the bar needed to be part of a hotel. Many of these hotels were poorly run, offering very basic meals, but the bars were always packed and there was an atmosphere of roughness, coarseness, foul language and few laughs – and women were not permitted to enter.

In downtown Joburg many of the white journalists from the *Daily Mail* and the Sunday papers spent much of their time drinking at the Fed, which was a mere three minutes' walk from 176 Main Street. It might have been that the racist apartheid state, the humiliation, the frustration and the violence in society towards black people, made for an escapist drinking culture – for both blacks and whites.

Casey Motsisi

Etricia gave birth to a baby boy on 22 November 1954 and we named him Wolfgang. Eight weeks later she discovered she was expecting again.

Our house in Edenvale was on a corner opposite a Dutch Reformed church. In our front garden there were two date palms and at the back was a yard with some fruit trees. A large portion of the backyard was tiled with cement, accessed from the kitchen. The property also had a chicken shed and an outhouse. The outhouse comprised a single room with a toilet and shower, and this was where our maid lived with her husband. The maid looked after the baby, cleaned the house and did all the washing, and her husband worked one day a week in the garden.

Although my work kept me extremely busy, Etricia and I also had a social life. Now and again we entertained over the weekend, when we would invite various friends and colleagues over for a braai (or barbecue). Ian Berry often turned up in his MG, wearing one of his dandy outfits. In this very conservative Afrikaans suburb, inviting black *Drum* colleagues over for these occasions was asking for trouble and so I chose not to. The Dutch Reformed church meant that there was a continuous stream of people walking past our house at weekends, for Sunday services as well as weddings and funerals. It was best not to attract unwanted attention.

Jazz remained my great love and sometimes I would invite Todd, Kippie and other musicians over in the evening. Kippie would bring his clarinet, Jacob 'Mzala' his double bass and, with Todd on the piano and a gallon of wine keeping us mellow, we had some most enjoyable jazz sessions that continued into the early hours. Sometimes I tried to play my guitar with them but I wasn't in their league and always gave up after a few tries.

I also took to dropping by Bill Papas's place, which was on my route home from Joburg, taking along short story ideas or Casey's column for Bill to illustrate. We would spend a couple of hours together going through the material, accompanied by rum and Coke and many laughs. Bill always managed to capture with his skilled drawings the mood and humour of Casey's words.

As time went by, my relationship with Etricia deteriorated. She grew increasingly intolerant and her jealousy, mistrust and suspicion grew too. She would routinely go through my pockets and question all my movements. 'Why are you late?', 'You smell of alcohol', 'You smell of other women', 'Why do you always play Eartha Kitt's records? What is it with you and Eartha Kitt?' These were recurrent refrains. One day she rushed up to me when I was doing some work in the garden, holding one of my white shirts in her hand and looking extremely angry. 'There's lipstick on your shirt!' she said accusingly. 'You were dancing with a woman.' Indeed there was a red smudge mark on the left side below the shoulder but it was from a red Chinagraph pen, used to mark contact prints, that was always in my inside jacket pocket. In the heat it must have rubbed off onto my shirt. Slowly, over time, I began to feel a sense of guilt if I talked to or photographed women. I tried very hard not to make Etricia jealous and distanced myself from female visitors and women at social events.

A new circulation manager, Ted, came to join *Drum*. He was a South African English speaker, about 40 years old, and a nervous, twitchy, skinny character, who often wore an outsize old coat that hung loosely from his thin frame. When Ted planned a trip to Durban to work on our circulation problems there and try to improve sales, I suggested to Sylvester that I drive down with him. I could spend time with our representative in Durban, GR Naidoo, and maybe do a story there.

Ted was also a very nervous, erratic driver, I discovered, and as we drove through the Valley of a Thousand Hills down to Durban I got rather worried. Plus, I observed with concern, there was a large bayonet at his feet, which slid from side to side as the car went round bends.

'What do you have a bayonet for?' I asked him.

'To defend myself,' he answered.

Fair enough, I thought, but against whom? I decided not to ask, preferring to let him concentrate on not plunging us off the hillside.

We arrived in Durban in the early morning. Ted dropped me off at the Goodwill Lounge, promising to return to pick me up in a couple of days once he'd done his rounds and had talked to the manager of the News Agency.

I received a hearty welcome from Pumpy Naidoo and his brother Nammy and was served an excellent curry breakfast. As I was sitting at their table, Pumpy on my right and Nammy on my left, I felt rather dwarf-like. They were both huge men. They told me the timing of my visit was perfect as they wanted me to meet the third Naidoo brother, who was on holiday in Durban. He was a journalist and lived in London. I would be able to meet him that evening at a special welcoming party they were giving for him.

After breakfast I went to my room, which was one of about a dozen rooms behind the Goodwill Lounge, and had a few hours of sleep, before I was woken by Nammy to tell me to get ready. The party was held in a large family house in an upmarket Durban suburb. It had a beautiful big garden and a high perimeter wall. I hadn't been there before but I presumed it was Pumpy's home. The party was in full swing when we got there with a few dozen, mostly Indian, guests mingling about with drinks in their hands. There were a few whites and coloured people among the guests. Almost all the guests were male, except for a small number of young women in party dresses. Nammy led me through the crowd and across a large room decorated with brightly coloured pictures of the Taj Mahal and stylised Indian dancers on the walls. We eventually found Pumpy and next to him a man who could have been his twin. He was as wide and heavy-set as Pumpy, except that he was half his height. Smiling, Pumpy introduced us. 'This is my brother Billy from London. He wants to know all about *Drum* and the work you are doing.'

In pinstripe suit and sporting a red bow-tie, Billy spoke the Queen's English. He told me he had been following the progress of *Drum* and was impressed by the fearlessness of its writers, especially Henry Nxumalo. He worked on Fleet Street and had recently met Tom Hopkinson, the editor of *Picture Post*, about which he talked enthusiastically.

As we chatted Pumpy led us into an adjoining room, leaving the party noise behind, where we sat down on green leather armchairs to continue talking. The room had bright-blue walls, the colour contrasting with the green to produce quite a strange atmosphere. When a young woman appeared in the doorway, Pumpy asked her to join us. He ushered her into the room with his arm around her tiny shoulders. She wore a low-cut girlish dress and shoes with very high heels. 'And this is my girl,' Pumpy said proudly. Up close, the young woman didn't actually look so young. Behind her eye make-up, powder and lipstick she seemed rather a tough cookie. When she started to talk to Billy, I noticed that she had a strong 'Cape coloured' Afrikaans accent.

Our conversation ranged across a number of topics and several hours went by. At one point Pumpy mentioned that he planned to launch more jazz concerts at the Goodwill Lounge and was hoping to bring out to South Africa the following year the clarinet virtuoso Tony Scott, and Bud Shank, who was in the West Coast jazz scene.

After a while Pumpy's girl – he called her 'Lovely' – left the room to get a drink and rejoin the party. As she opened the door, jazz music came blasting in from outside. Billy thought he might be able to sell some of my pictures in London, and he and I exchanged addresses. I then went and joined the crowd and got myself a drink. By now the room was packed full of people standing about smoking and drinking, and there was a buzz of chatter that blended with the sultry sounds of a saxophone blowing out a well-known piece.

Near the door to the garden a sudden commotion caught my attention. There seemed to be some shoving and pushing going on, accompanied by loud female shrieks. I pushed through the crowd to see what was going on. Pumpy's girl, Lovely, was in the middle of it. She and a dark-skinned Indian woman were pushing each other and shouting and swearing. Both started to push through the open door into the garden, to laughter and cries of encouragement from a group of Indian men, who seemed to be thoroughly enjoying the spectacle. The two women screeched and yelled at each other as they moved onto the lawn. Things got physical and they started to hit and slap each other. Goaded on by the group of men, they tore each other's dresses and eventually both of them ended up rolling on the lawn scratching, screeching, howling and ripping each other's clothes off until they were practically naked.

'Why don't you stop them?' I asked one of the characters who was clapping his hands and whistling.

He looked at me, puzzled. 'They are fighting over Pumpy – it's his problem,' he answered.

The two fighting women were now covered in blood with make-up smudged all over their faces and both were using extremely foul language. Eventually someone went into the house to find Pumpy and get him to come out and put a stop to the cat fight, but I decided it was a good time to take my leave. I managed to get a lift into town with another of the partygoers who'd had enough.

The next morning I went to the Durban *Drum* office to meet GR Naidoo, who had just been appointed head. He was a friendly, smiling fellow who, since the early fifties, had been doing freelance work for a number of Durban publications as a photographer-writer – I had met him on my first trip to Durban in 1952. GR was quite the charming ladies' man, sporting a thin moustache and a small goatee beard, and he always dressed very stylishly.

We were talking about some possible Durban stories for *Drum* when the door opened and a slim man with a moustache and wearing glasses came into the room. He had some cameras slung over his shoulder. This was Ranjith Kally, whose photos we had been publishing in *Drum* for the last five years. He was an excellent photographer, whose work I admired very much, and I was very happy to meet him in person. He was also the total opposite of the flamboyant and outgoing GR. Ranjith was reserved and retiring, preferring to stay in the background, the ideal personality for a journalist, who should be an invisible presence, in my view, a fly on the wall, to be able to capture and record the moment as an unobtrusive observer. All in all, I thought we had a good team in Durban.

Bob Gosani was also down in Durban. He had travelled from Joburg the previous Wednesday with the cast of the Jazz Parade troupe on the 'Jazz Train'. The plan was that Bob would photograph the atmosphere on the train, which was packed with musicians. The show had opened at Durban's Music Hall the night before and I was keen to hear how things had gone. I tried for some time to get Bob on the phone to find out if everything was okay but I couldn't locate him. Eventually I got through to Alfred Herbert, the show's promoter, who said he couldn't find Bob either. Apparently Bob had got very drunk the night before at the opening-night party after the show.

Since his car accident, Bob had become very unreliable. He was a talented photographer, who had produced some outstanding images, but often he didn't turn up for work at all, disappearing for a whole week at a time, and when he did appear he was usually drunk, or else he returned late and drunk from a photo shoot. It worried me, too, that despite losing a lung (something Bob always denied), he was still smoking heavily.

Alfred was happy to hear that I was in Durban. The cast wanted to go for a swim in the sea and they were all about to leave – would I come and take some pictures? he asked.

The cast were already in the sea when I arrived at the 'beach for Africans'. They were all fooling around, splashing, jumping and rolling around in the water. Dolly and Thandi were there, and the singer Gene Williams, as well as most of the dancers and musicians in the cast. I got out of the taxi, ran down to the water, threw off my shoes and started to take pictures. Dolly came out of the water and gave me some pin-up poses for fun. Everyone was enjoying themselves tremendously, splashing in the waves and laughing, and it occurred to me that many of them had probably never swum in the sea before or even in a swimming pool – I don't think any swimming pools existed for the non-white population of South Africa at that time.

Afterwards I strolled back to the Goodwill Lounge and decided to take a look at the Indian Market on the way, which was always full of hustle and bustle and the blended strong aromas of spices. I took lots of atmospheric pictures there. Then I walked down Grey Street to the corner of Victoria Street, the corner that had become notorious for the Crimson League gang fighting in the taxi war with the Salot gang.

Back in the Goodwill Lounge, Pumpy was sitting at his usual table. I joined him and we talked for a while. He made no mention of the girls' fight, but I felt I had to bring it up. I told him that I hadn't taken any pictures of the fracas as I was an invited guest at his home. He laughed and said I should have – they would have made some interesting cover pictures for *Drum*!

Later in the evening we were enjoying the soft background music provided by a small jazz trio when Ted walked in, breathless and nervous as usual. He'd made a satisfying tour of all the newsagents around Durban, he said, and he came and sat with us for a while. We were served some of the best curry in town and then it was time to return to Joburg. We said our farewells to Pumpy and Nammy and got into the car. Ted drove down Victoria Street and turned into Grey. There we saw a number of young men chasing a man down the road. We drove slowly, following them. When the men caught up with their victim man they started to beat him and threw him on the ground. Ted stopped the car about a hundred metres from where the man was being beaten, and I jumped out and ran towards the fellow, taking pictures as I approached. Unfortunately, I had to use a flashlight, but this didn't seem to stop the ruffians, who continued to kick the victim on the ground. When I flashed again, they suddenly noticed me. They came charging towards me – at which point I turned around and started to run as fast as I could to our car.

Ted was standing next to the driver's open door brandishing his bayonet above his head. He looked as if he was about to use it. I shouted to him to get into the car – we needed to make a quick getaway. As I jumped into the passenger seat, Ted started the engine and did a sharp, swift U-turn, narrowly missing one of the chasers. As we picked up speed, I looked back. To my great alarm I saw the thugs jump into a car that had driven up to collect them. They were now setting off in pursuit of us. We screeched to a halt outside the Goodwill Lounge, leapt out of the car and flew up the steps. Luckily Pumpy was standing near the door and immediately saw there was a problem. Breathing heavily, Ted and I staggered inside. When I'd caught my breath I stepped back outside and there at the entrance was the car that had followed us, filled with some very rough-looking characters. When they caught sight of Pumpy, they turned the car around and disappeared at high speed.

Pumpy laughed heartily. 'The Crimson League,' he said.

Back at the *Drum* office the next morning after our long drive home, I was sitting at my desk making the last pages for the printer when our driver, Peter Magubane, came to see me to have a talk. Since he often drove the writers on stories, he thought it might be a good idea if he could take some pictures of the people the writers were interviewing or the events they covered. He was very keen to learn about photography. What did I think of his suggestion?

Peter gave the impression of being quite a tough, streetwise fellow. His parents ran a vegetable business in Sophiatown and he owned a large American convertible, which he rented out for weddings. I thought it couldn't do any harm for him to have a go, so I got him a Yashicaflex camera, a copy of the Rolleiflex. Over the next few weeks I gave him some lessons on how to operate the camera, develop films and make enlargements. He was very enthusiastic and I liked his pictures, but he didn't have any idea about composition or structure, so his images looked rather cluttered and disorganised. I had a number of books on design and composition, and for about a year I tutored him once a week, usually on Monday mornings, to help him 'see'. I also taught him how to make prints in the darkroom.

After having been away from home for almost a week, I arrived to find a very grumpy and angry Etricia. 'I can't trust you any more,' she said. 'You must leave *Drum*.'

I tried my best to explain my work to her and to tell her about what had happened in Durban but she was simply not interested. She said I should get another job. She pointed out that she was expecting our second child. She'd had a plumber in to repair a leak and he had told her that he was doing very well, that there was no shortage of work in the area. I would do better if I took up plumbing, Etricia said. Later she also said she was fed up with studying the piano. She was going to take up writing instead. I could take it or leave it. Our arguing went on well into the night and I went to the office the next morning feeling drained. We were both young, I decided, and these problems would sort themselves out in time.

There were more staff changes at *Drum*. Humphrey Tyler was a new sub-editor. He was the exact opposite of gentle Joe Bloomberg. While Joe was unobtrusive, Humphrey had the ability to put everybody around him on edge. He was hyperactive, continuously on the move. He paced up and down the office between the desks, using his loud voice at full volume and clicking his ballpoint pen in a rather irritating way.

An ongoing concern of mine was the poor quality of the newsprint we used and of the printing press. We were supposed to be a picture magazine, but with such low-quality paper one could often not even identify some of the people and places in the photos. Our quality of printing and paper was worse than most South African newspapers, which were themselves of poor quality. I brought this issue up regularly at editorial meetings. Although Sylvester promised he would take it further and talk to Jim, most of the other members of the team did not appear to care.

There was a culture in South Africa which, as I later discovered, also existed in the United Kingdom, that writing, literature, poetry and theatre were paramount among the arts, whereas painting and photography were something you might do on Sundays, for amusement and fun. The writer and his work, ideas and vision tended to be absolute. In a climate like that, writers don't always understand, appreciate and acknowledge the value of the visual arts. In the fifties in South Africa, photography was not considered an art form and the photographer was viewed by the media world as a second-rate and inadequate journalist.

On 26 June 1955, 300 delegates from all over South Africa met in Kliptown to sign the Freedom Charter. The idea of drawing up a Freedom Charter came from Professor ZK Matthews, who had suggested the summoning of a national convention where all groups would be represented in a Freedom Charter for a future democratic South Africa. Many years later, in 1996, the Freedom Charter became the foundation of South Africa's constitution.

Es'kia Mphahlele (whom we called Zeke) and Humphrey Tyler, together with Peter and Bob, covered the event. The police arrived and proceeded to take down the names and addresses of everybody who was on the platform.

One day I was in the darkroom with Peter, showing him how to make enlargements, when we heard a loud commotion outside, with people shouting and yelling. Suddenly Cecil Eprile, the *Golden City Post* editor, came through the light trap into the darkroom. Even in the dim light I could see he was shaking like a leaf. He had a strong stammer and now was clearly struggling to get out a single coherent word. Peter and I dashed past him to see what was happening. Outside, big Hank Margolies, with a cigar stub in his mouth, was poking his finger into the chest of a huge fellow in a dark suit and hat, who was looking quite scared. Behind him, I saw, were several similarly dressed men, who also looked frightened.

'Don't come in here and threaten us! You're a bunch of hooligans and gang-sters. Now get out before I lose my temper, you pathetic, miserable bunch of hoodlums!'

The group looked like they were in a hurry to leave and, as they turned around and made for the door, Hank shouted after them, 'And don't bring your guns and knives in here! And next time – make an appointment!'

For the previous few weeks the *Golden City Post* had been reporting about the brutal Msomi gang, which ran a protection racket in Alexandra township.

They were notorious killers, known to have murdered a number of people by pouring petrol over them and setting them alight. They mutilated women and raped young girls. This morning they had come to the office intending to kill the editor of the *Post* to teach him a lesson. This was when Cecil had bolted into the darkroom, leaving tough guy Hank, with his heavy American Bronx accent, to deal with them. He had ordered them to put their guns and knives away and – as we'd witnessed – to get the hell out of the office.

All black men in South Africa had to carry a pass, or reference book – the *dompas* – and in 1955 the government moved to extend this to black women as well. On 27 October 1955, 2 000 women marched to the Union Buildings in Pretoria in demonstration against the pass laws. They were led by four representatives, one woman for each so-called race group – Rahima Moosa, Lilian Ngoyi, Helen Joseph and Sophie Williams. They carried letters of protest and a petition, which they left outside the door of the office of the minister of native affairs. The door was locked and there was no response to their knocking.

I went with Zeke to cover the story. He was a quiet character, different from the other *Drum* writers with their fast living. He was the first African to receive a higher degree, an MA in literature from the University of South Africa, which he earned with distinction. He didn't drink or smoke, was uneasy alongside the excessive flamboyant lifestyles of colleagues like Can Themba, Jim Bailey and others, and seemed somewhat uncomfortable working for *Drum*, which he believed did not challenge him intellectually.

A year later, on 9 August 1956, 20 000 women of all races protested again against the pass laws for women and marched once more to the Union Buildings in Pretoria. The second march was led by the same four women. They presented a petition addressed to Prime Minister Strijdom – and again there was no answer. It was one of the most spectacular demonstrations staged in South Africa by women.

I photographed the 1955 march to the Union Buildings in Pretoria, and Peter Magubane and Alf Kumalo photographed the 1956 march. These two marches would subsequently create unfortunate confusion and conflict among the *Drum* photographers.

Many years later I published one of my 1955 Women's March pictures in a

Women's March, 1955, with the author on the left

(PHOTOGRAPHER UNKNOWN)

book. I was criticised for this by Peter, who claimed I was using his pictures. I was obliged to prove to him that the pictures were mine, which we subsequently agreed on: in the 1955 march the four women leading the protest had worn different outfits from those they wore in the 1956 march. Helen Joseph, for example, had been wearing a light costume in 1955; for the 1956 march she wore a dark suit.

This was not the end of it, however. Some years later Alf Kumalo used some of my 1955 Women's March images in a touring show and book. The pictures featured Helen Joseph in the light suit, but when I pointed out the mistake Alf denied that the image was mine and insisted that he had taken it.

Another book published later on featured another of my 1955 Women's March pictures. It was credited to Bob Gosani by the photo agency BAHA. BAHA, which sells *Drum* photos, is run and owned by the son of Jim Bailey. In my experience, the agency made confusing mistakes in the captions and credits of the images they sold. At the time I did not take this confusion of credits seriously. However, it happened repeatedly many years later, which made me suspicious about the motive for creating this confusion, which created doubt about the rights and ownership of some of the photos.

Bloke Modisane was nicknamed 'Black Jesus' by some of the *Drum* writers because he had a tendency to preach on any subject that happened to be under discussion. In his capacity as the social editor, he wrote about showbiz, jazz and variety shows. I went to visit him in his Sophiatown room once – which he called 'Sunset Boulevard' – and I had to remind myself where I was, namely, in a rather run-down suburb with houses demolished all around us. Bloke dressed snazzily, with gold cufflinks and a bow-tie, and he served us cocktails with an olive on a toothpick in a cocktail glass. His room was immaculately tidy, with bookshelves packed neatly with scholarly and literary books, and *Esquire* and other magazines piled on a coffee table. We sat companionably in armchairs, Mozart on the record player, sipping our drinks and chatting.

Bloke liked to talk about his exploits and amorous adventures with a variety of young white women. White women, he said, found him irresistible. He would tell these stories with a wide smile, which I found quite confusing. It was as if his regular sleeping with white women was a type of spiteful and perverse revenge. I often discussed with him the dangers of relationships across the 'colour bar', which was a criminal offence under apartheid and could carry a prison sentence. He was an exceptional writer, I told him, with a bright future and I was sure his short stories would eventually be acknowledged internationally. He would get his recognition. After I left Bloke's room, I had the feeling that he was very bitter, especially towards whites, and was trying too hard to be admired and accepted as a sophisticated intellectual.

On my way back I stopped at Bill Papas', place to discuss the illustrations for Casey Motsisi's next batch of stories. How he managed to be so productive, churning out copy, while spending so much time in shebeens was a mystery to me. With our usual rum and Coke and much laughter, we went through the text while Bill made preliminary sketches. He unfailingly managed to produce the funniest and most fitting images of Casey's descriptive shebeen atmosphere. I invited Bill, his wife Aroon and her brother to come over to my place for our next session. I would provide the rum and Coke for a change. I thought it would be good to have them around and also that it might keep the peace with Etricia, who had become increasingly suspicious of my regular visits to the Papas home.

The Black Sash was a new anti-apartheid women's organisation, founded by a woman named Jean Sinclair. Its membership comprised white women, who regularly demonstrated in cities across South Africa. They were distinctive in the black sash they wore across their chests and often they held lighted candles in their hands on their silent vigils. They regularly demonstrated on the steps of the Joburg City Hall. On special days hundreds of women would stand there, but they were a constant presence throughout the year, even if there were only half a dozen of them at one time. Whenever I had an hour to spare, I would take a walk to the City Hall in the hope of getting some interesting pictures.

On one such occasion, when there were about a dozen Black Sash women standing in a line there holding anti-apartheid placards with slogans on them, they were suddenly bombarded with eggs and rotten tomatoes by a group of hooligans with hateful expressions on their faces, who mumbled and shouted abuse. The women refused to move and no one intervened. Some bystanders found the whole incident very amusing and stood by, openly laughing.

I squeezed myself in behind the line of women, thinking that I might get some good pictures of the hooligans throwing their missiles. Before I knew it I became a target too and found myself being pelted with flying fish, of all things (they must have got the fish from the nearby fish shop), which hit my camera and my shoulder. I kept clicking away – I was getting some excellent images of this angry mob with their ugly faces throwing fish and tomatoes at me. When I heard laughter coming from my right and left, I looked around and discovered that I was standing there solo. The Black Sash women had gone! I may have gone home that day stinking of fish and with very messy clothes, but I got some excellent pictures.

At our next editorial meeting we discussed our future programme. Sylvester put on the table an idea which I thought might be the lead story for the following year, 1956. 'Mr Drum Goes to Church' would see what happened if a black man went into a white church. Bloke Modisane, our 'Black Jesus', offered to investigate this story and plan the campaign.

Casey made the point that for the last five years we had been running an American cartoon strip about a black private eye, Don Powers – why didn't we produce our own strip, he suggested, featuring a South African detective character? I offered to get some ideas together with Bill Papas, and Sylvester gave this the green light. He also announced the winner of the fourth short story award. This was Nimrod Nkele, who, he said, would be working with us on Drum as a researcher in the advertising and circulation department. Nimrod came recommended as a skilled researcher who carefully double-checked facts and figures and already had experience from working for a few leading advertising companies.

Todd wanted to talk about the singer Miriam Makeba, who was now permanently singing with the Manhattan Brothers. He thought she would make a good picture story, and Sylvester agreed. He asked me to produce a cover picture of Miriam.

It was the hottest month of the year, early January, and I was driving in my little Beetle with the windows down through heavy lunch-hour city traffic with Miriam sitting in the passenger seat beside me. We were going to make the cover picture in a recording studio in an area called Industria, west of Joburg. Miriam seemed very shy and nervous. As we waited at a traffic light and I was trying to cheer her up by making a few jokes about the people crossing the road, suddenly a booming voice bellowed in my ear – 'Kaffirboetie!' Startled, I looked into a hate-filled face sticking through my window. The words were accompanied by a strong stench of alcohol. As the traffic light changed I sped off, leaving the objectionable character behind stumbling across the road. As we got into less busy traffic, I glanced across at Miriam. She looked terrified and was crouching low down in her seat trying to make herself invisible to the people passing by. I tried to reassure her, telling her not to worry about such foul-mouthed racist abuse. I regularly experienced this whenever I drove through the city with a black person, man or woman, sitting in the passenger seat.

The recording studio was in the basement of an old disused factory. It soon appeared that we were not being taken very seriously by the management. A young white Afrikaans woman, with blonde hair and a face plastered with make-up, came to meet us. She wore a short skirt and high-heeled shoes on which she hobbled unsteadily as she led us along a long narrow passage past several doors through which I could hear the sounds of musical instruments tuning up, and the beat of drums. At the end of the passage we walked into a room that might once have been a recording studio but was now full of junk. I spotted along the walls some music stands, an old piano, piles of record covers and an odd assortment of chairs. The painted face looked at me and said abruptly, 'The studios are all occupied. This will have to do.' Then she turned and left the room, closing the door behind her.

Miriam sat down on one of the chairs and looked at me. 'What now?' she asked.

I told her not to worry, put down my camera case and started sifting through the record covers, picking out the ones that were less tattered. The walls of the room were covered with the standard soundproof tiles perforated with holes. I looked over the heap of junk and found an old microphone and a couple of stands. Miriam and I got to work, pinning up the record covers on the wall and setting up the microphone. While I left the room to find some more pins, Miriam changed into her favourite dress. When I returned we started the shoot, which was somewhat difficult because Miriam was very unrelaxed. I don't think she had ever been photographed in such a bizarre situation before,

Miriam Makeba

and by a white man. Eventually, after some joking, performing and attempting to sing, totally out of tune as I am tone-deaf, I managed to get her to laugh and then I got some good pictures.

By now our second child, a daughter whom we named Martine, had arrived and Etricia seemed relaxed and happy. I had bought her a new modern type-writer and she spent much of the day typing away on a short story she was writing.

I had followed through on my promise to invite over Bill and Aroon Papas, and Aroon's brother, and late one afternoon on my way home I stopped at a bottle-store to buy a bottle of rum and a dozen Cokes for the evening we'd planned. It was going to be drinks and a brainstorming session to create a private eye comic strip for *Drum*. Our private eye was to be a funny character who wore a pinstripe suit and had a cigar permanently between his lips. He was followed around by a small tokoloshe – Bill's sketches made it look a bit like a rodent – and we called it Tikolosh, for fun. The private eye would investigate stories from selected current events going on in the country. He would frequently get pushed around by gangsters ... but he always made a comeback. Bill's fingers flew across the pages of his notebook and we were all laughing loudly, fuelled no doubt by the rum and Cokes we were getting through, as we thought up increasingly bizarre new stories for our character to investigate. We named our private eye Goombi. One of the stories was about Dolly the jazz singer getting kidnapped and how, after many adventures, Goombi managed to rescue her. It was after midnight when Etricia came to join us, telling us to keep our voices down so as not to wake the baby.

We now had a good set of ideas and drawings for the Goombi comic strip, which I presented to Sylvester the following day, despite my heavy hangover. Everybody on *Drum* was happy about our presentation, and with a few ideas from Casey and Henry we went ahead with the monthly comic strip. Goombi became a great favourite with *Drum* readers. He owed his creative origins to rum and Coke.

25

GOING TO CHURCH WITH BLOKE

Bloke came up with a list of churches we should visit and we began preparations for our first attempt at seeing what would happen when a black man tried to attend a white church service. I cut a hole into the pocket of the left side of my waistcoat where I put a Robot camera with an automatic spring winding system – on a full wind-up of the spring I could get 25 square frames on the 35 mm film. I put a cable release into my trouser pocket and set the camera on f2 and 4 metres, so the only thing I had to do was move my jacket aside with my left hand to expose the lens of the camera and, with my right hand in my trouser pocket, release the shutter as often as necessary.

One Sunday morning we all met up – me, Sylvester, Bloke and Bob – and drove to an Anglican church in a mixed English- and Afrikaans-speaking suburb. We arrived in good time for the service. Bloke was dressed in a suit and tie. Carrying a Bible in his hand, he walked into the church. As soon as he had disappeared inside I followed him, with my hidden camera under my jacket and a Bible under my arm. Sylvester and Bob waited in the car.

As I came into the church I spotted Bloke taking a seat in one of the pews already partly occupied by churchgoers. I took a seat about five rows behind him, on the opposite side, on the aisle. Most of the people were staring at Bloke as he sat down and then a rather hostile-looking man, who had been sitting behind him, got up, grabbed Bloke aggressively by his arm and pushed him out of the pew. He marched him back down the aisle and out of the church. In the meantime, was releasing my shutter and got the whole action on film. As I walked out of the church I saw Bloke standing next to the priest. The aggressive man was still holding him by the arm. There followed a heated argument between the priest and the man, while Bob, who was standing next to the car, took pictures.

The following Sunday we went to another Anglican church, this one in the predominantly English-speaking suburb of Kensington. We went through the same routine, but this time when I entered the church behind Bloke I saw a different scene. Bloke was sitting on a bench when the priest, carrying a Bible in his left hand, walked up to him and held out his hand. He welcomed Bloke to his church in a voice that was audible to the whole congregation. The service started without further ado. About 20 minutes into the service a car outside started hooting repeatedly. Eventually, I got up and quietly tiptoed out of the church. It was Sylvester with his hand on the horn, impatient to know what was happening inside. I told him and Bob what had happened. I added that if we only visited one church a week, we would never finish the story. Sylvester got more and more impatient, but there was nothing for it but to wait until the service was over. Eventually, after about another hour, we saw Bloke emerge, along with the rest of the congregation, looking very relaxed. He carried on chatting to people outside the church while Sylvester fumed.

We held a special meeting to discuss progress. Bloke was upset and annoyed at Sylvester's lack of understanding about this sensitive church story and even more so when Sylvester decided that Can should take over. After a heated argument I decided to intervene. In my view Bloke had acted properly in the circumstances, I said. He couldn't have walked out prematurely after the great welcome he'd received from the priest.

The following Sunday saw us at a Dutch Reformed church in the east of Johannesburg, where the congregants were all white Afrikaners. Can went ahead of me and I followed as before, with my hidden camera and Bible. I sat down six rows behind Can on the opposite side, on the aisle. The service started. Nobody seemed to take any notice of us and after about fifteen minutes I decided to leave. I got up and slowly tiptoed towards the exit door, which was closed. A large man stepped in front of me. Grabbing me roughly by the arm, he said, 'You can't leave. Go and sit with your friend.'

I tried to pull away from him. He barred my way.

'You can't leave,' he said again.

So I went back to my seat. The service was in Afrikaans, conducted by an elderly man in a dark suit and white tie. The church was bare, with no decoration or paintings, and a bare cross on the altar, with just a bunch of flowers at the foot. When the preacher finished, the doors opened and the congregation started to hurry out. I got up quickly, followed by Can. As I walked towards the bright sunlight outside I was met by a bizarre sight: policemen, their expressions grim, holding automatic rifles. Before I had a moment to think, I was grabbed and led at high speed down the rest of the aisle and out of the church. Then I was roughly pushed by two heavy-set cops into a police car. As I looked around, I saw Can getting much the same treatment from another two tough-looking cops and being manhandled into another police car. A number of police cars were parked along the road and the whole church was surrounded by officers with guns.

The two cops in the car with me asked me for my name and address and took me home. I later found out that they took Sylvester and Bob to the Special Branch headquarters, which was in a building on the corner of Main and Von Wielligh Streets, close to the *Drum* office. There they were interviewed by Major Spengler, the head of the Special Branch. Can was dropped off at *Drum*.

Apparently the church had phoned the Special Branch, believing that we were part of a political movement like the Defiance Campaign. Unfortunately, the *Rand Daily Mail* had got wind of our church story and an article appeared in the morning paper about our recent exploits.

The Seventh Day Adventist Church holds its services on a Saturday morning, and the following Saturday, undeterred, we set off to their church on the corner of Plein and Nugget Streets. Saturday was the busiest day of the week, and the city was buzzing with shoppers and traffic. We parked opposite the church and, as before, Sylvester and Bob waited by the car. This time Can didn't even get inside. As he was walking up the steps he was grabbed by two beefy, aggressive characters, who dragged him unceremoniously down the steps, passing a number of churchgoers, which included some ladies dressed in their church best and wearing floppy hats. They looked terrified at the sight of Can being dragged across the road and pushed into a car. A group of young men with Bibles in their hands then noticed Sylvester and Bob and started to grab hold of them. All this time I was busy taking pictures. Suddenly a churchgoer noticed me and pointed, shouting, 'There's another one!'

It was time for me to go. I turned and started to run, with a group of Seventh Day Adventist worshippers hot on my heels, still clutching their Bibles. We dodged through the traffic, brakes screeching all around, bumping into shoppers coming out of department stores laden with parcels. Somehow I managed to stay ahead of the mob. In Polly Street I dashed into the courtyard of the building that housed Beith Process, our block makers, and ran up three flights of stairs and into the workroom. Panting, I only had time to register their astonished faces, before giving my camera to the nearest person and asking him to hide it. Then I collapsed in a heap in the corner, exhausted and out of breath. I could hear shouts echoing up and down the staircase outside, followed by the sound of footsteps. I managed to gasp out an instruction to the Beith crew not to let anyone in, which, thankfully, they didn't.

When I was satisfied that the coast was clear, I made my way to the *Drum* office, where I gave my film to Victor to develop. Sylvester, Bob and Can turned up, looking beat. They had been taken for a ride into the countryside along some waste mine property where they began to fear they would be beaten up. But then they were taken to the Special Branch, where an angry Major Spengler told them there was nothing he could do. They should watch out, he said – one day they would go too far.

By now I had a splitting headache. Headaches had, in fact, been bothering me on and off for some weeks and, feeling very unwell, I decided to go home. When I got home I felt so sick, my head throbbing excruciatingly, that I went straight to bed. My moaning and groaning got Etricia so worried that she called the doctor, who, after examining me, immediately called an ambulance. I ended up in the isolation ward of the Johannesburg Hospital with encephalitis, where I spent six weeks in quarantine. Only after a very painful lumbar puncture to reduce some of the liquid in the spine, and therefore the pressure in my head, did things improve, but for a long time I could not even read. I was terribly bored. On my release from hospital and feeling rather unsteady, I returned home, where I stayed for another two weeks, recuperating and relaxing with the children in the garden.

When I returned to the *Drum* office, nothing had changed. Humphrey Tyler was still striding up and down the passages between the desks clicking his pen and pompously talking in a loud boisterous voice about some grammatical mistake or other made by one of the writers. Bob looked as shaky as ever and Henry was busy on his typewriter. After my weeks of silence and repose, I felt I was well and truly back in the *Drum* world.

26

SPIES, LIES AND LITERATURE

In 1956 Alf Kumalo was doing regular freelance work for the *Golden City Post*, and one day I went into the darkroom and found him making prints. When I had a look at some of the prints washing in the water dish, I was somewhat taken aback – they were of people obviously in a European city and showed scenes of revolutionary activity, with burnt-out tanks and guns. I asked Alf if they were his pictures, and he got quite embarrassed and evasive. Then he told me that Cecil Eprile had sent him to Hungary to cover the uprising there and he had just returned. What became known as the Hungarian Revolution, the nationwide revolt against the government and its Soviet-influenced repression, shook Europe during October and November of 1956. I pressed Alf for a more detailed explanation about the connection between a revolution in Hungary and *Drum* publications and he told me in a pedantic tone that Cecil had given him cash to book a flight to Budapest to photograph the revolution and interview some of the leaders of the uprising. I found the whole story unbelievable but, at his request, promised to keep it confidential, provided he found out what was going to happen to his pictures.

In Sylvester's office I ran into Jim. He wanted to have a chat and asked me to join him for a drink. I had to finish preparing the last pages for the press, so I suggested instead that he come for dinner at my place. We set on the following evening at 7.30. That afternoon I left the office early to pick up some ingredients for a curry, and Etricia and I had everything prepared. Etricia had not met Jim before and she was rather nervous. She put the children to bed so they wouldn't disturb us. I opened a bottle of wine to breathe. Seven thirty came and went. So did 9.30. We waited and waited. Then it was 10pm and still no Jim. I phoned the Rand Club in case he was there, with no luck. At 11pm we decided to eat the curry and drink the wine and then we went to bed. I had already dozed off when the doorbell rang. I looked at the bedside clock – 12.30.

Jim was standing outside the door. He looked even more unkempt than usual. 'Could I have a bath, old boy?' he said.

I warmed up some leftover curry while he was in the bathroom (where he left his dirty socks) and then we sat down. I was disconcerted when I realised what it was Jim had wanted to talk to me about. He asked me what I thought of Sylvester. Was he a good editor? Did he have enough command over the staff? Could he, as a South African, understand 'the black mind'? In essence he was asking me to comment on my boss behind his back, which not only seemed disloyal but also undermining of Sylvester's authority. Jim had done something similar to me when he had called Gopal into his office and questioned him about me and how much money I was spending – was I wasting too much time, and were we overstaffed in the photo department? This had resulted in Gopal adopting a rather cocky attitude towards me and had undermined my authority over the photo department.

I told Jim it wasn't my place to discuss Sylvester's work with him, at which point Jim burst out laughing. He carried on guffawing and spluttering for a while, and when he calmed down he told me he was trying to get Tom Hopkinson to come to South Africa to edit *Drum*.

For a number of weeks I had been going through the pages of *Golden City Post* but found no reports or photos or any mention of the Hungarian uprising. So one day I cornered Alf and asked him what had happened to his pictures. Alf said he was not supposed to talk about it. Eventually, after my insistent probing, he made me promise to keep quiet and not mention what he told me to a soul. After he had given the prints to Cecil Eprile, Cecil asked him for all his negatives, which he gave him. Cecil gave him £50 in cash on the condition that this was all totally confidential.

Nothing was ever proven, but there had been several rumours among the journalists at the *Post* about Cecil working for the CIA, and this whole business got me wondering. Years later, in early 1967, these rumours were still circulating when

Cecil was appointed managing director of Forum World Features, an international news feature service located in London. *Time Out*, a London weekly, broke the news that Forum was (even at the time the story broke) a CIA front. This story was followed by corroborating stories in the London *Observer* and a number of other newspapers. It was also reported that British Intelligence approved of the CIA-run Forum.

Brian Crozier, a British journalist, was the programme manager for Forum and was Eprile's superior and boss. Crozier was a great supporter of Spain's Franco and also of Chiang Kai-shek, and both Crozier and Eprile were distrusted throughout the media world. Eprile left Forum after four years and, in poor health, retired to Silver Springs in Maryland. He was made a United States citizen by a special bill and given a pension by the John Hay Whitney Foundation. John Whitney was the chairman of Forum.

Anyway, I thought I'd better keep the Alf–Hungarian issue to myself and that's what I did.

Time-Life had opened a bureau in Johannesburg, and one day I got a phone call asking me to come and meet the new bureau chief, Mr James Bell. James knew about some of the work I was doing and asked if I would be interested in supplying pictures to *Time*, on a freelance basis, especially on stories related to the anti-apartheid movement and the ANC. He suggested I keep him informed about the stories I was working on. As I believed their interests to be the same as mine and *Drum*'s, I gladly agreed – and, also, they paid well.

When I told Etricia the good news, she was peeved. It would mean I would be out of town and travelling a lot of the time, an idea she disliked. Then she suddenly said, 'What about plumbing?' I thought she had forgotten about that idea! To keep the peace, I decided not to get into an argument about it.

Sylvester had hired some fresh blood. Two promising young journalists from *Ilanga lase Natal* were about to join *Drum* – Lewis Nkosi, aged 21, would be starting in the photography department under my guidance, and Nat Nakasa, aged 20, would be working with Cecil on the *Post*. Lewis Nkosi arrived on the next train from Durban, before Nat, and came to see me. He was a slim, well-dressed young man in a tweed jacket, white shirt, conservative tie and shiny shoes. The first time I met him at the office he was carrying under his arm a hardcover copy of James Baldwin's *Go Tell It on the Mountain* – which never left him during his first few months on the *Golden City Post* and *Drum*.

I showed Lewis around the darkroom, but to be honest he didn't seem very interested. After trying for about six weeks to teach him how to develop films and make enlargements, I gave up and so did Lewis. 'I am a writer, I'm an intellectual,' he would say grumpily. I offered to talk to Sylvester and Cecil about moving him to another department and eventually he moved on to the *Post*. Arthur Maimane was still filling in there as news editor, and he and Lewis didn't get on, which led to continuous friction between the two.

Lewis became a heavy drinker and was very popular with a shebeen queen named Aunt Suzie in Fordsburg, where most of the *Drum* chaps used to hang out after office hours (and before them). He didn't like living in Sophiatown and after a while he moved to Parkview, a white suburb, where he lived with a white girlfriend. A few months later I noticed he was still carrying a book under his arm – only Baldwin had been replaced by Jean-Paul Sartre.

Many years later I was in a crowded train in the London subway when I suddenly found myself standing opposite Lewis Nkosi. He was wearing a cape over his shoulders, the type policemen used to wear in the early twenties, a very popular fashion item during the sixties. We greeted each other and then he did something rather astonishing. From beneath his cape he produced a glass of brandy, gave me a smile, and took a sip!

Nat Nakasa came to Joburg a couple of months after Lewis. Can Themba agreed to put him up, and he went to the station to collect him and a fellow writer, Obed Musi. Can said that Nat arrived with a suitcase and a tennis racquet – an unlikely image for a tough and gritty *Drum* journalist. Nat stayed with Can at his 'House of Truth' in Sophiatown, where he observed a busy social scene peppered with alcohol and girls. Later Nat went to live with friends in a flat in white Hillbrow or sometimes stayed in a house in Parktown. Occasionally he ended up sleeping on the floor of the *Drum* office.

Nat had a young friendly face, full of smiles and laughter. He was short and slim, usually smartly and sportily dressed, often wearing a tie, and gave the impression of a confident young man about town. He only spoke English. I never heard him speak Zulu.

For the first year Nat and Lewis worked almost exclusively for the *Golden City Post* under Cecil, but they often joined us at our monthly *Drum* conference, offering story ideas. One day Nat talked to me about Nadine Gordimer, whose work he admired. He said she had invited him to a dinner party and he asked me to come along. Nadine was an admirer of *Drum* and of Nat's writing. A week later we went together to her house in Parktown. Petite and gracious, she welcomed us and took us through to dinner. The other guests were already seated at a long and elaborately laid dining-room table. Nat was the only black person there. Nadine introduced him as a promising young African writer.

The evening was very formal, with dinner served by waiters in white gloves. Can would have described the guests as 'typical white liberals' but Nat felt relaxed and was very entertaining, talking happily about his adventures as a black man living in a white world. One story he told was that when talking to officials on the phone they thought he was white, treated him with respect and were helpful. When he gave his surname they thought they had misheard it and presumed it must be something British like 'McKenzie'. When he spelt out his surname they almost always asked his nationality. That was the moment when their tone changed and they became angry and insulting. Some of the dinner guests reacted with embarrassed laughter on hearing this and similar stories.

Early on 5 December 1956 I was woken by a phone call from Robert Resha, who hurriedly explained in a breathless voice that the police were swooping down on and arresting many political leaders and searching the ANC offices. He expected to be arrested at any moment. Then the phone went dead.

I drove as fast as I could into town and found that within a few hours 150 leaders had been arrested and charged with high treason. Almost all the people arrested had been at Kliptown in 1955 and had been instrumental in the creation of the Freedom Charter. They were members of the ANC, the South African Indian Congress, the Communist Party and the Congress of Democrats, and were of different race groups. They were accused of planning to overthrow the government to create a communist state, and instigating a revolution. In total 156 people were alleged to be involved in this 'political plot'. The preparatory trial opened in the Drill Hall in Johannesburg two weeks after the arrests. There were large demonstrations in front of the Drill Hall and I went along with Peter Magubane to photograph the happenings, which had also attracted the international press.

When we got there, a number of local photographers were running about taking pictures of the protesters, who had started to sing the ANC anthem 'Nkosi Sikelel' iAfrika', when the police made a sudden baton charge into the crowd and chased the people into a side street. I saw Ian Berry in the crowd, jumping about taking pictures, and another photographer, Tom Sharpe, with a couple of Leicas around his neck and a large camera bag full of lenses over his shoulder. Tom was a keen photographer who lived in Pietermaritzburg and taught English at one of the boarding schools in the area. He used to travel by motorbike to Joburg whenever there was an interesting political event. He would later become famous for his satirical novels.

The protests lasted all morning, with the police chasing and dispersing the demonstrators, who regrouped, returned and sang again. I, along with the gang of photographers, followed the action and got some good images. I noticed that a couple of ill-tempered-looking policemen were chasing Peter, who fled to try and get away from them. When I saw this, I pushed my way through the crowd of demonstrators towards him. Peter had been cornered in a doorway by four policemen, who were all beating him angrily and ferociously with batons. He had his arm up to protect his face and head. I was furious. I saw red and took a dive, with all my cameras flying round my neck, ending up on top of the four policemen, kicking and shouting at them and emitting a high-pitched war cry. Everyone dispersed and for a moment the policemen looked frightened. They quickly recovered themselves and grabbed me. They led me down the road, followed by Peter, who was also being led by a number of policemen. All the photographers around started to photograph this spectacle.

We were taken to Marshall Square, where we had to hand over our cameras and I had to take off my tie and belt. I was escorted by a guard down a few long passages with cell doors on either side. Then the guard opened up a cell and pushed me into it. Cross-legged on an old mattress on the concrete floor, rolling a cigarette, sat an untidy bundle of a man. He was unshaven and, I reckoned, about 50 years old.

'Smoke?' he said as I sat down next to him.

I saw that he had only one eye: where his left eye should have been was a hollow empty space.

I offered him one of my Lucky Strikes, which he readily accepted.

'So what have you been up to?' he asked, lighting our cigarettes with a match.

Just then loud footsteps came echoing along the passage. They stopped outside our door and we heard a key being put into the lock. As the door opened, a voice shouted in Afrikaans, 'Jürgen, kom!'

At the charge office I was given back my cameras, tie and belt. Peter, who appeared a few minutes later from the non-European cells, was given his. We got a taxi and went straight back to the Drill Hall – to the great surprise of the police and the press – and continued taking pictures. I made some enquiries as to why we had been released so quickly, and it appeared that a journalist from the German Press Agency had seen the whole arrest and had called the German embassy, who then got in touch with the Justice Department – that was why. The following day we were charged with 'obstructing the police in the execution of their duties' and given a date to appear in court.

The local newspapers covered the story and carried pictures of our arrest, which became the talk of the town. About a week later, just before Christmas, I got a letter from Lady Bailey. She bemoaned the terrible things happening in South Africa and felt sorry for me for having been pushed around and arrested by the police. If I ever wanted to stay in Cape Town, any time, I and my family would be very welcome as her guests, she said.

When I showed Lady Bailey's letter to Etricia, she got very excited. 'We need a holiday!' she said. 'Let's go!' It was the weekend before Christmas and she kept on chirping about it, even telling the kids about the trip, who also got very excited. We hadn't had a holiday for about four years and I thought that, actually, it might be a good idea. I phoned Sylvester the next day. If it was okay with him, I said, I'd like to take a couple of weeks off. I'd be back at work in early January. Luckily, thanks to a cancellation, I managed to book train tickets to Cape Town for the four of us, and I sent a telegram to Lady Bailey.

We spent ten enjoyable days in Cape Town as guests of Lady Bailey – who insisted again that we call her Mary. She put us up in the butler's flat, gave us the use of her car, a Chrysler (which had been standing on blocks in her garage), and was extremely generous and charming.

A couple of days before we were due to head back home, I received a phone call from Sylvester. He said he'd been trying for some time to contact me; he hadn't known I was staying at Lady Bailey's home. Had I heard the news? And then came the most horrific shock: Henry Nxumalo had been murdered just before Christmas. I was speechless, completely distraught. Henry was my best friend, my only friend. Poor Henry, a man of great courage, personality, character and humour – I was devastated. When I got back to the *Drum* office, I found that I had missed his funeral.

Sylvester was doing his best, making numerous enquiries, to find information about Henry's murder, which was proving difficult. All he had been able to discover was that Henry had been investigating a story about a white doctor attached to the Sophiatown police station. The doctor had a clinic in Sophiatown where, it was reported, a large number of botched abortions had taken place. Henry's murder was never solved and no one was convicted for the crime.

One day Ian Berry called me on the phone and invited me and Etricia for a drink at his new flat – and to meet his fiancée. His apartment was in a new building in the now fashionable part of Hillbrow. The young, rich and trendy people (whites) flocked to Hillbrow. The European-style cafés, like Café Wien in its main street, were well patronised and there were many entertainment venues – the Montparnasse, the Chelsea Hotel and a variety of jazz clubs, night clubs and strip joints. It was the sort of trendy place where I would have expected Ian to live. Although the foyer downstairs was quite grand, the flat itself was just a two-roomed one, small and sparsely furnished. Nevertheless, Ian looked his usual dapper self in beige corduroy trousers, tweed jacket, suede shoes and a silk scarf under his blue-striped shirt. 'Good to see you, lad!' were his first words as he opened the door. 'Meet Shirley.'

There, with a cocktail glass in one hand and a cigarette in the other, stood a pretty young woman in a figure-hugging dress and high heels. She had long black hair cascading in curls down one side of her face and very red lips. Ian told us Shirley was from Benoni on the East Rand, where she had recently celebrated her débutante 'coming out' party. He seemed very proud of his conquest. The engagement party a week later – Ian had asked me to prepare one of my famous punches – was a happy occasion. And the more of my punch the guests drank, the happier they got. At one stage one of Ian's friends, a commercial artist named Arthur Goldreich, got up and started telling stories. His stories got funnier and funnier, the audience's laughter louder and louder, and Arthur more and more animated – waving his arms about to ever-increasing gales of laughter. Arthur left eventually, with a skip and a wave goodbye at the door, having thoroughly entertained us all – no little thanks, I thought, to my punch!

Not too many years later Arthur Goldreich would be arrested, in July 1963, at Lilliesleaf Farm in Rivonia, where he was a tenant of the property. He lived there quietly with his family as a cover for the ANC freedom fighters. When police raided the farm, Arthur was arrested together with the underground leadership group of the ANC and was held, awaiting trial, under the 90-day detention law at Marshall Square. Civil rights lawyer Harold Wolpe was also detained. They eventually managed to bribe an unsuspecting young warder and escaped on a Saturday night. Despite a nationwide manhunt the two men, dressed as priests, managed to escape to Francistown in Botswana, where they waited for a Dakota to fly them to Lusaka in Northern Rhodesia. When the plane arrived in Francistown to pick them up, the South African Security Police had got wind of it and blew up the plane. The two escapees hid in a priest's house, hounded by the South African and international press, and it was only some weeks later that they finally got away, under cover of darkness, and off to safety in another light plane.

In February, Peter Magubane and I went to court to face the charges of obstructing the police in the execution of their duties. After a long time waiting on a bench outside the courtroom, the prosecutor came out and spoke to our lawyer. We were told that the state's witness had been unable to appear and so the case was postponed. On our next court date we sat waiting on the bench again. The arresting officer arrived and joined us on the bench. He passed round a packet of cigarettes and lit our smokes for us. Then he began telling us his life story, saying how unhappy he was working in the police force. Leaning across Peter and me, he asked our lawyer if he could help him get a job, maybe in security. Just then the courtroom door opened and a number of people came out, including the prosecutor, who approached us.

'Where is Sergeant Potgieter?' he asked the arresting officer.

'I don't know. I think he's in Krugersdorp,' said the policeman.

'What is he doing in Krugersdorp? He should be here.'

Like our dejected arresting officer, the prosecutor was a young man, probably in his twenties. He was wearing an ill-fitting double-breasted grey suit and
an untied bright-blue tie. We could see he was irritable and short-tempered.
'You have made a mess of the case!' he yelled at the policeman, who looked
very embarrassed. 'I'm going to drop the case – there's no point working with
your department – I'm going to talk to your commanding officer!' He ranted
on for a while and then Peter and I were excused. The soon-to-be-unemployed
policeman trailed after us. Outside the courthouse he asked our lawyer for his
phone number.

In mid-1957 Sylvester announced at an editorial meeting that he would be
leaving towards the end of the year to go to West Africa and run the *Drum* office
there. Tom Hopkinson would be taking over from him in early 1958. He also
announced that he was taking two weeks' leave. Can would be acting editor
while he was away.

One of the cover stories we were planning to work on for the next issue
was about the first black tennis champion, Althea Gibson, who in July 1957
received the trophy from Queen Elizabeth at Wimbledon for winning the
Women's Singles – her opponent was fellow American Darlene Hard – and
Doubles finals. We decided to use a picture on the cover of Althea Gibson holding the trophy and being given a congratulatory kiss on the cheek by her blonde
white opponent.

We were still working on the layout and text while Sylvester was on leave and
Can was supposed to be in charge. However, Can seemed to have got lost. He
hadn't shown up at the office for five days and chief sub Humphrey was performing his pompous peacock act, talking loudly and strutting up and down the office,
clicking his pen, and arguing over trivial points and petty matters. I eventually
got tired of his behaviour and called him a bullshitter, which kept him quiet for
a while until the next arrogant outburst – when I called him a bullshitter again.

Jim had returned from one of his regular world tours and he asked to see

Can Themba

the layout of the next issue. He took one look at the cover design of the Althea Gibson story, a black tennis player being kissed by a white tennis player, and hit the roof. His face contorted into a disgusted grimace. Shaking his head vigorously from left to right, in his most commanding voice, he said, 'Drop the cover!'

'Why?' I asked, taken aback.

Jim gave me his comradely smile. 'We don't want the paper closed down, do we?' he said.

'I have to speak to Sylvester,' I said. 'He's the editor.'

Jim's expression changed to one of tired annoyance. 'Sylvester is a tedious clot,' he said. 'Now get on with it. Find a new cover picture.'

Can turned up at the office looking knackered but behaving as though nothing had happened. I told him and Humphrey about Jim's instructions. We were in limbo about the cover – what to do? I tried to get Sylvester on the phone and, after a fruitless day of attempting to track him down, finally managed to get the number for the hotel north of Durban where he was staying. When I told him what Jim had instructed me to do, he was livid. His message to Jim was clear: if the picture was removed, he would not return to the *Drum* office, nor would he work for *Drum* in West Africa. That was final. Then he hung up.

Humphrey's head started to swell again and he became more puffed up than ever – I had to repeat my bullshitter comment a few more times to keep him calmer but eventually we found a replacement cover picture.

Jim called Can to his office and told him he was in charge until Tom Hopkinson arrived the following year. In the meantime, he said, he wanted to see the *Drum* schedule and all the text and picture layouts. This was fine, I told him, except that he was only in the office one week a month, so how would that work? Plus, it would also be difficult to make contact with him as he was constantly travelling – to West Africa, Kenya and elsewhere.

'Between you, Can and Humphrey, you will have to manage,' Jim said imperiously.

And we left it at that.

27

CUCUMBER SANDWICHES

Drum moved offices from 176 Main Street to bigger premises a couple of blocks away in Troye Street. The building was Samkay House and we occupied the whole of the first floor, along with the *Post* and all the administration staff. Our darkroom was also there.

One day Zeke Mphahlele asked me to accompany him to an interview he was doing with a civil rights lawyer and take some photographs. Fortunately, I was free at that moment and we walked together along Commissioner Street to His Majesty's building. As we walked into the foyer and were about to get into one of the four lifts, we heard a loud voice from behind us.

'No! No natives in this lift!' The voice was that of a Zulu man in a security guard uniform and he was full of self-importance. 'Natives go in the goods lift,' he said.

Zeke looked very upset but he began walking towards the goods lift. 'See you on the fourteenth floor,' he said to me over his shoulder.

'No way,' I said. We would both go in the goods lift. As I was about to get in behind Zeke, I heard the security guard shouting again. 'No, baas, no, baas! You are not allowed in this lift! You must take the lift for the masters!'

I had had just about enough of the man and the whole apartheid farce. I could feel myself getting worked up. I grabbed Zeke by the hand, pulled him out of the goods lift and led him across the foyer to the staircase. 'We walk!' I said. Zeke gave me a small smile and up we went. When we reached the tenth floor we were both out of breath and sat down on the steps to recover. Zeke was totally relaxed, which was most unusual for him. This time I got a genuine smile. 'That was tremendous,' he said.

Zeke was an outsider in the *Drum* group of writers as he didn't participate in their drunken parties and excessive behaviour, which was their way of escaping from apartheid racism and the pressures that came with it. To me Zeke seemed a bitter man, who had a deep hatred of all whites – and yet some of his hatred was directed towards himself for accepting Western culture as an intellectual. Most of the other *Drum* writers managed to hide their real feelings by adopting quirky behaviour. Henry Nxumalo and Casey Motsisi were the exceptions. They seemed to have risen above tribalism and racism.

On floor fourteen Zeke got his interview and I my photo and then, step by step, we walked down the stairs to the ground floor. For the first time I heard Zeke laugh heartily – in fact, we both ended up in fits of laughter after our minor defiant, triumphant, comic escapade.

Can, Humphrey and I, the three musketeers, together with the rest of the *Drum* crew, managed for six months to produce and bring out *Drum* magazine – from mid-1957 to the end of that year. We had our differences, with Can continuing to disappear for days, and sometimes he had too much skokiaan, and Humphrey needing regular reminders from me about his bullshit behaviour, but in general we all got on well together and produced some reasonable pages.

I had started to use Ian Berry for a number of our picture stories, and some of his pictures were outstanding. One day he brought in a set of pictures he had taken of a riot in Benoni. Black garment workers had been demonstrating about wages and the mostly black cops were beating them up with long wooden clubs. One old man was on his knees with his hands raised up to protect his face from being viciously bludgeoned. I was standing at my desk with Joe Bloomberg and Can, looking at Ian's pictures and discussing what space and copy we should give them, when Humphrey came swaggering in. Behind him was a man in his late fifties with a gentle expression on his pale face.

Humphrey bellowed, 'Hello, boys! How are you – all busy, I see? Excellent! And what have we here?'

I had my head down, looking at Ian's pictures, when suddenly Humphrey turned around to the stranger and announced: 'This is our new editor, Tom

Zeke Mphahlele

Hopkinson.' Then he waved around at the editorial office and made introductions – 'my chief sub, Joe Bloomberg, my assistant editor, Can Themba, and my
pictures editor, Jürgen Schadeberg. Now they are yours!'

Tom Hopkinson seemed embarrassed by Humphrey's theatrical performance. He shook hands with all of us and took a great interest in the pictures
on my desk, going through them all carefully. He asked me if they were mine
and I told him they were from our freelance photographer, Ian Berry. 'Buy the
set!' Tom said immediately. 'An excellent set of photos.'

I found out later that Humphrey had known about Tom's arrival for a while
and had gone on his own to pick him up from the airport, introducing himself
as the current editor of *Drum*. He told him he had been editing the magazine
since Sylvester left six months before.

My first impression of Tom Hopkinson was of a mild-mannered, soft and
gentle person, who could easily be taken for granted. However, when he held
his first staff meeting a few days later he quickly showed his tough, determined
side. When he started, he had no idea about how we had worked with our previous editors and on what terms. His style, however, was that everyone on the
editorial staff should know exactly what was going on and what the plans for
our next issues were. Everyone would have a say about every issue. We would
have regular meetings, like this one, where anyone could put up suggestions
and ideas for the following issue and contribute story and photography ideas.
Everyone should feel free to comment on and criticise the ideas of others. Our
day should start at 8.30 every morning – in his week as editor, he said, he had
noticed that the staff turned up late and at irregular times. Also, he wanted everyone to work on stories for the whole month. We had a small staff and there
was no excuse for leaving the work to the last minute, scrambling bits of copy
together. We wanted a paper that was original, well written, and with great
photographs, superior to any daily or weekly paper around.

Tom asked me to work out the assignments with Can and said we were free
to consult him at any time. Time permitting, he wanted to get to know everyone individually and bring out their abilities and talents. Those members of the
team with no apparent abilities were not suited to work on *Drum*, he said, and
he would have no hesitation in firing them. He regarded all of us as journalists

and he would be relying heavily on us to do our jobs well.

After the meeting Tom asked me about Bob Gosani. He had seen many of Bob's pictures and thought him a very talented photographer – what was he doing? Why hadn't he seen him at the office? I told Tom that Sylvester had fired Bob because of his continual drunkenness and unreliable behaviour and that Bob was now freelancing for the *Golden City Post*. A week later, after a long session with Tom, Bob was working for *Drum* again. I was told that Bob made a promise to Tom to stay away from alcohol.

One day a young man, about eighteen years old, with a shy manner and a slight limp turned up at the office to see me. He carried a large camera bag and had a black rangefinder Nikon over his shoulder. He introduced himself as Ernest Kole, a photographer looking for work. Then he produced out of his camera case an 8 x 10-inch box, which he opened and passed to me. Inside was a set of about 25 prints. Looking through them, I was pleasantly surprised. There were some excellent photos among them – weddings, portraits and family groups – and some outstanding prints. Ernest told me he was making a living from social photos but was more interested and involved in documentary photography and photojournalism. I told him I was very interested in his work and would see what I could do after speaking to the editor and Jim.

After lots of arguments and ums and ahs from Jim, I managed to get him to agree that Ernest could be my assistant while receiving picture editing training from me. Ernest was delighted and, after I had him working in the darkroom for a few weeks, teaching him the fundamentals about developing and printing, he helped me on the picture desk. I found him to be friendly, enthusiastic and helpful but shy. He confided that he was about to change his racial classification on account of the continual problems he had with the police, who always stopped him to see what was in his camera bag. To prove that he had legitimately bought his equipment, he carried with him the receipts for all his cameras and lenses. He wanted to be reclassified from 'African' to 'coloured' and had been working at this for some time, getting all the right papers and practising what to say at the interviews at the Racial Classification Board. He planned to change his name from Kole to Cole and life would be much easier for him.

After Tom's stern lecture at the last meeting, everybody turned up at work before ten in the morning. Tom had arranged a final meeting with Can and the editorial staff for the following Monday at nine. I came to the office at about 9am and found Tom alone. The editorial room was still empty, except for Joe Bloomberg, who was working at his desk. Tom came out of his office, stood at the open door, looked around and went back into his office. At about 10.30 one of our writers, Butch Molotse, came into the office, looking rather red-eyed, shaky and fuzzy. Tom came out of his office again.

'Where is everybody, Butch?' he asked irritably. 'We have a meeting this morning to get started on our new issue!'

Butch looked around vaguely, licking his lips as if he was about to have a drink. 'Casey's not here,' he said and, looking around some more, 'Bob's not in,' and, looking at me as I got up from my desk and walked over to them, 'Can's not in, Mr Hopkinson ... Maybe they are all a little bit late this morning, being Monday, Mr Hopkinson ...'

I told Tom our colleagues must have had a great weekend and were probably sleeping it off. 'We probably won't see any of them today – or tomorrow, in my experience,' I added. Tom looked furious. He asked Butch if he knew where his colleagues lived. Butch hesitated a bit but then said he thought so. Tom decided they should go and get them from their homes there and then. As Tom and Butch started to leave, Tom turned to me and said, 'Jürgen, you come too!'

So there the three of us were, squashed together in the front seat of Tom's car. I took the middle spot while Butch sat on my left with the window wide open. As we drove into Sophiatown Butch kept leaning out of the window, smiling and greeting people. At this time of the morning the roads were busy with people, children and dogs crossing back and forth, and Butch kept up a constant volley – 'Hey, man! Hey, Samson! Hey, Moses!' Later when Tom asked me why Butch had kept on waving and shouting out of the window, I explained: he was worried people would think he was sitting in a car with two white cops.

'But we don't look like cops,' Tom said with a puzzled expression.

'All whites are cops to them,' I replied.

We found Can lying naked on his stomach in his house across a mattress on the floor. He actually looked unconscious. Butch tried to turn him around and lift his head. Can's eyes opened briefly and rolled around for a second. Then he sank back into oblivion. There was no point, I told Tom. We wouldn't be seeing Can at work for a few days. Next we went to Bob's house, where his young wife made an effort to get Bob on his feet. He peered at us with bleary eyes, then stumbled about trying to drink the coffee his wife had made for him.

'There's no point,' I told Tom, repeating what I'd said at Can's place. 'He won't be able to focus.' Then, trying to add a note of humour, I added: 'He's totally out of focus.' So much for Bob's promise to stay away from alcohol. We gave up and left.

As we were getting back into the car to go and look for Casey, Butch said that as Casey tended to sleep in different places every other night, it was bound to be a fruitless search. Then he turned to Tom and said brightly, 'Would you like a drink?' Tom, who seemed rather fed up and disheartened by the morning so far, agreed that a drink might not be a bad idea in the circumstances. I had to agree.

Butch took us to the home of a girlfriend, Mabel, who was a shebeen queen. She readily invited us into her living room and we all sat down at a long table. The room was neat and well kept, with a couch covered by some patterned blankets and lots of cushions. Mabel produced half a bottle of gin and a couple of quart bottles of Lion beer and Butch got busy pouring drinks into glasses. This was something of a new cocktail – beer topped up with gin – but Butch seemed to have no problem with this strange concoction. Tom and I needed to get acquainted with the taste first, but after a few glasses we all seemed to feel much more relaxed. Butch kept filling up the glasses.

Mabel sat next to me, getting rather close. 'Why are you not at ease, Mr Schadeberg?' she asked, giving me a long look. 'Why cannot you be at ease too?'

I told her that I was quite at ease and very happy.

'No, you're not happy, Mr Schadeberg, and you are not at ease.'

In the meantime Butch was filling up our glasses again and gulping down his own drinks in one go.

'Only Mr Schadeberg is not at ease,' Mabel repeated. She gave me a big smile and then burst out laughing.

I must admit I was rather fed up with the day's performance of looking for *Drum* colleagues and ending up drinking in a shebeen ourselves, and I felt sorry for Tom, who seemed thoroughly perplexed by his new staff. When it was time to leave, Tom took out his wallet.

'No,' said Mabel. 'You are my guests and my friends.'

I was about to get up from my chair when Mabel came up to me, put her arms around me and, leaning over, whispered in my ear, her large breasts squashed into my face. 'Come and visit me again and I will make you at ease and you will have good time.' And then she kissed me on the ear. Behind me Butch had settled down full length on the couch. He had a peaceful smile on his face but I could see he wasn't coming with us.

Two days later, when everybody was back in the office, Tom called a special staff meeting. Looking from one person to the next, he said, 'We need to make a successful, best-selling magazine with a small staff we can depend on, a staff that stays sober at work. We need new regulations at work about drinking.' Everybody was silent. 'From now on anyone who gets drunk at work, and this applies for all office hours, will be suspended for a week without pay. Anyone who gets drunk a second time will be suspended for a month. Anyone who is drunk for the third time gets fired.' This applied to black staff and white – no discrimination there. Those were the regulations from now on.

We had a new member on the editorial staff – Matthew Nkoana. He was in his mid-thirties, rather messy-looking with his frayed collar flapping about, wore double-thick glasses on the end of his nose, had brown misshapen teeth and spoke with a high-pitched intellectual-sounding voice. His first assignment was to interview Robert Sobukwe, the leader of a group of disillusioned ANC members who had taken part in the Defiance Campaign in 1952. The group called themselves the Pan Africanist Congress and they planned to break away from the ANC, which they felt had been infiltrated by communists. Sobukwe was about to lead this group of angry young men to create the PAC, which believed that only two groups had an inherent right to South Africa – the blacks and coloureds. Whites and the Indians were foreign minorities. The PAC was also going to abolish the pass laws.

I was impressed by Matthew's interviewing skills. He seemed, to me, to be on a par with a journalist like Henry Nxumalo. He and I talked about the idea of an investigative story we could do together: 'Mr Drum Returns to Bethal'.

Can and Bob were about to leave for Kimberley. With John driving them in the Land Rover, they were going to cover a conference there of the combined African churches which, maybe for the first time during the apartheid period, were becoming political and making their anti-apartheid voices heard. They would be gone for three days. A day later we got a phone call from the police station in Potchefstroom, saying they had three of our employees in custody. They needed bail money – £60. The three had been arrested outside Potchefstroom for drunken behaviour, drunken driving, illegal possession of alcohol and resisting arrest. When they eventually returned to the *Drum* office we got some very muddled and confusing versions of the events. Needless to say, they never reached Kimberley.

This was what happened on the drive down, more or less.

The road to Kimberley went through the town of Potchefstroom and it so happened that there was a fire in the Woolworths department store, next door to which was a bottle-store, which was about to catch fire. The three stopped and Bob got out of the Land Rover to take some pictures. When they saw a white man carrying bottles of liquor out of the bottle-store to safety, they thought he might need some help. In the confusion they managed to take half-a-dozen bottles of brandy and put them in their car for their trouble. They then climbed back into the Land Rover and drove off onto the road to Kimberley. John, the driver, wanted to get rid of the six brandy bottles and throw them out of the car, and an argument ensued. Can and Bob had a better idea. They insisted John help them drink the brandy – why throw good brandy away? Bob and Can, together with a reluctant John, had almost finished four of the six bottles when they were arrested by the police who, it seemed, had been following them for some time. There were several variations on this story. It also appeared that a fourth person might have joined them on this trip but we never got to the bottom of that.

Tom Hopkinson was beside himself with anger. Bob Gosani was fired on the spot and Can was suspended without pay for a month and stripped of his position as assistant editor, resulting in a reduction of his pay. The following Monday evening, when the editorial staff had left the office, Butch was found by a general manager, whose name was Weatherstone, to be dead drunk, rowdy and unruly, which behaviour was reported to Tom. Tom said he was going to sack Butch, but the manager, disgruntled though he was, told him this wasn't possible. Butch owed the firm £30, a loan he had received a few months before, and was paying it off at £5 a month. 'You can't fire him until he's paid off his debt in six months' time.' Tom objected. Surely it was better to forfeit the £30 and get rid of troublesome, useless staff? 'I have to balance my books!' said Weatherstone. And so Butch got a reprieve.

In September 1958 Etricia and I began packing up our Edenvale home and got ready to move closer to town. We had rented a house in African Street in Norwood, which was in a more central spot. We also had a new addition to our family, Frankie, who was now six months old, and Etricia was expecting again. We'd both decided that four children was a good number and we were looking forward to seeing if number four would be another girl, making it two pairs of each. Our relationship, however, was still difficult, with Etricia continually distrustful of me, resulting in many a jealous outburst, and our family life was gloomy. Whenever I worked late or stayed out of town for a couple of days for work, I returned to Etricia's jealous tirades, which had the rebound effect of giving me an irrational guilt complex. In the end and in the hope of keeping the peace, I resorted to phoning Etricia before my late returns to describe in detail the various events at work that were keeping me.

In the last few days in Edenvale the Papas family visited again. We were running out of stories for the Goombi cartoon strip and it was going to be a long and intense brainstorming and rum and Coke session. By about six the next morning we were still at it, still laughing and joking, but had not yet produced much in the way of new ideas. Admittedly, we were all quite tiddly and the rum bottle was close to empty when suddenly Aroon said: 'What about Sputnik?' Bill looked at her as though she were mad. 'What about Sputnik? Are you moonstruck?' he asked. But through my tipsy stupor, somehow I got the message. 'Goombi goes to the moon on Sputnik!' I shouted. And right there we solved our problem.

The launch of Sputnik in May 1958 was on everybody's mind at that time – I'd even named my new dog Sputnik. The Americans were upset that the Soviet Union had been the first to launch a satellite into orbit. So Goombi's cartoon would be very current and topical.

I thought that it might be better to have Ian Berry join the staff since, after Bob had been fired, we now had only one photographer, Peter Magubane, and he couldn't manage all the work on his own. I was using Ian regularly anyway, as a freelancer.

I was so busy working on production and picture editing that I could only manage one or two main stories a month myself. Getting Ian on the staff was something of a battle, however. Tom agreed but Jim didn't want to know. After a good deal of arguing with Jim, and with Tom's support, we eventually made it happen and of course Ian was delighted. Now he had access to the main apartheid events and stories which could be channelled to Magnum, his photo agency in Paris.

On 13 October I was finishing off the November issue and as usual had two pages to complete – we always left these open for any last-minute emergency events – before we went to press. Suddenly Tom burst out of his office and came hurrying over. 'Jürgen, send two photographers to Pretoria! Something is going to happen at the Treason Trial – now! And hold the last two pages!' I dashed off to find Ian and Peter. Peter was out on a job, so I decided to go with Ian myself. Nat Nakasa was the only writer in the office at that moment, so the three of us jumped in my Beetle and raced to Pretoria.

We arrived at the Old Synagogue, which was where the Treason Trial was being held, just in time to see the accused pouring out of the exit with big smiles on their faces. They proceeded to shake hands and light cigarettes. Ian and I got busy with our cameras, moving from one group of big smiles to another. I spotted Nelson Mandela and managed to get a number of images of him and Moses Kotane as they left the yard through the Synagogue gate.

It was a mild, cloudy Pretoria morning when the leader of the Crown team addressed the court: 'Your Lordship, I withdraw the indictment against the accused.'

Dumbstruck, the courtroom was completely silent. When the 91 accused, men and women of all races, there to fight the charge of high treason, recovered from the shock, there was a roar of laughter and applause. The relief on the faces as they left the courtroom could be seen in the beaming smiles, thumbs-up signs and much handshaking. Some weeks later most of the accused were rearrested and the Treason Trial continued for another two years when, again, a not-guilty verdict was returned.

Many years later I produced and published some of my Mandela pictures in a number of my books about South African history. One day I received a call from Peter Magubane. He asked me to meet him at the office of lawyer David Dison

Nelson Mandela outside the Old Synagogue, 1958

the following day. When I arrived at Dison's office I was led into a boardroom. There, sitting next to Dison at the end of the boardroom table, was Peter, with a stern look on his face.

David greeted me with 'Hello, Jürgen, sit down, please', but before he could say anything else Peter interrupted him. In a harsh, steely voice, he said: 'The Mandela picture, where he comes out through the gate of the Synagogue at the Treason Trial with Moses Kotane, is my picture and you have to return the negative to me and also pay me for any previous sales of this image.'

Peter claimed that he had been at the Old Synagogue in Pretoria on 13 October 1958, but in fact, as I explained and reminded him, he couldn't have been. He was doing a story on Josias Madzunya, the bus boycott and school boycott leader, in Alexandra township that day. I also described the circumstances in which I had taken the picture. Dison seemed satisfied with my explanation but Peter was unconvinced at the time and called me a liar. The matter was only resolved years later. Years on I found one of my Mandela 1958 images credited to Alf Kumalo and, in other publications, credited to Bob Gosani. It was disheartening and I almost gave up fighting to prove that this picture was mine. Then I saw the image on sale on the BAHA photo agency webpage – credited to various photographers other than myself. In the end, ownership was resolved and the judgment of a Berlin high court forbade BAHA from selling my pictures outside South Africa.

Matthew Nkoana's research for 'Mr Drum Returns to Bethal' was well under way. He was building up his contacts in the town and had researched some of the farms most notorious for ill-treating their labourers. In the meantime I got, on loan, some land-surveying equipment – a surveying tripod, impressive-looking levels and transit levels equipment and a surveying distance-measuring wheel. I hired an Afrikaans-speaking reporter, George, and gave him instructions to wear khaki shorts and shirt and a floppy farmer's hat. All set, we then loaded up the Land Rover and, with John at the wheel, we drove to Bethal.

In the town we enquired about the farm Matthew had picked out as one of the worst, and people suddenly became uncomfortable, giving us suspicious looks, but we managed to locate it. We saw some workers in a field digging up potatoes and throwing them into large baskets. I instructed John to drive through the gate, and onto a rough piece of farmland where some workers were digging. They stood up and watched us intently. George and I got out and began to set up the surveying equipment. I looked through the lens equipment while George held up the numbered rod a couple of hundred metres from us. A few minutes later a bakkie sped over the field towards us in a cloud of dust. It stopped next to me.

'What are you doing on my farm?'

The farmer got out of the truck. He was a large, burly man – needless to say, in khaki shirt and shorts and floppy hat – and the half of his face we could see was dark brown and sunburnt. He leant into his bakkie and pulled out a shotgun, which he put under his arm. He looked angry. He glanced at George, who was slowly approaching us with the surveying rod. Speaking in Afrikaans, George said something about telephone lines and how the farmer should have been informed. Fortunately his words seemed to calm the farmer down. Mumbling irritably to himself, he got back in the bakkie and drove off, leaving another cloud of dust settling around us.

Once the farmer was safely gone, Matthew got out of the Land Rover and walked across the field where he talked to the workers, some of whom seemed no older than about fourteen. I followed behind and took photographs. They all told the same story I had heard with Henry so many years before, of being beaten, starved and forced to buy their foodstuffs on credit from the farmer's store. This arrangement meant that when their contract was due to end, they could not leave because they were in debt to the farmer. They were consequently forced to sign up for a further nine months. Many of the farmworkers were in this perpetual vicious circle of never being able to leave. The farmer withheld their passbooks, too, telling them that they would be arrested if they ever left without paying their debt. Being found not to have a pass was a criminal offence under apartheid and caused untold problems for those who were caught. We went to visit other farms in the area, using the same trick of posing as land surveyors, and heard the same stories.

When we returned to Joburg, Tom was disappointed that I hadn't got any photos of the notorious prison farm in the district of Bethal. He decided I should go back the following Monday to find some farm prisoners – and then he decided to go with me himself. On Monday morning he turned up at the office ready for our trip – in a safari outfit! I stared at him, speechless. 'This way I look like a British tourist,' he explained, looking rather pleased with himself.

'The only thing missing is a tropical helmet!' I told him.

I got my camera case and we went to his car, which was parked outside the office. I was surprised to see it was the old Plymouth, the one I'd crashed into the ox in 1952 ... I hadn't seen it since 1953 or '54 – I'd wondered what had happened to it. Anyway, Tom was driving, I was sitting next to the passenger door and in between us on the seat was a pair of large binoculars, which I thought was a very good idea to spot farm prisoners from a distance. After about two hours' driving through flat open country, Tom turned his binoculars on a clump of trees on top of a hill, the first hill we had seen since we left the city. Tom turned onto a dirt road that seemed to lead towards the hill, and parked on a path next to a tree. 'Let's have tea!' he said.

I had no idea what he was talking about. There was no tearoom within a hundred miles. Even in Bethal we would have been hard pressed to find a tearoom or coffee house – only some bars. Tom trained his binoculars on the treetops again. He looked disappointed. 'No birds here,' he said. Then he walked back to the car and opened the boot. He took out a basket, which he placed beside the tree, and a blanket, which he spread on the ground. What with the out-of-place tropical outfit and now a picnic, it seemed, I could hardly believe my eyes.

Out of the basket Tom took plates, a teapot, a flask and some wrapped cucumber white bread sandwiches. When I recovered from my astonishment I took some pictures of Tom Hopkinson serving tea and cucumber sandwiches on the South African highveld in his safari suit. Tom was genuinely disappointed that there were practically no birds around and kept scouring the treetops with his binoculars while we had our tea.

We found the prison farm eventually and I managed to get a few pictures from a distance of labourers at work, with a guard with a rifle watching over them. Tom had approached the Farm Prison Department for an interview some days before but they had declined, saying that under no circumstances could we interview anyone. We returned that evening to Johannesburg disappointed but not altogether empty-handed, and Tom dropped me off at our house in African Street.

The cucumber sandwiches were delicious.

South Africa in White and Black

David Pratt, who shot HF Verwoerd, in court

28

NEW FOCUS, NEW DIRECTIONS

Etricia and I and our four children – our daughter Bonnie was born on 17 October 1958 – were quite settled in our Norwood home. It was a pleasant house on a big property, over 2 000 square metres, with enough space for all of us and a small darkroom. The property had outhouses at the back, which were occupied by a maid, who worked for us full-time and looked after the children.

Etricia had given up the idea of becoming a writer and had started to take an interest in gardening. She redesigned our garden in African Street, planting new bushes along the wall facing the street and making new flower-beds. She also planted peach trees and a patch of mealies behind the house along the wall. Within a couple of months of our being there, Etricia had transformed the outdoors into a beautiful garden. She worked non-stop from early morning till sunset, furiously digging and planting. I was surprised at her energy and focus. It didn't last, however. After a while I noticed that many of the flowers were dried up and the bushes and trees neglected. When I tried talking to Etricia about it, she told me her plans had changed. She had been to visit Fritz Isaac, from Werner's Studio, and was going into business with him – a partnership selling ladies' underwear! In due course they intended to open a shop and she wouldn't have time to look after the garden.

Etricia was very excited about her new business venture. She suggested that the time had come for me, as the head of the family, to think seriously about our future. I should leave *Drum*, give up photography, and go into business with her. I was dumbfounded. I had learnt from bitter experience that there was no point arguing with her, so I said I would think about it. In the meantime, please could she arrange to have the plants in the garden watered so that they stayed alive.

In fact, I had been thinking about leaving *Drum* for some months. Eight years, I thought, was enough. Most of my old friends and colleagues had left or were about to leave – the magazine or the country or both. Henry, Arthur, Zeke and Bloke were gone, the others soon to follow. Also I was not so happy with Tom.

Tom and Jim had frequent disputes, not only over finance but also about editorial content. It seemed to me that Tom was trying to turn *Drum* into *Picture Post* from a British Labour Party perspective. Under his editorship the visual and design aspects of the magazine had certainly improved but in the process *Drum* had lost its jazzy, lively character and inventive African touch. Now it looked more and more like a well-produced English publication – which didn't seem to suit African readers.

So in early 1959 I gave three months' notice as *Drum*'s photo editor, production manager, head of the photographic department and art director, but I offered to continue my service as a freelance photographer, with an improved payment arrangement. (I heard that after I left *Drum* they employed three people to fill my multi-tasked role.)

So that was that. Now I had to set myself up as a full-time freelance photographer.

I got in touch with Taubie Kushlick again. She had just formed a new company with Leon Gluckman, the Kushlick-Gluckman Company, and was producing a play called *Half in Earnest*, a skit on *The Importance of Being Earnest*. They promised me continuous photographic work. I was also approached by *Panorama*, a magazine produced by the National Party government that catered for the tourist market. I was worried about working for the government, even on a freelance basis, but the story they wanted me to do, which I photographed in colour, seemed harmless enough. It was about paintings produced by 4–6-year-old children in a progressive nursery school which promoted creativity in young children.

I also managed to get some work from the *Rand Daily Mail* and the *Sunday Times*. Joel Mervis was the editor of the *Sunday Times* and known for his success in vastly increasing the paper's circulation. It was the biggest-circulation paper in

Africa, selling over one million copies per week. Johnny Johnson, whom I already knew, was news editor. Johnny was a tough fellow, with complete control over his ten reporters, who were terrified of him. The chief photographer at the time was Pat Smith, who, in my opinion, was an outstanding news photographer, but he seemed to be out of favour with Mervis and Johnson, which I found difficult to explain, except for the fact that he was an enthusiastic parachute jumper and devoted much of his energy and time to jumping out of planes. I started to get regular work every Saturday with the *Sunday Times*. James Bell at Time-Life also sent work my way. In no time at all I became a busy freelancer.

Despite good and regular work coming in, I needed something else, a change from the usual daily routine of news stories. I needed to find a story or project that would personally inspire me.

I had begun reading widely about South Africa and its history, and in my reading I came across a book by Laurens van der Post, *The Lost World of the Kalahari*, which was about his failure to make a film about the Kalahari Bushmen or San. This started me thinking and I did some further research into the San people. The history that was available to me at the time was that the San people had lived in southern Africa since ancient times and were the first occupants, living as hunter-gatherers for thousands of generations. They lived off the land in small mobile groups. They were also talented artists – their graphic cave-wall paintings bore testimony to this. I was told that in the Cape some two thousand years ago the San people began to herd goats and sheep and later cattle and were also called the Khoekhoe, or Hottentots. Archaeologists agree that modern man (*Homo sapiens*) is the descendant of the San and shares the same gene pattern, which dates back to over 100 000 years – we are all descendants of the San people.

The colonising of the Cape brought with it many ills, the repercussions of which are ongoing in South Africa today. Conflict, disease and forced migration were some of these, but land and its ownership would become a much longer-term battleground. The San people came increasingly under pressure and their livelihood and lifestyle were constantly under threat, from their fellow human beings as well as from nature. At one time they were ruthlessly hunted as game and years of drought and land incursion also took their toll.

I became increasingly interested in learning more about the San. Professor Phillip Tobias, who was the head of the Anatomy Department at the University of the Witwatersrand in Johannesburg, was engaged in deep research in this field, and when I heard that he was leading an expedition to the Kalahari in 1959, I wrote to him. I said I would very much like to join his team and would try to meet him on Friday, 16 June, in Ghanzi. This was a small town in then Bechuanaland (now Botswana) in the Kalahari Desert where, I had been told, someone from the expedition went to the store every Friday to take and collect post.

At this time I was driving an old Peugeot. It was a very long drive, but I set off from Joburg optimistically thinking I would be able to get there in time. When I arrived in Gaborone, the small capital town, I was told there was no road for the 400-plus miles to Ghanzi, only a sand track. There was no way I was going to get there in my old car. After some asking around, I managed to get a lift with a farmer who was driving to Ghanzi the next day. I sat on the back of his bakkie with two of his labourers and we got thoroughly jostled around during a rough ride through deep sand. When there was a steep hill, we had to get out and push.

Halfway to Ghanzi, we stopped for the night and slept around a fire. Early in the morning we heard loud noises, which sounded like dogs barking. The farmer got his rifle and started to walk in the early morning light towards a clump of bushes. I followed him with my camera. I saw some shadows rushing away from us. Then the farmer started to shoot and I saw an African wild dog fall to the ground. There was a strong wild animal smell in the air. The farmer took out his hunting knife and cut off the wild dog's tail. 'I get ten shillings for each tail – they are vermin, you know,' he said, smiling. As we returned to the bakkie, I heard the dog panting. It was still alive.

It was very hot in the back of the bakkie as the sun climbed into the sky. At one stage we had to stop for about 20 minutes to wait for a vast herd of wildebeest, followed by herds of springbok and some giraffe, to cross the road.

Ghanzi was not much more than a small village, with a few buildings dotted around. There were no tarred roads. The farmer dropped me at the store, where a strange-looking vehicle was parked. It had very large wheels, a cabin in the front and a large space in the back high above the ground. I reckoned it must be one of the expedition vehicles. I asked the storekeeper and he pointed past the shelves to a short bearded man dressed in khaki reading a letter. The man turned out to be Professor Phillip Tobias himself and the letter he was reading was mine! He had just got to the part where I'd said I was arriving that very day – and there I was in front of him.

We drove some 30 kilometres in the expedition's large contraption of a vehicle, which I learnt had been specially built for it, and arrived at a tented camp in a small green, treed area. I was introduced to the group of 20 or so scientists and researchers, among them Professor Nussbaum, from Harvard University, and a couple named John and Lorna Marshall, who were specialists in the San and their language.

I also had my first introduction to a San family. Families consisted of 40 or so people living under shelters covered with branches. The San were very small in stature – beside them, the white people in the expedition looked like giants. They wore leather coverings and cloaks and each member of the group that was the subject of Tobias's research here wore a two-and-a half-inch white disc round his or her neck with a number on it. These identity discs were distracting for my pictures. When I printed these images up much later for a book, I retouched the white disc to make it look like a shell. Some years after the book was published, I received a very angry phone call from a United States university professor who had done much research on the 'shell' – which was not known ever to have been discovered in the Kalahari. When I explained, the professor got even angrier.

Different members of the expedition team had different tasks. Some were charged with weighing the San, some with taking measurements of their skulls, jaws, teeth and noses. Tobias and one of his female colleagues took one of the San girls into the bushes to measure her genitals. Another activity was to give them a tray filled with sand and ask them to draw various objects presented to them. One such object was a large urn. Interesting to me was that they drew the urn 'intellectually', as viewed from above, with one small and one large circle (a round object with a hole in the middle), quite different from a Western perception.

One day some of us were sitting in a row on a dead log when one of the researchers produced a small container. Inside it was a scorpion. He called a couple of San youngsters over. In one hand he held up the container with the scorpion and in the other hand he showed them a small silver coin – a South African tickey. For each scorpion they found, he told them, he would give them a tickey, at which the boys began laughing. They held their hands out to us and asked us to get up and turn around. Then they pulled the bark off the log we had been sitting on and revealed dozens of scorpions of all sizes. This created tremendous laughter all round.

There seemed to be quite a lot of disharmony among some of the learned scientists. There were frequent disagreements and some hot tempers. I found this quite surprising, embarrassing even, especially in front of the gentle, peaceful San.

After a week there was talk of a full moon. This was when the San traditionally carried out their ritual night healing dance called the Dance of Exorcism. I asked the leader, whose name was Katchu, for permission to photograph the dance. After much discussion, and an offering by me of some tobacco and a spare pair of shorts I had with me, he agreed.

Just before sunset the next evening the San started to hum and dance. As the sun set and it grew darker, Katchu made a fire and the women settled in a circle around the flames, some of them with babies on their backs. They started to clap their hands in rhythm and sing in high voices. Then the men formed an outer circle behind the women. They wore shells around their ankles, which made a rattling noise as they shuffled their feet in the sand and danced around the women, moving rhythmically one behind the other. With Katchu leading the group, singing loudly, they began to mimic the sounds of wildebeest and monkeys to pay tribute to the animals. By now it was pitch dark. Phillip Tobias held a small paraffin lamp for me while I took my pictures.

While the women sang in harmony with the men and created a pulsating rhythm with their clapping, Katchu started the healing dance by sucking evil spirits out of the women's navels, mouths and ears, going deeper and deeper into a trance-like state. When he had absorbed all the evil from the group, he attempted to throw himself onto the fire to burn the evil spirits. As he was beginning to pass out, the women pulled him back from out of the flames. When the women started chewing roots and spitting them in his face, Phillip Tobias moved in and took Katchu's pulse. He was shocked to find that for about five minutes the leader had no pulse. Then he came to. As the sun rose on a new day the San group slowly dispersed, going off to their shelters to sleep. The following day Katchu was proudly wearing my shorts and smoking a pipe. I thanked him and all the others, who reacted with loud laughter and broad smiles.

On the next Friday I went with Phillip Tobias and the Marshalls to the store in Ghanzi on the regular post and provisions trip. Here we met the district commissioner, who was dressed in khaki uniform and tropical helmet. He seemed very pleased to meet some people from the 'outside world' and he invited us to stay the night. He wanted to give us a party and meet a few of the locals. We accepted his invitation and went to his house in the evening, where we drank gin and tonic and listened to classical music from his record collection. The district commissioner told us that 'Doc' would be coming to meet us. To my surprise it was Doc from Andy's printing shop in Joburg, the former South African Air Force hero and medical doctor. It was good to catch up with him — and in such an unexpected place.

Doc had gone to England, where he had married an Englishwoman. He was now running a small clinic in Ghanzi. He was much more relaxed than I remembered him and he was delighted to see me. He invited me to visit his clinic the next morning, which I was pleased to do. The clinic was a round building in the style of a huge rondavel. He told me he had two waiting rooms — one for the San and the Africans and one for the Afrikaner farmers. The farmers, he told me solemnly, had to wait. The image amused us both.

Whatever the nature of the conflict between the learned whites, it grew worse, resulting eventually in a decision to split the camp into two. One group, with Tobias, moved to Lonetree, which was on the route from Lobatse to Ghanzi, and set up camp there, and the other group stayed where they were. In the new campsite we met a new group of San people. The site had a borehole, with a diesel pump. We made camp under some trees and went to the borehole for fresh water, only to discover that the pump didn't seem to work.

The professors each had a go but were unsuccessful. No water – what to do? Then in the distance over the horizon came two leather-thonged San hunters, carrying their bows and arrows. Greetings were exchanged and the two men stood silently by, watching us struggle with the pump. After a few minutes they started laughing. Then one of them moved Professor Nussbaum gently aside, pulled at a few levers, loosened a screw here and there, and voila! The pump started working. The professors didn't seem all that amused, but I couldn't help joining in the laughter of the two hunters. So much for 'civilisation', I thought.

Back at the camp the Afrikaans driver had got a big fire going. While we were at the borehole he had collected masses of firewood in his truck. Two of the San men came up to us in a very distressed state, saying that they wanted to leave. We discovered this was because we were burning their wood unnecessarily. Wood in the area was sparse, and in order to preserve it, the San only made very small fires. The fire at the trance dance had been an exception. We did our best to placate them and apologised for our ignorance.

After three weeks it was time for me to go. I got a lift to Gaborone with two young British government officials. They had their own servants, and when we stopped for the night the servants produced a table set on a canvas carpet on the sand. The table was laid with a tablecloth and drinks and food, and the officials made themselves comfortable on folding chairs. Since there was no extra chair, I watched the proceedings from my sleeping bag, and contented myself with some biltong (dried meat) for my supper. I soon fell asleep, woken briefly by the sound of lions roaring loudly nearby.

In Gaborone I collected my old Peugeot and drove back to Joburg.

29

WINDS OF CHANGE, WHITE JOURNOS AND THE CAMEL BORDER PATROL

Robert Sobukwe was now the leader of the Pan Africanist Congress and the organisation's first order of business, in late 1959, was to launch a major campaign against the hated pass laws.

On Monday, 21 March 1960, thousands upon thousands of African people assembled in front of police stations to burn their passes.

In a town near Johannesburg called Sharpeville, 300 policemen and a number of armoured cars faced a crowd of 5 000 people who had assembled in front of Sharpeville police station and begun to sing and burn their passes. The police started to panic and opened fire, some shooting from the top of armoured vehicles. Sixty-nine people were killed, most of them shot in the back as they were fleeing, and 180 people were seriously injured.

On the same day, many people gathered and demonstrated outside Langa police station in the Cape, and after the police gave a command for the crowd to disperse they made a baton charge. Some people started to stone the police and the large crowd surged forward. The commanding officer ordered his men to fire. Two people were killed and many were injured.

It was a day the country never forgot.

Humphrey Tyler and Ian Berry were in the middle of the massacre at

Sharpeville and their report was published in *Drum*. Unfortunately for me, I was covering the story at another police station, but I wanted to cover the funeral of the victims, which was scheduled to take place a week after the tragedy. The 69 victims were to be buried in a long row, a priest standing in front of each individual grave. I decided that in order to show in one photo the scale of people being buried and highlight the enormity of the massacre, I had to take the photo from a high point, as the burial site was on flat land. I chartered a small plane, had the passenger door removed and, wearing a safety harness, took photos leaning out of the passenger seat. For close on two hours we flew around the funeral procession as it moved from the church service in Sharpeville to the burial ground, where I eventually got my photo of the row of graves and the trucks carrying the coffins arriving, the priests standing in front of the graves.

Flying around in circles and sideways had its challenges – for the pilot, who had to be especially careful as another plane was also circling overhead filming the event, and also for me, leaning out and taking pictures. I got quite airsick, but it was worth it. Being able to record that sad and historic day was an important milestone for me.

A few weeks later Johnny Johnson, with a big mysterious smile, asked me to go and see Joel Mervis in his office. Mervis, the famous editor of the country's biggest-circulation newspaper, offered me a job as chief photographer on the *Sunday Times*. Pat Smith had left the paper. I was delighted to accept. It meant regular pay and no more hustling for work.

My first assignment was a feature picture story of the Rand Easter Show. This was an annual trade show visited by thousands of people. I spent several days walking about the show and funfair and produced a set of pictures of people enjoying themselves, eating ice cream, admiring the latest luxury cars and new technology from all over the world. After I had handed in my prints to the news editor, I was called to see Joel Mervis. Johnny was with him, only this time he wasn't smiling.

'Sit down, Mr Schadeberg,' Mervis said. Then, in a disapproving tone, he said, 'Our readers on a Sunday morning do not want to see black faces over breakfast in the *Sunday Times*.'

The Sharpeville funeral procession

I wasn't at all sure what he meant.

'I understand that you have been working for many years for a paper that caters to black people,' he went on, in a kindlier voice, 'but you have to realise that you are now working for a paper that caters to white people only.'

It dawned on me that my pictures of the Rand Easter Show had been of a mixture of whites, blacks and Indian people who were visiting and enjoying a day's outing. I couldn't for the life of me see what the problem was in that, but I could also see there was no point arguing. I told Mervis I understood and promised in future to take pictures of white people only.

A few days later I was summoned to the editor's office again. This got me worried. Sitting again opposite the great Joel Mervis behind his imposing wooden desk, I had no idea what to expect and I wriggled around nervously. He noticed that I was ill at ease, smiled and then, in an earnest tone, said, 'Tomorrow, Saturday, 9 April, Prime Minister Dr Hendrik Verwoerd is going to spend the day visiting the Rand Easter Show. It's the last day of the show. I want you to be next to him at all times, following him everywhere he goes.' I was very surprised at this assignment and, as I got up to leave his office, Mervis said, 'Keep it to yourself.' I nodded and left.

I was at the entrance when Verwoerd and his entourage arrived and I dutifully followed him closely all day, never leaving his side, not even to drink, eat or sit down. It made me realise how busy a politician has to be to get publicity and promote himself to his supporters. The last event was in the evening in the main arena, where various farm animals, cows and sheep of good breeds, were paraded. Together with other VIPs, Verwoerd sat in a box among the rows of benches in the audience. I hung around with some other press photographers, among them Ian Berry, who had also been at the show all day taking photos.

The show was coming to an end, and as people began to leave the arena, we thought we could call it a day. Verwoerd and his entourage stayed in their box, some of them standing and chatting, while the camera crews packed up. I left with the rest of the press people and went to a bar behind the stadium for a well-deserved drink. We were all standing about drinking beers and smoking, enjoying our first break since morning, when one of the freelance *Rand Daily Mail* reporters came rushing up to us, looking very agitated. He was a small, timid man named Dennis Bagley, who had an unfortunate stutter. He tried to talk to us but struggled to get the words out.

'V-V-V-ver — Ver — Woerd — sbeen — sh- sh- sh- sh- ot!'

'Go away,' Ian said, laughing. 'Stop being funny.'

'No — no — no — b- b- been — sh — sh sh sh-ot!'

At that moment we heard a siren ...

The news flew round quickly. A local farmer, David Pratt, had walked into the VIP box as everyone was leaving, grabbed Verwoerd by the neck, put a low-calibre pistol to his head and shot him twice in the brain. Verwoerd survived and was able to leave the hospital within a few days.

A state of emergency was declared. It stayed in place for six months and over the next few weeks 20 000 people were detained.

If I had thought my *Drum* colleagues operated in an alcoholic haze, I was in for a surprise. The reporters on the *Sunday Times* were even worse.

During the week I worked with various journalists in the newsroom on a variety of assignments, except on Saturdays, when the *Sunday Times* operated like a daily paper and employed freelance photographers. Each reporter specialised in different areas of the news, ranging across gossip, sport, political events, entertainment and the arts. Although they called themselves 'social drinkers', many of these writers were heavy drinkers, and some of them were certainly alcoholics. For the most part I saw them as drunks.

Allen Loxton was a journalist who specialised in finding gossipy, humorous and entertaining stories from the countryside and he made weekly trips to small towns to the north of Joburg to unearth these quirky tales. He was a pleasant-faced man, a bit overweight and a bit jowly, with a somewhat put-on upper-class English accent. One Tuesday morning I was assigned to go with him to Mafeking (Mafikeng) to cover a memorial celebration of the Relief of Mafeking, which marked a significant point in the Anglo-Boer War. Among the dignitaries due to attend was Major-General Freddie de Guingand, a former chief of staff of Field Marshal Montgomery. Also there would be Major-General Friedrich von Mellenthin, who had served in North Africa in the Afrika Corps.

We requested a car from the office car pool. I was then informed that Allen had been banned from driving any office car after leaving several wrecks in his

State of emergency, 1960

wake, so I was the one who was responsible for the car and the driving. On the way in the car Allen began telling me about the battle he'd fought in the Sahara during the war, how he'd been in Tobruk and fought against Rommel. He went on and on.

Our first stop, though, was Rustenburg. Here Allen asked me to drop him off at the town hall because he wanted to talk to an official there who was a friend of his and had a story for him. He'd be about half an hour, he said. He told me to wait for him at the Lions Bar down the road. I found a corner in the bar, away from the usual half-dozen or so barflies sitting at the counter clutching their drinks, and had a Coke. An hour later Allen came charging through the bar's swing door. He whizzed straight past me to the counter and ordered a double whisky. I got up, picked up my drink and strolled over.

Allen poured his whisky down his throat in one gulp. 'Ah, there you are, young man,' he said, sliding his empty glass down the counter in the direction of the barman. 'Another double,' he said. He slapped me on my shoulder and boomed, 'And another double for my photographer here!' Before I could say anything I had a double whisky in front of me and Allen was off on his desert exploits again, telling the barman and everybody else in the bar all about them and how he was going to reconnect with his famous fellow comrades-in-arms in Mafeking the next day. I finished my whisky slowly, while Allen ordered a cold beer. Then, because I was driving, I had another Coke. The more Allen drank the louder he got. He continued to regale all and sundry with his war stories, which did not seem of the slightest interest to anyone in the bar except him. The barflies were oblivious. They all ignored him, while the barman automatically replenished their drinks. Eventually he turned on the radio for the news in Afrikaans, which successfully drowned out Allen's stream of chatter.

Back in the car, with Allen breathing heavily beside me in the passenger seat, we drove towards Zeerust. As soon as we were moving, Allen fell into a deep sleep, snoring softly. After about 40 minutes' driving, I saw a signpost up ahead and slowed down. Allen woke up with a start.

'Where are we?' he shouted.

The signpost indicated a right turn to Groot Marico and another sign, in front of us, said 'Hotel – Bar'.

'Stop here!' Allen said excitedly. 'We must stop at the bar – there's a crow that drinks whisky!' He grinned at me. 'And I need a drink.'

True enough, there was a black crow in the bar. It waddled up and down the counter making funny noises and putting its beak into Allen's whisky glass. When it lifted its head to the ceiling and wriggled its neck and body, it looked as if it was drinking. The crowd in the bar, all of them plastered, thought it was hilarious. We spent about an hour there, watching the crow behave in an increasingly ridiculous fashion, until it finally fell asleep. By this time I had to help a well-oiled Allen into the car.

The road to Zeerust was a rough, dusty, gravel one, with potholes that required nifty driving from me. Allen was fast asleep again but woke up as we got into town.

'Stop here – at the church!' he instructed me.

'What now?' I asked.

'I have to see the priest about a story,' he said in a drunken, sleepy voice.

'Are you about to confess your sins?' I asked jokingly, but Allen didn't answer.

I waited in the car while Allen went into the church. After a short while he returned, saying that only the verger was there and he had wanted to talk to the priest. The story was to do with a murder that had taken place about a month previously in the churchyard.

'Let's just stop at the bar for a beer,' Allen said. 'I know the owner.'

Allen managed two beers in about half an hour, and then it was back to the car for the last leg. My companion beside me in a deep sleep, snoring loudly, I drove to Mafeking and found the Central Hotel. I went in and booked a couple of rooms. Then I got back in the car and woke Allen. He looked at me rather dazedly, got out and walked unsteadily round to my window. 'Sorry I can't ask you in … you know what my wife's like,' he said. Then he turned around and walked into the hotel.

We had arranged to meet Major-General Freddie de Guingand in the lounge of the hotel the following morning at ten and I was there promptly. De Guingand introduced himself and the gentleman he was sitting with, who, it turned out, was General Von Mellenthin. Von Mellenthin had apparently come to the Relief of Mafeking celebrations specially to meet de Guingand. The two men were well groomed and refined, immaculate in tailored suits and polished shoes, although somewhat out of place in the African countryside.

Then Allen arrived. For some reason he was wearing a furry Cossack hat, which he had bought on a two-day promotional trip (courtesy of Lufthansa) to Moscow. He had on a tweed jacket and a red tie. 'Ah, you met my photographer,' he said, coming up to us. 'I am Allen Loxton from the *Sunday Times*.' We sat around for a while, talking and drinking, and then Allen asked if he could have a picture of the two distinguished military men in the countryside outside Mafeking, somewhere sandy, somewhere that might resemble the Sahara Desert.

I organised a kombi from the hotel and quickly found the ideal spot for a photo just outside the town. I had taken a number of pictures of the two generals, including them shaking hands, when Allen wanted a picture of himself with the generals. He pushed himself between the two men, put his arms over their shoulders and smiled into the camera. 'The Three from the Desert!' he shouted.

As we got back to the hotel we had a phone call from the office. Johnny Johnson was on the line. We were to charter a plane to fly to Tshabong in Botswana, where the British High Commissioner would be inspecting the border guards of the Bokspits Border Post the following morning. At short notice we managed to find a pilot who could take us, although he asked if we could take another pilot, a friend of his, to help navigate over the semi-desert. We took off the next morning, with Allen and me in the back of a small Cessna behind the pilot and navigator. An hour into the air we were flying around the Tshabong landing strip. Looking down, I saw a line of camels and men in uniform in front of them. The men were standing to attention. There was a car, with its top open, and a man standing inside it wearing a khaki uniform and a tropical helmet. The pilot brought us in to land, and as we taxied along the landing strip towards the group, the man in the helmet approached the plane in his car. Loxton was onto the wing of the plane in a flash. Still wearing his Cossack hat, he jumped down onto the tarmac and greeted the man. 'I am Allen Loxton from the *Sunday Times*.' Looking over his shoulder at me and the two pilots as we clambered out of the plane and jumped down, he continued:

'Let me introduce you to my staff – this is my pilot –' pointing at each of us in turn as we walked over '– this is my navigator ... and this is my photographer.'

The man in the tropical helmet introduced himself as the district commissioner. Gradually it became clear that everyone thought Allen was the High Commissioner, whom they were expecting, but he didn't disillusion them. Instead he began to inspect the 40 or so men standing in front of the camels, walking very slowly past the line of men standing to attention and giving them the salute. I took out my camera and I began photographing his performance.

The Camel Border Patrol from the Bokspits Border Post patrolled hundreds of miles of desert along the Molopo River, which at Bokspits joined the Nossob River, which was the border between South Africa and Botswana.

Poachers from South Africa drove herds of game across the river, especially when the rivers were low or dried up, sometimes using a Tiger Moth plane. They drove thousands of wildebeest across to South Africa, where they shot them and cut them into strips, hanging the strips up to dry in the hot sun to make biltong, which they sold locally and abroad. Over the years most of the game in the southern part of Botswana was killed off.

When Allen had finished with his charade, we all walked across to the nearby barracks. Here a young man in a khaki uniform reported that he had just received a radio message, saying that the High Commissioner had been held up in Gaborone and would have to delay his visit because he had an urgent appointment in Maun. He would call back in about two weeks ...

The district commissioner invited us for a cup of tea in his lounge. On the wall hung a large photo of the Queen and a number of small framed photos – group pictures of uniformed men and the camel border guards. We made ourselves comfortable in armchairs and a settee, and a young African man, barefoot and wearing a typical African servant's outfit and a colourful scarf wrapped around his forehead, served us tea and scones. These, we realised, must have been prepared for the High Commissioner.

Then Allen called out to the waiter. 'Hey, boy – bring me a whisky.'

The waiter looked bemused. He looked at his boss.

'I'm sorry, Mr Loxton,' the district commissioner said, 'unfortunately we have no whisky. But you are welcome to a gin and tonic, if you like.'

'Make it a double,' Allen responded, looking rather pleased. And then he proceeded to tell everybody the history of Indian tonic with gin until finally our pilot interrupted the flow. We should leave if we wanted to get back to Mafeking that night, he said, as it would be getting dark in the next two hours. It was too risky to navigate at night because there was no lit-up landing strip in Mafeking and they would have to arrange flares. Outside the window I saw the guards mounting their camels. I got up, grabbed my cameras, and excused myself. I got some good pictures of the camel border guards moving out.

We arrived at Mafeking's airstrip just as it was getting dark and drove to the hotel. Allen went straight to the bar to, as he put it, 'refresh himself', and I went to my room, where I lay down on my bed and instantly fell asleep.

The next morning after an English breakfast Allen was in a hurry to get back to the office. We drove through Zeerust without stopping – to my relief. However, when we passed the sign to Groot Marico Allen suddenly came to life and my heart sank. 'Stop here at the hotel bar,' he said. 'I need a drink. And we want to see the crow.'

In the bar we found the crow apparently passed out, sitting in his corner with his eyes shut. The barman told us the crow had drunk a lot of water after we'd left last time, fell over and hadn't moved much since. Allen had a few double whiskies without his feathered companion. He told me how he had hated the gin and tonic at Tshabong. Eventually we left, got back in the car and I drove straight through to Joburg.

30

SOCIAL ENGAGEMENTS AND THE SUNDAY PAPERS

Not all the reporters and column writers on the *Sunday Times* were drinkers. Desmond Blow, for example, who wrote general stories about the Joburg scene, covering entertainment, crime or society gossip, had many reasons for his absences. He was a very short man, and thin, with a goatee beard, and he laughed a lot, especially about himself. One morning Johnny Johnson was tearing about the newsroom in a bad mood, shouting out, 'Where is bloody Blow? He was supposed to hand in his story this morning.' When Johnson went on the rant, everybody was a target. He carried a short leather whip around with him and he'd whip the desks as he went.

About an hour later Blow turned up in the newsroom, smiling at all the surprised faces. Johnson came out of his office and glared at him. 'You'd better have a good story,' he said angrily. 'If not, you will get the whipping of your life!'

'I ran out of petrol on Louis Botha Avenue, during rush hour, had no money, and I was in my pyjamas, and barefoot ...' Blow rattled off with a smile on his face. Of course the whole newsroom burst out laughing but Blow, undeterred, continued. 'I was taking my kids to school and they were late – and so was I ... I ran around in my pyjamas to get some petrol to get home.'

'Okay, okay!' Johnson snapped to shut him up. 'Go to your desk and write the story we're waiting for!'

Blow was always getting into crazy situations. He lived in a house in Orange

Grove with his wife and two children. His suburban house was next to a main road, about ten metres above it, and with a steep drive up into his garage. On the other side of the road was a shallow river with small rocks. One day he came home and left his car on the sloping driveway, and because he was in a hurry he left the car in neutral and the handbrake off. His car slowly started to move down the slope. Desperately chasing it down the drive, Des tried to stop it. He fell on his face as he tried to grab the front bumper, injuring himself in the process. The car careered across the main road into the river. Des showed up in the office next day with his face all patched up with bandages. His car was at the panelbeaters.

Johnny Johnson was, in my opinion, an outstanding professional journalist and an excellent news editor. He did have some rather quirky ways of keeping discipline among his reporters, however — one being his leather whip. When trying to discipline one of his writers, he would first give him a dressing down in the newsroom about his poor copy, its late delivery or some other infraction and then he would ask the miscreant to come into his office. He would close the door and instruct his victim to shout out in pain while he cracked his whip hard on the desk. Of course, the whole newsroom could hear the goings-on in Johnson's office, and although we all thought the pantomime very funny and no one was fooled, our respect for Johnson's authority as news editor remained.

Leon Bennett was another entertainment reporter on our team. One day he and I were sent to cover an art exhibition featuring local and international artists at the Adler Fielding Gallery. The gallery was on the top floor of a high-rise building in Commissioner Street and was owned and run by two gay men, who could often be seen walking around clutching their miniature poodles under their arms. The invitation said 'Evening dress required and medals may be worn'.

As we approached the main entrance of the building we saw the red flashing light of an ambulance. In the foyer a small crowd had gathered, all dressed in evening outfits. Sitting on a chair with his left leg suspended and being bandaged by a paramedic was a rather miserable-looking man. His face was covered in blood, his trousers were torn and his tuxedo was dripping wet – he looked a mess. Bennett made some enquiries. It seemed that the man, a guest, had lost his balance, slipped and fallen into a small pond next to the entrance of the gallery on the top floor. The pond, which was about twelve inches deep, was covered with water lilies, and the drenched man, rather dazed after falling in, then proceeded to walk through the glass door that led to the lifts and cut his face and his legs on the broken glass.

Up on the top floor the gallery was packed. The guests were all glamorously dressed – the women wearing low-cut long evening dresses and bedecked with sparkling jewellery and strings of pearls, the men in black tuxedos. I spotted the lily pond in a small alcove which was lit with colourful lights.

As I walked about photographing the social scene, I saw a distinguished-looking man in a burgundy dinner jacket, with a group of admiring ladies clustered around him. I noticed that he had a number of medals on his chest and I took some pictures of him and the people around him, including a shot of a lady who seemed to be giving him a royal curtsey.

A little later it was time for the speeches and the guests crowded around, looking up at the row of artists and at Mr Adler, who had his little poodle tucked under his arm. The speeches took some time. I happened to be standing behind the distinguished-looking man. He turned around, saw me standing there and gave me a nod of recognition. As the speeches were coming to an end I saw him do something I'd never seen before – the distinguished man was wiggling his ears!

Back at the office Leon thought we might be able to get the story of the accident-prone man into the late edition for the Sunday morning paper. Apparently he was quite an important personality and Leon had got a quick interview. He suggested I process my pictures. I included a print of the regal-looking man with the medals and the adoring ladies. When Leon saw it he burst out laughing. 'Did you have a close look at the medals?' he asked me, shaking with laughter. 'They weren't real medals. One said Deputy Sheriff and some of the others were metal cut-outs from food tins.' Then he told me the man's name was Adam Leslie, a famous South African actor and theatre producer. My picture of this joker was on the front page of the paper the next morning, along with the accident-prone VIP.

Thinking about that photo later on, I realised something important about photojournalism. In concentrating on 'the moment' or 'encounter', the photographer has little time to take in the finer details. That was the reason I hadn't noticed the medals were phoney.

Leon Bennett had a somewhat bizarre family life. One day he invited me to accompany him to an afternoon barbecue in the suburb of Houghton. He picked me up at the office in an old Citroën that had seen better days and long ago lost its sheen. Inside, the car was strewn with litter and cigarette ends and it reeked of stale tobacco and beer. Leon put his foot down and we spluttered and jerked forward, leaving a cloud of black smoke behind us.

Leon and his family lived in Kensington. 'We have to go to my place first to pick up the meat and the boerewors and a case of beer,' Leon said. When we got to his house, he asked me to come and meet Violet, his wife, and I was happy to get out of the four-wheeled ashtray. As we walked up the steps, a woman appeared at the front door with a small child on her arm, followed by three more children, ranging from about three to seven years old. Leon introduced me to Violet and told me the names of the four children. Then Violet said she was coming to the barbecue.

'No, you're not,' said Leon and he went inside.

Violet took the children down the steps and ushered them to the car. She opened the back door, and just as she began pushing them one by one into the back seat, Leon appeared at the front door with packets of meat and a case of beer. 'No! No you don't!' he shouted, and came bounding down the steps. He put the barbecue things into the boot and then he opened the back-seat door on the other side and proceeded to pull the now crying children one by one out of the car. The children ran round to their mother on the other side, who promptly pushed them all into the back seat again. This went on for some time until the kids stopped crying and began to enjoy the game, giggling and scooting from one side of the car to the other. Violet just got angrier.

It was a bit like a Laurel and Hardy scene and I started taking pictures, which diverted Violet's anger towards me. 'This is all your fault!' she shouted, and all the children started crying again. Leon carried them back into the house. By now I was almost hysterical with laughter but I didn't stop taking pictures. I couldn't help it. On a small rusty table near the steps stood a dozen or so terracotta flower-pots. Violet became incensed and shouted at me, 'You're the troublemaker!' Then she picked up one of the flower-pots and bashed it on my head. The pot disintegrated, covering my head and face in soil and plant. It made me laugh even harder. I picked up another pot, handed it to her and held my head in her direction. Violet grabbed the pot and bashed that one on my head too, and kept bashing until it, too, disintegrated.

I have to say those terracotta pots couldn't have been very strong. My head survived the whole tableful. Violet flung all twelve at me, soil, seedlings and all. Afterwards she looked utterly exhausted. I brushed the soil and plant remnants off my clothes and joined Leon in his car.

The whole comic circus wasn't even worth it in the end – the barbecue, which was in an upmarket part of Houghton, proved to be a flop and was full of boring people. Leon mentioned later that his wife had a habit of attacking strangers, whom she always blamed for making him work late. He thought the barbecue might not have been suitable for his over-active kids and, anyway, he was planning to do a social story on the party. I still have a vivid memory of Violet standing by the gate shaking her fist at us as we drove off.

Allister Sparks was the editor of the *Rand Daily Mail*. He offered Nat Nakasa a job on the paper as a regular column writer. Since Nat and I worked in the same building at 176 Main Street, we sometimes met in the canteen. I found Nat quite changed. This normally happy young man had become very depressed by the ever-increasingly rigid apartheid laws, which severely limited his life and writing. He was also beginning to feel uneasy because of being watched by the Security Police, who had been making enquiries about him after spotting him at various ANC meetings. Nat mentioned that Lewis Nkosi was about to leave for the United States, having been offered a Nieman Fellowship at Harvard. Lewis was going to leave the country on an exit visa, which meant forfeiting his South African citizenship. Nat was also upset that many of his other friends and colleagues had already left South Africa. Todd Matshikiza, Bloke Modisane, Arthur Maimane and Sylvester Stein had all gone, and Can Themba had gone to Swaziland to teach. So now Nat was thinking seriously of applying to study in the States and leaving the country too.

A few months later I met Nat again. I had read some of his outstanding columns in the *Rand Daily Mail* and congratulated him on his literary skills. On this occasion he seemed more enthusiastic about life than the last time we'd met. He was planning to start a literary magazine called *The Classic* with the help of Nadine Gordimer. The intention was that it would feature stories and poems by African writers. Nat was confident about getting finance from the American sponsor John Thomson via the Fairfield Foundation. He also told me that Peter Magubane was starting to work as a freelance photographer for the *Rand Daily Mail*.

I took this as a good sign. It meant that it was becoming possible for black journalists and photographers to work on white papers.

31

POSITIVES AND NEGATIVES

By chance I bumped into Ian Berry's wife, Shirley, in the foyer of the office one day and we went for a cup of tea to catch up. We hadn't seen each other for a long time. She told me she and Ian had been living for a few years in Paris, where Ian was very busy working for the Magnum photo agency. Magnum was run and owned by the photographers themselves, most of whom worked in documentary photography. They also had an office in New York. Shirley and Ian had an apartment in Paris and were very happy, except that Shirley had recently suffered a miscarriage, which was a big blow for them both. Happily, she was pregnant again, and because Ian was often away working on stories, she had decided to have the baby in South Africa. I suggested she come for dinner and say hello to Etricia.

Shirley and Etricia got on famously. Etricia had recently developed an interest in writing again and the two women had two topics of interest in common – children and journalism. They got on so well that at the end of the evening Etricia told Shirley she was welcome to stay with us until the baby came. We had plenty of space and a comfortable spare room. A week later Shirley moved in. She and Etricia spent hours talking. Etricia was especially fascinated by Paris, and enjoyed Shirley's stories about life there, so much so that she said I should join Magnum and we should all go and live there. I felt a little tempted, but with four children such a big move would have lots of challenges. Plus it wasn't easy to be accepted into Magnum. Ian had worked at this for over eight years.

At the regular Tuesday morning meeting one week, Joel Mervis gave me and Carel Birkby instructions to fly to Maun in Botswana. We were to leave immediately, from a small airfield south of Johannesburg. The Secretary General of the United Nations, Dag Hammarskjöld, was expected to fly in from Katanga the next day to investigate the plight of the Herero people. A deputation of Herero people would be meeting him. Carel was to interview him and I was to take pictures.

Carel was our chief reporter, a slim man in his fifties with a moustache and rather fragile demeanour as a result of too many pink gins, something I had concluded and witnessed first-hand on a story we'd covered together just after I joined as chief photographer.

When we arrived at the airfield we found that most of the available planes had already been booked by the many journalists and international television crews who were going to cover the event, but luckily we got seats on the very last plane. The pilot, however, had agreed to take some of the TV crews' equipment so space was limited, which caused some problems for us, especially when it came to loading Carel's large bag, which I'd noticed clinked ominously when he'd loaded it into the car. When the pilot opened the bag, the clinking was explained: it was filled with large bottles of gin.

The hotel in Maun was full of international journalists and the bar was heaving with drinkers and thick with tobacco smoke. Accommodation was going to be another problem. With Carel's considerable powers of persuasion (another thing I'd personally witnessed), he managed to get a small room for himself in the attic. Fortunately, I had brought my sleeping bag with me and I found myself a spot to sleep on the sandy bank of a nearby river. In the middle of the night I woke up and got a huge fright when I saw a number of long black shadows slowly coming out of the river. I was convinced they were crocodiles. To my relief they were actually tree-stumps being washed up by the tide.

It was September 1961 and the news at the hotel was that Hammarskjöld in his Douglas DC-6 plane would be arriving at about three that afternoon. Journalists and cameramen assembled on the landing strip of the small airport along with representatives of the Herero people, who stood in a corner by themselves. Some of the women wore very colourful nineteenth-century-style outfits and towering headgear made up of intertwined scarves.

After about half an hour the news came through on the radio in the airport hut that there was a delay. There would be a news update in an hour. Most people repaired to the hotel and the bar. I spent a bit of time walking around. Behind the hotel at the bar's back entrance was a mountain of empty beer cans – I had never seen such a sight! – which I thought would make a good picture. There was a lot of noise coming from the bar inside and the smell of alcohol and cigarette smoke was strong.

Suddenly I saw people running out of the front of the hotel and up the road in the direction of the post office. I saw Carel coming out. 'What's happening?' I said as I started jogging alongside him.

'They killed him!' Carel said. 'They shot down his plane!'

In the post office there was total chaos and a huge commotion going on, with everybody talking and shouting at once and the journalists queuing up to use the one and only phone. The atmosphere was electrifying. The Hammarskjöld plane had crashed near the Zambian border after having left Katanga, and the rumour was that the Douglas DC-6 had been shot down by supporters of the mining company Union Minière.

It was Friday evening, and once the excitement had died down everybody assembled back in the bar. Most planned to leave the following morning. The journalists who had come in Land Rovers decided to take their time driving back to South Africa via Francistown. Carel was insistent about flying back to Joburg on Saturday morning but the pilot was worried because he knew that the Francistown airfield was closed over the weekend and there would be nobody there to turn on the beam. He also said we didn't have enough fuel to fly directly to Joburg and he didn't think we could refuel in Francistown. Carel, who must have had quite a few pink gins by then, was having none of it and he got very angry. I thought it best not to argue but wait till the morning when he would be more rational and agree to wait till Monday to fly out. In the meantime, the pilot tried to get through to Francistown on the only phone in Maun but there was no connection. It was the same with the radio.

But in the morning Carel hadn't changed his mind. He insisted we fly back to Joburg. The pilot's reluctance was obvious and again he explained the problems. A loud and angry argument ensued until finally, in a commanding voice, Carel said: 'I am in charge and I must get back to Joburg this afternoon or the airline will lose the *Sunday Times* contract!'

Shortly after take-off Carel fell sound asleep. At one point the pilot told me he was slightly off course but fortunately he found his direction back to Francistown, where we landed at an airstrip about noon. Carel woke up as we taxied along the small runway towards an office building, where we all got off the plane. The place was totally deserted. There was a dirt road, which presumably led to Francistown, but virtually no traffic. Carel decided to walk along the road in the hope of getting a lift into town, and although the signs were not very encouraging, nevertheless off he trudged. Soon he was out of sight.

After about an hour the pilot got back in the plane and managed to make radio contact with someone who could bring us some aviation fuel. It took a while but it arrived eventually and, a little later, so did Carel. He reeked of alcohol. It seemed he had succeeded in getting a lift and had spent the time he was away drinking in the local hotel bar.

We were ready to take off for Joburg, but now it was getting late and our pilot was getting worried all over again. He radioed the airfield to the south of Johannesburg but there was no response. It would be dark by the time we arrived and he didn't have a licence for night flying. And if the airfield didn't put on the runway lights for our landing ... well, let's say he was an anxious man at that moment.

We took off and began our approach to the city after the sun had set and it was getting dark. The pilot was becoming visibly agitated. Carel, oblivious to it all, sipped peacefully from a bottle of gin, which he passed to the pilot, who also took a swig – which started to make me nervous. As we saw the city lights ahead, the pilot radioed Jan Smuts, Johannesburg's main airport, for permission to land. He was looking quite distraught by now and the tension in the plane tightened a few notches. Then the Jan Smuts air traffic controller came on the speaker and started giving instructions. I allowed myself to let out my breath a little bit, but it wasn't over yet. After a number of hard bumps and being shaken around crazily, we finally landed, only to discover that the pilot had brought the plane down on the wrong airstrip! He must have misunderstood the instructions at some point.

Once we were safely inside the airport terminal Carel headed straight for the bar and had a drink. The pilot had to report to the airport administration where, I later found out, he was given a stern warning and had his licence suspended for two years.

When I arrived home that night, there was a big drama and Etricia was in hysterics. 'Why didn't you come home last night? I couldn't reach you – I had to take Shirley to hospital!' I didn't know what was going on until she calmed down enough to tell me that Shirley had had another miscarriage. She would be flying back to Paris the next day.

About a week later I got home very late one night after doing a story with journalist Roy Christie, and not altogether sober. I walked into the living room to be greeted by two angry women sitting on the settee with a bottle of wine on the coffee table in front of them: Etricia and Shirley. I was bewildered. I thought Shirley was safely home in Paris with Ian, but it seemed that something had gone wrong and she had come straight back to South Africa. Etricia's eyes were full of resentment and anger, while Shirley's had a tormented, wounded look.

'You photographers are all bastards,' Etricia said in a voice filled with hate. 'You are all treacherous, deceitful and unfaithful bastards!'

Then Shirley started to cry and I got the story. 'The bastard cheated on me. I took the night flight to Paris and arrived at our one-roomed flat. It was just getting light and they both were fast asleep in our bed.' She took a gulp of wine. 'He was with Renate, his photo researcher from Magnum.'

After Shirley had gone to her room, Etricia said coldly, 'Why are you late? You were going to be home early this evening.'

The evening with Roy and a dubious Hollywood film director called Erik-Erik was a complicated one, but before I could open my mouth I got a stream of abusive insults about photographers like Ian and myself, committing adultery, going off with dancing girls and having lots of women when we travelled while pretending to work on stories. I knew from long experience that it was no good trying to talk to Etricia. I left the house at sunrise and went to the office darkroom to catch up on making overdue enlargements.

Shirley went to stay with her parents in Benoni and life at home went on quietly for about a week, Etricia behaving relatively normally. She didn't mention her recent outburst. By the end of the week, though, she was acting rather mysteriously. Then she asked me to meet her at Shirley's lawyer's office in town. Shirley had decided to begin divorce proceedings against Ian. When I got there Etricia was sitting on her own in the waiting room. She looked as if she was in a bad mood and ignored me. As I was wondering where Shirley was, we were called into the lawyer's office. Behind a large desk sat a short bald man. He got up, greeted us briefly, and pointed at the two chairs facing his desk. He handed me a folder. Looking through the papers I found out to my surprise and astonishment that these were divorce papers all right but they had nothing to do with Ian and Shirley Berry. They were my divorce papers and Etricia was suing me for desertion. She was asking for maintenance for the children of £50 a month and, among other things, stipulating that I could only see them one weekend a month. I sat with the folder on my lap trying to get my head around this turn of events.

The lawyer had moved around to my side of the desk and now he was standing next to me, smiling, with a pen in his hand. 'The only thing you have to do is sign here and you will be divorced in six weeks,' he said.

For a moment I thought this was some sort of bluff by Etricia. Then, without saying a word and without hesitation, I signed the papers. I walked out of the office feeling strangely happy.

I took two weeks' leave and went to Cape Town, where I spent most of my time on the beach. I had been bamboozled and tricked by Etricia and was upset at being separated from my children, but the truth was our marriage would not have lasted much longer. Living with continuous tension and Etricia's fits of jealousy and never knowing what she would do next had become a terrible strain. I was very happy and relieved to be on my own. When I returned to Johannesburg I found a new place to live.

In 1963 I got a cable from Black Star in New York, a photo feature agency to which I offered stories and prints from time to time. They asked me to go urgently to Dar es Salaam and cover the unrest that was happening there. There had been an uprising in Zanzibar which had spread to Tanganyika.

I had to get a re-entry visa on my German passport, which proved to be problematic. Previously, I had had a multiple visa for travelling to British protectorates such as Bechuanaland (Botswana), Lesotho and Swaziland but it had expired. I went to the relevant government department to sort this out and was told I could pick up my multiple-return visa the following day. When I went back they said there was a delay. This worried me because I needed this type of multiple visa for my international work. I went back again the following day, to be told that the visa was being held up by State Security – in other words, the Special Branch – and I would have to pay them a visit. I had already booked my flight to Dar es Salaam and time was running out.

I was shown into a small, bare room with a long table in it. There was an upright typewriter on the table and a couple of In and Out baskets with piles of folders. When I entered, two Special Branch officers were sitting at the table, their shirtsleeves rolled up, ties and top buttons loosened, and their jackets hanging on the backs of their chairs. They sat paging through folders, chain-smoking, ignoring me totally and talking to each other in Afrikaans. An ashtray on the table was full of cigarette stubs. I couldn't understand a word they were saying, so I just sat there, waiting.

Suddenly the younger of the two men held up the folder in his hand, looked at me and said in a loud voice and a deep, guttural Afrikaans accent: 'Jorrgen Scadeberg.'

The older fellow took the folder away from him and looked at it with consternation before fixing his gaze on me. 'So you're the troublemaker?' he said. Then he turned to his colleague and, in an authoritative voice, said, 'Kom, Jannie,' and they both left the room. As the door closed behind them, I heard the key turn in the lock.

Now I'm for it, I thought. I'm locked in a room at the Special Branch headquarters. I really was getting worried. Maybe it was time for me to leave the country. About half an hour later I was getting impatient and increasingly anxious when I heard the key in the door and the two characters reappeared. The older man was carrying a large box full of folders containing newspaper cuttings. He put the box on the table and took out a folder, which he opened. He extracted a cutting and laid it down on the table. It was one of my double-page spreads from *Stern* magazine, showing a man on a horse carrying a whip in a mealie field with black labourers picking mealies.

'Now, Jorrgen, listen to this: "Afrikaners whip and beat their African workers to death". What do you have to say to that, Jorrgen?'

I looked at him. I told him I was dyslexic.

'What's that?' he asked.

'I can't write,' I said.

This caused a deep, puzzled frown. 'Jorrgen, man, you are cheeky,' he said and his face grew red.

'I can give you a doctor's certificate. My eye nerves are twisted,' I told him.

His eyes narrowed. 'Maybe it's you who are twisted.'

Then he called his partner into the room. 'You wait here!' he said, and left. After about ten minutes he came back and sat down again. 'Jorrgen – we have been keeping an eye on you and we are not happy with the pictures you publish. Man, you are a German! And you are hanging around with all these natives and commies. And what do you want to do in Dar es Salaam – where there are lots of ANC agitators and British liberal commies?'

I didn't know where this was going or what was going to come next. Were they going to lock me up? He gazed silently at me, with an evil expression on his face. I didn't say anything. There was no point talking to people like this man. What came next, however, surprised me.

'Now get out!' the security officer said. 'Next time I see you, you better watch out. You can't hide behind your German passport forever.'

I left in a hurry – out of the room and along the narrow corridor. I took the stairs four at a time, ran down four floors and out of the building. No re-entry visa. Nothing for it, then: I would have to go without one.

I went home and packed a large suitcase, putting essentials in it. Then I went to the *Drum* office library, where I took out a few of my important negatives. After that I went to the *Sunday Times* darkroom, where I took some more of my negatives. I would get the rest another time, I thought. I was worried that the Special Branch would confiscate my negatives at the airport. That evening I flew to Nairobi, taking only an overnight bag and my cameras with me on the plane. The large suitcase I checked straight through to London.

Leaving South Africa was the right decision. I knew that over the last few years the Special Branch had been on my back, tracking my movements, and that I was often followed. They had also visited some of my friends, asking questions about me. One day I had lent a friend of mine my car for the day, and when he returned it two days later he said: 'I'll never borrow your car again – I must have been crazy!' Apparently the first day the police had followed him several times and also stopped him several times, asking him for his papers and the name of the owner of the car. A day later he was followed again, this time by an unmarked car with two plainclothes policemen inside, taking notes of where he parked and whom he visited.

I got off the plane in Nairobi and found a flight in a Dakota to Dar es Salaam via Zanzibar. I thought I was very lucky to find a connection so quickly. The plane was an old crate which flew low over a small mountain range and bounced about, making me sick. When we landed in Zanzibar, we were told we couldn't get off the plane but, thanks to some sort of commotion at the back, I managed to slip off, to try to get the story and take photographs. I was walking swiftly across the tarmac when I was caught by two security guards and promptly marched back onto the plane.

I arrived in Dar es Salaam later than I'd hoped and I tried to find out what was happening. I found out that the HMS *Centaur* aircraft carrier was anchored off the coast and that a company of Royal Marines from No 45 Commando had just landed by helicopter and had captured the mutineers of the Tanganyika Rifles.

President Julius Nyerere had appealed to the British government after the Tanganyika Rifles had used the Zanzibar uprising as a convenient opportunity to start a mutiny. The country's military had rebelled and the British High Commissioner was detained, but in the end most of the strategic points had been captured by the Royal Marines. Most of the mutineers had quickly surrendered, so it was too late for me to photograph any action. I did, however, photograph some of the Royal Marines cleaning up the city, arresting some stray mutineers.

There wasn't much else I could do in Dar es Salaam, so I took the next flight to Nairobi, shipped my films to Black Star in New York with an explanation for my delay, and got my connection to London.

Europe

Andalusia beach

32

LONDON – BERLIN – LONDON

I left my case at St Pancras station and walked around London, not knowing what to do or where to go. I could have phoned Anthony Sampson but I felt that might create complications, so I thought about tracking down Arthur Maimane – but how to find him? I wandered around Piccadilly Circus for a while. It was early morning rush hour and I watched hundreds of people in bowler hats, with umbrellas under their arms, rushing up and down the steps to the Underground. Distracted, I bumped into someone. I looked up to apologise and we stared at each other in utter surprise – it was Sylvester Stein!

We were both very excited at this chance meeting and we went and had coffee together at Patisserie Valerie, where we sat talking for hours. Sylvester wanted to know everything that had happened at *Drum* after he left; he wanted to hear about all the *Drum* characters. I told him that Arthur and Todd were now both in London.

Sylvester told me he had a small office in Dean Street in Soho and that he was publishing magazines, including one called *Camera Owner*, which was aimed at amateur photographers. He was looking for an editor. Might I be interested?

I got myself a tiny basement flat in Fulham, where I somehow also managed to find space for a small darkroom, and got stuck into my new job. Sylvester had agreed that I could take off from time to time to do my own photography on a freelance basis. The staff was tiny, just a young girl, a secretary, and a Mr Brown, an elderly South African man I had met before at Sylvester's house in South Africa. Mr Brown was the book-keeper. I found out much later that book-keeping wasn't the only job of 'Mr Brown': he was running the explosives and weapons route to Umkhonto weSizwe (MK) in South Africa.

The existing material for the next issue of *Camera Owner* wasn't very good. The syndicated text was dated and simplistic, as were the photos submitted by the amateur photographers. I decided to use some of my own photographs from South Africa to illustrate how to take better pictures. I also used a set of pictures from the South African photographer Sam Haskins to show how to photograph models. I met a representative for Ilford Film, Bill Jay, who was very helpful and arranged for me to get better pictures and text. Over time the quality of *Camera Owner* improved.

The photojournalism scene was changing rapidly, mainly due to the introduction of colour TV, which led to newspapers losing their print advertising as clients migrated to television. To counteract this, the London *Sunday Times*, the *Observer* and the *Weekend Telegraph* now all produced colour magazines, which they sold with their main paper, a trend that was taken up by many papers in Europe.

Photographers had switched from rangefinder cameras to single-lens reflex cameras, which were noisy, the mirror jangling up and down during the exposure. Many cameras had motors which could shoot frame after frame, exposing masses of rolls of film. The advantage of the reflex camera was that you could see through your lens, which was especially necessary when using colour film when one had filters on the lens.

So no more black-and-white as far as the London magazines were concerned.

My first freelance assignment was for the *Observer* and it was a big one: the funeral of Winston Churchill on 30 January 1965. The pictures editor asked me to come into the office for a briefing. I hurried along, very pleased and excited to get such a big assignment. When I arrived at the meeting, to my surprise I found ten photographers standing in front of the pictures editor's desk. Each photographer was given a spot to cover along the funeral's procession. Some spots were at a specific window in a building, others were on street corners on ladders, and everyone had to be in position two hours before the start of the procession. We were to stay for the duration and wait till after the funeral for the motorcyclists to collect our rolls of film from us. My position was at a government building on the corner opposite Westminster.

On the day of the funeral I arrived at my allotted building and was taken onto the roof and locked out there, together with a number of film makers. It was early, still dark, with a cold wind blowing. There was not much of a view to the street below and we all huddled together in a corner, waiting for daylight and for the procession to start. Not the most glamorous assignment, after all!

One day I got a call from Ernest Cole, who said he was coming soon to London on his way to New York and would like to see me. He was currently in Sweden, where he had been given a travel document. I was pleased to hear from him, and when he got to London we set up a day and time to meet at my small flat. Ian Berry was in London and I invited him and another photographer, David Hurn, to come along too.

When Ernest arrived, Ian and David were already there. Ernest was his usual shy, self-conscious self, and we all sat facing each other on the floor. Ernest then produced a 10 x 12-inch box of prints, which we passed around. He wanted to publish them in a book in New York about apartheid. There were 150 prints in the box. I was enormously impressed. I thought they were the most moving set of prints I had ever seen about South Africa under apartheid.

Ernest explained the different subjects and themes he had covered – from mineworkers to nannies, from 'locations in the sky' (these were small rooms on the roofs of apartment blocks to house the 'house-boys and maids', domestic servants of the white people who lived in the apartments) to white life to street children who turned to crime living on the streets of Joburg.

Neither Ian nor David seemed particularly impressed by Ernest's prints or interested in them, and as we passed the photos around they started talking about other things. Both David and Ian were members of Magnum and I had thought that they might be helpful to Ernest when they saw how powerful his work was. I was disappointed by their attitude and I could see Ernest was discouraged. I did my best to reassure him, praising the rich quality I saw in his work and telling him I was sure his book would be a big success. About a year later I read in an international photography magazine about a book just published book entitled *House of Bondage* by Ernest Cole, with text by Joe Lelyveld of the *New York Times*, and a few weeks later I received a copy in the post. Ernest enclosed a note thanking me for my support. The book made a big impact and earned Ernest well-deserved fame worldwide. Almost all the photo magazines and newspapers reviewed it, proclaiming it the most important book to come out about apartheid South Africa.

In 1966 I came across a report in the German magazine *Die Zeit* about Jewish families resettling in Germany – in Berlin, Frankfurt and Munich. I thought this would make an important story and made some enquiries about getting contacts. I then made an appointment to see the editor of the *Telegraph* Sunday Supplement, John Anstey.

John Anstey had a reputation of being something of an eccentric. I'd heard he was once a racing-car driver, among other diverse activities. I sat across his desk from him and he passed me a glass of whisky clinking with ice cubes and told me he liked my work. He was a ruddy-faced man of about 50, and I could see that behind the smile and friendly demeanour was a tough character. He asked me to go to Berlin and make contact with the neo-Nazi party and then follow the story to Frankfurt and Munich. Once I had the information and photos he would decide on an appropriate journalist to join me.

I finished the next *Camera Owner* issue and Sylvester agreed that I could be away freelancing for a couple of weeks, leaving enough time to work on the next issue on my return.

And I was off to Berlin.

The first thing I did was go to the famous synagogue in Fasanenstrasse. The synagogue was burned down by the Nazis during Kristallnacht in November 1938 and then what remained of it was bombed by the Allied Forces in 1943. After the war it was rebuilt in a modern style. I introduced myself to some officials in the office, who were delighted to help me in my story, especially as it was for a major British publication. I was lucky as it was the annual Purim holiday celebration and there was a gala evening with dancing the following day, where I would be able to meet members of the Jewish community in Berlin and take some photos. I booked into the Kempinski Hotel across the road. Kempinski was renamed Borchardt during the war because the Kempinski

Hotel was run by a Jewish family. In my youth my mother and I often went for a meal in their restaurant.

The following evening I went to the Purim celebrations and found the community hall packed with about 250 people of all ages, from teenagers to men and women in their eighties. People were eating and drinking at tables around the dance floor, where couples were dancing to the music of a band on the stage. Everyone was stylishly dressed in evening wear and black tuxedoes, enjoying the gala celebration. It was a jolly atmosphere and I moved around the hall documenting it all on film.

While I was taking photos, a distinguished-looking man with thinning hair and a friendly face approached me and introduced himself. Artur Brauner was the president of the Jewish Society in Berlin and a well-known film maker, who had made films about the Nazi regime and the suffering of the Jewish people. Not only had he survived Auschwitz but he had escaped from the notorious concentration camp. Artur asked who I was taking the photos for. When I explained that I was doing a story about the Jewish community in Germany for the London *Telegraph*, he was delighted and he asked me to join him at his table. I got some interesting information from him, and after we had some wine together he introduced me to his guests. He also told me a bit about the new neo-Nazi party that was beginning to rise in Germany. If I visited him in his Grunewald home, he said, he would be able to give me some leads. He could also help me with Jewish community contacts in Frankfurt and Munich.

I took up his kind offer and visited Artur Brauner in his villa. By the time I left I was loaded with information. Next I went to Frankfurt, where I visited the Jewish Cemetery. I found some abandoned gravestones with names like Rothschild and Goldsmith engraved on them. One thing I found very moving was the many graves inscribed to sons, brothers and fathers who had died fighting for their fatherland, Germany, in the First World War. In Frankfurt I met many members of the Jewish community who had returned to the city. Many of them considered it their home town and all of them were optimistic about their future in Germany. In Munich I found the same attitude and I took pictures at a progressive Jewish nursery school and youth club.

Back in London I went to see John Anstey. I gave him all the information

I'd gathered about the neo-Nazis, much of it gleaned from the generous Artur Brauner. Anstey seemed satisfied and we decided that I should return to Germany with a writer.

James Cameron was the writer/journalist who would be joining me on the neo-Nazi story. He was well known in England as one of the top investigative journalists, one of the first to interview Ho Chi Minh in Hannoi, from where he had just returned. We met for lunch in a restaurant in South Kensington and we got on well. He was very keen to work on the story with me for the *Telegraph* and we decided to leave for Germany the following week. He confessed to me that the neo-Nazis gave him the horrors. He promised to try not to blow up when we interviewed some of these characters but I should keep an eye on him, he said. I thought James was just the right person and journalist to work on this story. In some ways he reminded me of my old friend and colleague Henry Nxumalo.

I had just enough time to finish the next issue of *Camera Owner* as well as complete the story of 'Jews in Germany', which was published as we left for Berlin. When we arrived I phoned Artur Brauner for an appointment. He said he would pick us up after 7pm at the bar of the Kempinski Hotel. This gave us enough time to visit the NPD (National Democratic Party of Germany) office, which was in an old working-class suburb of the city. The office was small and it reeked of stale tobacco. Posters with racist slogans were plastered on the walls. The only person there was a young skinhead, who was sitting at an untidy desk – papers, newspaper cuttings, beer cans and a large ashtray full of cigarette stubs covered most of its surface. We had been hoping to interview the district manager, but the young man, who introduced himself as Rudi, said he wasn't there and didn't know when he'd be back.

Back at the Kempinski we settled at the bar to wait for Artur. James pointed at a row of about 30 liquor bottles – schnapps, whisky, and brandy – in front of us on a long shelf behind the bar and smiled. 'How long would it take us to taste that row?' he asked me. 'At least a week,' I said. I hoped he wasn't planning a crazy binge. James ordered us a tot each from the first bottle in the row ...

After a very strong slivovitz and then a tot each of schnapps, I began to get worried. On the fifth bottle I was about to resign from the contest when Artur arrived, accompanied by a pretty young lady, Maria, his wife. He seemed very pleased to see us (although not as pleased as I was to see him) and welcomed us warmly to Berlin.

At the Brauners' home in the Grunewald we were invited to make ourselves at home on comfortable armchairs in the conservatory. Maria produced a special bottle of Polish vodka and we made several toasts to the success of Artur's new film, *Die weisse Rose*. Talking about the film took me right back to my boyhood and Aunt Doris and running errands in Berlin for this underground anti-Nazi group, delivering messages back and forth on my bicycle.

By this time I was fairly tipsy. Maria got in the mood and gave us an impromptu dance performance, frolicking round the palms, joined by James, while Artur kept filling up our glasses. The evening turned into quite a drunken event. Quite how things transpired I don't remember, but I ended up sitting in an aeroplane next to James without any idea how I'd got there or where we were going. James, the more experienced vodka drinker, explained to me that we were on a short flight to Hannover to meet the Nazi leader, Adolf von Thadden.

In contrast to the small Berlin office, Von Thadden's was spacious and neat. He was a tall slim man, hair cut short and wearing a dark suit. He welcomed us and invited us to sit on chairs arranged around a low table. He sat down opposite us and started his party line.

'The National Democratic Party of Germany is a party for Germany for the Germans. I can reassure you that the Jewish problem no longer exists,' he said, looking intensely at James. 'It has been replaced by the Israel problem.' There followed a long period of silence. Then he continued: 'Don't you see – it's the problem of Israel; it's diplomatic blackmail. We have already paid the Jews endless fortunes in indemnities – what is called "restitution". They never stop moaning about the past. They demand more and more.' He carried on like this in a long monologue. 'We want Poland to give us our German province back and we need a bigger and stronger army.' His talk became more bitter and hateful, and when we left about two hours later James and I were both very depressed. Probably the fact that we both had hangovers was a good thing.

We took the next train south to Frankfurt to cover an NPD meeting in the township of Langen outside Frankfurt. In a large room long tables were laden with bottles of beer and a young speaker talked about the thirties with great emotion, the men sitting at the tables nodding occasionally and giving staccato barks of approval. We travelled on for a few more days, meeting other neo-Nazi groups. In Karlsruhe we covered a conference where the six executive members of the NPD were in attendance. They sat on a large stage and were joined by Von Thadden and party chairman Fritz Thielen. All six of the executives had held high rank in the SS. The national anthem was sung and the auditorium was packed to capacity, predominantly with middle-aged men. Outside the conference hall almost 20 000 people took part in an anti-NPD demonstration, holding anti-Nazi banners.

After our story appeared in the *Telegraph*, it was followed up by *Paris Match* and several other newspapers, but only then did the German newspapers publish this story seriously. Most of the neo-Nazis were eventually taken to court and the NPD party seemed to disappear.

I stayed on in Germany, while James returned to London rather shaken by the experience of meeting German Nazis who were alive and well. After he had flown home, late that evening I drove to the Teutoburg Forest near Detmold where the Nazis were celebrating a victory over the Romans in AD 9. The event was held at the Hermann Monument and later that night the songs and speakers became more and more vitriolic and sinister, and uniformed members of the neo-Nazi group held up burning torches and gave the Nazi salute.

On the plane back to London my thoughts turned inwards. I took myself back to Germany in 1950, all that I and the country had been through, and the circumstances in which I had been living. I knew that leaving had been the right decision for me. I remembered arguing with German Jewish friends in South Africa about the Nazi regime. Somehow they continued to believe that German society was a cultured society which had produced great literature and art, and that the Holocaust was just a freak moment in German history that would not be repeated and was only brought on by the humiliation of the Versailles agreement. I wasn't so optimistic about Germany's future but I hoped I was wrong.

33

ANDALUSIA

During the next few years I did a number of stories for the colour magazines in London and for *Die Zeit* in Hamburg. In 1968 I did a photo study of the removals of the depressed township of the Gorbals in Glasgow and a story about Heathrow airport.

I was growing tired of the rain and grey weather in London, and the thought of another winter was dispiriting.

I read an article in a magazine about a town in Andalusia called Torremolinos, and how it had been one of the most fashionable high-society centres in Spain. In the early sixties Frank Sinatra had been arrested in a brawl at the Hotel Pez Espada there, having been framed by a crooked photographer. After spending a night in a cell he angrily said that he would never visit Spain again. After the affair the hotel opened Frankie's Cafe in honour of the famous crooner. In the fifties the film star Rita Hayworth had spent her holidays in Torremolinos, soon to be followed by other film luminaries such as Elizabeth Taylor, Diana Dors, Grace Kelly, Laurence Olivier and, later, the writer Graham Greene.

When the holiday package tours started to invade the Costa del Sol in the late sixties, with themed holidays such as 'painting holidays' and 'photo holidays', Torremolinos became the main attraction for the regular British holidaymaker. Many people from the United Kingdom (those who tended to drink from morning till dawn) became permanent residents. In 1965 Sean Connery, Sophia Loren, the King of Spain, and Spanish and international statesmen moved to Marbella which, with its original Spanish atmosphere, became the new jet-set location.

With all of this in my mind, I decided to investigate the famous Costa del Sol. And so I left London and its cold winter behind and went to take a look. I ended up living in Spain for some years.

Torremolinos had little left of the original charm that had attracted the high-flyers, but the Bar Central was still there and it offered rich opportunities for photographs. Here you could sit and watch the tourists pass by. Always on duty was the local policeman directing the traffic, waving his arms about and blowing his whistle. Often the village buffoon, a friendly fellow who was known by all, would take over from him for a spell, while the policeman stood aside and watched with tolerant amusement. One day an American painter, dressed in a traditional Spanish outfit, rode up to the bar on a black thoroughbred horse. Moving his left leg over the horse's rump and sitting side-saddle, he called the waiter to bring him a sherry, which he sipped slowly as he inspected us sitting with our espressos at tables out front.

Then there was the pub restaurant called the Galloping Major. This catered for 'the Brits', the ex-colonials who had settled in or near Torremolinos and who came from the former British colonies in East Africa or the Bahamas. The Brits were good drinkers and from 11am every day the Galloping Major was full of pale-skinned people drinking pink gins, gin and tonics, whiskies and lagers. You would often see the same characters there every day.

One day in the private bar, which was on the first floor with three large floor-to-ceiling open windows to let the breeze in, I got talking to a sportily dressed gentleman. In an exaggerated upper-class accent, he declared: 'The Labour Party is the downfall of the British Empire.' And then, pointing his finger at me, he said, 'You must have another drink, young man!' The barman, who had a long pointed moustache, poured us two more whiskies. 'He is a Guardsman, you know,' the barman said to me, as if I hadn't shown the man enough respect. 'He's in the Hickey column.' (This was a gossip column in the *Sunday Express*.) The Guardsman finished his drink in one gulp, stood erect and said, 'I must be off, old boy!' and marched straight out of the window. The barman and I rushed to the window and looked down anxiously. Luckily the man had fallen into some bushes. He was brushing himself off. We watched as he swayed unsteadily down the road.

There was an English-language radio programme on the Costa del Sol and I got to know the presenter, Jane Holtman, quite well. She was a cheerful English lady who was nuts about dogs and horses. She told me about how she had fought for years with the Málaga authorities to cover the heads of the coach horses with small umbrellas to protect them from the hot summer sun. These horses were a tourist attraction and they spent hours in the sun walking up and down the Málaga promenade. Jane also picked up lost dogs from the streets and she kept these strays on the small plot outside Torremolinos where she lived. Regular features of Jane's programme were news items about the latest celebrity visitors to the coast and, of course, the weather. She also played British hit songs.

One evening as Jane was driving home in heavy traffic, she saw a donkey in the road. It was running from one lane to another, with cars swerving in the dark to try to avoid it. She parked at the side of the road and attempted to catch the donkey, but this only made the problem worse because the creature kept running away from her. Brakes screeched and drivers shouted. Jane didn't give up, however, and after a long chase she saw the donkey trotting up the wide stairs of one of the luxury coastal hotels. It ran into the foyer, Jane in hot pursuit, where it caused general pandemonium. It ended up in the dining room with Jane trying to protect it while some of the waiters and guests flapped at the animal with table napkins. They then tried to push it back into the foyer using dining-room chairs. Eventually order was restored and the donkey was led away. Jane was charged with disturbing the peace for her troubles and asked to pay costs for the damage caused!

I went to see an English-language magazine called *Look Out*, which catered to the foreign residents on the coast. The editor, Ken Brown, was a former Fleet Street journalist. I found him a personable, friendly fellow who agreed, after I had shown him some of my work, to use me as a freelance photographer on the coast. This gave me an entrée to interesting situations and people, as well as a small income.

About 25 kilometres west of Torremolinos was a tiny fishing village called Los Boliches and here I rented a small house. The village was unspoilt and I found it idyllic. In the evening I would walk on the beach and see the shadows cast by the setting sun of the fishermen repairing their nets and roasting sardines on a fire, watched by sleepy dogs lying on the sand.

There was one English bar in the village, Bar Santiago, which catered for expatriates, mostly English, but some German and Dutch too. I didn't spend much time there – its patrons were your typical barflies – but preferred spending time in the village's tapas bars, where I sampled the most original and delicious Andalusian dishes, and discovered some good inexpensive local wine.

During the seventies there was a dispute between Spain and Britain over the ownership of Gibraltar, with the Spanish trying to claim it back from Britain. As a result Spain had isolated it by closing the border to Gibraltar. This upset the British living on the coast because they couldn't get their bangers (pork sausages), their unsalted butter, Worcestershire sauce, English bacon, Ceylon tea and Woodbine cigarettes. An Indian entrepreneur came to the rescue, smuggling in to order the required goods for the deprived Brits. Once a week he came to Bar Santiago bringing new supplies. The place was always crowded with Brits talking about their problems, especially the 'Spanish' problem. It seemed to me they thought the British Empire was alive and well.

Torremolinos had definitely lost its romantic reputation of the fifties. The night life was rough and tough; drunks staggered in and out of the many bars. I took pictures of white-faced, sweaty, sickly-looking teenagers, many of them from Scandinavian countries, where alcohol was restricted. These kids couldn't handle the unlimited booze in Spain but they did their best to try. Discos, with their loud, thumping music, went on into the early hours. At El Bierkeller, German tourists raised their glasses and belted out drinking songs. Tiffany's was the 'in' discotheque (it had stereophonic sound) and the King Club offered flamenco shows and a swimming pool. The beach was always full, sunbathers packed together like sardines in a tin.

In February the Verdiales of Málaga took place. Hundreds of pilgrims would toil up a winding road in the hills behind Málaga to a tavern to watch musicians from different villages compete, presenting their 'Fandangos de Málaga'. Ken wrote about this in *Look Out* and I took pictures. 'Somewhere in the crowd are a dozen groups of village musicians warming up for the contest. Suddenly a group starts up to our left. We stand tip-toe, craning our necks, and spot the fantastic Verdiales headgear – straw hats festooned with flowers, tiny mirrors, all manner of baubles, bangles and beads, and multicoloured ribbons – bobbing above the sea of faces … the groups, one after another, are to perform before a table of judges.'

Manuel Blasco Alarcón, Picasso's second cousin, ran an antique shop in Málaga. He started painting late in life, at the age of 60, and his pictures brought back to life a vanished epoch. They showed the old Málaga and the traditional festivities and were not for sale, but exhibited in major museums around Spain.

Ronda, a town from the Middle Ages with a long history, is situated in the hills 80 kilometres west of Málaga. It is said to have the largest and oldest bullring in the world, dating back to 1784. I didn't know much about bull-fighting but, intrigued by a new experience, I decided to go along and take photographs. The crowds were a mix of Spanish and Anglo-Saxon foreigners. I noticed that many of the foreigners, who did most of the screaming and shout-ing during the fight, were drinking wine out of large two-litre bottles and lots of them were very intoxicated. I concentrated on the fight itself, but first I had to learn about the ritual, so I sat watching for a while as one bull after another was brought into the ring. After the sixth fight I began to get a better idea of what it was all about and began to take pictures. I felt especially sorry for the horses, who were often mortally injured by the bull.

Later I showed some of my bullfight prints to a number of bullfight experts, who accused me of taking the worst bullfight images they had ever seen. They did not see in the pictures the elegance or courage of the matadors. I left it to the viewers to judge for themselves the value of my bullfight pictures.

I returned to London at the end of 1971, where I started to freelance again, but I found it more difficult than before my move to Spain. *Camera Owner* had been bought by a company Bill Jay worked for and the magazine was renamed *Creative Camera*. In the United States *Life* magazine, *Look* and *Holiday*, as well as many others, had closed down, which meant that a large number of photojour-nalists were out of work worldwide, including me. As it became increasingly difficult to get assignments, many photographers took on teaching jobs. I got a part-time position at the Central School of Art and Design in London. For the next fifteen years this was where I taught photography three days a week.

Africa in Full Colour

'The Lord is my shepherd' truck

34

PRAYERS AT SUNSET – FROM SENEGAL TO MALI

Early in 1973 I had the idea of doing a photographic trip through Africa. I had lived in South Africa for fourteen years but had never really seen the rest of Africa. In attempting to become a white Western country, South Africa was politically, socially and culturally isolated from the rest of Africa. I had seen an article in a German magazine about a group of young journalists who had hitchhiked on the cheap through India and had produced a book about their adventures, and this inspired me to embark on this African journey. Also I was badly in need of some sun after many grey, wet London winters.

I went to see John Anstey again. I tried to interest him in the idea of a photographic hitchhiking tour across Africa but he wasn't very keen, saying, 'It's too dangerous. Amin in Uganda, problems in the Sudan – and the *Telegraph* can't send an expedition to bail you out.' I countered this argument, saying I thought it would be interesting to do a study of the realities of daily life in several African countries. I said I was prepared to pay for my own airfare and travel costs, that all I was asking him for was his editorial support. After a few whiskies in his office John agreed to pay my return airfare, £200 in expenses, and sponsor some colour film, but he made it clear that the *Telegraph* bore no responsibility for what he still saw as a risky trip.

The very next day, 28 January, I started to make enquiries at Africa House about conditions in the various African countries I was planning to visit and began organising the requisite visas. Most of the countries I had on my itinerary were suspicious and unwelcoming of journalists, so my cover story was that my interest was in photographing African traditions and the natural world. I had a problem with getting a visa for Zaire (DRC) and had several visits to an official at the embassy, who was a large, very dark-skinned man in his late fifties. The second time I saw him he asked me where he could buy a 'chicken fry', which completely threw me. I didn't have a clue what he was talking about. Then he explained: it was a chicken roasting machine, a rotisserie. He explained that he was retiring soon and was planning to open a roast chicken shop in Zaire. I promised to try to find him a second-hand fryer and, in fact, I did my best. I scoured the United Kingdom for a machine, to no avail. Eventually I found one near Hamburg in Germany and the embassy official was thrilled. I got my visa for Zaire. I was unable to get a visa for Nigeria. The embassy said it would take too long but I was welcome to try again when I got to Ghana.

After a tiring time dashing across London from one African embassy to another, on 19 February I was in the air on a flight to Dakar, Senegal. I was feeling tense but prepared for my train journey from Dakar to Mali, which should give me three days in Dakar. I landed in Dakar at three on a Monday morning. I tried to cash a £10 sterling traveller's cheque but a lone man behind the money exchange bar said in broken English that he could only take dollars, Deutsche marks or French francs. He didn't know anything about British pounds. There was no bus at the airport but I found a rather dilapidated taxi with a driver in a long white shirt and sporting a colourful cap. He took me to a small third-class hotel with first-class prices. I paid the taxi driver with my last £2, which resulted in a long argument over the price. The tiny room had a concrete floor, a small sink in the corner with a dripping tap, and a bed with a dirty mattress and an old blanket. Luckily, I didn't need the blanket – the heat, even at that time of the morning, was unbearable. I was too tired to worry about anything, so I fell onto the bed and sank into a deep sleep.

I woke to bright sunshine coming through the curtains at around 9am. I located a bank, where I queued for 20 minutes and cashed some traveller's cheques (UK£1 = 550 francs). Then I had coffee at the Hotel Centrale café in the street in the main square of Dakar, Place de l'indépendance. I was pestered

by a stream of shoe polishers, watch sellers, and jewellery and sunglasses sellers, who immediately saw in my white untanned face that I was a newcomer
and foreigner. Next I went to a travel agency, where I was told the train to Mali
left on Tuesdays at 6.30pm. I would either have to take the train the next day or
wait until the following Tuesday. After two visits to the Ministry of Information
I eventually got a permit to photograph in Senegal. It was very hot and my
skin was starting to burn, so I put sunscreen on my face and started walking.
I walked through the maze of Dakar's streets, taking pictures – of women in
colourful traditional dress, men in long kaftans and decorated houses.

I found the Mali embassy, where I was told that I had to wait for my visa till
5.30pm the next day, which would be very close to the time of the departure
of my train to Mali. The following morning, after an uncomfortable sleep in
my cell-like hotel room, I got up early and took a ferry to Gorée Island. This
was the island, fought over by the French and British, which became the centre
for the slave and gold trade. It was quite commercialised and the place was full
of tourists – I noticed that the island inhabitants stayed at home behind closed
shutters.

Back in Dakar I got my ticket to Bamako (6 450 francs) and then wandered
back to the Place de l'indépendance, where I got into playing chess with some
locals and took some pictures until it was time to go back to the embassy and
collect my visa. Then I took a taxi to the Dakar railway station, the starting
point of my trek, stopping first at the hotel to collect my bag.

The station was a lively, busy hustle and bustle, with all sorts of activity
going on. Tall dignified women in colourful dresses strolled by, selling sunglasses, watches, cheap jewellery and peeled oranges. Other women, in bright
clothes and striking headwear, were preparing to board the train. Hugging their
baskets to their chests, which were filled with supplies of food for the journey, they gave me wide friendly smiles as I climbed aboard. The coach had a
central passage and seats on either side. Bags of onions, cabbages, and fruit
boxes covered the floor and people selling bananas and oranges clambered over
them, going back and forth along the passage. The train itself was as bustling a
marketplace as the platform outside. A man with a board displaying all types of
sunglasses passed me, and then another selling jewellery and cheap perfume. In

one corner a woman sat on a bench with several chickens clucking and crowing and running between her legs, trying to escape her clutches.

By 6.30 the carriages were packed. The engine gave a warning hoot, the pedlars disembarked and we jerked into motion. We pulled out of the station and slowly chugged past shanty towns on the outskirts of the city. With the train whistling continually, changing pitch as we went, we rattled our way over the last junction point and then we were off with a steady rhythm into the African dusk.

On the seat nearby, a boy was saying his prayers, humming in an even tone, and a blind man walked slowly past me singing and snapping his fingers. He stopped for a silent moment, then walked on, resuming his humming. A Mauritanian man dressed in white robes sitting opposite me looked at his watch, got up and unfolded a small carpet, making space on the floor by shifting some bags. He laid his carpet down, stood up and, unfolding his arms, murmured in prayer. He knelt on the carpet, bent over and, in a prone position with his face on the floor, remained still for a few minutes. Then he got up and repeated the ritual. All this was happening together with constant traffic along the passage. More blind men passed through, singing. A stout lady handed one of the men a banana, which he ate in silence as he continued on his way.

By now it was dark outside. Two weak lights in the ceiling threw shadows on us. A man in an orange headscarf got up and prayed, and the train rocked us gently through the dark night. Having removed their shoes, most people were sleeping now, and there was a pungent odour of sweaty feet, oranges and bananas in the carriage.

Suddenly I had a strong feeling that someone was watching me from the bench behind. I turned round to see a very large goat with big horns and a tufty beard standing in the passage, staring fixedly at me. It had huge black pupils and its gaze never wavered. The animal was on a lead held by a small boy sitting on the floor between the benches behind me. It gave me the creeps.

A woman came along the passage and stopped in front of me. She had a baby on her back and the baby looked at me, stretching its arms out and saying, 'Banana, banana, banana.' The mother laughed at the baby and strolled on. There was a farm smell in the air and it was getting very stuffy with all the

Train to Mali

windows closed. Tiredness came over me and, looking out of the window into the dark night, I fell asleep.

I was awoken by loud voices. It seemed the train had stopped at a station. It was still dark outside but there was much movement, chatting, shouting, babies crying, parcels, boxes, bags and chickens being moved. And the boy with the goat was leaving. As I watched him walk away along the passage, the goat turned its head and gave me a final stare.

We started to move again and soon the train had resumed its steady, rhythmic pace. It was getting light outside and people were settling themselves on the floor, some sitting on their bags and starting to eat – chicken, fruit – while others woke up slowly to the dawn. We chugged through dry, flat landscape with a few large, strange-looking trees here and there and scrubby bushes. The trees looked as if they were part of a stage set.

The last town in Senegal was Belle. At the siding station women and children were selling fruit, nuts and fried goat meat wrapped in banana leaves.

Soon after crossing the Senegal–Mali border, we arrived at the town of Kidira. Here I and four other white passengers were asked to leave the train and go to the police station. We filled in forms and were asked to wait for the commissioner, who had to stamp our passports. It took a long time for him to turn up and we began to worry that the train would leave with our luggage but, in fact, it stayed in the station for several hours. One of the other white passengers was a young American fellow in his early twenties with a short military haircut. He introduced himself as Jeffrey Hutcherson Hall from Lexington, Massachusetts. He said he was a student and this trip was part of his final year of studies. Eventually the commissioner arrived. We got our passports stamped and returned to the train, where I settled down in my seat, which my fellow passengers had kept free for me.

After a while I noticed a certain amount of confusion among the passengers – luggage was being passed out of the windows and some people were getting up. There was a lot of shouting outside. I worked out that our coach was going to be disconnected, so we all had to get out and climb on another coach. I hurriedly got my bag and handed it down through the window to someone. Then, seeing that the doors were jammed with people, some trying to get in and

Fruit selling on the roadside in Senegal

some out, I followed my bag through the window and into the coach opposite like everyone else, hoping I was doing the right thing and we were still going to Bamako. Everyone resettled in the new compartment (which was exactly the same as the previous one), and the same people sat around me with all their belongings. After another interval the train set off again. By this time it was almost full daylight outside.

And then it was night again and we were getting close to the end of our journey. We had spent over 40 hours in the over-crowded train. Everyone seemed to be getting edgy, protecting their limited territory jealously and eyeing one another nervously. When someone stepped on another person's foot, angry words were spoken and tension in the carriage mounted. When we finally arrived in Bamako it was just after midnight.

35

NESCAFÉ, CONDENSED MILK AND TINNED SARDINES

Outside Bamako station I spotted two men holding a board that said 'Bus to Abidjan'. They told me there was a bus leaving first thing in the morning, the price £6, and if I wanted to catch it I should accompany them. At this point I was joined by Jeffrey, who also wanted to travel to Abidjan. One of the two men led us through some dark streets to an open square where we saw half-a-dozen minibuses parked in one corner. Behind the driver's cabin were four rows of wooden seats or benches – each could hold four or five people – and there was a roof-rack for luggage. We put our bags into a bus with the name 'Super Yanky' emblazoned on it in large colourful letters. We were told to wait until more passengers had been collected and then we'd be taken to a house where we would spend the night.

Jeff and I looked around for somewhere to eat and get a drink. Not far away we saw a low table lit by an oil lamp and strolled towards it hopefully. It turned out to be an outdoor café and we sat down on the only bench and were greeted effusively by the owner. We discussed the price of a Nescafé and after much misunderstanding agreed a price of 75 francs for two glasses of coffee and two pieces of French bread. Our host then proceeded to make the coffee himself. From a pot over a fire, he poured a brown liquid through a sieve into two glasses, put eight large cubes of sugar into each glass, followed by a teaspoon of Nescafé and some condensed milk from a tin. All this was done in slow motion with great precision. The coffee tasted delicious.

There were eight passengers now in the bus and our driver, who was the young man from the station, indicated that we were ready to go. We hadn't gone far, bumping along some dark roads with small houses on either side, when the bus broke down. There was much clanking of tools and voices outside, then some pushing of the bus, but eventually we arrived at the house where we were to spend the night. We were shown down a dark passage and into a courtyard. On a small veranda, also lit by an oil lamp, we climbed into our sleeping bags.

When I woke up it was 6am and there was much commotion around me as people got up from their sleeping spots and began to get ready to leave. I got a small bowl of cold water and washed and shaved as best I could. Then the owner arrived. He was a very short man, straight out of a forties gangster movie – he was silent, never smiled, and wore a hat and an old raincoat that he never seemed to take off. I paid him 3 000 Senegalese francs, for which he gave me a receipt. He told us we would leave for Abidjan at 10am. I went to look for a toilet and eventually found in the corner of the yard a contraption about one and a half metres high without a door where you had to sit on a wooden beam and do your business in the hole below. I made the mistake of glancing down and saw the hole filled almost to the top with millions of maggots wriggling about. Somehow I managed.

We all got back into the bus and drove off to the market square. Dozens of stalls were already set up, selling everything from fruit and nuts to dresses. There were open-air barber shops and blacksmiths fixing bicycles. The early sun was already blazing hot. I counted about 30 buses parked in the square, all with roof-racks packed with bags. Four Mauritanians in turbans and long loose kaftans, clutching many bags, joined our group and we settled down in our seats. I had chosen a window seat, but there was no glass in my window. Then I saw that none of the buses had windows. I presumed this was because of the heat. The bus was full and we were all ready to go but nothing seemed to be happening. It was extremely hot, and some of us got off and walked around. A rumour started that we would leave at 12, then at 1pm. Then our two drivers appeared with some packages, which they put on the roof, rearranging the luggage already there. When we asked them when we would be leaving, they said, 'Later.'

Bus from Bamako

Meanwhile, a self-confident, chain-smoking young boy from our bus was doing business with the black market money dealers. He had quite a large amount of Mali money in his pocket, which he changed into Ivory Coast currency. Suddenly a large man appeared, grabbed him by the neck and marched him off, which caused quite a stir. Later we discovered that the boy had stolen the money from his mother and it was his brother who had caught him.

At about 4pm someone changed a wheel on the bus. I went around to take a look and to my horror saw that both front tyres were worn right down to the canvas. A little later one of the drivers changed the oil in the gearbox. Most of the other buses in the marketplace had already left and Jeffrey started to get impatient. He began shouting at our driver, who remained totally calm and unmoved, as did the other passengers, who just sat patiently, a glazed look in their eyes.

Shortly after 6pm there was some action. The driver got into his seat behind the wheel, the unsmiling bus owner in his raincoat and hat turned up, and we all sat up expectantly. Helpfully push-started by a few people and with a lot of hooting, we drove to the end of the square. There we stopped for petrol. As we eventually moved on and out of the square I looked around and noticed that, although it was full, the four Mauritanians in their white robes who had been with us earlier were missing, but the bag belonging to one of them (an elderly man, who had been sitting next to me) was still at my feet.

On the outskirts of the town we pulled up beside two policemen sitting at a table on the roadside. The boss (Jeffrey and I called him the Mafia Man) got out of the bus and showed them some papers and after a few minutes we were crossing the Niger River. Finally, I thought, we were on our way … but no. First there was another police control point where all our passports and personal papers had to be checked. Then, after a few pushes by some of the passengers, we continued on our way. A few miles later we were stopped again by the police for a bus roadworthy check. It was a mystery how Mafia Man managed to get through the check with those worn tyres but he did. Jeffrey was getting angry again (he seemed given to rants and tantrums) and started shouting at the Mafia Man. Like everybody else, the boss just ignored him. By the time we were through the last police check in Bamako it was getting dark but it seemed we had another stop to make.

Looking out of my glass-less window, I saw eight shadows appear out of nowhere. Suddenly we had four new passengers, plus the four missing Mauritanians. With these additional people the bus was now very over-crowded and extremely uncomfortable. The old Mauritanian was again sitting next to me, his friends behind. Squeezed up close together, we bumped about as the bus drove over potholes and I tried not to think about the tyres. I had to keep my eyes closed with the dust blowing into them, regretting that I had chosen a 'window' seat.

I suspected that the reason for the delay in Bamako was actually to allow the four extra people and the four Mauritanians time to walk round to the pick-up point to avoid the police checkpoints at which we'd had to stop on the road. Either they didn't have the right papers or else the bus wasn't allowed to carry more than 25 passengers.

In spite of the cramped conditions and the cool night wind blowing dust into my face, I found myself lulled by the Mauritanians' quiet Arabic chanting and I dozed off.

It was after midnight when we stopped again, this time in a dark square at what was the African equivalent of a roadhouse. I counted eight buses beside ours. All around the square were low huts, each with large pots of meat and rice boiling over fires in front of them. Mafia Man told us we were stopping for a meal and then we would drive on through the night. We sat down at a table and had Nescafé and French bread. We were given some meat with boiled rice and sauce served on metal plates.

Afterwards Jeffrey and I walked back to the bus. To our surprise many of the passengers had taken out their grass mats and were sleeping on the ground around it. There seemed to be no sign of us continuing on our journey. Jeffrey and I went to look for Mafia Man. We found him sitting in a dark corner, a cigarette in his mouth. Jeffrey demanded to know what was happening. The boss told us we had run out of petrol and would have to wait till morning to fill up. He promised we would leave at 6am. Then he got up, spread out his grass mat, lay down in his raincoat and hat, covered himself with a blanket and turned his back on us. We had no choice but to lie down in our sleeping bags, covering ourselves against the onslaught of the ever-present mosquitoes.

We woke up as dawn broke. Around us the Muslims were facing east, murmuring their prayers. Some had small waterpots with spouts, from which they poured water into their hands and washed their faces. I got myself a bowl of water and washed my hands and face as well as I could, and then shaved under the curious scrutiny of a group of onlookers. Around 7am I saw someone repairing the tyre on our bus. Other buses were leaving.

When we eventually left about an hour and a half later, we were eight passengers short. As we got out of the village we were stopped by a police checkpoint, where we were told to take our luggage off the bus and line it up on the side of the road. The police were only interested in the large bags belonging to the missing Mauritanians. They opened these bags and threw their contents onto the ground. This looked like nothing but bundles of short thin sticks – the local equivalent of toothbrushes (you took a short piece of the stick and chewed on it until it became soft and then you rubbed it against your teeth – the fine fibres did the cleaning) – so whatever it was they were looking for clearly wasn't there. The policemen seemed disappointed.

We continued on our journey, and after driving a few kilometres, just over the brow of a hill, we came across our eight fellow passengers, waving and smiling. They climbed back on board amid much chatter, which I couldn't understand, and laughter. Jam-packed again, we set off. After an hour of driving through the fine dust I could hardly open my eyes. We drove through a small village and stopped at a border post, where everyone had to get off and show their papers. We were minus eight passengers again, of course, but by now I understood the pattern and accepted that it would be a little while before we would continue our journey.

Jeffrey and I got ourselves stamped and returned to the bus, which was parked on the side behind the border post building. Three policemen and a number of children were sitting in the yard in a hammock under a grass roof eating rice with a hot sauce out of a large dish. I went over to ask for water and they invited me to sit on the hammock and join them in their rice meal, which I gladly did, eating African-style with my right hand, using the thumb and two fingers to make balls of rice which I stuffed into my mouth. One of the boys filled up my water bottle and another made some delicious tea, pouring it from a tiny teapot on a fire.

I started to take a few pictures of us all eating together when the policemen shouted, 'No! No!' Obviously they did not like being photographed. Then I got my bag from the roof of the bus and took out my Polaroid camera, which I had brought with me just for moments like this, and I started to take some pictures of the children – which created a sensation when they saw the prints coming immediately from the camera. Suddenly we were surrounded by people all wanting their photographs taken. The soldiers all posed for their pictures and one of them ran into the border post building to show the pictures to his boss. He returned swiftly and said that his boss would like to be photographed too. I should come to the front door and wait for him. Two of the policemen and Jeffrey joined us, and I positioned myself in front of the main entrance, waiting for the boss to appear. Quite a few people had now assembled outside the entrance, and then one of the policemen came out, pushing a small moped, which he positioned in the open space in front of the door. A little later a short, rather fat man came through the door – he was in full uniform: white boots, white belt, and white shoulder strap across his chest. In his hand he carried a white helmet, which he proceeded carefully to put on. He then climbed clumsily astride the moped (which was much too small for him), placed his boots firmly on the ground on either side, looked at me and smiled, showing a perfect set of white teeth. Everybody behind me clapped and I released the shutter. He was very happy when I gave him the final pictures.

With a friendly 'Bon voyage!' we finally drove off in our bus with everyone on board, except the eight, of course. Five minutes out of the village they all came walking down the side of the road – except this time they had an escort: a policeman pushing a moped. Mafia Man got out to talk to the policeman and there was a lot of arguing and shouting and hand waving. It appeared that our eight companions were illegal in the Ivory Coast and were being returned to Mali – where they also had no legal papers. The driver took their luggage off the roof and they walked disconsolately away, carrying their bags.

After about two hours of driving we stopped again, this time at a small resthouse by a river. Until now we had been driving through dry bush country but the landscape was slowly changing to thicker scrub and more trees. The resthouse was run by a ferocious woman who shouted continuously at everyone and threatened us with a large spoon, to the amusement of many. We settled down on low stools under a grass roof and were given tin plates of rice stew. Later Jeffrey and I made a small fire, borrowed a pot, bought a tin of Nescafé, powdered milk and sugar, and made ourselves lots of coffee. Meanwhile, the fan-belt on the bus had broken and the driver was trying to fix it, digging through a large tin box full of old car parts, screws, rubber pipes and other old bits and pieces.

At 3am we were woken up and told that we were about to continue our journey. We dressed quickly by torchlight and packed up our things. Then we joined the line of shadows walking across the river over a dilapidated bridge and up the hill – we were told the bridge might not be safe for a full bus. From there we all stood and watched the bus slowly and carefully cross the bridge and come chugging up the hill – and then we all climbed back in. About two and a half hours into our journey, which took us along a dirt road through dense forest, we heard a loud bang and the bus started to slide along sideways. We ended up facing the direction we had come from. There had been a blow-out of one of the front tyres.

We all got out of the bus and immediately found ourselves under attack by millions of tiny flies. They flew into our noses, eyes and ears – they were everywhere! Some passengers fled into the forest where they sat on a fallen tree trunk like a row of pigeons, each having picked some large leaves, about half a metre long and wide, from a strange-looking plant. They waved the leaves in front of their faces to fan the flying insects away. The driver was still fixing the wheel, so I went and joined them on the log. Then I saw Jeffrey. At the onslaught of the insects he had dived into his sleeping bag head first. He had been stumbling about on the road in the hot sun with his sleeping bag over his head, but now he seemed to have fallen over. He was on the ground, not moving. I thought he might have suffocated or had passed out, so I rushed over to him and pulled him out of the bag by his legs. I got a bottle of water we had kept for ourselves and splashed water on his face and he returned to life.

A bus came up the road and stopped. It looked to me in a better state than ours and I asked the driver if he had enough space to take Jeffrey and me to Abidjan. He said he did, and we went to collect our luggage and talk to Mafia

Breakdown in Ivory Coast

Man about a refund. He refused point-blank and walked away. Jeffrey became enraged and charged after him. He took hold of him and dragged him along the ground, shouting at him at the top of his voice in French about what he thought of him and his bus. This shouting went on for a while. Eventually I managed to get some money back from one of the drivers and we boarded our new bus – but our satisfaction was short-lived. We broke down twice, the second time stopping for the night by the roadside near some huts, where we were given a large variety of hot sweet potatoes for supper. While we were eating, the 'Super Yanky' arrived. Needless to say, there were a few giggles from our former companions.

During our meal I heard rhythmic drumbeats and singing coming from somewhere in the bush. When I enquired I was told that it was the 'dance of the witches'. I asked if I could watch and take some pictures, and after some discussion was told that I could if I went alone. A young man led me along a path to a circle of huts in an open space with a large fire in the centre and an empty chair. Eight men clothed only in loincloths made of leather and beads were dancing around it. Dancing with them was the witchdoctor, wearing a cloak made of beads, a headdress of beads and a mirror as a face plate. I walked over to the chief, who was elaborately dressed in leather and beads. He welcomed me and gave me permission to take photos.

I got a few shots using colour film. The light was low for a group picture, so I asked a couple of young dancers to cut some of the tall grass and hold it high up and light it – the flames gave a warm light for my pictures – and I got busy. When I saw the two fellows standing stoically, but now with worried expressions on their faces and flames engulfing their arms all the way up to their hands, I quickly put a stop to that idea.

We continued on our journey, and after about four hours of uninterrupted driving we pulled up near some shops for a break. I went into a store and bought four tins of sardines, which I thought would be good for the journey. The storekeeper offered to open the tins for me but I explained that I wanted the sardines for later that day. He said he only had one tin opener but sent someone off on a motor scooter to get one for me – he never returned. During our journey we couldn't find any fruit such as oranges or apples – only bananas or plantains, which, in our innocence, Jeffrey and I had bought thinking they were bananas. When we tried to eat them they were tasteless. Only then did we realise: plantains have to be fried.

Towards midnight the following day we finally arrived in Abidjan, the capital of Ivory Coast, tired, unshaven and with our hair and faces covered in powdery red dust. Abidjan was humid and hot. We were dropped off at the bus terminal in the market square. I said goodbye to Jeffrey, who had decided to stay and sign up on a ship, and took a taxi to a cheap hotel.

36

'WELCOME TO GHANA'

The following morning, 29 February, I decided to move on to Ghana, where I could speak English again. As I walked through the town of Abidjan, passing the upmarket part with beautiful large houses and gardens, then several bars and casinos, I realised that Abidjan was the playground of the French colonial world. I made my way to the bus terminal in the market square where two buses and several cars were busy loading passengers for Accra. I took a Peugeot taxi for 500 francs, which would take me to Ghana. We were five passengers in the Peugeot and the road we took north, skirting around the river delta, was all on dirt tracks. I'd heard there was a road along the coast and a ferry that transported traffic across the river mouth but apparently it was old and no longer operating.

At a police checkpoint, a hut surrounded by tropical jungle, a row erupted over the paperwork of the woman sitting next to me. She did not have a passport but only a piece of paper from the Ghanaian authorities. It looked quite in order to me but the police seemed determined to make an issue of it and a heated argument developed. The two policemen strode officiously up and down, throwing their arms about and ordering the driver to take the woman's luggage off the car. After about fifteen minutes they relented and the woman was allowed to put her luggage back. But as she was about to get back into the car, she said something rude about the police and it all started again. Eventually, after another fifteen minutes and a lot of apologising from the woman, she was allowed to continue her journey with us.

About ten miles from the border we were dropped off under a tree on the outskirts of a small town. Here we met up with other travellers with luggage. After a while some taxis from Ghana appeared and we all piled in – our taxi driver passed on part of the fare to the Ghanaian taxi driver. At the border I got out and took a picture of a sign saying 'Welcome to Ghana', but as I crossed over the barrier on foot I was rushed at by three policemen in battledress who demanded my camera. I had taken pictures of their post, which apparently was not permitted. I attempted to explain but soon realised that I wasn't getting anywhere, so I took the film out of the camera and gave it to policemen. The soldier who took the film cassette held it up triumphantly over his head and announced in a ringing tone: 'I shall burn it to ashes!' Then he marched purposefully away. The other two took my arm and followed him into a building where I explained myself to a senior officer. The film was returned to me with apologies. In the immigration office I found the officer with his head on his desk. I had to wake him up to get my passport stamped. This done, he went straight back to sleep. I couldn't fathom how he could stand it – the office had no window and was as hot as an oven.

We hadn't progressed more than a few metres when we were stopped in front of the customs office and asked to put our luggage on a long metal table. A powerful-looking lady in a smart military uniform indicated that I should open my bags, which I did, provoking a cloud of red dust that caused her to step back smartly. Brushing her hands over her uniform, she got so worked up, crying out loudly and dramatically 'Do not dirty my uniform!', that she forgot to look in my bags.

In the market square in Berekum, the first town in Ghana, our driver put us onto a bus, passing on part of the fare, and in a few minutes we were off again, stopping now and then to pick up or drop off passengers. At one bus stop there was a little hut with a grass roof beneath which drinks and food were displayed – curried chicken served on banana leaves, a type of bun fried in oil, palm wine, beer and a ginger drink that was very strong but delicious. Later that afternoon we arrive at Sunyani where again we were dropped off at the market square. We were told there was no more transport to Accra that day, so I booked into the driver's union rest-house where all the door handles were upside down so one

The 'Welcome to Ghana' sign that saw the author's film being confiscated

had to push the handle up to close or open the door. It was very hot and sticky, so I found my way to a bar nearby. This was an open room with wooden tables and benches under a thatched roof. I cooled off with some excellent Ghanaian beer. The only problem was the scratchy loud background West African pop music and after a while I had had enough. I was about to leave when a friendly young waiter, who had told me he was studying engineering, asked me if I would like to look at his home. He invited me for dinner and said his brother would join us.

I walked with him along a dark dirt road through the township, passing small houses with tin roofs and people cooking over fires, plumes of woodsmoke filling the air. The thick smoke mixed with the oppressive heat, the children and goats running about, women washing dishes and cooking in front of their houses, men sitting on benches chatting and loud pop music blaring everywhere – this was a heady mix. My host told me of his ambition to visit the United States to study engineering and economics. He worked all day from 7.30 in a store and then in the bar in the evening. When we got to his house we sat in his tiny cramped room, which was also as hot as an oven, and he showed me his books – *Teach Yourself Economics*, *Teach Yourself English*, *Teach Yourself Electronics* – and some pictures of his family. Then his younger brother arrived (he was also studying and also wanted to go to the States) and served us dinner – margarine on dry biscuits, a small tin each of condensed milk, a loaf of bread and a glass of the ginger drink.

The next morning at five I got a bus to Komati, a two-hour drive. In the very busy market square, African pop music blared from loudspeakers and drowned out all other sound. All the buses and taxis had brightly coloured slogans splashed all over them, 'None Shall Pass', 'God Is King', 'They Talked – What They Don't Know', and I took lots of pictures.

Soon I was sitting in another kombi taxi. The last 280 kilometres took us on a tarred road. The landscape here was tropical bush, with giant trees. Huts lined the roadside, where people were selling peeled oranges, boiled eggs, and chicken. Our driver had great affection for his horn and pop tunes belted from his radio at full volume. All bus drivers hooted and waved at each other when they passed. It was quite a noisy journey but finally it was over. We arrived in Accra in the afternoon.

'Envy No Man' kombi taxi, Mali

My impression of Ghana's capital was of a sprawling city, more like a group of large villages, very run-down and messy, rather unattractive, I thought, and very noisy. Cars and buses hooted continually, and all the vehicles looked rusty and in need of paint. The people, however, were generally charming and hospitable.

I went to visit the *Drum* office and met the editor, Joseph Mensah. He took me to a hotel near his home. I discovered that there was little hope of my getting a visa for Nigeria. *Drum* journalists told me they didn't easily let people into the country – especially journalists and people not living in Ghana and travelling around, which they would see from my passport. I had to plan a new route.

I got a visa from the French embassy for Cameroon, which bordered the Central African Republic, and found a travel agent, where I booked a seat on a cargo ship, the *Bia River*, which would take me to Douala, the capital, the following week, on 7 March. When departure of the ship was delayed to 10 March, and I discovered that the hotel was full, Joseph put me up in his home, where I enjoyed some splendid Ghanaian food. The main dishes were porridge, which one scooped out of a bowl with one's hands and dipped in a plate of spicy fish soup. Meat was rare in this part of Africa so people mostly ate fish. Joseph's wife cooked these lavish meals in a tiny bare room no bigger than 2 x 2 metres with a small gas fire on a concrete floor, some pots and no running water. I slept in my underwear in a room with grass mats, no blankets and closed windows. It was hard to sleep with the heat, the mosquitoes and the smoke from an insect-repellent stick which burned all night.

One afternoon Joseph took me to visit his brother in his small tin-roofed hut, one of a number of huts arranged round a square that formed the family compound. Joseph's brother was much older than him. He sat on a large lounge chair while we sat on small stools facing him. He welcomed us in Ghanaian fashion – shaking hands then pressing the other person's index finger against your thumb and your index finger against his thumb and making a clicking sound. I discovered this required some practice. If my clicks were sufficiently loud, this was usually accompanied by much laughter. Joseph's brother then produced a bottle and three small glasses and poured some clear spirit – made

THE WAY I SEE IT

from palm oil – into each glass. He then made three splashes from his glass onto the ground, an offering to the earth, to God and to us, and drank the liquid down in one gulp. We did the same. After three rounds and listening to some conversation between the brothers in a Ghanaian dialect, we said goodbye with the Ghanaian handshake. Later on we visited another of Joseph's brothers and went through the same procedure, by which time I was feeling a bit under the weather. My head spinning, as soon as we got back to Joseph's home I went to my little room and fell into a deep sleep.

Strange things happened in Ghana, I decided. Whenever I took a stroll around the market or walked on the beach, several people, especially teenage girls, would come rushing up to me and run their hands over and along my arms, legs and head. Then they would laugh and walk away. Sometimes young teenage girls made a hissing sound as I passed by. I found out later that they were intrigued by the hair on my body (most West African men have no body hair) and they were also curious about my white skin and fair hair.

Before I left, Joseph told me a story from African folklore about why mosquitoes buzz in one's ear at night.

At the time when man was not yet a whole man, only independent parts – the ear, the arm, the leg, the eye – they went out hunting in the forest. Suddenly the ear asked them to be quiet. After a moment of silence the ear said he could hear the game and told the eye where to look for it. The eye then saw the game and told the leg, which ran to the game, and then the arm killed the game. Then there was a quarrel over who had the rights to the game and when they couldn't agree they took their grievance to the council. The council agreed that the ear had the right to the game as it had heard it first. The mosquito, who was the messenger of the council, was sent to tell the ear – and that is why, when the mosquito buzzes by your ear at night, the hand comes up to slap it.

37

BIRTHDAY IN CAMEROON, BEER IN BANGUI

I left in the morning on 10 March on the Ghanaian cargo ship *Bia River*. All the other passengers were Ghanaians on holiday, cruising to Cameroon and back. There were two army officers with their wives, both stout ladies and each with a small boy, and a businessman and his wife.

The sea was calm with now and then a burst of sunlight through the humid haze around us. Sailors banged away at rust on the deck, the sound of their hammers echoing. After weeks of living rough I was suddenly in luxury – I had my own cabin, air-conditioned, with a shower and a proper bed, and regular real meals I could order from a menu. How much I needed and depended on these simple luxuries was revealing. For weeks I had been sleeping on floors in rooms so hot I lay in pools of sweat, burning foul-smelling anti-mosquito coils, eating little and strange food, drinking sickly tasting water, and quenching my thirst with juicy whole pineapples, coconuts and mangoes. Now, I discovered, I was longing for a cup of 'proper' tea. I asked the waiter when tea would be served and he replied with a big smile: 'A few time.'

To pass the time I played darts with the kitchen staff and a waitress, and the passengers were shown a film about police and crime, which seemed totally out of place in our surroundings. I had two paperback books in my bag that I'd started reading in London and had found interesting, *Portrait of the Artist as a Young Man* by James Joyce and *I, Claudius* by Robert Graves, but now in this world I found both books dull fare.

We docked in Douala in the early morning of 15 March. After breakfast we were told by the immigration official that all passengers had to go to the police station to fill in forms and have their passports stamped. We duly presented ourselves at the police station but had to wait about two hours before the right official turned up. I said goodbye to my fellow passengers and took a taxi to the railway station. That night I was on a train to Yaoundé, the capital of Cameroon. The train wasn't very full and I had a bench to myself to sleep on. Later that night I went to the bar, where several people were drinking beer and listening to African pop on a transistor radio. A blue-uniformed conductor, his cap worn rakishly on the side of his head, came down the passage. With shining face and beaming smile, he danced down between the seats of the passengers, checking tickets. He went cha-cha dancing down the corridor, clapping his legs together in rhythm to the pop music, beaming all over. When he got to me he grinned and said, 'I was a much better tap dancer when I was younger.'

In Yaoundé I had to change trains. At the terminal I sat waiting on a bench, where I eventually fell asleep. The train to Bélabo arrived early the next morning. This train was full of soldiers and policemen. The atmosphere throughout the journey was very lively – there was a man walking around selling beer and cold drinks and there was lots of singing and radio music. Towards late afternoon, about 30 kilometres from Bélabo, the train broke down at a small station. Everybody got out and started to walk up and down the platform. The engine driver came out of his cabin and talked to some people. It turned out that there was no phone at this station, so they decided to send some fellow on ahead on a moped to the Bélabo terminal and organise either another engine or a technician. So the fellow went off on his moped with everyone shouting an encouraging 'Au revoir!'

In the meantime I was curious and I asked the driver if I might take a look at the engine (although I knew nothing about engines). He took me into his cabin and then along a long passage with a massive engine. As we walked by, he gave the engine a kick, showing off, at which the huge machine started to burn and murmur. The driver gave me a look of astonishment, then hurried back to his cabin, with me following behind. He came dashing back towards me with a spanner in his hand. He opened a metal plate on the engine, turned some pipes with the spanner, and the machine was fully in action.

The passengers were ordered back onto the train, which slowly started to move off, everyone looking out of the window waving and shouting to alert and stop the messenger on the moped who would be driving on a dirt road in the dense forest near the train line. The driver blew his whistle as we raced through the jungle, bottles of beer were passed around in celebration, and everyone was smiling.

About 40 minutes later we arrived in the terminal, which was the depot for heavy trucks and buses carrying goods or people to the border of the Central African Republic and from there to the capital, Bangui. It was Friday evening and I had almost run out of money. There was no hotel in Bélabo and I was told that there were no buses or trucks going to Bangui before Monday. So I bought myself some tins of sardines and corned beef and some bread. Then I went to a store, which was about to close, and asked if I could sleep on their veranda over the weekend. I think they thought I was a bit crazy, but after some humming and hawing they agreed. So after the town closed down and everything was quiet, I settled down on the cement for the night.

The bright twin beams of headlights shining right at me startled me awake. I sat up and saw a bakkie stopped in front of the store. A big man in shorts and a T-shirt got out and approached me. He spoke to me in French, and when I indicated that I didn't understand he switched to broken English. 'You are not to sleep here – you will wake up with your throat cut!' he said. I explained my problem to the man and he offered to take me to some place where I could safely spend the weekend. There was a bungalow belonging to a German volunteer who was away at the moment and I could spend the weekend there. He would pick me up again first thing on Monday morning.

We drove for about ten minutes through heavy jungle up and down hills and arrived at a thatch-roofed rondavel with a veranda enclosed by mosquito nets, similar to some old South African country houses and farmhouses. The Frenchman, Monsieur Endier, introduced me to a tall man in a long white shirt wearing a white cap. 'I am Nigerian,' the man said, and after the Frenchman had introduced me, he again said, 'I am Nigerian.' Those were the only words he said to me.

The Nigerian carried my bag into the bungalow and I thanked Monsieur Endier. 'Call me Maurice,' he said and with that he drove off. On the table in the rondavel, to my surprise I found a couple of books on photography, and a German photo magazine lying open at an article about me and my work, with a photo of me. I found this quite freaky.

There was a hammock in the rondavel, and this was where I slept, soundly and undisturbed, until morning. It was Saturday, 18 March, and I suddenly remembered that it was my birthday. A monkey – which I later learned was tame and had the run of the place – came through the open door carrying a banana, which he presented to me, for all the world as if he was giving me a birthday present! But no – after I had peeled it, the monkey carefully took it away from me and ate it. I found a village down the hill where I bought some mangoes, bananas and pineapples. I still had some sardines and corned beef so I was all right for the weekend.

I had now reached a state where I was accepting of the timelessness of Africa, where no one was ever in a hurry. The sound of the bush at night had a harmony, rhythm and pulse. I often heard the sounds of drumbeats as if they were talking or communicating with other drums many miles away. The second night it started to rain and there was a heavy thunderstorm. I decided to sleep outside on the veranda as it was too humid inside. I fell asleep in my sleeping bag with the monkey beside me. Some time in the night I woke with a fright to find the Nigerian man in his long white robe leaning over me. He was lifting my head up with his hand and placing a cushion beneath it.

When I left I wrote a note to the owner of the rondavel thanking him for his unwitting hospitality and signed my name on the magazine page with my story. On Monday morning Maurice came back and drove me into town, where I quickly got a lift in a truck to the border town of Garoua-Boulaï. I sat in the cabin with the driver and co-driver. The road was so rough, full of pot-holes and stones, that we couldn't drive faster than 25 kilometres per hour. We arrived at Garoua-Boulaï in the evening and I booked a room in a run-down hotel. The young man at reception was drunk and loud pop music blared in the background. I took a short walk around the town, and on a roundabout in the centre I saw a large pole with a number of signs sticking out from it in different directions. On closer inspection I saw the directions, with the distances in miles, pointing to Cape Town, Nairobi, London, Cairo, Accra and other destinations. I took a picture of this unusual signpost and was promptly grabbed from behind by a soldier wearing a helmet and battledress. He told me I was a spy and, grabbing me by the neck, walked me off to the police station, where I was interrogated. Why had I taken pictures of the road sign? Was I from the CIA? Who was I working for? This went on for a while until I managed to get the upper hand by becoming more assertive, telling them I was a free man, and after a while they let me go.

The next morning I walked across the border, filled in the usual forms and got my stamps. I now realised that I would have to rely on free transport because I had very little cash left and only one traveller's cheque. I sat in the shade under a tree and waited for a lift. It wasn't long before a truck pulled up and stopped. It was 480 kilometres to Bangui and it took three days to get there. I was very careful during this time not to take any pictures. I was in the Central African Republic and had been told that several journalists had been locked up for no reason other than being journalists.

On 22 March the truck driver dropped me off at the market square in Bangui. It was mid-morning and busy, with lots of colourfully dressed people milling about. After asking around, I was told that the best place to camp was at the beach of the river that flowed through Bangui. I found what looked like a military personnel carrier, only much bigger and painted bright orange. I saw a few camping tables and several men sitting around in deckchairs. I noticed that, strangely, they were all bald. I introduced myself and they told me they were academics from Warsaw, Poland, from different universities, on a study tour through Africa. When I asked them why they were all bald, they laughed and said they hadn't wanted to appear to the locals as long-haired hippies – and now they were all sunburnt on top!

On their advice I went to the tourist office nearby and got myself a tourist visa, which was an impressive little card and made me feel like a VIP. I was again told to be careful when photographing in the country, which was run as a police state by its dictator and self-styled emperor, Jean-Bédel Bokassa.

I slept on the beach and had coffee with some of the Poles, who were sitting around exchanging addresses. One of the academics was very interested in photography – we hit it off immediately – and we decided to exchange addresses too. On a piece of paper I wrote 'Jürgen Schadeberg, Central School of Art & Design, Holborn, London', while he wrote his details on another. Then we exchanged our pieces of paper. I looked at his in astonishment: 'Mr Schadeberg, Teacher of Art & Design, Warszawa, Poland'. We raised our heads and just stared at each other. With such an unbelievable coincidence, we promised to stay in touch.

I walked through Bangui to find the road to Bangassou and noticed a large group of police and some military activity going on. People were being picked up in the street and pushed onto trucks. I kept quietly out of the way. People went silently about their business, but I sensed a great deal of civilian tension in the air.

In the afternoon of 29 March, I hitched a ride outside Bangui in a bakkie, which took me the 240 kilometres to Sibut. The owner of the bakkie, Monsieur Louis, was a middle-aged man, very jolly, who told me he was a businessman and minister of the rural council. His wife was travelling with him and, in addition to the driver, there were another six passengers in the back, along with several large bunches of bananas. We travelled fairly fast over a reasonably good dirt road and soon we all had our faces caked in red dust mixed with sweat. At dusk we stopped at a beer garden in a little town, where Monsieur Louis ordered many bottles of beer and wine. Our glasses were continually being filled up to the point of overflowing while we chatted to our fellow passengers. One was from Zaire Radio, another a government official – and they were all fascinated by my trip and treated me with great respect, especially when I showed them my fancy Central African Republic tourist visa. Monsieur Louis seemed to have overdone it and eventually he passed out.

Later that night we were dropped off at the town of Sibut under a tree where a large lady was making and selling coffee by the light of an oil lamp. There was no street lighting in the town and, except for the lady with the lamp, the whole place was pitch dark. Two young men walked by and stopped to have a chat.

They told me in broken English that they were medical assistants at the local hospital and suggested I should come with them – they could find me a place to stay at the hospital. They led me along a path through thick bushes until we came to some buildings which in the dark looked like a row of barracks. I saw strange shadowy shapes moving around. They took me to a dark building past sleeping bodies lying on the veranda floor into a room, where I unrolled my sleeping bag and lay on the concrete floor. I fell asleep but woke up later when I heard the sound of drums beating a slow, soft rhythm somewhere. Then other drums joined them and the sound got louder, deeper and faster, building to a climax. Then it slowly died away before softly starting up again. The drumming went on all night.

As it grew lighter I saw that the shadows I had seen the night before were long-legged black pigs. One of the young men had brought me a bucket of water and I gave myself a rudimentary wash. Besides the pigs there were a great many goats, I noticed, walking in and out of the building, going where they pleased. One reason all this livestock could walk about so freely was that there were no doors. I realised these must have been removed for firewood or building material (there were no window frames either). The floorboards were also gone. I heard people groaning and moaning somewhere in the hospital, but it seemed that there were no doctors or nurses, just the two medical assistants looking after the sick.

I walked back to the big tree along the road and the lady making coffee was still there. After waiting for about half an hour drinking fresh coffee, a bakkie pulled up. It already had several passengers, but the driver was going to Bambari and he asked if I wanted a lift. When he asked me for money I explained to him that I had none, but he said I could sit in the back anyway. He stopped at a beer garden outside Bambari. We had been driving for about three hours by then, over a very dusty rough road, and everyone needed a drink and wanted to wash their faces, which once more were caked in red dust. We settled around a large table and everybody ordered beer. I had a locally made drink which was a mix of ginger and honey – it was absolutely delicious.

My fellow passengers and the driver, who was also the owner of the bakkie, then started firing questions at me. Where did I come from? Was I with the

CIA? Why was I travelling in the Central African Republic? Was I a mercenary? I started to get rather worried and asked if I could get my bag out of the bakkie. They said the bakkie was now parked at the owner's home, which was eight kilometres down the road. This was getting scary – if they thought I was a mercenary, I wasn't at all sure what they would do. They were beginning to give me angry and suspicious looks. I had no way to explain myself and couldn't run away or ask anyone for help.

I was just starting to look through my wallet to see how much money, cash, I had left when one of the fellows looked over my shoulder. Spotting my Central African Republic tourist visa card, he asked me if it was mine. I pulled the card out and showed it to him. Some of the other passengers, government officials, had the same type of visa cards. When they held them up, everybody started to relax. We had some laughs, drank some more beer, and they gathered round me and slapped me on the shoulder in friendship. After a number of drinks they fetched the bakkie and took me to a hotel on the top of the hill with a beautiful view overlooking the river and surrounded by an overgrown garden. The owner of the bakkie came into the hotel with me and told the girl at the desk that I was a very important person and they must give me the best room. I said goodbye to my new good friends, noting that by now they were all somewhat under the weather.

The hotel looked very run-down but the room the girl led me to along a veranda was pleasant. It had a wooden balcony overlooking the river. I tried out the toilet to see if it worked. It immediately overflowed onto the floor, producing a sickly smell. And there were living things in the murky water. I asked the girl to show me another room, which she did, but this one didn't seem to have any running water at all. In the third room there was a trickle of water, so I decided to take it. When I asked her the cost of the room, she said the boss, the bakkie owner, had already paid for the room for the night. I was very grateful since I didn't have enough cash to pay and would have had a problem.

As there wasn't enough water to have a shower, I decided to take a look at the plumbing. The girl seemed to have left and there was no one else about. The only evidence of life was the blaring pop music, which, I'd accepted by now, was everywhere. I took the shower to pieces and tried to clean the pipes.

After half an hour of fiddling I put all the pieces together again and turned on the water. With much grumbling and gurgling, the pipes coughed out a mucky brown trickle of water, along with some leaves and other bits and pieces. I don't think anyone had looked at those pipes for years.

The following morning I walked to the main road going out of town and sat down under a tree opposite some huts to wait for a lift to Bangassou. Many people passed me with goods they were taking to market – bundles of fire-wood, bananas, baskets of mangoes, large dishes of liquid porridge – and they all greeted me. Some of them stopped to shake hands and have a chat, asking me where I was from and where I was going. As the day passed, I shifted around the tree trying to keep in the shade. There seemed to be no traffic on this road whatsoever – except on foot! When it grew dark I decided to sleep under the tree, where I was savagely attacked by mosquitoes. In the morning I managed to get a lift on a truck and that evening arrived at Bangassou, where I slept in front of a store.

The next day I walked through a bush track down to the Mbomou River, where I saw two men sleeping on the grass beside a couple of canoes made from large carved-out tree trunks. There was no bridge anywhere, and no ferry – I must have missed the main road that led to the river – and nothing else to do but wake up the sleepers and ask for their assistance. I could see a number of houses and stores on the other side of the river and what seemed like a white man in shorts looking in my direction. So I woke up the sleepy duo, who jumped up and were obviously surprised to see me. I asked if they could take me across the river. Five francs, one of them said, to which I quickly agreed. One fellow got busy pushing one of the canoes into the water. Then he held out his hand for the money. I got into the canoe with him and he started to paddle. The river was very calm, but as we got closer to the centre I saw a hippo. It was very near to our oars but the canoe paddler skilfully avoided it and we reached the other side safely.

I was now in the Congo (formerly the Belgian Congo and now Zaire).

The figure I had seen from the other side of the river was indeed a white man.

'Man,' he greeted me, 'I'm glad to see another human being. I've been stuck

A truck in the Central African Republic

here for the last six days and there's no transport – only jungle – and some stores that have nothing to sell.' He was smoking and I caught the unmistakable aroma of marijuana. He introduced himself as Robert Baron from New York and told me he was studying folklore at Philadelphia University in Pennsylvania. Before I could introduce myself, we heard the sound of a truck coming from the road through the jungle.

A big truck emerged from the jungle and we asked for a lift to the next town, which was Manga. The driver wanted 10 francs each if we sat in the back – and he said he would leave in a few hours. Manga was the first town in Zaire – 50 kilometres away – where we needed to have our passports stamped.

While we waited we sat down by the river where there was a pleasantly cool breeze, watching the water move silently by. We could see a man doing his washing on some rocks, a canoe with one paddler drifted by noiselessly, and away in the distance we could hear the pulsing throb of a diesel engine. The truck left at long last, with two of us sitting in the back, but we hadn't been moving for more than five minutes when the driver pulled up in front of a little settlement and a group of people standing on the road with a large pile of palm roof materials. Measuring one metre square, a roof consisted of several palm leaves knitted together into an almost solid piece, making a roof 'tile'. There were a few makeshift shelters dotted around and hundreds of palm trees, and all the members of the settlement came to watch and help put the palm tiles onto the truck. The driver gave the leader of the settlement a receipt for the number of palm tiles loaded on the truck and off we drove. We stopped every five or ten minutes to load more palm coverings until eventually we were sitting quite high up on top of a pile of palm leaves, giving us a good view. A couple of women and some children had also joined us as passengers and late that afternoon we were dropped off on the outskirts of Manga. The truck driver went on to drop off his load, to return and then repeat the trip.

38

WAR AND PEACE –
ZAIRE, RWANDA, KENYA

Robert and I walked along a sandy road towards the village centre, passing on either side of the road once elegant homes from the Belgian colonial era, built for the white ruling class, and now uninhabited, dilapidated and crumbling. Trees and vegetation grew out of the windows and rusty roofs, and the shutters on the windows were all broken.

Manga was like a ghost town. We came to a small store, where we found the shelves empty except for half-a-dozen tins of South African sardines, which we bought. We were told that the immigration officer lived a few houses down the road – we couldn't miss it: it was the house in good condition. We found the immigration officer on his veranda drinking beer. There was a monkey sitting on the wall and Robert went up to it and blew some marijuana smoke in its face, which made the monkey angry. It snarled, bared its teeth and made grunting noises at him. I, meanwhile, had gone up to the officer and introduced myself. He stamped my passport and gave it back to me without saying a word, but when Robert came up to him with his passport he was given a mouthful of swear words in French.

The officer called a young man from inside the house and told him to take us to the courthouse where we could spend the night. Our guide took us along the street near a river to a small square in front of a large building with a flagpole. As we got closer to the building we saw that the door had gone, as had the door frame. All that was left was a large opening (the windows and their frames were also gone). Inside, the courthouse had been totally gutted. The wooden floors had been ripped up and there were piles of rubbish everywhere. We found ourselves a clear spot in the corner and settled down in our sleeping bags. Early the next morning we were woken by some scruffy-looking characters. There were about ten of them. After we'd exchanged greetings they told us to follow them outside. Here we all formed a line and stood to attention while a man wearing a suit and tie, but barefoot, raised the Zaire flag up the flagpole. Then everybody sang the Zairean national anthem – totally out of tune.

Down by the river I saw small boys doing washing on some rocks and I went over to have a closer look. The river water was very dirty and polluted – definitely not suitable for drinking. I decided to have a look around the village to see if Robert and I could get something to eat and drink. Everyone I asked pointed in the direction of the jungle. They showed me a narrow path into the jungle and after about 300 metres I came across some people from the village, who all greeted me with friendly smiles. Now I saw where all the missing doors, shutters, windows and wooden floors had ended up. A sort of shanty town had grown up in the few open spaces here, with people dwelling in huts that were all poorly constructed out of not much more than a door and palm leaves. I found this return to the jungle mystifying.

With my remaining few francs I bought some large pineapples and mangoes from the villagers. When I returned, Robert had found a tin of corned beef at the store so we had an acceptable lunch. Robert knew by now that I was short of cash (except for my £10 last remaining traveller's cheque) and he offered to lend me some – which I eventually returned to him some months later when he visited me in London.

The next morning, after we had had to stand to attention again at the flag-raising ceremony, we looked for a lift. Luckily, before long we got a ride in a van which was going to the town of Bondo. The road there was not much more than a track, snaking through tall stands of bamboo on either side. By the time we reached Bondo we were hot and tired. When we made enquiries about where we might find something to eat or drink, some fellows took us down another long jungle path, where again we saw how the jungle had taken over the areas where once the colonial houses had stood with their spacious grounds. People shouted greetings to us – 'Jambo! Jambo!' – from the tops of palm trees where they were tapping the palm wine. Some of them seem to have been sampling it as they worked and were so far gone they couldn't get down from the trees. In a hut – a jungle restaurant – we were served a delicious meal of game cooked in a spicy sauce. Afterwards we were directed to the local drinking spot, which was in a clearing in the jungle, where several huts sold palm wine. Everybody there, including a bunch of soldiers in uniform, was very drunk.

Our boots became a great topic of conversation and were greatly admired and discussed. Mine, which I had bought in London, had lightweight soles and zipped up to the calf and they were made from very light, soft leather. I was getting worried the drunks might grab them off me there and then, so Robert and I decided we should leave.

We had been told that there might be a train to Aketi, so we set off to find the station. I think it was the smallest station I have ever seen. On further enquiries we learnt that there hadn't been a train for three weeks but that maybe one might come the following day. The gauge of the railway was very narrow, not much bigger than a fairground or mine rail. We couldn't imagine what sort of train might use it but we decided to stick around and see.

That night we camped on the floor of the telephone room. It looked as if it must once have been an impressive switchboard office, but the switchboard had had its guts ripped out and there were cables hanging in a tangled muddle. Amazingly, one phone line was still working and throughout the night we were woken up by drunks in underpants rushing in and fumbling with the wires, making phone calls and enquiring about the whereabouts of the train. Finally, the train arrived the following afternoon. It looked more like a converted bus than a train and had only one coach. As it arrived it drove onto a circular turnaround where one wheel became derailed, which proved a big problem. The train was due to leave in an hour, at 3pm, so some of the rail assistants rushed to the village to find a jack to lift the coach back onto its track. About two hours later the coach was back on the track, but we then discovered that this 'train' was not really a passenger train but a government train for officials making payments to government employees up and down the line. This meant, happily, that we didn't have to pay a fare.

The two of us climbed into the driver's cabin. In the coach behind us were about a dozen officials. As we slowly made our way through the jungle we stopped frequently for people to buy drinks or do official business at a tiny post office or other local offices and the cabin slowly filled up with bunches of bananas, game meat, and bundles of sugar cane. Once we stopped for someone who wanted to shoot a monkey he had spotted. A little later, as we approached a raised embankment and the train slowed down to walking pace, everyone became very quiet. The driver told us this was a very dangerous section, and when I looked out of the window I could see why. We were driving over a makeshift bridge, below which were huge rocks and a rushing river. When I looked ahead I could see the rails shifting, lifting and wobbling. We crept over the bridge with everyone very tense and wide-eyed, and there was a sigh of relief and much opening of beer bottles when the train sped up again. Radios were turned up, with the usual pop music once again blaring forth, and there was much laughter and chatter on the rest of the journey to Aketi.

At the station there was a long goods train, which was about to leave for Isiro, but we were told we needed a document from 'the director' to be permitted to board it and he wasn't in his office, which was closed for the evening. However, we found a Greek man on a scooter who took us to the director's home, who also turned out to be Greek, and for 100 francs we got our bits of paper and managed to board the train. We were put into a carriage with a rough, rusty iron floor and settled at the back, making ourselves as comfortable as possible. Two fellows joined us, introducing themselves as the guard and his assistant, and they sat themselves down at the front of the carriage, facing us. The carriage had large sliding doors on each side, which we kept open to allow the hot air to flow through.

Eventually, with much jerking, the train started to move slowly forward and the rusty floor began to rattle and bump. We passed through miles of green jungle. It was extremely hot in the carriage, the sun belting down on the metal roof, even with the doors open, and after a while Robert and I sat by the open door with our legs dangling down. Later there was a heavy rainstorm and dense sprays of water came sweeping through the open door on one side and out the other. The guard immediately stripped off his clothes, grabbed a piece of soap

Goods train to Isiro

and had a wash and shower. That night we saw millions of glow worms sparkling in the dark sky. The train sped down hills and crawled up hills and it was very uncomfortable in our carriage – we had now been travelling for 36 hours.

In Isiro we stocked up on tinned food and decided to continue our journey by road. We noticed that there were very few Belgians in Zaire. The majority of the white residents were Greek – they were storekeepers, plantation managers or directors of companies. We got lifts on bakkies and trucks. One was a beer truck, where we crouched under a canvas tarpaulin almost choking with the fumes, dust and heat. Another time, when we were in the back of a truck with several other passengers, we were caught in a storm and got thoroughly drenched while the truck swayed and bumped wildly. Neither Robert nor I had washed or shaved for days.

One day we were dropped in the jungle under a tree and waited in its shade all day, trying to avoid the glare of the sun. In the evening a Land Rover pulled up and offered us a lift. There were two tough-looking characters in the front and they both stepped out to relieve themselves. As they passed by, I noticed that each had a revolver in his belt. They told us to get in the back, and as they opened the back door we saw another man already inside. He was sitting silently on some steel boxes, hanging onto a rifle. We took our seats, also on steel boxes, and as the truck drove off with the two of us and the man with the rifle not saying a word, we began to get nervous. Had we been kidnapped by warlords? It was pitch dark outside – the only light I glimpsed through a small wire-grilled window was the headlights of the Land Rover streaming onto the jungle. There was dust everywhere. After travelling for a couple of hours, we got onto a tar road and we could see some lights. Then we stopped. We heard voices outside and people walking up and down and around our vehicle. Then the back door opened suddenly, and the man with the rifle jumped up and out into the road, pulling one of the boxes and giving me a sign to help him. I took the handle of the box and jumped out. Robert was asked to help one of the other men with the other metal boxes. We found ourselves carrying the boxes into a bank. It turned out that we had been given a lift in a van delivering money to the bank in the town of Nia-Nia.

Next we got a lift in an oil truck (sitting on top of greasy oil drums) that was going to Mambasa. We arrived in the town on 12 April and, after a long wait for further lifts, eventually managed to get to Butembo, and after that we got a ride in the back of an empty truck. Leaving the jungle behind, the road climbed up and up and over a steep mountain. Before us was a beautiful panorama of part of the Ruwenzori National Park with the volcano Karisimbi in the far distance. As we drove down through the valley we passed a herd of elephants and later saw a couple of lions and other game. Driving along the banks of a quiet flowing river with flowering bushes, we could see the humps of hippos rising from the water. We arrived in the village of Goma in the late afternoon of 14 April. The view of Lake Kivu – the water still, with a slight mist rising over it – was breathtaking. This was the last night Robert and I would spend together. From here he was going south and I was going east.

Robert was a seasoned hitchhiker and he was a relaxing travelling companion. He had hitchhiked in India and in the States. When I watched him stroll lazily towards an oncoming truck and energetically wave it over, I realised there was definitely a trick to it. While we were waiting for lifts, Robert would disappear into his book – he was reading *War and Peace*. We had a last meal together at a restaurant in Goma and toasted our goodbyes with some good French wine. I was going to miss him.

I crossed the border into Rwanda, where I changed my money and got a lift to the capital, Kigali, on a beer truck. We were at quite a high altitude and the air was crisp. Sitting on top of crates of beer, I had a good view of the most beautiful hilly country. People working in fields waved as we passed. I saw healthy-looking cattle, fat sheep and many banana plantations.

I was dropped off in the centre of Kigali, where the first thing I needed to do was find a bank as the money Robert had loaned me was almost finished. I discovered it was a public holiday and the bank was closed, so I decided to keep going. I walked to the end of the town to see if I could get a ride to Rusumo Falls, the border town between Rwanda and Tanzania. A local priest kindly gave me a lift in his car. He talked the whole way in Swahili, which I didn't understand a word of, but I was grateful for this lift, as by now it was raining heavily and I would have been soaked to the bone on an open truck or bakkie. The priest dropped me off at the border post.

A winding road in Rwanda

In the immigration office I handed my passport to a very drunk officer, who shot me some aggressive, angry looks and asked me a string of questions. I tried to explain in a mixture of poor French and some English that I couldn't understand what he was asking and he began shouting at me, emitting strong alcoholic fumes. I was getting anxious about the state of my passport, which he leafed through roughly, turning the pages back and forth, but eventually he stamped it, several times, and returned it to me. I hurriedly exited his office.

Having left Rwanda, I got a ride to Rusumo, Tanzania. Panting up a steep hill along a dirt track, I saw what looked like a farmhouse. Here I found a friendly man who introduced himself as the immigration official. He pointed me to some lights in the distance and told me I could see him there the following morning to get my passport stamped. I walked towards the lights and found a group of 20 or so people standing around in the centre of a brightly lit circle of tents and Land Rovers, eating spaghetti out of stainless steel pots. They were a mixture of Australians, white South Africans, British and Americans who were on an organised safari tour through Africa. I introduced myself and told them about my travels and they offered me a plate of spaghetti. They all looked very clean, neat and organised – certainly in comparison with me! When I had polished off the spaghetti, I thanked them and went to the immigration house, where I chatted for a while to the two customs and immigration men. They were also interested in hearing about my trip and asked many questions. They offered to let me sleep on their veranda that night and also invited me to join them around a fire outside for some roast chicken. I took up both offers and we spent hours talking about Africa. I must say it was a relief to talk English again.

I was woken in the night by the sound of crunching bones. I looked up and saw a shadow by the extinguished fire where we had been eating chicken. I thought it must be a dog eating the bones. This would be bad for it, as bones splinter in dogs' guts, so I got up and slowly walked towards the animal. When I got within a few metres, it noticed me and I hesitated. Then it made a loud hissing sound, turned around and went off into the darkness. In the morning I told my friend the immigration man, whose name was Simon Nkuwama, about the incident and he burst out laughing. 'I should have told you,' he said. 'It's the leopard. He often comes out at night and looks for something to eat!'

The safari group was getting ready to leave. With many goodbyes and waving of farewells, I watched their kombi drive off on the road to Rwanda. There was no traffic going east all day, so I had to spend another night at the border post. Simon took me down to a nearby store in his official car and very generously bought me some tins of sardines, a tin of corned beef and a tin of peaches, as he realised that I had no cash.

The following morning as we were sitting on a tree stump talking and smoking, a rather neat-looking kombi drove up. It was going east – my direction – and Simon remarked that I was very lucky to get a ride. Inside the kombi were a young Swiss couple and their dog. I asked if they would give me a lift to the next town, and to my surprise they refused, saying they never gave lifts to hitchhikers. I pointed out to them that we weren't on a European motorway … but they made some excuse about not having the right insurance in case of an accident. The customs man asked them to drive around to the back of the house.

About half an hour later a Land Rover arrived, with two couples, one from Australia, the other from the United Kingdom. I had seen them before, in the Central African Republic. Although they were overloaded and the vehicle was in bad shape, they offered me a lift to the next town. This was Biharamulo. The spoken language there was English and I should also be able to cash my cheque there. Tony and Colin went inside the office to fix up their papers and passports while their wives made some sandwiches for the journey. Half an hour later my bag was loaded onto their roof and I went to say goodbye to my friends at the house. Simon took me to the window at the back of the house and pointed. There the Swiss couple were, both of them scowling angrily, laying out all their bags and cameras on a table to be checked, including the checking of the numbers of their cameras. Simon winked at me and said, 'African justice!'

It took a good couple of hours on the dirt road to travel the 60 kilometres or so to the next town, Biharamulo. On the outskirts of the town I saw a big store and asked my companions to drop me off there. I asked the Indian store owner if he might cash my cheque for me, which he did with pleasure. I also got a cup of tea and a young boy to show me the way to the village bar; he carried a bowl of chilli bites for me to nibble on as we walked down the street. When I got to the bar I thanked him and he returned home. I bought the half-a-dozen or so people in the bar a round of drinks and they all wanted to know who I was. I found out from them who the village boss was and afterwards I went off to the square to meet up with my travelling companions. I found the women fixing a sun cover over the Land Rover and setting out some deckchairs and a table.

Colin and Tony came walking towards us with plastic petrol containers in their hands. They looked rather despondent. 'No petrol – no beer,' Tony said. They had tried in vain to get petrol and beer. In their opinion, the people in 'this godforsaken village' were unpleasant and hostile. I took them to the nearest café and we sat down and had a coffee. I told them in as polite a way as possible: 'You just arrived in this village and spread your camping gear in the middle of a public square without asking for permission from one of the elders or officials. If you had introduced yourself to the community first, you would have got all the petrol and beer you needed.' Then I took them to the bar and told them to buy a round of drinks and introduce themselves – and from then on they had no problems.

I said goodbye to the couples at the market square in Biharamulo and caught a night bus to Mwanza. This required disembarking from the bus early the next morning and getting on an over-crowded ferry to Mwanza. There I boarded another bus to the Kenyan border town of Namanga. In effect I was trying to finish my trip as quickly as possible now, partly because of my dwindling funds, but also because I had been experiencing malaria symptoms, which were worsening, and I felt unwell. I could get some money wired to me in Nairobi.

On the bus I met up with a pair of friendly but reserved Japanese hitch-hikers who had travelled from West Africa. The following morning we arrived at Namanga and discovered that we would have to walk along a dirt road for ten kilometres to get to the border post. The hitchhiking pair were students from Tokyo and, unfortunately, spoke poor English, so communication was heavy going. About halfway we stopped for a coffee in a little roadhouse in the village. The landscape was open dry country with thorn bushes and some strange-looking trees which appeared flat, hollow and other-worldly. I walked around and took some pictures near a house, which turned out to be the local party office. Suddenly several men appeared and angrily told me not to take pictures and insisted that I accompany them to the police at their office. 'We want to establish whether you are a good man or a bad man,' they said. I explained that I was a tourist. The two Japanese men, who had been watching all this from afar, came running over to assist me. After much explaining and some muddled conversation between the Japanese men and my suspicious official, everybody ended up shaking hands. I thanked my Japanese friends for coming to my rescue and together we walked a further five kilometres to the Kenyan border, all of it uphill. They decided to camp next to the border post under some bushes, but I decided I would walk on a little. I had seen some lights further on and I gravitated towards them. Here I discovered a noisy safari camp, with a bar, 100 metres down the road. A dozen or so people, mostly couples, were sitting around a fire drinking beer out of bottles and there was much chatter and laughter. They greeted me with curiosity, and after I had introduced myself they told me that they were leaving the following morning for Nairobi and en route were going to visit a Masai village, a trip which had been organised by the tourist board. The group was mostly English with some Scottish and Australian people plus a South African couple from Johannesburg. The South Africans said they knew my work on *Drum* and the *Sunday Times* and they offered me a lift to Nairobi. There was space in their bus, they said, which was parked nearby. This was a stroke of luck and I was very happy to accept their offer. We spent many hours late into the night talking about Johannesburg.

Early the next morning, with an orange sun rising in front of us in the east, I was on the bus sitting with the South African couple as we travelled through a landscape of bushland and wide open spaces. After a couple of hours we arrived at Lake Magadi and under a group of trees found the Masai village. There were three buses parked nearby and dozens of tourists, dressed in their khaki outfits with cameras dangling over their large stomachs, were milling about. When a group of 24 young Masai men, their bodies painted in red clay, and holding spears, performed obligingly for these somewhat stereotypical tourists, jumping up and down, everybody crowded round to take pictures.

Some young Masai women, also in red body paint, clapped their hands and sang, while other Masai sat on grass mats on the ground, selling and displaying their handcraft work – beadwork, wooden carved figures and multi-coloured

Masai dancing

mats. I found the commercial exploitation of the Masai people rather unpleasant and went back to sit in the bus after I had taken some photos. I was also experiencing more malaria symptoms and not feeling at all well.

In Nairobi I booked into a hotel where I cleaned myself up – shaved and showered – and made myself look like a city dweller. I found that it took some time to get used to walking on an even floor, inside and outside in the street. The sensation was similar to that after having been on a long, rough sea journey.

I found an English bank where I got some money wired to me from my London bank. I had to rest a lot at the hotel and eat some good and plentiful food to cope with my malaria attacks. When I looked at myself for the first time in a mirror, I was surprised to see how skinny I had become.

After a few days I was ready to travel the last leg of my trip. I got a Peugeot taxi to Mombasa, securing a seat in the front next to the driver for 35 shillings. We left early in the morning and the trip was about 500 miles on tarred roads. The only surprise event of the trip was meeting a bull elephant in the middle of the road – he wouldn't move, and when the driver hooted, the elephant started to raise its ears, about to charge. We reversed very quickly, the elephant stopped, and we had to wait half an hour until it decided to leave.

We arrived in Mombasa in the late afternoon. After dropping the four other passengers off at the town square, the driver took me to a beachfront hotel outside the town. The hotel was fully booked, but when I told the receptionist that I had come all the way from West Africa and gone through all the countries I had travelled across, she found me a little room that was usually reserved only for staff.

I went down to a totally deserted beach, and after a good swim in warm, clear water I settled down beside a palm tree and fell asleep. I was woken up after what must have been hours by a local man selling coconuts. I bought one for a shilling. Using a large knife, which he swung with tremendous force, the man cut the top open for me so that I could drink the refreshing milk there and then. It was delicious, so much so that I asked him to get me half a dozen more. I was sitting leaning against the tree drinking when a family of tourists passed by and stopped to take pictures of me. When one of the cameras didn't work, I got up and sorted it out for them.

Mombasa beach

After a few days of hanging around the beach, I went back into the city and booked a ticket on the first flight to London. From the airport I went straight to the Hospital for Tropical Diseases, where I spent ten days undergoing treatment for malaria.

Much later, reflecting on my journey through Africa in the seventies, I came to the realisation how difficult it was at that time – almost impossible – to travel by road. This was mostly because of the long distances. The main cities had airports and four-star hotels to ensure that political leaders, businessmen and tourists were able to visit. The only road travellers, really, were the safari tours, so the countryside in Africa was underdeveloped and poorly serviced.

Jung was once asked, after a short trip to Uganda, what Africa meant to him. He repeated what an elderly African man had said to him while they were sitting on a tree stump: 'Africa is not people's country. It's God's country.'

United Kingdom, United States, South Africa

The author and Nelson Mandela

39

MEETING CLAUDIA AND
A WINTRY WORKSHOP

Settling back in London took some adjusting to, and recurrent bouts of the malaria which I had picked up on my African travels didn't help. I recovered slowly and got myself back into some interesting projects. One of these was organising an exhibition for the Whitechapel Art Gallery about the Jewish community in the Whitechapel area. One member of my team was the photographer Leonard Freed, whom I had first met in Antwerp during the 1966 student riots, when we were both running about photographing the action while his German wife stuffed sugar cubes into our mouths to keep us going. The Whitechapel Gallery show was a great success with a display of over 250 images.

Thanks to the sponsorship we received from a new insurance company, my students from the Central School of Art and Design and I organised a show entitled 'The Quality of Life' as part of the opening celebration of the new National Theatre complex on London's South Bank. I rented an old warehouse in Tooley Street near London Bridge, which was a four-storey building that used to be a toy factory. There was enough space for a large darkroom, a meeting room and rooms for some of us to stay during the three-year project. The exhibition featured images by ten young photographers who travelled to the United States, Africa and many parts of Europe, as well as around the United Kingdom, to capture what 'the quality of life' meant to them in these diverse societies. The exhibition had a successful opening at the National Theatre complex, was on show for three months and then travelled to France.

One day I had been at a party with two friends. It was a sunny, warm summer's day and we were going to visit another friend, Claude Davies, whom I had known from the *Drum* days many years ago, when he had been an accountant. As we passed the wall of his house, we heard voices and laughter coming from the garden. I thought I would surprise Claude and his guests. I picked a few leaves from some ivy growing nearby and wove them into a crown, which I stuck on my head. Then I climbed up and over the wall, jumping down into the garden to the great surprise and much amusement of the group of people sitting around a table drinking wine. I was fascinated by a young woman among Claude's guests, who had the most beautiful auburn curly hair and a gorgeous face, with seductive smiling eyes full of humour. I thought she looked like Bette Davis. I got a bit of a fright when she started talking – she had a strong BBC accent.

Having lived and worked in the United Kingdom for years, I had never thought about or paid much attention to the class system, but I had come to realise how much it defined people. The way you speak, your diction, your lifestyle, where you live, and the school or university you attended put you into a certain class. Now I understood better why the first thing people often asked me when we met was 'What do you do?' and 'Where do you live?' My answers would place me in a social group or class. However, because I was a 'foreigner' and had a slight accent, they always found it difficult to identify my class and background.

Anyway, Claude produced a bottle of champagne and introduced everyone. The beautiful redhead's name, funnily enough, was Claudia. From the way Claude introduced me to her I suspected that they were somehow involved, so I thought I had better leave things for the moment.

In 1979 I had an exhibition of a study of faces in the Air Street Gallery in the centre of London, and to my pleasant surprise Claudia was one of the guests at the launch. After the show we went for a drink at the French Pub in Dean Street. It was getting late and the bar was about to close but we sat in a corner, surrounded by photos of famous film stars, sports stars and other celebrities who had visited this pub, and talked. Not only did I find Claudia very beautiful, indeed gorgeous and ravishing, but, going by the way she looked at me, I thought she might be interested in me too.

As it happened, and frustratingly now, I was booked to fly to New York the following day to give a course in photography at the New School, and then to join a workshop in Millerton in upstate New York. I would be away from London for about six months or more. Suddenly it was 'Time, gentlemen, please' and Claudia and I had no option but to part.

On the flight to New York I couldn't stop thinking about Claudia. I also berated myself for being an idiot – I hadn't asked her for her phone number or address so I wouldn't be able to contact her while I was away. For once I had met a woman I was really interested in and here I was flying to a different continent. Maybe we'd meet again in the future. I put my trust in fate.

Teaching photography to a group of mature students in New York, I was struck by one thing: their concentration span was extremely short. After fifteen or twenty minutes they became restless. One student even asked me if he could smoke during classes. After a while I decided to have small breaks every 20 minutes and this worked like a charm. Everyone lit up, relaxed, talked about the weather and appeared happy. I put this short attention span down to United States TV programming, which was divided into short sections, interrupted by commercials, to avoid long sequences.

At the weekend I took a train from Central Park Station to Millerton where one of the members of the Apeiron Workshop picked me up. The workshop was on an isolated farm next to a forest. The farmhouse was attached to a large barn, which had been converted into about a dozen small darkrooms and the same number of bedrooms, plus a lounge with a TV set and a few armchairs. The partitions were made of thin wood or board and were not noise-proof, so you could hear every sound coming from all the rooms. Each room seemed to have a radio constantly blaring, especially the darkrooms, where the students often printed or developed films all night. The noise made it very difficult to sleep at night.

Apeiron was run by a curious fellow. About 35, he had a pale face and a Clark Gable moustache. He was fast-moving, hyped up and irritable a lot of the time. When I arrived he proudly and confidently showed me his portfolio. The album itself was very impressive and expensive. It was made of dark green leather and had his name, John Daido Loori – Apeiron, embossed in large letters on the cover. As he paged through his portfolio, I have to say I found his photos, which were mostly of weddings, sports events and a few portraits, rather boring. They could have been press or newspaper photos. Then he came to a photo of a corner of a ceiling in a room and said, astonishingly: 'This was the moment when I became abstract!'

Including John, myself and two other teachers, the workshop group comprised fifteen people. One of the students had a ponytail and dressed in a fancy 'Red Indian' outfit, complete with colourful headband, leather-tasselled clothes and leather sandals. Another wore a cowboy outfit with a wide-rimmed hat, high-heeled boots and an elaborate leather belt and walked like John Wayne, swaying from side to side. I thought he looked as if he had something stuck in his trousers. One of the women students had long black hair and wore long brightly coloured skirts. She spent the whole night in the darkroom making one print for her master's degree. In the lounge after classes the topics of discussion were Zen, the Mexican poet and philosopher Octavio Paz, and Carl Jung's theory of symbolism. There were many Paz and Jung titles on the bookshelf, as well as a lot of books on the occult.

Every Friday we had a meeting to look at everybody's work. The students pinned their prints on a long board and we all sat across from it, looking at their pictures and discussing them. These sessions were led by John or one of the instructors. On one of these Fridays, John pointed at an image and, looking around at everyone, said, 'This is a very religious picture.' The photograph was a wide landscape image of open flat country with a wooden fence on either side disappearing into the distance. 'This is symbolic of your psychic process,' he said, referring to one of the young students sitting next to me, who was obviously the author.

'I don't understand,' I said.

John looked at me. 'Don't you see it?' he said in a sarcastic tone.

'No, I don't,' I repeated.

John then put it to the group. 'Do you see it?' he asked. They all nodded. Yes, they could see the religiousness. 'Look at the vanishing point,' John said, fixing his eyes intently on me. I looked at the picture more carefully. At the centre of the photo the fence had a small gate and one of the wooden poles was rising above the others, and a length of wood crossed the pole, which, from a distance, could look like a cross.

The next picture John discussed was of a white wall of a small building. In the centre of the wall was a small round window with a couple of bars across it. The wall had the shadow of a tree trunk that forked upwards, passing the window on either side. John looked at it for a while and then asked whose picture it was. A young girl no older than seventeen shyly said it was hers. John walked up to her and, with a worried expression, said, 'You have very serious sexual problems, young woman!' The girl blushed bright red with embarrassment and crumpled up in her chair as if she wanted to disappear. I felt sorry for her.

'Aren't you going too far with your imagination?' I asked John.

He looked at me angrily and quoted Jung. 'Archetypal union of opposites by means of the integration of opposing polarities, conscious and unconscious, reason and instinct, spiritual and materialism.' Then he looked around. 'Who's next?' he asked.

The woman who had been printing all night got up with a pile of photos under her arm and put the photos side by side along the wall. There were twelve prints in total. Each photo was of the same set of rocks splashed by the sea, but each had a different splash, some high, some more gentle. Everybody looked puzzled. 'What does it say?' John prompted. The woman looked annoyed. 'Why? Can't you see it?' she said. Everybody kept quiet, but some got up to take a closer look at the pictures. Still no one offered anything. 'You don't see it?' the woman asked, getting more frustrated. 'Okay,' she said and then, in a loud voice: 'It's an orgasm!'

One day John Daido Loori told me that the founder of the Apeiron Workshop, Peter Schlessinger, was due to visit us. He also asked me to take over a group of students and start a workshop with them. 'You've been with us for two weeks now and should have acquainted yourself with our aim and directions,' he said.

There was an old tree behind the farmhouse which was covered in snow, its bare branches making some interesting forms and shapes, altered hourly by the changing winter light. When the sun was shining, the snow on the tree reflected tiny crystals and had the appearance of an illuminated Christmas tree. Black clouds in the evening made the snow look grey. I chose six students and asked them to arrange their cameras on tripods to photograph the tree, or parts of the tree, every hour, starting one hour before sunrise, leaving the cameras in position, and exposing a frame every hour until one hour after sunset. In case of snow they should leave some towels over their cameras. The idea was that the final result would give the students an idea and understanding of how light changes from hour to hour, which in turn changes the meaning or form of the image.

When I checked on the students at lunchtime to see how they were doing, I found that they must have got fed up with the idea and had decided instead to decorate the tree with a dozen or so rolls of toilet paper, making a farce of the whole object of the exercise.

Peter Schlessinger duly arrived and John introduced me to him in the kitchen. He was a slim man with long hair down to his shoulders and a wrinkled suntanned face. He asked me a lot of questions about my background and life, especially what I did during the war during the Nazi period – had I been a member of the Hitler Youth, for example. It wasn't much of a conversation and my feeling about him (and the other members of the workshop) was that they didn't have any idea about Europe or the wider world outside the United States.

Oddly, Peter then asked me if I could do some carpentry work for Apeiron. I explained that I was a photographer with a wide experience in photographic teaching, the details of which I had already related to him clearly during my grilling. I got the impression that for some reason he didn't believe me. Peter and John then left, leaving me standing, quite speechless, in the kitchen.

One of the projects we did proved to be fun and worthwhile. A group of six of us had to get into the back of a van with no windows at six in the morning when it was still dark outside. Inside were two long benches. We each had one camera, one tripod and four rolls of film and we weren't allowed to talk to one another. The van drove off, destination unknown. After a rather boring, silent three-hour drive we stopped. We opened the back door and stepped out into a white landscape. The van had stopped on the edge of a frozen river near a small village. The instructor told us that we should set our watches since we had to return within two hours and all four rolls of film had to be exposed. If anyone was late returning they wouldn't wait for us. It turned out that we were on the Hudson River near the village of Athens. So off we walked in four different directions and started our hunt for images. Two hours later, frozen and red-cheeked, we all returned to the van. I had found some interesting images in the village – wooden houses and large snowed-under cars – and made, for me, some new and different images.

The following week we went to a football field beside an ice-rink, which I found to be more difficult for interesting images. In the third week we went on another mystery trip – this time the van parked us in the middle of Manhattan next to Central Park. As we climbed out I noticed that some of the group were hesitating. The John Wayne fellow with the cowboy big hat and fancy boots decided to stay inside the van. I tried to coax him out to join us, saying that his big boots could kick off any unwelcome approaches, but he wouldn't budge. So the rest of us went into Central Park, which was a paradise for photos, with hippies, roller-skaters, and people playing ball games and making music. Some had painted faces, there were acrobats clowning around, and an assortment of jugglers and other colourful characters. In no time I had filled up my four films.

One day I found a tome of a book on the kitchen table. Over 600 pages, it was an encyclopedia of American foundations and companies that funded projects. I asked one of the teachers, a young man by the name of Jimmy, what it was used for. 'It's our Bible!' he said. 'We go through the companies, banks and foundations that support and finance projects in the arts and find ideas that fit in with their requirements. Then we tailor our projects to their interests.'

The workshop over, I left Apeiron and returned to Manhattan, where I tried to contact Ernest Cole. There was no response at his address or from his phone, so I went to see Joe Lelyveld, who had been a patron of Ernest and had written the text for his powerful book. Joe told me he was very upset with Ernest because he had decided to give up taking pictures. He had gone into a deep depression and it had become almost impossible to help him. He had often found him sitting on a bench in a park where he would spend the night because he had been thrown out of his room by his landlord. Also Ernest seemed to have lost all his negatives.

I eventually managed to track Ernest down in the flat of one of my South African friends, Joe Gumede, who was working as an interpreter at the United Nations. Ernest was sitting in his room in silence, looking out of the window. I tried to cheer him up by talking about the great success of his book, but it didn't seem to help. He was isolated and lonely and couldn't return to South Africa to see his family, mother, sister, and his friends. His African American friends in New York had no sympathy for his plight and he couldn't relate to them. It made me very sad to see Ernest this way.

I began preparing to return to London. Claudia was much on my mind and I hoped that she might still be interested in me. I had been away for almost a year.

Back in London, I managed to get in touch with Claudia and we went for a drink. She was pleased to see me again but now she was about to travel. She was working on some stories about an IRA bomber. We arranged to meet whenever we were both next in London. I did some more teaching at the Central School of Art and Design, spent some time in Hamburg teaching a course at the School of Art there, and then worked on a number of stories for *Die Zeit*.

40

'IT'S A BIT OF A SHAMBLES'– THE *DRUM* ARCHIVE

At the end of 1982 I took a flight to South Africa to find and collect my negatives of the pictures I had taken in the fifties and sixties, which I had been forced to leave behind.

It was 20 years since I had been in the country.

My mother and John now lived in a small suburban house in Randburg with their three poodles. John was an independent debt collector for medical doctors. His temperament hadn't changed but he seemed to have shrunk in size. He still didn't look pleased to see me.

I noticed many changes in the country and there was a definite change in the atmosphere. On one side there was talk of business leaders holding meetings with some leaders of the ANC, while on the other many suburban whites feared a bloody revolution. The leader of an extremist right-wing movement, Eugene Terre'Blanche, made a fool of himself when he fell off his horse when leading a small group of his followers through Pretoria.

On the street I observed many small shifts in people's interactions. In Hillbrow on Saturdays there was a festive atmosphere, with groups of musicians playing in the street, informal traders with fruit and vegetable stands, and a vibrant flea market. I saw two policemen standing at a corner, one lighting the cigarette of another – one was black and one white. I saw a couple holding hands – one was white and the other was black. At the public swimming pool in

Sea Point, in Cape Town, I saw black and white kids splashing happily together in the water.

One day I went to the bar of the Federal Hotel. It was dark inside and almost empty, but who should I see there, nursing a bottle of beer, but Desmond Blow. I walked over, sat down next to him and ordered a beer. For a while he didn't say anything. Then he glanced sideways at me and said, 'Serious problems with my wife – she's beastly unpleasant to me.' It was as though time had stood still and he hadn't noticed that I'd been away for 20 years. Some people had not moved on in South Africa. It was as if they were trapped in a time warp.

The *Sunday Times* had moved to a new building in Mooi Street. Here I met with the chief photographer, Jimmy Soulier. He didn't have good news for me. Just after the *Sunday Times* had moved, there had been a flood in the darkroom and all my negatives had been destroyed. I spent some time searching in the storage rooms but I couldn't find any of my negatives for my many years of work for the paper. Next I went to the *Rand Daily Mail*, where I tried to locate the *Drum* archives. *Drum* had gone bankrupt in the seventies and the archives, or so I'd been told, had been handed over to the new owners, the *Rand Daily Mail*, which was part of SAAN. I then discovered that when the *RDM* moved offices they had no space to keep the *Drum* archives. Instead of destroying them, they had offloaded them onto Jim Bailey. These 'archives' were now stored on his farm in Lanseria.

I took a drive out to the Bailey farm. Jim looked much older, his face creased with wrinkles. To my surprise, his wife was none other than Barbara, the young girl with the violin. Although she was now about 45 years old, Barbara still looked and behaved like a tomboy. Later I was told that she had been married for several years to singer Jeremy Taylor before she married Jim. I asked Jim about my negatives. 'It's a bit of a shambles,' he said. 'They must be at the farm manager's office ...'

Shambles was an understatement. I found a chaotic mess. Stuffed into four large filing cabinets, one of which was lying on its side, the negatives spilled out in all directions.

'Help yourself,' Jim said. Then he turned and walked away. I didn't know where to start, but I opened one of the sliding drawers. It was packed with piles of dust-laden negatives with no protective envelopes or any numbering. I spent about three days at the farm looking through all the files, negatives and prints. I found some of my negatives, but many were missing. I asked Barbara if she knew where the other negatives of the 'archive' were kept and she told me to look in the barn. There were piles of boxes with photos and 'other *Drum* rubbish' in there, she said. She was fed up with Jim and his *Drum* and was going to have the boxes picked up soon by the garbage collectors. So I should take a look before they were thrown out.

The barn was a large low building, in the corner of which were about a dozen bulky cardboard boxes crammed to the top with photographs, negative sleeves filled with negatives, sets of photo cartons and contact sheets, all mixed up and in a big heap. I spent some time looking through this mess and eventually found some more of my negatives. Then I went to see Jim in his study. I showed him what I had found and what I was going to take. He showed no interest whatsoever in the negatives. We chatted a little and agreed vaguely to meet up sometime in London.

I flew back to London, where I started to print my negatives from the fifties and make up a dummy book on South Africa. I gave it the working title *The Black and White Fifties*.

I phoned Claudia, who was back in London now too, and we arranged to meet in a few days – she said she would phone me with a date. She chose 18 March, my birthday. I wondered how she knew … I later found out that she is an incredible researcher. It was my best birthday ever. Claudia had arranged a surprise dinner with champagne and candles, and from that moment our loving relationship began. In no time Claudia moved into my flat and we never looked back. We shared the same ideas about life, society and history, which were mirrored in our separate but uncannily similar collection of books.

Until Claudia came into my life and my heart, and stayed there, my personal life had had its fair share of ups and downs. After our divorce and my departure from South Africa in 1964, Etricia brought up our four children and, sadly, I saw them infrequently. I got married again, to a Portuguese woman. We lived together for six months before we got married and then, inexplicably, she suddenly became aggressive and jealous, which led to my speedy departure. Then, when I was living in London, I had a common-law wife, Sandra, with whom I had a son, Leon, who is now a photographer in Bangkok. Sandra was somewhat anti-social and spent her days reading romance novels. She took no interest in my work and in the end we parted amicably. Then there was a cheating girl-friend, another whose mother disliked me because I was German, poor and therefore unsuitable for her Jewish daughter, and then a dope smoker ...

And then I struck lucky and met Claudia.

I spent the next few months seeing publishers in London and Amsterdam, both cities having had strong anti-apartheid movements, showing them my dummy book. Even though at the time there were new moves to bring South African business and government together with the ANC, which gave the book a topical edge, they weren't interested.

One day I was walking across Chelsea Bridge when I saw a man with longish hair coming towards me. I noticed he was wearing an identical long herring-bone overcoat to mine. It was none other than Jim Bailey – a surprise meeting in an unexpected place. We had a few laughs and agreed to meet the following day in a wine bar in Mayfair. I took the dummy of my book to show him. He suddenly became very excited and urged me to come back to South Africa and sort out the archives. I was hesitant. I told him I needed to think about it.

Claudia and I were both fed up with the grey, damp and cold British climate and we'd begun thinking about moving to the South of France. We also decided to get married. We wanted to do this in the village town hall and began the process of getting together all the many papers the French required, including health certificates, family details and even school reports. This became com-plicated as papers were only valid for three months, after which they had to be renewed, and so, facing a never-ending cycle of doomed paperwork, we then decided to get married in London instead. Claudia and I were married at Marylebone Magistrate's Court on 21 April 1984. With France on the back burner, we discussed the idea of going to South Africa for a while to sort out the archives on Bailey's farm and I wrote a letter to Jim with a proposal. I would organise the *Drum* archives in his farm, identify and sort out the thousands of negatives and prints, and produce three books using this material to tell the his-tory of South Africa in the fifties. I would self-fund my trip there, but Jim would contribute to my living and accommodation expenses, paying me R1 200 per month, which was roughly half my expenses. Jim accepted the proposal. It was agreed I would retain all my personal negatives which I had taken as a freelancer on *Drum* and which I had left in the archives for safekeeping in 1964 when I'd exited the country to avoid confiscation of my work by the Special Branch.

Claudia and I flew to Johannesburg. John, my stepfather, came to the airport to pick us up. His first words to me were: 'You have to do the cooking. Rosie is not very well.' Despite this odd caution, the house was full of cooking smells when we arrived. John led us to the small second bedroom. Before we had put our luggage down, he said, 'You can't stay long.' Then my mother appeared in the doorway. 'Come and have something to eat,' she said. 'You must be hungry after such a long trip.' I introduced Claudia to my mother. John kept going on about the cooking, with my mother contradicting him and saying she was quite happy to cook. I told John not to worry – we'd be moving out soon. Claudia was three months pregnant and we wanted a place of our own anyway.

The next day we rented a car from 'Rent a Wreck' and arranged to meet Jim at his farm in Lanseria. He invited us for lunch and we all sat in the kitchen round a large wooden table and enjoyed a simple meal of green salad and brown bread, accompanied by a glass of red wine. Jim confirmed his agreement to the terms of work I had proposed in my letter, and I said I would start organising the mess of the *Drum* archives in about ten days' time, once Claudia and I had found a place to rent in the vicinity. Jim offered us a place on the farm, but when we saw it, we declined. Even if it had been suitable, which it wasn't, I didn't want to live on the job. We found a place not far away that both of us liked. This was a little thatch-roofed cottage with a small garden (it was actually a converted chicken run). I bought an old Japanese car and some bits of furniture, and Claudia and I set up house.

I went back to the Baileys' farm to make a start. Jim took me along a path away from the office building, his library and living area to a dilapidated farmhouse. 'You can set yourself up here,' he said. Then he walked away across a field towards his library. The place was small and had clearly been untouched for decades, but it had two rooms and a bathroom and it would have to do. It took me two weeks to clean it up and make it a workable space. I converted the little bathroom into a darkroom, one room into an office with some filing cabinets, and in the other I put a large light table for viewing negatives and some more cabinets and files. I persuaded Jim, with difficulty, to invest in these necessary changes to the building and I also got him to fund an assistant to handle the captions and archival files. Annamie Gardner became my enthusiastic, professional and good-humoured assistant. She helped lighten the mood and the load of what became a very arduous task. I busied myself going through the tens of thousands of unmarked negatives on the light table, identifying each negative, where possible, with the author, date, subject and event. After eight hours of this laborious work each day, I began to suffer from image fatigue and eye strain, but nevertheless I continued.

41

BOOKS, FILMS, MUSIC

After twelve long months of this exhausting work, having identified the bulk of the negatives, I began to put my first book together. This was a collection of some of the best photos from the newly organised archive, which I had created from chaos, and I called it *The Finest Photos from the Old Drum*.

Our son Charlie was born on 19 February 1986. He had Claudia's red curly hair. On the day he was born, while he was lying on his stomach, I was surprised to see him do a few vigorous press-ups and turn his head around, surveying his new world. Claudia was relaxed and happy and spent quality time with Charlie in our converted chicken run while I toiled away organising the archives and producing books. Charlie brought much joy into our lives over the coming years.

One of the strong interests Claudia and I shared was film. Claudia had an amazing knowledge of film history, directors and actors. Given our similar creative thought processes, already in London we had begun to write film scripts together for dramas and documentaries, and we continued this collaboration. Later on, when Charlie was a little bigger, Claudia worked at the SABC on a film review programme, which made use of her TV talents and experience and her wide knowledge of the world of films.

The new owner of *Drum* was Nasionale Pers and the magazine had been incorporated into its stable of magazine publications. It was now a glossy, popular, gossipy magazine covering social events, sports, love stories, film stars (international) and scandals in Hollywood. I thought it dull but I went to see the editor anyway. He was as bland as the magazine, I thought, and displayed no vision for the publication. He seemed a safe front man for the new owners. I had thought of suggesting some investigative stories to them but realised immediately that they wouldn't be in the least interested.

I then went to see an old friend, Stan Motjuwadi, the editor of *City Press*, the sister paper of *Drum*. He seemed to be happy in his job and managed to cover some in-depth stories. Claudia and I often went to the Market Theatre complex for drinks in the Yard of Ale, which became our regular socialising spot. It was a cultural, multi-racial island of liberals, intellectuals and artists who all mixed happily together and discussed the state of the country and its future. For us it was an island of sanity.

Stan asked me if I would have a look at the *City Press* photo department to try to improve their rather poor photography output. I spent a few days talking to the photographers and found that only one of the three staff photographers had a fair idea of what photography was all about. He knew his equipment and produced some good pictures, but the other two were hopelessly incompetent. One of them had been working for *Drum* and *City Press* for over ten years but he still didn't understand how his flashlight worked or how to make prints in the darkroom. It was a frustrating and disappointing state of affairs. The darkroom was filthy and one of the enlargers had never been cleaned, so all the prints were fuzzy and couldn't be used in the paper. I tried my best to help, but what they badly needed was a thorough course in photography.

Behind the Market Theatre was Kippies jazz club, named after Kippie Moeketsi. It was a small, intimate space – the building was a redecorated Victorian toilet – and it became the leading jazz venue of Joburg, featuring all the best jazz groups and singers. Claudia and I and our friends spent many evenings listening to great jazz in this tiny, smoky, crowded venue. The whole Market Theatre complex buzzed with new and progressive ideas for a new South Africa. There was the playwright Barney Simon, who produced innovative plays, which until recently would have been banned, and there was Athol Fugard, whose production of *Waiting for Godot* was groundbreaking. Change was in the air – change was happening – and people were whispering and hoping for a new South Africa.

Claudia, the author and Charlie

I managed to get Penguin Books to produce, with Jim Bailey, *The Finest Photos of the Old Drum*, which I had just put together. Sadly, Annamie had to leave and she was replaced by Maureen Isaacson, who worked in the archives writing the text for some of the other books, including the next one, *The Fifties People of South Africa*.

Claudia and I were working on a documentary 35 mm film, *Have You Seen Drum Recently?* and we put together a five-minute pilot. The only thing we needed was some good voice-over commentary. We found one of the best documentary voice-over writers in Richard Beynon, and I spent many hours with him at his home in Orange Grove going through the material from *Drum* and events of the fifties. A year later when the film was finished, using 700 photos, archive footage and 35 pieces of original fifties music, it was accompanied by Richard's outstanding and excellent commentary.

I now needed someone to make prints in the darkroom for the books and films we were working on and came across a young man who had come to see me for guidance in photography. His name was Santu Mofokeng and I thought he showed great promise. I employed him as a darkroom assistant and he was soon making some very good prints. He stayed with us for over a year, making all the darkroom prints. From time to time I gave him a tutorial on his photography, which he practised over the weekends. Santu eventually became an internationally known and successful photographer.

We had secured some financial interest from a film distributor in Joburg for the *Drum* film, which gave us added impetus to get it made. I started to select 700 photos from the archives to be used in the film and had them printed up and mounted on board. They were divided in sections – for example, sets of images of pennywhistlers in Joburg, the Defiance Campaign, the Treason Trial, and the *Drum* staff. Over each print I attached a sheet of transparent paper on which I marked the detailed timing for the rostrum camera for each print – full frame 2 seconds, zoom 1 second, hold, zoom 2 seconds, move from left to right etc. All were marked with colour coding.

I did some research at the Pretoria Film Archives and found a film called *Zonk*. This 35 mm film had been made during the late forties by the government to entertain the returning black troops from the war who were kept, supposedly for security reasons, in camps over several years before they were demobbed. They didn't want to release them all in one go as they believed that these tens of thousands of soldiers who had seen the world outside might create an unsettling situation. *Zonk* featured the best African musicians of the time, groups, large bands and singers, with such top names as Kippie Moeketsi, the Inkspots from Springs, Makay Davashe, Dolly Rathebe, the Manhattan Brothers and many of the famous pennywhistlers, who were all filmed on large stages in a large hall with space for elaborate dance numbers. The material was a gold mine for our film. Next I arranged for the 700 prints to be filmed with a rostrum camera, and Claudia and I selected a number of film clips.

The enthusiastic financier we had found in Johannesburg was moving to Cape Town, where he had several partners with whom he planned to finance our *Drum* film. Jim was curious about the film, and when I told him we were going to use 700 photos from the *Drum* archives, he wanted to see the pilot. Then, when I told him that we had some possible financiers in Cape Town, he looked thoughtful. Next thing he proposed that he finance the film.

I realised that Jim wanted to take over the whole project, but I suggested he rather co-finance with the Cape investors on a 50/50 basis. I suggested a 33 per cent stake for him, 33 per cent to the Cape investors and the remaining 33 per cent to be held by myself and Claudia. We arranged for him to go down to Cape Town and meet with the financiers.

Next for Claudia and me came the interviewing of people who had been involved in and knew about the fifties and *Drum*. We approached Peter Magubane and Alf Kumalo, who both turned me down. They didn't want anything to do with the film. Don Mattera, a former Sophiatown leader of the Vultures gang turned educationalist, agreed to be interviewed, as did Jackie Heyns from Cape Town and Coco Cachalia, daughter of Yusuf and Amina Cachalia from Joburg. Arthur Maimane in London, who was one of the few *Drum* writers still alive, agreed to be interviewed, and so did Todd Matshikiza's son John, who was also living in London. Claudia flew to London where she hired a local crew. She did an excellent interview with Arthur, but at the last minute John Matshikiza changed his mind. For some reason he got suspicious about the film, especially as it was being made by whites.

Meanwhile, Jim came back from the Cape saying that he'd been unable to meet with the financiers. When we looked into what had happened in Cape Town, we discovered that the financiers had met with him but had been alienated by Jim's arrogant behaviour. Jim repeated that he wanted to finance the whole film himself. 'I'll foot the bill,' were his words. He'd already had a contract drawn up by his lawyers. All we had to do was sign it.

The contract stated that Claudia and I were not partners in the film but rather Jim's employees and we would get a fee of R3 000 each for producing and directing the film. We would receive 12 per cent of the profits – but only once all the costs of the film, including distribution costs, had been paid off. It was a ridiculous document but we were between a rock and a hard place. By then Claudia and I had already spent two years on the project and had invested heavily in the film. Using our own funds, we had done the research, made the pilot, filmed the London interview, and committed ourselves to the rostrum camera work. There was no turning back. We signed the contract.

Years later, when the film had won many awards and was shown worldwide in festivals and on TV, all organised by Claudia, the unpaid distributor, we submitted the total budget, which was just below R150 000, to Jim Bailey. To our surprise and shock, we discovered that he had fictitiously doubled the budget by including a fee for himself as producer and fees for several other unrelated people, including his farm manager. We came to the sad realisation that we would never receive any royalties from the film. To add insult to injury, we had to fund ourselves the transfer of the 35 mm film to video as well as the production of a music and effects track, which was necessary for selling to non-English-speaking countries. You could say that this experience was a great baptism by fire!

The Finest Photos from the Old Drum had now been printed and I arranged a book launch with the publishers at the Market Theatre. I hired a professional 'hot dog' truck, which we placed in the foyer. Book launch guests and theatre audiences could stuff themselves with the finest free hot dogs. In the space upstairs I organised an exhibition of photos from the book. I had asked Jim to say a few words about the book at the function and the theatre was packed with enthusiastic friends, supporters and members of the media. When it came time for Jim to give his talk, everybody went upstairs. When Jim started to talk the room went quiet. He talked at length – about the *Drum* writers in Joburg, Can Themba, Casey, Arthur and Henry and so on, about the *Drum* writers in West Africa, Nigeria and East Africa. Then he returned to the subject of South African *Drum* writers, those in Durban like GR Naidoo, and in Cape Town like Jackie Heyns. He droned on and on. People began wandering off downstairs, where they quickly cleaned out the hot dogs. In 40 minutes Jim never once mentioned photography or the *Drum* photographers – although the focus of the book launch was photos. Despite this, the exhibition was well received and the launch went well. I arranged for similar events in Cape Town and then Durban – without Jim.

After much arguing we settled on a title for the film: *Have You Seen Drum Recently?* We showed it for the first time to a private audience at a film lab – and it was well received. Jim took no interest in the distribution and publicity side of things, so Claudia and I handled these together, starting with presenting the film at various film festivals worldwide. Eventually the BBC bought it for one showing. I had to fly to London to sort out a technical query the BBC had raised about the voice-over. We'd used Richard Beynon for the pilot and General Duze, the famous guitarist from the fifties, with his husky tobacco-whisky tones, for the film. One of Duze's front teeth was missing, which meant his pronunciation of the letter *s* had a slight lisp, whistle or hiss. This was what worried the technical department of the BBC but I managed to sort it out.

Our next book, *The Fifties People of South Africa*, was now ready for publication. Heinemann were the publishers this time. It was a collection of profiles of about 60 people from the fifties who had made important contributions in the world of politics, sport, music, painting and social change. We included *Drum* editors, writers and photographers. Each individual had two pages, but some, such as Henry Nxumalo, Nelson Mandela, Robert Resha, Dan Twala and Job Richard Rathebe, merited more space. There was a short text for each person and photos with captions. When the book was published, the people of Soweto viewed it as their own personal photo album, since it was the first time they had seen their role models, acquaintances and friends published in a book.

One day I got a call from a police colonel. He seemed polite and friendly but then surprised me by saying that I could go to prison if I distributed any photos in the book of political prisoners. Photos of Nelson Mandela and Walter Sisulu were proudly in the book. I consulted the legal department at Wits University and eventually, after a stern warning from the police, somehow we managed to get away with it and the book wasn't banned. It got me worried about the film, though, which we were about to launch at a cinema in Johannesburg. Of course it featured a number of images of Mandela, and also Walter Sisulu and Ahmed Kathrada, who were all still in jail. So I put the 35 mm copy of the film on the cutting table and with a black felt pen made some lines over each frame that featured political prisoners. When the film was eventually launched on the big screen and it came to the inked-out frames, one was able to see through the scribbles and easily identify those 'blacklisted' prisoners. The film was a great success.

I then started on my third book, *The Rise of the ANC*, which was a collection of *Drum* stories and pictures about the ANC from its birth to the present day. It included sections from the Defiance Campaign of 1952, the Treason Trial and many other events and personalities. When I showed the book to Peter Magubane to check that the captions and credits were correct for his pictures, he became very angry. He said I had no right to publish a book about the ANC. I told him I had sent the dummy of the book to Oliver Tambo in Zambia and that we had his blessing – after which Peter kept quiet and sulked.

I decided it was time to stop working with Jim on the farm. Claudia and I were unhappy with how we had been treated by Jim generally, and especially on the feature documentary film, and we had decided to consult lawyers. Our lawyers sent letters to Jim explaining our unhappiness about the way he had hijacked our film and how we were denied any royalties. On top of this we were still spending our time and money promoting the film. Jim never replied to the letter.

Claudia and I were now working on several film scripts. The first script was for a full-length feature film, *Mr Drum*, which was about my friend and colleague Henry Nxumalo, the brave investigative journalist who on many occasions had been prepared to risk his life to expose the injustices of the apartheid regime. The film also encompassed the social, cultural and political scene of the time and *Drum*'s anti-establishment team.

We also wrote some lighter comedic scripts, such as *I Love Soweto*, which was about a character who, through a series of misunderstandings in Soweto, ends up being mistaken for a hospital doctor and a shebeen bootlegger. *A Chase in the Sun* was another light-hearted feature film script in which an unemployed clerk gets a job as an entertainment manager in Sun City. Still on a creative roll, our next comedy script, *There's a Hippo in My Pool*, followed a pampered white Joburg family into a series of improbable and farcical situations.

While I improved the *Mr Drum* film script with several rewrites, Claudia worked on fundraising and distribution. We approached various South African film companies and producers to partner us on this project but there was little or no interest. It was time to approach the international market. We met a Hollywood producer who expressed interest. When he returned from a trip to LA, he said, 'I have some good news and some not so good news. The good news is that Paramount Pictures would like to make the film but the bad news is that you would not be able to direct it, nor have any say in the possible script changes.' We decided to pass. We would continue our search for finance in Europe.

In October 1989 Walter Sisulu, Ahmed Kathrada and a number of other prominent ANC leaders were released from Robben Island. A huge celebration was held at the FNB Stadium near Soweto and I went to cover this landmark historic event with a camera crew. Sisulu was one of the main speakers and the stadium was packed to capacity, with people singing freedom songs and waving ANC flags. The atmosphere was electric and exhilarating. Not long after this memorable event I met Walter and showed him the *Mr Drum* script. A few days later he sent us a letter supporting our film.

By chance we came across a French film producer, Lise Fayolle, from Paris, who expressed great interest in *Mr Drum*. She said it was just what she was look-ing for. Lise Fayolle was short, plump and very energetic. She was always on the go. She had a booming voice – if she spoke to you on the phone, you'd have to hold the receiver well away from your ear. After a number of visits to South Africa she told us she had raised US$6 million for our film, but there was a problem in that the French Finance Department didn't permit French currency to leave the country unless there were special circumstances.

On 11 February 1990 Nelson Mandela was released from prison. It was one of the most electrifying and thrilling moments in the country's history and the whole world celebrated his release. I managed to meet him when he returned to his home in Soweto and we spent some memorable moments reflecting on the fifties and *Drum* magazine. He was slimmer than when I'd last seen him and he spoke in a more unhurried, measured, calm and steady tone. His 27 years in prison isolation must have had a profound effect on him. The world he now entered was a much-changed one, the zeitgeist and political climate having moved from after the Second World War to the Cold War. Relationships between peoples and countries had altered completely.

I was very impressed by Mandela's generosity when it came to his interaction with members of the media. When he entered a room full of press people and television crews, he would greet everyone personally, shaking their hands, asking them how they were and, in many cases, remembering their names. When he made a speech he would read his talk wearing glasses, and when he finished he took off his glasses and improvised. This second part was more relaxed and usually interspersed with jokes and personal anecdotes. His audience was always mesmerised. One time when I was filming his talk to some young students, he finished the scripted part, took off his glasses and talked more personally. He said, 'There are three types of people. Type one you will never remember after they have passed away, not even their names. Type two people you remember by their bad deeds, by their crimes and destructive behaviour and the death and horror they have left behind. And then there are those who will be remembered for their good deeds and the work they have done to improve society and people's lives.'

I told Mandela about our *Mr Drum* feature film and the problems we were having in getting the money out of France. He immediately gave me a letter supporting the film, which eventually led, along with the letter of support from Walter Sisulu, to the French President François Mitterrand declaring the film to be French – which then released the French funds. We now had to find some French actors and crew, which I thought was good, as we would get some very experienced and talented people to work on the film. And when a portion of the funds arrived we started pre-production.

We found a perfect base for our film, a large disused hotel in Randburg, the Ridgeway. Five storeys high and still furnished, it was available to rent. It had a large dining room and kitchen, a ballroom with a stage and dance floor, and a spacious foyer and lounge area. And there were 80 bedrooms. We started to build two soundproof sets in the dining room – one the *Drum* office and the other a shebeen – and a French sound expert visited us to advise us on the best way to soundproof them. Our production office and rehearsal rooms were in the foyer and lounge, and some of the bedrooms were used by the art department for wardrobe, make-up, props, and accounts offices.

At the same time the search for locations began, one of the first being the Fort, Johannesburg's notorious prison, where Henry Nxumalo spent two weeks as a prisoner to write his prison story for *Drum*. This now disused prison was a sinister, terrifying place, resounding with the spirits of past tortured victims. We found a corner of the prison that matched Henry's description of where he had been held.

Then casting began. We found a young singer to play the part of Dolly Rathebe, who was coached by the indomitable Dolly Rathebe herself. We also cast the Elite Swingsters, a famous jazz group from the fifties, which had been out of the music scene for over 30 years owing to the stringent apartheid laws, bought them instruments and rehearsed them on the hotel stage for over three months. In the beginning they were very discordant, but after some weeks they improved dramatically and their original swinging fifties sound returned. Most of the group were well over 50 years old but still managed to produce a young and fresh original fifties sound. This would be the soundtrack for the film. Finally, we cast Patrick Shai as Henry and rehearsals began.

In order to get visas for the French crew and actors we had to submit a script to the minister of home affairs. We were two weeks away from filming when I received a phone call from the ministry. I was told that we could not make the film and that we would get written confirmation of this final decision. We were horrified – this was dreadful news – and there were angry reactions from the cast and crew, who all believed strongly in the film and its message. We thought hard about what to do. I phoned Home Affairs in Pretoria to arrange a meeting so that we could state our case and defend our film. Two days later we received a call from Lise Fayolle in Paris. She had just been to the South African embassy there and she was very angry. They had been abusive towards to her and had refused to renew her South African visa, neither on a tourist nor work basis. She would not be allowed to enter the country. I had to hold the phone well away from my ear for that call.

Claudia and I went to Pretoria for a meeting with the censors at Home Affairs. We sat in a boardroom around a large oval table with five Afrikaans civil servants. These included their spokesperson, a Mr Engelbrecht, who had a reputation as a bitter, extreme racist and was one of the main media censors. We were served tea in floral teacups and then began the hostile part. 'Mr Schadeberg – in the fifties we did not use the term "apartheid" but called it "separate development",' Engelbrecht said. Then he proceeded to go through our film script with a fine toothcomb, taking issue with much of the dialogue. Then another member around the oval table took over. 'The film *Cry Freedom* has just been shown in South Africa, which has created a lot of unrest. We had to ban the film. You see, there is no point making your *Mr Drum* film. We will have to ban it. You're wasting your money.'

We spent almost two hours with these narrow-minded, discourteous, aggressive and steely civil servants and in the end felt there was no hope. These apartheid apologists had made up their minds. In their eyes our film, which was based on fact, was a danger to South African people and had to be closed down. We were devastated.

The Rise of the ANC was shortly to be published, by Jonathan Ball and Ad Donker in South Africa and Bloomsbury in London. Bloomsbury asked me to change the title to *Nelson Mandela and the Rise of the ANC*, redo the cover and add some photos of the release of Mandela and other Mandela images. They also added a short text at the end of the book by Professor Njabulo Ndebele. One day we had a visit from a French man, Alain Guenon, who had a French news agency in Johannesburg selling TV programmes to the SABC. He told me he had bought a copy of the book and was interested in my making a film about the ANC for his company. We went to see him at his office to talk further, where he had a number of employees busy writing and editing, and also visited him in his home in an upmarket suburb, which was luxurious and furnished with antiques. We were served coffee from silver coffee pots by a black butler while two Great Danes lay elegantly on fine Persian carpets. Alain arranged for the financing of the film and I flew to London to source the historical and more modern footage which we needed and which was held by the major television companies and news agencies.

Although it looked as if apartheid was on its way out, it was still dangerous to bring this type of material into South Africa, so Alain organised for a lady to collect the bag with the footage from London, take it to Paris and then somehow get it smuggled into the country. I edited the documentary in secrecy in an editing suite with the door locked. The finished programme was titled *War & Peace* and Alain was very happy with it. Claudia and I retained the rights to the film and years later we updated the programme several times, with Claudia doing the voice-over. We later found out that Alain had given financial support to Winnie Mandela for her new Orlando township mansion and a new Mercedes, and he had also handsomely supported Tokyo Sexwale and Chris Hani. Years later we were informed that Alain had been working for the French arms industry.

While we were busy closing down our *Mr Drum* feature film and producing the new book, South Africa was being rocked by major unrest across the land. Townships were seething cauldrons and many erupted in flames and violence. Police combed the townships street by street to find those responsible for the chaos. Violent street battles between Inkatha supporters and ANC members claimed many lives. There was a pervasive mood of anger, violence and distrust between different groups. Government and municipal officials suspected of being informers were targeted. Their homes were torched and some were subjected to the brutal practice of 'necklacing' – where rubber tyres were placed round their necks and they were doused with petrol and burnt alive.

I now began writing a pilot for a film script about a present-day African news magazine in Johannesburg with the working title *Drum Beats*. I planned a television series, comprising six one-hour episodes covering social, cultural and political stories in the new South Africa. At the same time I was also busy working with Claudia on a feature documentary film project about the history of Robben Island, which looked at the history of this prison island from

1600 to the present day. I designed the layout for an accompanying book, to be published by Ravan Press. While the book was ready to go, the one-hour film was proving difficult to finance. After many years of chasing finance, but determined that this important South African story be realised, at last Claudia succeeded in securing 50 per cent of the funding in the United Kingdom from BBC TV. Now she was looking for the balance from South Africa – but, sadly, nobody seemed interested.

It was Christmas 1990 and we were having a break after several years of concentrated work on various film and book projects related to social, political and cultural history. Our finances were low, not only because we had tried to self-fund some of our projects but also because we were still clearing up the financial mess following the closure of our doomed *Mr Drum* feature film project in which we had spent so much energy, time and passion. Our French finance had stopped and we were left alone to pick up the pieces, pay outstanding bills, honour contracts and say farewell to a dedicated, despondent and disappointed crew and cast. They had all put their hearts and souls into this film. As one of them said, 'This film is the story of our lives.'

Out of the blue we received an unexpected invitation to celebrate New Year's Eve with Nelson Mandela and his family. We arrived a little early on the evening of 31 December 1990 at Mandela's new Soweto home. Mandela welcomed us warmly and we sat down on his large terrace and talked. Our discussion and reminiscences ranged across many topics – from life today and our multicultural society to the fifties and how society had changed so dramatically since those days. Soon a joyful, happy Winnie appeared, bringing us drinks, and more guests arrived, most of them former Robben Island prisoners. The atmosphere was relaxed and informal and there was much laughter and jollity. After helping ourselves to a variety of delicious spicy African dishes prepared by Winnie herself, we sat around the table and heard many entertaining, inspiring and also amusing stories about Robben Island. The evening passed very quickly and at midnight we celebrated New Year with many toasts – the first of 1991 with Nelson Mandela and Winnie, who were seated across from me and Claudia. It was a memorable clinking of glasses and an unforgettable evening.

Claudia had organised a number of exhibitions of my photographs in

Germany and France – one show being 'The Black and White Fifties' with an accompanying book published by Protea Boekhuis in Pretoria. Both Claudia and I were regularly flying backwards and forwards to Europe, where I was often invited to give talks about the apartheid system in South Africa and how it affected the daily life of black people. In Germany we exhibited in museums and town halls across the country, and in France we started our exhibition tour at the House of Photography in Chalon-sur-Saône, the home of Nicéphore Niépce, one of the famous French inventors of photography.

Groote Schuur, the official residence in Cape Town of South Africa's presidents, became the venue for talks between the government and the ANC in preparation for ending apartheid. It was where the National Peace Accord was signed by representatives of 27 political organisations to prepare for the Convention for a Democratic South Africa (CODESA), which opened at the World Trade Centre just outside Joburg in 1992, to work on how a new democratic South Africa would be shaped.

The next film project Claudia and I embarked on was a television series about the history of South African music and its evolution, from early San singing and dancing to disco pop. Our idea was to do a seven-part series musical extravaganza entitled *The Seven Ages of Music*, dedicating each part to a particular section of music. Again, however, we had fundraising problems, so in the end we produced only a one-hour documentary, funded by an investment company, and the film condensed all sections into one production. I wrote a rough script, we selected and booked the hundred-plus musicians, dancers and singers, and shot the whole film in a studio in ten days, thanks to Claudia's skilful producing and organisational skills. Our son Charlie, then six years old, was in charge of the smoke machine so the production became a family affair. With the talented actor David Phetoe presenting each section, we featured a string of the best musical talents of South Africa, including Dolly Rathebe, the Inkspots, Jonas Gwangwa, Hugh Masekela, the Elite Swingsters, Ntemi Piliso, Mike Makhalemele and the Street Beat Dancers.

During this time I received a letter from BBC Channel 4 asking me to do the voice-over for a documentary they had made about my pictures and pictures of other *Drum* photographers. I had just finished reading the letter when

I received an angry call from Peter Magubane, who somehow assumed that it was I who had made the film and that I had not informed him. After I explained that I had had nothing to do with it and was, in fact, as surprised as he was, we both decided to contact Channel 4 to find out what it was all about. It turned out that they had signed a contract with Jim Bailey for a one-hour programme about *Drum* photos, which would feature my images from the early fifties, including images of Mandela, the jazz scene and Sophiatown, as well as some of Peter Magubane's photos of the June 1976 uprising in Soweto. Channel 4 wanted Peter and me to talk over and describe our pictures. As they had already paid Bailey a fee of £20 000 for this usage of our images, unless Bailey paid us from the fee he received, we would receive no money for our work.

Of course Peter and I marched along to Jim Bailey, asking for a percentage royalty for the use of our photos, but he just laughed and refused to pay us anything. I noticed that since my departure from the archives, a collection which I had painstakingly created, and since I was no longer working on the farm producing books and projects, Jim had become more bitter and unfriendly towards me and towards Peter. Despite his great wealth, he had developed a very mercenary, exploitative streak.

Claudia had now managed to raise the remaining 50 per cent funding for our Robben Island documentary feature, which would be a co-production with the renowned BBC Arena programme. It was decided that Claudia and I would produce the film and retain the copyright, and the BBC would choose a BBC director – Adam Low. Pre-production started immediately and we began organising the filming dates.

During this time I received a call from Jeremy Ractliffe, the head of the Mandela Children's Fund. He asked if I would take some pictures of Mandela receiving a cheque from a sponsor. This was the start, for me, of several years of documenting, on a voluntary basis, the numerous sponsors from all over the world donating funds to this charity. These presentations were made in different venues, sometimes at Mandela's residence in Houghton, at a school or at the Children's Fund's office. Each personal meeting with Mandela earned over US$100 000 or more for this charity.

42

ROBBEN ISLAND AND A NEW ERA

Between 1992 and 1993 battles raged continuously between the warring Inkatha and ANC groups while the CODESA talks were ongoing. It remained a volatile and troubled time – with the Boipatong and Bisho massacres and then, on 1 April 1993, the cold-blooded assassination of MK and Communist Party leader Chris Hani. This murder sent shockwaves through the country and came very close to derailing the peace process.

Claudia and I produced some short half-hour films about various social and human rights issues. These included homelessness, abandoned children with AIDS, teenage pregnancy, adult literacy, and ballroom dancing (which was slowly becoming desegregated). *Voices from Robben Island* was our main production, however, at this time. Most of the filming was done on Robben Island and in Cape Town and, as co-producer, I spent time in Cape Town to take stills of the shoot for the film and book while Claudia had to oversee the production from Joburg, and liaise with the BBC in London and the crew in Cape Town. She also managed the accounts.

I and the crew spent a few nights on Robben Island, which was still a prison for common-law prisoners, and we were treated with great suspicion, discourtesy and distrust by a particular power-happy prison warder who, after three days of shooting, told us to stop filming and leave the island. It was a Friday evening and we needed to do some more filming, so this presented a real challenge. The future of the film, which had taken seven years to fund, was under threat. The following day I decided to call the head of Nasionale Pers whom I had met years before when the group had bought *Drum*. I explained our problem to him. He told me to phone Adriaan Vlok, the minister of law and order. I should pick my time carefully (just before he went to church) and tell him he had suggested I call – and I should flatter him as much as possible. So on Sunday morning I phoned Minister Vlok, explained our problem, and asked for his help to continue our filming on Robben Island. His response was friendly and he said he would fix things on Monday morning. So on Monday morning we took the ferry to Robben Island and went directly to see the warder, who rebuked us loudly for disobeying his orders and daring to return. He started on a long lecture about the difficulty of his job and was telling us that we would immediately be escorted off the island by an armed guard, when the phone rang. The warder suddenly sat bolt upright in full attention mode, and his legs began shaking. 'Ja, meneer,' he kept saying in a distinctly nervous tone. After he put the phone down he looked at us with wild eyes and a red face. Then he swallowed hard and said, 'Would you like some tea?' We were given all the time we needed to complete our filming.

One of our filmed interviews was with Nelson Mandela at Shell House, the ANC headquarters in Johannesburg. We set up in the morning and, with the interview planned for 2pm, Adam Low and I went for a quick lunch nearby. As we strolled back to Shell House after lunch, deep in conversation, we were just passing some fruit and vegetable stands on the pavement when suddenly a young black boy, no older than sixteen, approached me with an outstretched arm and closed hand. I saw the flash of a flick-knife pointing straight at me and at the same time two other youngsters with knives directed at me came from either side. One of them grabbed my camera, which was slung over my shoulder. I held onto the strap while the youngster pulled the other end and put his hand into my trouser pocket. Holding onto the strap for dear life with my left hand, I pushed the young fellow on my right, who fell to the ground with his hand still in my pocket, which tore my pocket and the side of my trousers wide open. The third fellow in front of me had his knife at my throat – so I let go of the camera strap, which the fellow on my left was still holding. He started to run, followed swiftly by the other two. Adam had run off, leaving me to fight my battle alone.

Claudia and I had now been living and working in South Africa for several decades and we felt it had become our home. We decided to apply for citizenship. We believed in the 'rainbow nation' concept, as envisaged and first articulated by Archbishop Desmond Tutu, and so in February 1994 we became South African citizens.

For some years Claudia had been looking after Dolly Rathebe's professional affairs on an informal, non-payment, friendship basis, booking gigs, ensuring that Dolly was well paid and promoting her singing talents. Dolly was delighted that Claudia could handle this and they had many laughs as they planned future concerts and shows. We also tried to help the Inkspots, the immensely talented close-harmony singing group from Springs, who were struggling to survive. We decided to make a documentary, called *Dolly and the Inkspots*, about these musical legends who had sung together in the fifties but, again, there was no possibility of financial support. Realising the historical and musical importance of this project, we took a chance and shot it without any backing. I filmed it myself on Betacam, did the sound and editing on our edit suite, and Claudia did the research and interviews. We found a closed-down underground jazz club, the Zanzibar, in Braamfontein with a stage and bar where we could film at no charge, and we shot many scenes and musical numbers there. The film was interspersed with clips of Dolly in *Jim Comes to Jo'burg*, *The Seven Ages of Music* and the film *Zonk*.

Early in 1994 Mandela and some of the Rivonia Trialists planned a visit to their former prison on Robben Island. There was going to be a sizeable press contingent covering this historic event – it was the first trip back for many of the prisoners – so I didn't think I should photograph it. It would be covered extensively by the local and international press. Claudia insisted I go, however, and so I went along to the harbour.

I arrived at the pier from where the Robben Island ferry left and saw a plethora of press people and international television crews already boarding. When I got to the gate, I wasn't allowed on. This, I was told, was because I had no official press commission and I wasn't on the staff of a news agency or newspaper. I was just a freelancer. After much arguing, they called the PR office and summoned the 'salad lady' (this was Gill Marcus, the spokesperson for the Mandela Foundation, so called because she used to run a salad bar in London before she was an ANC activist). Gill looked very busy and she had little time for me. She dismissed my request to join the media group. I sat on some steps by the pier, having given up, when a photographer friend, John Rubython, approached me. Some years before, John had emigrated to South Africa from the United Kingdom. He was based in Cape Town, where he ran a press club for members of the overseas press. I told John my sorry tale, where-upon he rushed down the steps to the ferry and somehow – I still don't know how – persuaded them to let me get on. I remembered this generous gesture some years later when I heard that John had been stabbed to death in his home by a fourteen-year-old intruder.

On the Island there was an emotional reunion of some of the former Rivonia Trialists, in particular Walter Sisulu, Denis Goldberg, Ahmed Kathrada and Andrew Mlangeni. The international TV units got busy filming this historic reunion, some climbing up the ladders they had brought with them to get a better view. Mandela was totally surrounded by media people and there was much shoving and pushing by the press people, who aggressively elbowed their way through the crowds. A lunch with Mandela had been arranged, and again he was engulfed by journalists asking him to recount some stories of his time on the Island. After lunch we all followed him to the yard outside the cells where the political leaders had been held. TV crews were allowed two minutes each to film Mandela in his former cell and they went in one by one. Then it was time for the photographers – there were only three of us and luckily I was the last, so I had some more time. Mandela was pleased to see me and happy to pose for me. He patiently stood still, in one position, as I requested.

On 29 March 1994 about 20 000 Inkatha supporters marched to Shell House through downtown Johannesburg in protest against the election, which was scheduled to be held on 27 April. They carried spears and clubs and many were in traditional Zulu dress. The powerful singing and rhythmic stamping of feet resounded off the building on all sides. Terrified passers-by quickly got out of the way of this war-like group. At the ANC headquarters they started bang-ing on the closed gates. The guards inside the building, upon hearing gunshots from the outside, became panic-stricken and they started firing. They claimed

Nelson Mandela in his cell on Robben Island

that the Inkatha group was about to storm the building. Nineteen people were killed there that day. Subsequently, a commission of inquiry was ordered and amnesty was granted to all concerned.

After days and weeks of rumours about the possibility of a bloody revolution and violent threats from the AWB, the Afrikaner right-wing group, South Africa's first democratic election, miraculously, took place peacefully on 27 April 1994. I filmed a number of polling stations to record this historic moment and found that despite the long queues everyone was relaxed and patient even though they had to wait for hours to cast their votes. Black and white, housekeepers and housewives, people from all walks of life, young and old, talked to each other, without any apparent discord, as the queues moved slowly forward. It was a remarkable and amazingly happy event. At the Union Buildings in Pretoria, on 10 May 1994, Nelson Mandela was sworn in as the first black democratically elected president of South Africa. The moment was greeted with tumultuous celebration and great optimism. The post-apartheid era had officially begun.

EPILOGUE

Claudia and I left South Africa in 2007. We moved to Normandy, where we lived for four years, producing a book and show about our village and holding many exhibitions in France. Then we went to Berlin, and spent two years there. We also exhibited widely there, especially shows about South African history, and I also produced more books – about Germany over six decades and Great Britain in the sixties.

Claudia and I had always been attracted to the Mediterranean lifestyle, the people, the colours and the humour, so in 2013 we made a move to Spain. Charlie had left for London several years earlier; he was studying psychology and enjoying life in a big city. We chose for our home in Spain a little mountain village south of Valencia and settled very happily there. Over time we had several shows in Madrid, Valencia, Gandia and various small towns. All of the shows were extremely well received, and in Valencia, to my great surprise and pleasure, in 2014, a year after our arrival, I was honoured with a doctorate by Valencia University.

Not long afterwards, in 2014, I was again surprised – this time by the Institute of Contemporary Photography in New York, who honoured me with a Lifetime Achievement Award. It was immensely rewarding to see that my work was being recognised internationally by such a prestigious organisation, and Claudia and I travelled to New York together to accept the award.

We published two more books: *Spain Then and Now*, featuring my images of Spain in the sixties and today, and *Viva Europa Viva!*, a tribute to the values and lifestyle of pre-Brexit Europe. I began training two young talented Spanish assistants to help with the daily running of our large photographic archive, print room and darkroom, and the many requests we continue to receive regularly from around the world from galleries, museums, universities and collectors.

Currently we have four touring shows in Germany and Spain – including a Mandela show in large format on metal – and we are in the process of scheduling shows and book projects for the next couple of years. *Portrait of a Spanish Village*, which is a study of the people and lifestyle of our little mountain village in Spain, was published in 2017.

RECENT AND SELECTED PORTFOLIO

Individual Photographic Exhibitions

2010   'Voices from the Land' – Journees Solidaires, Coutances, France

South African Images – Nelson Mandela Mediatheque, Vitry, Paris, France

Felix Nussbaum Museum, Osnabrueck, Germany

New Colour Images of South Africa – large format – Freelens – Hamburg, Germany

Berlin 1961 – The Building of the Wall – Erdmann Contemporary – Cape Town, South Africa

'Voices from the Land' – Goethe Institut Johannesburg and film screenings, South Africa

The Fifties – Mediatheque Benoite Boulard, Le Port, La Reunion

2011   Solo Show – Berkeley University, California, USA

Portrait d'Un Village Francais – Salle de Fetes – Pin La Garenne, France

All That Jazz – 60 years of South African Jazz– Goethe Institut, Brussels

Retrospective – Timeless Moments – 65 years – Willy Brandt Haus, Berlin

South African Fifties – Douarnenez Film Festival, Brittany, France

Le Voleur d'Images – Paris – The Defiance Campaign 1952

Portrait d'Un Village Français – Institut Francais Berlin

The Black Fifties – Pasadena Library, USA

2012   Solo Show – Frankfurt Leica Gallery, Germany

Solo Show – Oldenburg Kultur Lounge, Germany

Solo Show – Aachen KUK Centre, Monschau, Germany

Solo Show – Argus Gallery, Berlin, Germany

Solo Show – Carpentier Gallery, Berlin, Germany

The Black & White Fifties – Hong Kong and Beijing

2013   Solo Show – Peter Herrmann Gallery, Berlin, Germany

Kunstraum Dreieich, Frankfurt, Germany

University of Gandia, Spain

Solo Show – Mandela and The Fifties – St Ouen Town Hall, Paris

2014   Solo Show – Flo Peters Gallery, Hamburg

The Retrospective – Kunsthalle Darmstadt

Photography Centre – Goerlitz, Germany

Retrospective – Universitat Politecnica, Valencia, Spain

Jazz – Photokina, Koln, Germany

Retrospective – Gandia House of Culture, Spain

The Black Fifties – Biberach, Erbach, Germany

Mandela – Belgravia Gallery, London

2015   The People of Barx Village, Barx Casa Cultura, Spain

Nelson Mandela & The Fifties – Kulturhaus Osterfeld, Pforzheim, Germany

Retrospective – Railowsky, Valencia, Spain

2016   Viva Europa Viva – Museum Goch, Germany

Selected Moments – Huleva Photo Festival, Spain

Selected Moments – PhotoEspana, Spain – Blanca Berlin Gallery, Germany

Major Retrospective – Hopital Antigua, Madrid

Mandela – 6 decades – Wuerzburg University – Africa Festival, Germany

Mandela – 6 decades – IGMetall, Frankfurt, Germany

Timeless Moments – Silvertone International, Johannesburg, South Africa

Selected Images – Cullera University, Spain

Selected images – Albarracan, Spain

Viva Europa Viva! – Sylt Foundation, Sylt, Germany

Viva Europa Viva! – Uberlingen Museum, Germany

Three shows: San of the Kalahari 1959, Retrospective, Tales from Jozi, Casa Cultura – Gandia, Spain

Group Exhibitions

2010	South African Images – Polka Gallery, Paris
	Virginia Museum of Fine Art 'Darkroom'
	Coutances, France – Voices from the Land
2011	Birmingham Museum of Art, Alabama
	Young Gallery, Brussels
	Africa – Polka Gallery, Paris
	Chris Beetles Fine Art Gallery, London
2012	'Apartheid' – ICP New York
2013	Group African Show – Monaco
	'Apartheid' – Haus der Kunst, Munich
	Chris Beetles Fine Art Gallery, London
2014	Apartheid Show – Museum Africa, Johannesburg
2016	Retrospective – MUVIM Museum, Valencia

Books

Jürgen Schadeberg (Photographers' Gallery, 1981)

Kalahari Bushman Dance (Jürgen Schadeberg, 1982)

The Finest Photos from the Old Drum (Bailey's Photo Archives, 1987)

The Fifties People of South Africa (Bailey's Photo Archives, 1987)

Nelson Mandela & the Rise of the ANC (Jonathan Ball/Donker, 1990)

Drum (Rogner & Bernhard, 1991)

Voices from Robben Island (Macmillan, 1994)

Sof'town Blues (Jürgen Schadeberg, 1995)

South African Classics (Macmillan, 1995)

The Black & White Fifties (Protea Boekhuis, 2002)

Soweto Today (Protea Boekhuis, 2002)

The San of the Kalahari 1959 (Protea Boekhuis, 2002)

Witness: A Retrospective of 52 years or work in Africa, Europe & USA (Protea Boekhuis, 2004)

The Book of Life: A Look at the UNDP Aids Programme in South Africa (United Nations, 2004)

Voices from the Land: Farm Life and Farm Conditions in South Africa (Protea Boekhuis, 2005)

Jürgen Schadeberg: Photographies (IAC France, 2005)

Jazz, Swing & Blues: SA Jazz over Six Decades (New Africa Books, 2007)

Tales from Jozi (Protea Boekhuis, 2007)

Jürgen Schadeberg: A Retrospective (Hatje Cantz, 2008)

Horizon d'Esperance (Editions Verlhac, 2010)

Portrait d'Un Village Français (Editions de l'Etrave, 2010)

Great Britain 1964 / 84 (Mitteldeutscher Verlag, 2012)

Schadeberg Visits Germany: 6 Decades (Mitteldeutscher Verlag, 2012)

Six Decades of South African Photography (Unisa Press, 2013)

Spain 1969 – 2014 Then and Now (Museum Goch / Pagina Verlag / The Schadeberg Collection, 2015)

Viva Europa Viva 2016 (Museum Goch / Pagina Verlag, 2016)

Portrait of a Spanish Village (Jürgen and Claudia Schadeberg, 2017)

Films

Have You Seen Drum Recently? The Black Fifties in South Africa, 1987 (35 mm, 77 mins)

War & Peace: A History of the ANC, 1989 / 1992 (Video, 56 mins)

The Seven Ages of Music, 1992 (Video, 46 mins)

Drumbeats, 1993 (16 mm, 56 mins)

Ballroom Fever, 1994 (Video, 26 mins)

Voices from Robben Island, 1994 (16 mm, 90 mins)

Dolly &The Inkspots, 1994 (Video, 26 mins)

Jo'burg Cocktail, 1995 (Video, 56 mins)

Halala Bomane!, 1996 (Video, 56 mins)

Ernest Cole: 1940–1990 Photo Journalist, 1999 (Video, 52 mins)

Drumbeats, 2000 (Pilot for drama series, 52 mins)

Deadline, 2000 (Drama series, 6 x 52 mins)

Looking Back, 2011 (Video, 26 mins)

ACKNOWLEDGEMENTS

All my thanks to Claudia for her encouragement, work and advice on my memoir. She was my permanent partner on this project, having transferred and corrected my longhand writing onto the computer over a five-year period.

I thank Nick Snelling for his support and valued opinions.

I would also like to thank the Pan Macmillan team for their creative support – Alison Lowry for her considerable editing skills in putting the book into shape, Andrea Nattrass for her valued literary input, and Terry Morris for accepting the memoir in the first place.

CPSIA information can be obtained
at www.ICGtesting.com
Printed in the USA
LVHW091716170119
604295LV00002B/262/P